The
Complete Martial Arts of Japan
The Complete Series

撃剣・柔術・剣舞
Gekken・Jujutsu・Kenbu

Published 1898

By Sadamoto Sugawara

Illustrated by Fujiyama Shibu-un

Translated by Eric Shahan

武勇館蔵版

武藝全書 撃劍

菊判　全壹冊　正價貳拾五錢　郵送税　四錢

本書ハ柔術ニ係ル居合、抔捌ヨリ劍術、槍術、弓術、
馬術、水泳術ニ至ルマデ師ニ就カズシテ獨稽古ノ出來ルヤ
ウ深切丁寧ニ圖解シ僻郷師ニ乏シキ地ノ壯者ト雖モ武藝上、
右ニ記ス課目ノコトハ學ブコトナ得ル無類ノ寶典ナリ、抑又
流儀ハ各著名ノ流儀ニシテ柔術ニ係ルモノ及ヒ劍術ハ關口流
槍術ハ大島流、弓術ハ日置流伴道雪派、馬術ハ大坪本流、水
泳術ハ和歌山派ナリ方今尚武ノ世、壯者ノ必ズ一見チ經ベキ
モノナレバ諸ヲ隨覽アリテ其必要ナルチ諒シ給ハンコトチ

1898 Advertisement for
The Complete Martial Arts of Japan: Gekken

This volume contains techniques that are correlated with Jujutsu. Specifically introducing sword drawing, how to respond to a person grabbing the handle of your sword as well as sword techniques, spear techniques, archery, equestrian and swimming techniques. This book was designed as a self-training manual so you can train without a teacher. Detailed, easy to follow illustrations and explanations are included for those that reside in areas without access to qualified martial arts instructors.

It will also serve as a unique resource of martial arts knowledge. Further all the Ryugi, or schools of martial arts, will be listed according to their official name. The Jujutsu and Kenjutsu techniques are from the Sekiguchi School. The spear techniques are from the Oshima School. Kyujutsu is Dosetsu order of Heichi School. The equestrian arts are from Otsuka School. The swimming arts are from the Wakayama order. At present we live in a world where martial arts and bravery are very much at the forefront of society, therefore taking the time to examine this volume would be of great personal benefit.

The Complete Martial Arts of Japan
Volume One: Gekken

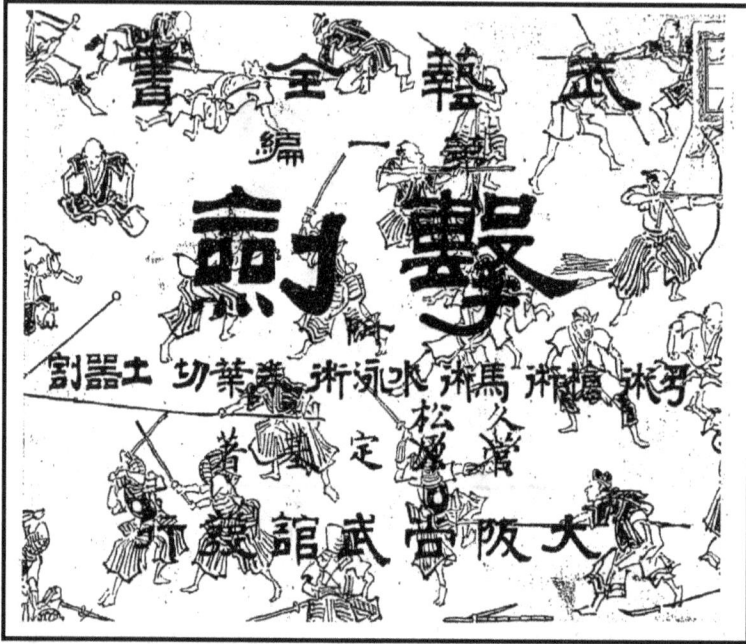

Written by SUGAWARA SADAMOTO
Illustrated by Fujiyama Shibu-un
Translated by Eric Shahan
Published 1898

弓術 Kyu -Jutsu Archery
槍術 So - Jutsu Spear Fighting
馬術 Ba -Jutsu Equestrian Arts
水術 Sui - Jutsu Swimming
巻藁切 Maki-Wara-Giri Test Cutting
土器打 Dokki Wari Clay Pot Challenge

Preface

THE COMPLETE MARTIAL ARTS OF JAPAN・武芸全書

自序

今也尚武之世也矣既在尚

武之世而不修武技猶病不

欲食滋品爲夫人不食滋品

缺除血液血液貧缺體弱體

而底弱何以立世一朝有歟

何以拒之雖然止于一人者

耳在此尚武之世而不修武

技其將如此國何人或曰有

陸軍矣有海軍矣胡爲要他

其言然矣雖然砲銃者通隊

與共者也異日倘從軍亂軍

單騎搭鬮則無其屬一己武

技可乎般鑒不遠優遂東之

役有淺川大尉搭鬮如此時

專恃砲銃可乎弓馬劍槍者

古來六藝中除砲銃二藝之

他武夫必修之技也謂之長

物者抑亦不思耳予雖謝劣

爲壯者稿之豈有他哉一意

思國故耳聊叙徵衷以冠首

端

明治戊戌春三月

浪速處士　菅原定基　撰

9

Preface

Nowadays great import is being placed upon the fighting arts and the military. However, the sight of people not developing their military skill and instead seeking only to consume decadent foods, is like to make one weep.

The blood that flows in one's veins can make you either stronger or weaker. What would you do if called to action? If one morning the enemy should appear, by what means will they be repelled? Without the acquisition of *Bugi*, martial skill, what then is to become of our country?

There are those that say, "Well, we have the Army," or "We have the Navy." This is correct. However, cannons and rifles are used by *people*. The armed forces must be a single, unified organization. Every member must move in accordance with the rest. If it were to become every man for himself, it will become a riot.

There is, of course, the famous charge lead by Captain Asakawa. This is a prime example. Expertise is not limited to artillery and rifleman-ship. Archery, Horseback riding, Swordsmanship and Proficiency in spear are all important as well. From long past these have been known as the Riku-gei, or the six arts. In addition to artillery and the use of the rifle, these four skills are of essence to a Samurai.

It is reasonably said that these are the things that a person who seeks to become a General must know. Nothing will come of someone who just listens absently to what is being said. One should consider what needs to be done and what action needs to be taken.

Of late, when considering the state of my country I have become anxious.

March, Spring of the Boshin Year of the Meiji Emporer 1868
Composed by a *Nami wa sho shi,* or Citizen of the Lands of Osaka :
Sugawara Sadamoto

Translator's notes:

This introduction was written in Kanbun 漢文. A style of Japanese writing that used all Chinese characters, that would then, in turn, have to be reworked by the reader into standard Japanese.

I would like to express my deepest thanks to Manaka "Unsui" Sensei, Head of the Jinenkan School of Kobudo for his assistance translating this Kanbun into standard Japanese.

The following paragraph detailing Captain Asakawa's exploits is from:

Heroic Japan: A History of the War Between China & Japan, F. Warrington Eastlake and Yamada Yoshi-aki, Sampson Low, Marston & Company, 1897.

13.—MUTUAL AID.

As noted above, the conflict between the reconnoitring Cavalry of the Second Column, while on the march to Port Arthur, and the large body of Chinese—certainly not less than 2300—whom they encountered at Tuching-tse, was exceedingly fierce. By sheer force of numbers Chinese succeeded at one time in surrounding the Japanese on three sides, with very little hope of escape. At first Captain Asakawa with his Company of troopers led the van; but on seeing that the fight had become general, he rode over to the right, in order to render assistance in this direction. Noting this the Chinese made a furious attack on that side: so rapidly and fiercely engaging the Japanese that those who had not yet mounted were rendered incapable of doing so; and the cavalry-men had to fight on foot like all the rest. The Brigade Commander now ordered Captain Asakawa to disperse the rapidly increasing enemy, and, with only 40 or 50 troopers, the latter charged into the ranks of the Chinese. At this moment a shot disabled his left arm, while his horse was killed beneath him. He was on the point of falling into the merciless hands of the enemy

CAPTAIN ASAKAWA.

KIMURA GEMMATSU.

SERGEANT KOBAYASHI.

when Kimura Gemmatsu—a third-grade trooper,—notwithstanding a severe wound he himself had received in the abdomen, caught sight of his Captain's peril and made through the press to his aid. Dismounting, he said: "Sir, as the head of my Company, please get on my horse!" The Captain with the help of his sword and Kimura's arm was just barely able to mount, and, owing to his wound, incapable of managing the reins. Seeing this Kimura grasped the bridle and despite the agony he was suffering ran the horse through the storm of bullets until he reached a little knoll some five or six hundred metres distant. Captain Asakawa was now so far restored that he could manage his mount, but Kimura, sick and faint, could no longer keep his feet. Just then Sergeant Kobayashi Shun-ichirō, a comrade of Kimura, rode up, dismounted, and helped the wounded officer on his own horse. Being still within the range of and exposed to the enemy's fire, Sergeant Kobayashi led his comrade four miles to the rear to a place called Shwangtai-kau, where there was no danger of meeting with Chinese. Here they halted, and the Sergeant temporarily bandaged Kimura's wound, thus ultimately saving the brave man's life.

The above story is a simple one. It shows none the less the devotion of the Japanese soldiers to their officers, their own disregard of personal pain and discomfort, and the strong fraternal feeling existing among the soldiers themselves. "Of these things," says Japanese journal, "we feel we have a right to be proud."

The Abbreviated History of Amaha Setsuo Sensei

天羽拙翁先生之略傳

天羽拙翁先生ハ紀伊侯之臣ナリ八代将軍徳川吉
宗公未ダ将軍タラズ紀伊侯タリ宗家徳川氏嗣ヲ
闕ク吉宗公入リテ宗家ヲ嗣グノ前藩臣東都ニ随
従シ請フ者衆シ公断ジテ曰ク早晩儀式ヲ立テ宗
家幕府ヨリ上使ノ来ルアルベシ其日当直ノ者ニ
限リテ許サント先生其日直ニ当ラズ為ニ随従ノ
志ヲ得ズ快々トシテ過光ス一日感ズル所アリ
然ラ致仕シテ所謂ル浪士ト為リ浪華ニ来リ玉造組
與力等ノ師ト為ル先生ハ關口流ヲ善クシ劔槍其
他柔術ニ達ス其名夙ニ揚ルヲ以テ隣國ノ士多ク
之ガ門下タラントコトヲ翼フ尼ヶ崎藩士殊ニ篤シ
是ニ由テ先生坂尼両地ヘ交互教授ス柔術ニ於テ
ハ玉造組與力中之ヲ受ケ後々石川氏アリ尼ヶ崎
ニ於テハ某氏等之ヲ受ケ一宮氏之ヲ嗣ギ中馬氏
亦タ之ヲ嗣ギ予ハ之ヨリ受ケタリ先生多湖氏ヲ

主トス因テ以テ此家ニ卒ス多湖氏ノ香華院谷町
寺町ニ在リ先生ノ碑此ニ存スト云フ
因ニ云フ吉宗公東行ノ際随従シタル者ノ中抜擢
ノ榮ヲ荷ヒタル者ハ田沼侯ナリ侯若シ随従ノ幸
アラズンバ依然トシテ紀伊家ノ臣ナリ即チ陪臣
ニシテ所謂直参ニアラズ何ノ幸カ上使到着ノ日
當直ノ員ニアリシヲ以テ旗下ト為リ列侯ト為リ
父ハ老中子ハ若年寄ノ榮ヲ荷ヒ一旦事アリ減祿
スト雖モ歴然タル華族ニ列ス嗚呼先生ノ歎固
ニ以テアルナリ倘シ先生ニシテ其日當直ノ員ニ
アラシメバ安ゾ知ヲ旗下ト為リシヲ、不幸
シテ浪華客中ニ歿ス哀シイ哉

後進　定基　謹誌

The Abbreviated History of Amaha Setsuo Sensei

Amaha Setsuo Sensei was a Kerai, or retainer, of the Tokugawa of Kii Domain, present day Mie and Wakayama Prefectures. At that point Tokugawa Yoshimune had not yet been installed as the Eighth Tokugawa Shogun, but was the Banshu or Lord of a Domain.

When the lord was beginning his transfer to Edo, present day Tokyo, there were many that sought to join the retinue. Lord Yoshimune pondered this then decreed,

Should he come late or should he come early, when the envoy fom Edo arrives to announce the ceremony, only those on duty that day may accompany me to Edo.

As Amaha Setsuo ws not among those on duty that day, he was not eligible to accompany lord Yoshimune to Edo. After spending several days under a gloomy cloud, he realized that something must be done. He made his decision one day and became a Roshi or Ronin and made his way to Roka, present day Osaka. There he became an instructor of the Yoriki or auxillary fighters of the the Tama-tsukuri Gumi an Osaka based group.

Through his knowledge of Sekiguchi School martial arts, he taught Kenjutsu, or swordfighting, Sojutsu or spear-fighting as well as Jujutsu, in which he was adept. Eventually, Amaha Sensei's name began to draw Bushi from neighbouring countries who reqested Deshi-iri, or to become a personal student of him. The head of the Amaga-Saki Han, comprising the areas around Kobe City, was a particularly dedicated practitioner. For this reason Sensei conducted Keiko, or training, in Osaka as well as in Amaga-saki.

With regards to Jujutsu, Mr. Ishikawa took over the instrucion of the Yoriki of the Tamazukuri Gumi, while Mr. Ichi no Miya took over teaching in Amaga-saki. From there Mr. Chuma took over from Mr. Ichi no Miya. I received instruction from Mr. Chuma and then from Mr. Tago, when he became head, until he passed away.

Mr. Tago's family temple is in Tani-machi-tera-machi in Kyoto. It is said that Sensei's Ishi-bumi or stone monument bearing an inscription is there.

Looking back, of those selectted to accompany Lord Yoshimune back to Edo, a Mr. Tanuma later became quite prominent[1].

Those that were not permitted to make the transfer are no doubt still retainers of the Kii Han. So, despite being retainers, they were no longer able to directly attend to their lord.

What luck was it for those who became Kika, or Samurai directly under the Shogun, to have been on duty the very day the envoy from Edo arrived! You would become a Daimyo, your father a Roju or elder advisor to the Shogun, your son a Waka doshi yori or younger advisor to the Shogun.

Though with the advent of the Meiji Restoration there would have been some reduction in status, overall the family would be stable and prosperous.

Alas! Amaha Setsuo Sensei had tragic luck all around. This could well have been his destiny. If Sensei had been on duty that day he would have become a Kika, but he did not wallow in this turn of fate.

He used this "poor luck" to make his way to Roha, or Osaka, and his chance to become a top retainer to the Shogun passed away. Such a tragic tale.

But he is now retired and has now handed over his responsiblities.

Transcribed with solemn care,
Sadamoto Sugawara

Translator's note: I would like to thank Konno Sumire San for checking over my Japanese interpretiation of this section of rather tricky old text.

---

[1] Likely referring to Tanuma Okiyuki who transferred to Edo along with 200 other Han Samurai to Edo. His son Tanuma Okitsugu became a Roju to the Shogun and introduced monetary reform. *His regime is often identified with rampant corruption and huge inflation of currency. In 1784 Okitsugu's son, the wakadoshiyori (junior counselor) Tanuma Okitomo, was assassinated inside Edo Castle. Okitomo was killed in front of his father as both were returning to their palanquin after a meeting.*

The Complete Martial Arts of Japan
First Scroll：Gekken

Direct Transmissions from Amaha Setsuo of Sekiguchi Ryu
Writer: Sugawara Sadamoto
Illustrator: Fujiyama Shibu-un
General Overview of Gekken or The Sword Arts and Fencing

武藝全書 其の巻

關口流天羽拙翁正傳

菅原定基著

藤山紫雲畫

◉擊劍總説

敵手の透を見て打込み開々と掛聲を掛くるうち斯く來れば斯くすると目算をすること肝要なり其目算をするに木刀或は竹刀の搆へ方肝要にして此搆へ方によりて損益あれば能く此搆へ方を心得べし又た兵法に虛實あるが如く劍法にも虛實あり卑怯なる事をせず能く虛實を圖るべし其虛實を圖るに付きて一話あり

昔時板倉侯京都所司代たりし時大内に散樂の御催しありたり散樂は能狂言なり此時衆庶にも拜觀を許されたる事故京洛中の者は申すに及ばず洛外其他近圍より拜觀に出る者夥しく板倉侯即ち所司代は御所を守護する役目故其日出張して非常を制せらるるに此日拜觀に人の内に京都の染物屋にて吉岡建法と云ふ者あり此者は中々の擊劍家にて達人との噂高し

然るに斯る群集の中にて建法は無禮を致す故非常を制する官吏は之を制せしに吉岡建法を大に怒りて自宅へ歸り刀を懷ろにして再び出來り前きの官吏を見て斬り付け之が爲めに拜觀人は事起りたりとて上を下へと騷ぎ立ち鎭まるやうは見えざりければ所司代は此時日華門に詰合さるる夫々指揮して取抑えしめらるるに板倉侯の臣下にて太田忠兵衛と云ふ者亂暴人を探ぬるに紫宸殿の此方にて吉岡建法に出遭ひ建法を呼かけて其罪を責め蒐らんとせんとするに建法は刀を拔きて斬て蒐らんとせんが物に躓きて仆れたり然るに忠兵衛は之を斬らず起きて立上るや否や斬すてたり此事を主君板倉侯へ申せしに板倉侯は奇異に思はれ忠兵衛に向はれて其方は何故建法が仆れたるを機として斬らざりしぞ建法は敵の使人と聞く若し過て彼れ手に權らば辱ならずやと曰はるゝ忠兵衛之に對へて臣は聊か物の虛實を心得あり建法が仆れたるは仆るゝは虛にして擊つに實あり依て臣は斬らず起上る時は擊つに虛にして起上るに實なり故に臣は其虛を

16

Upon seeing an opening in the opponent, you should enter and strike while calling out with a *Kake-goe*[2] of *Ya-ya*-! Conversely if your opponent decides to advance, it is essential to have formulated a response. An important aspect of this calculation is the Kamae you take. This applies if you are holding a Ki-gatana, wooden sword, or a Shinai, bamboo sword. Depending on the Kamae you choose, you will have strong points and weak points, thus you should examine these Kamae carefully.

Kyo-jitsu, Lie and Truth or Feints and True Attacks, is part of the arts of war, so Kyo-Jitsu is also part of Kenpo, The Way of the Sword. Kyo is a feint, a lie to deceive your enemy while Jitsu is truth, your real attack. You should remain calm and judge the appropriate time and manner in which you launch your Kyo-Jitsu. Let me tell you a story of a man who used Kyo-Jitsu.

^{In days past} Long ago when Lord Itakura[3] was the Shoshi-dai of Kyoto there was an occasion where a Sangaku performance was to take place within the O-uchi[4] of the palace. Sangaku resembles the Kyogen of Noh Theater.[5] As the general populace had permission to view the performance, excluding those living in the city center or

---

[2] Kake-goe 掛声 A shout that unifies the body and spirit.

[3] Three members of the Itakura family to served as the Shodshi-dai. This is referring to an incident during the era of the first Itakura.

板倉 勝重 Itakura Katsushige (1545 –1624) Served 1601-1619

板倉 重宗 Itakura Shigemune (1586 –1657) Served 1619-1654

Some other unrelated dude (1607 –1677) Served 1654 -1668

板倉 重矩 Itakura Shigenori (1617 –1673) Served 1668-1670

The Shoshi-dai was responsible for maintaining order in Kyoto, and keeping a watch on (ie. spying on) the royal household, nobles and the various Daimyo in Western Japan.

[4] This part of The Kyoto Imperial Palace. The Dai-dairi is the Great inner and outer portions of the center of the palace. The O-Uchi is referring to the inner part.

[5] Sangaku 散樂 is a Chinese-style circus with everything from acrobats and sleight of hand to people imitating the sounds of animals. It later evolved into comic storytelling that was presented during the intermissions between Noh theater performances.

Kyoraku chu, multitudes of spectators from outside the city center or Raku-gai as well as people from neighboring countries arrived for the spectacle[6]. Lord Itakura, or the Syoshi-dai as he was known, was not in attendance as he was tasked with guarding the royal court as well as maintaining general order that day. Amongst the spectators that day was a man from a dyer's house in Kyoto by the name of Yoshioka Kenpo. It was fairly common knowledge that this fellow was an expert in Gekken. However, as it happened, someone in the throngs of people accused Kenpo of being rude.

The official in charge of keeping such matters under control brought things to a halt. This only enraged Yoshioka Kenpo, who returned to his house, stuffed his Katana in his belt and returned to the scene of the altercation. Seeing the official who had chastised him, Kenpo drew his sword and cut him down, which immediately threw the spectators into a panic. In the aftermath of that incident nobody knew quite what was up and what was down and it didn't appear that things were going to calm down anytime soon.

This day Lord Itakura, the Shoshi-dai, was at the Nikkamon Gate and unable to break away, so he ordered his retainer Ohda Chubei to find and deal with the violent outlaw. In the area of Hall for State Ceremonies Chubei came across Yoshioka Kenpo and told him he was to be taken into custody and held accountable for his crimes. Kenpo drew his sword and gathered his power for a cut. Suddenly, Kenpo caught his foot on something, stumbled, and fell over. Chubei did not, however, move in to attack but, instead, waited until Kenpo had stood up again before cutting him down.

When Chubei was reporting this incident to his master Lord Itakura, his Lord found this sequence of events to be peculiar and turned to Chubei and asked,

"Why did you not seize the opportunity to cut Kenpo when he fell over ?"

Chubei replied, "I heard that Kenpo was an extremely skilled sword-master, if I got caught out by his trap I would be shamed."

Chubei went on,

---

[6] 京洛中 Kyoraku chu or "downtown Kyoto" and 洛外 Rakugai or "outside Kyoto City." The character 洛 means "town," but is used to refer to different parts of Kyoto.

"I have some small knowledge of Kyo-Jitsu. When Kenpo fell flat on his face, I determined that what I saw before me was Kyo, the lie. Were I to have struck then, thinking it was Jitsu, the truth, it could have been my downfall. Therefore your humble retainer did not cut. As he stood, I struck at the Kyo, the lie, which had become Jitsu, the truth, as he rose.

Lord Itakura was mightily impressed upon hearing how his retainer achieved a win by striking at Kyo, the lie. In the end he offered fine Sake as a reward and added his achievements to the record.[7]

---

[7] I was able to locate various versions of this story in 日本武術神妙記 or *Fantastic Martial Arts Tales of Japan* by 中里介山 Nakazato Kaisan. All seem to take place in the first twenty years of the 17th c. In summary:

Yoshioka Kenpo is insulted by a 雑色 Sasshiki or Zo-shiki, the lowest rank of peasants, and he ends up returning to kill the Sasshiki as well as many others who try to avenge their friend. Chubei is also variously armed with a Naginata or a Bisento (basically a large Naginata) but in the case of the latter abandons it in favor of the sword.

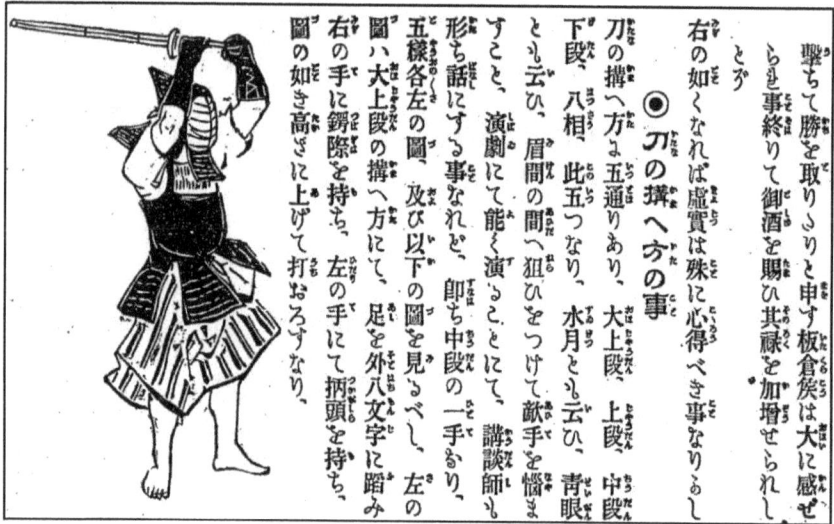

撃ちて勝を取りしと申す板倉殿は大に感ぜ
られ事終りて御酒を賜ひ其禄を加増せられ
し

とか

右の如くなれば虚實は殊に心得べき事なりとし

◉刀の搆へ方の事

刀の搆へ方ゝ五通りあり、大上段、上段、中段、
下段、八相。此五つなり。水月とも云ひ。青眼
とも云ひ。眉間の間へ狙ひをつけて歟手を悩ま
すこと、演劇にて能く演ずることにて。講談師も
形ち話にする事なれど。即ち中段の一手なり、
五樣各左の圖、及び以下の圖を見るべし。左の
圖ハ大上段の搆へ方にて、足を外八文字に踏み
右の手に鍔際を持ち、左の手にて柄頭を持ち、
圖の如き高さに上げて打おろすなり。

◎ **The Kamae, or Stances, with the Katana**

There are five Kamae or stances of the Katana, and they are as
follows. The five are Dai Jodan, Jodan, Chu-dan, Ge-dan and Ha-so.
Worry the opponent by putting pressure on places like Suigetsu, the
solar plexus, Seigan, or on the eyes, or Miken, between the eyebrows.
Storytellers might even find this of help to their set-tales, maybe
something that occurs just before the climax. People of all stripes
should look at the illustration to the left, and all the illustrations
below as well[8].

The illustraion above shows Dai Jodan Kamae, Upper Stance.
Your feet are planted outward in the shape of the character for eight,
hachi 八. Your right hand should be just below the Tsuba, or sword
guard, and your left hand should hold the Tsuka-gashira, or pommel.
Your sword should be held at the height shown in the illustration
and you should cut down from there.

---

[8] 五儀 *Gogi*, or the "five types" refers to both the ranks at court:
公 prince/ 侯 Daimyo/ 伯 Count/ 子 Viscount/ 男 Son
A second "five types" are the kinds of people in the world:
聖人 Saint/ 賢人 Wise man/ 君子 Man of high rank/士人 Samurai/
庸人 Common man.

左の圖は上段の構へ方なり、右の足を後へ引き、少し体を反して、圖のごとく上げ構ふるなり、左の足を向ふへ出し、

左の圖は中段の構へ方なり、足は少し廣く外八文字に踏み、少し反身になり、圖の如く竹刀を向ふ上に持ち構ふるなり、

The illustration on the top right shows how to hold Jodan Kamae. Your left leg should be planted out facing your opponent. Your right leg is back with your body leaned slightly back. The Kamae should be as pictured in the illustration.

The illustration on the left is the way to hold Chudan Kamae, Middle Stance. Your legs are planted in a slightly wider, outward facing Kanji for 8 八. As shown in the illustration, in this Kamae your Shinai, or bamboo sword, is held angling upward toward your opponent.

左の圖は八相の構へ方なり、此右構へは左の右の足を後ろにし、何時にても右足の足を前へ出し、前へ出し、せしや打拂はうにしんとして、圖のごとく構へるなり。

左の圖は下段の構へ方なり、足つきは前に異らず、体は尋常にて、竹刀先を圖のごとく下ろすなり。

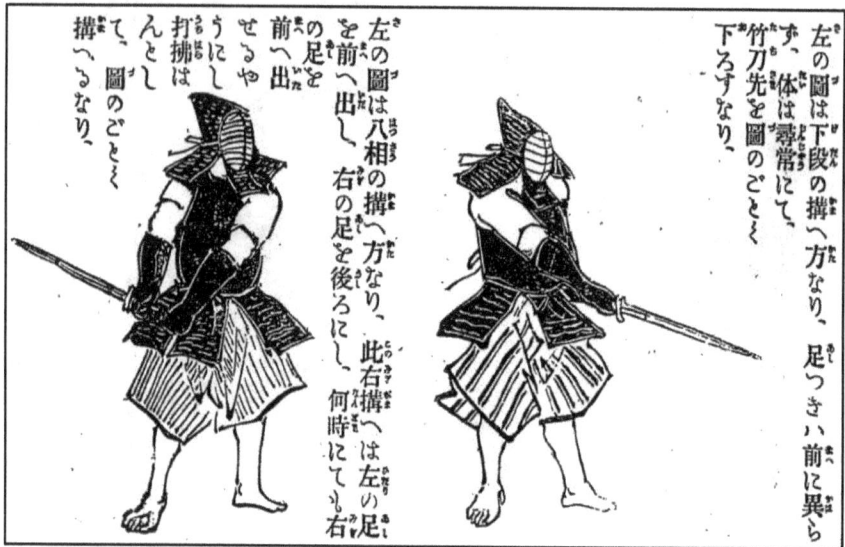

The illustration on right shows how is the way to hold Gedan no Kamae, Lower Stance. Both your feet should be equally spaced, with your body held naturally. The end of your Shinai should be pointed down as depicted in the illustration.

The illustration on the left is the way to hold Haso no Kamae, Side Back Stance. For this Kamae your left foot should be out front while your right foot is placed behind. You are ready at any moment to step out with your right foot and strike with a sweeping motion. You should stand as shown in the illustration.

Translator's Note:

The following techniques contain around 7 steps each. The author's writing style is to summarize the previously introduced information and then add the next step. So some of the same information will repeated several times. The author labeled the two combatants Tsukai-te "The User" and Uke-te "The Reciever," however for clarity I have labeled the combatants *you* and *the Opponent.*

圖 一 革

◉劍術 抜口 第一形

此試合の初めは、木刀もしくは竹刀にても、眞劍ならば鯉口の所を持ち、右の手を右の膝頭に下り、噂踞り、其の手を双方立ち上る間に、夫より第三圖の如くごく小手の左の第一圖のごとく、左の手にて、各々左の手にて鍔下を持ち、(立ち上る時足は第二圖のごとく、尤も此時足は圖の如く、夫より抜打にて人の小手を打つと同時に、抜打とは手首を謂ふなり)又人の小手を使人は右の足を踊むなり、とく外八文字に置き、夫より下を持ちたる手にて鍔下を放さず、(小手とは手首を謂ふなり)使人は左の足を出して右の足を切付け、素早く使人は左の足を出して右の足を切付け、(素早く)四圖のごとく、

◎ Kenjutsu Nuki-Kuchi, Draw and Cut
First Kata
<u>First Illustration</u>

    This 試合 Shi-ai or match begins as is depicted in the first illustration. Both combatants are squatting down with the left hand just below the Tsuba, or hand guard, of the Ki Tachi, wooden sword, or Shinai, bamboo sword.

    If you are holding a Shin-Ken, or real sword, your hand should be in the area of the 鯉口 Koi-guchi, the opening or "carp's mouth" of the scabbard. Your right hand should be atop your 膝頭 Hiza-gashira, or kneecap. From there, as is shown in the second illustration, both sides stand up with their left hands holding the sword below the Tsuba (The left hand does not release the sword while standing.)[9] Again, your feet should be planted as shown in the illustration, resembling the bottom of the Kanji for 8, 八.

    From there, as is shown in the third illustration, you step out with your right foot and do a 抜打 Nuki-uchi, a rapid draw and cut onto the Kote of the Opponent. (Know that by "Kote" we are referring to the wrist).

---

[9] All brackets are from the original text.

圖 二 第

の足に繼ぎ、（繼ぐとは並べ揃ゆるなり）足を繼
ぎ、圖のごとく刀を振り上げ、又た左足を出して、右足に
とくと右の足を出して、第五圖のご
繼ぐと同時に斬り下げ、左の足を一足引き、
の掤元へ右の手の指を延べ伏充て持ち、第七圖に
のごとく左へ七ひ上げ、左の手の食指拇指に及び刀を右に
背を擦りて右へ引き、此形は誠に神速にして、
受くる後え落たに收むるなり、鞘口を持ち、
後人は刀を抜く間も無きこと、能く想ひ見るべ

Second Illustration

Next, as the fourth illustration shows, you rapidly step out with your left foot and then slide your right foot up beside it in a moved called Tsugi 繼ぎ (Tsugi means "to bring together and line up.") The moment your feet come together, which is shown in illustration 4, raise your Katana up. Step with your right foot as shown in the fifth illustration. Follow that by stepping with your left foot. The moment your left foot lines up with your right in a Tsugi, cut down and drop your left foot back about a foot's width. Do the same with your right foot.

Your Katana should be held as shown in illustration six. The fingers of your right hand, which is holding the 柄元 Tsuka moto, or just below where the handle meets the hand guard, should be extended turning the Katana upside down almost parallel to the ground.

As shown in the seventh illustration, bring the Katana to the left and, using the 食指 Hitosashi-yubi, or pointer finger, and the 拇指 Oya-yubi, or thumb, grip the 背 Mune, or back of the blade. Pulling with your right, allow the blade to slip through your fingers while your left hand holds the opening of the 鞘 Saya, or scabbard. Stepping back, sheathe your sword.

第三圖

此の第三圖は、前の第二圖のごとく、鯉口を持ち、右の手を下げ、使人は足を双方左右の八文字に踏みて透を見合するが、使人の小手を透さんや否や、斬り付けたるとあるなり。斬くして使人は受人の小手をザックリと斬り込むとき、再び誠に左の足を出し、刀を振り上ぐるや、継ぐや、神速に次の第四圖のごとく刀を振り上ぐる。右の足に継ぎ、素早く左の足を出し、此圖受人を小手を斬り込むとき、斬る駿速の斬りに受人の肩をザックリと斬るべし。斬り込むとき、斬り上ぐる、間髪を入れず、上げて右の足を出し、込ひては、受人の開きあひをも見るべし。受人は茫然たるべし。

Third Illustration

This Kata should be done with Shin-Soku 神速, or "Divine Swiftness" in order to prevent the Opponent from having any chance to draw his own Katana. This should be committed to memory.

This illustration follows the previous. Both combatants are holding the Katana left-handed at the Koi-guchi, the opening of the scabbard, while the right hand hangs down. Their feet are planted out like the base of a Hachimon-ji, or the bottom of the Kanji 八, waiting for the moment that a Suki 隙, or opening, presents itself.

Upon seeing a Suki in the Opponent, you step forward with your right foot and, at the same time, do a rapid Nuki-uchi, Draw and Cut, to the Kote, or wrist, of the Opponent. Next, you rapidly bring your left foot up even with the right in a Tsugi movement, and, as shown in the fourth illustration, raise your Katana overhead. Step out with your right foot again and quickly bring your left up beside it. Then cut down deeply into the shoulder of the Opponent with a *Zakuri!* sound.

There should not be the slightest gap between these movements, not even a single hair should be able to fit in the gap between them. As can be seen in this illustration, when the Kote of the Opponent is being cut, his legs are spread apart. You have done an explosive cut that the Opponent receives and it leaves him utterly dumbfounded.

第四圖

此第四圖は、前の第三圖のごとく、使人が受人の小手を右に出しさま抜打に斬りてより、直ちに左の足を出して右の足に繼ぎ、繼ぐや其刀を受人の肩を斬らんとして、振り上げたるところなり、繼ぎたる足の寄り矩合を能々視よ。是よりは神速に右の足を出し、左の足をそれへ繼ぎ、受人の肩を斬るなり、卽ち次の第五圖の体勢より次の第五圖の体勢にうつる間は、實に間髪を容れざる程に速くす べし。此第四圖の体勢より次の第五圖の体勢にうつる間は、實に間髪を容れざる程に速くす。

Fourth Illustration

This fourth illustration follows what occurred in illustration three. You have stepped forward with your right foot and cut to your Opponent's wrist with a Nuki-uchi, Draw and Cut. You next slide your left foot up beside your right foot in a Tsugi movement. After that, immediately cut down into your Opponent's shoulder. Understand that as soon as your feet come together your sword should be raised fully overhead. This is shown in the illustration. This illustration shows the proper position after you have brought your feet together and should be studied carefully.

Next, step with your right foot using Shin-Soku, or Divine Speed, and slide your left foot up beside your right. Then cut down into the shoulder of your Opponent. You should move with such speed that a single hair cannot be slid into the interval between the position shown in illustration four and the position shown in illustration five.

此第五圖は、前の第四圖のごとく、受人の肩を續いて斬らんとして刀を振り上げ、神速に右の足を出し、左の足をそれに繼ぎ、受人の肩を斬り下げたる所なり、是にて使人は勝ち、受人は負けなり、是までの使人の働きは、烈風の吹き來るがごとく迅速なりしを以て、受人は刀を援くこともならず、やみやみと肩を斬り下げられたり、眞劍ならんに受人は直ちに仰反り仆るべし、是より使人は後へ引きて刀を收むるなり、其の收め方は次に示すべし。

Fifth Illustration

This fifth illustration follows what happened in the fourth illustration. Your aim is to cut into shoulder of your Opponent, so you bring your Katana up and with Shin-soku, Divine Swiftness, and step forward with your right foot. Slide your left foot up beside it and cut down into the shoulder of your opponent.

In this fashion you win and the Opponent is the loser. Throughout this technique your movements should be fast like a violent wind. The Opponent, meanwhile, has no chance to draw his Katana, thus cutting through his shoulder is done with an easy *Yami-yami* sound. If you had been using a Shinken, real sword, your adversary would have been instantly blown back.

After cutting, you step back and sheathe your sword. The Osame Kata 収め方, or way of sheathing the sword, will be described on the next page.

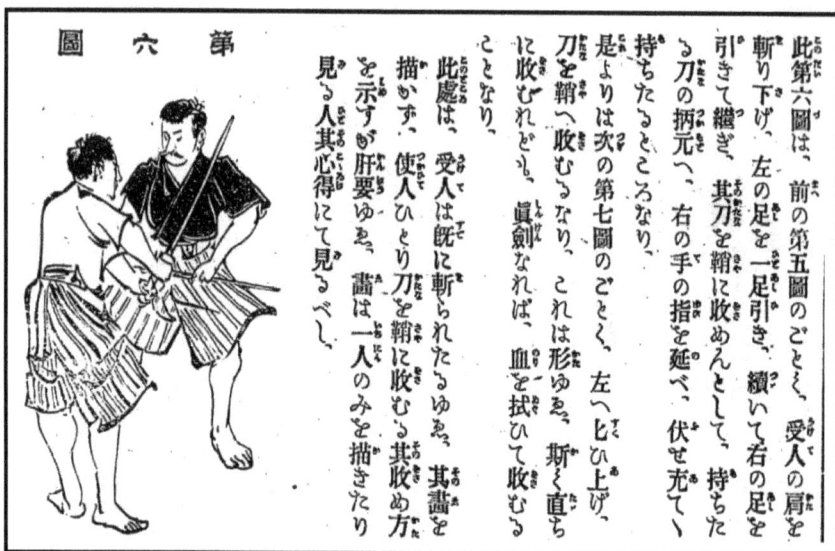

此第六圖は、前の第五圖のごとく、受人の肩を斬り下げ、左の足を一足引き、續いて右の足を引きて繼ぎ、其刀を鞘に收めんとして、持ちたる刀の拵元へ、右の手の指を延べ、伏せ充てゝ持ちたるところなり。是よりは次の第七圖のごとく、左へヒひ上げ、刀を鞘へ收むるなり、これは形ゆゑ、斯く直ちに收むれども、眞劍なれば、血を拭ひて收むることとなり。此處は、受人は既に斬られたるゆゑ、其畫を描かず、使人ひとり刀を鞘に收むる其收め方を示すが肝要ゆゑ、畫は一人のみを描きたり見る人其心得にて見るべし。

Sixth Illustration

The sixth illustration follows what happened in the fifth illustration. After cutting into the Opponent's shoulder, pull your left foot back one step, then slide your right foot back beside it in a Tsugi movement.

Sheathe your Katana in the Saya, or scabbard, by first extending the fingers of your right hand, which is holding the Tsuka-moto of the Katana. Next, lay your sword it on its back, blade up, on the end of the sheath.

The next step is as shown in the following seventh illustration. You flip the end of your Katana up and over onto your left side and sheathe it in your Saya, or scabbard. As this is a Kata the sword is immediately sheathed, however if it were a Shinken, real sword, the blood would first be wiped off before sheathing.

At this point as the Opponent has already been cut there will not be a drawing of him. He sheathes his Katana on his own. As this Osame-kata is the Kanyo, or the essential point, only one person will be depicted. When studying this illustration keep in mind this is how both practitioners should sheathe their swords.

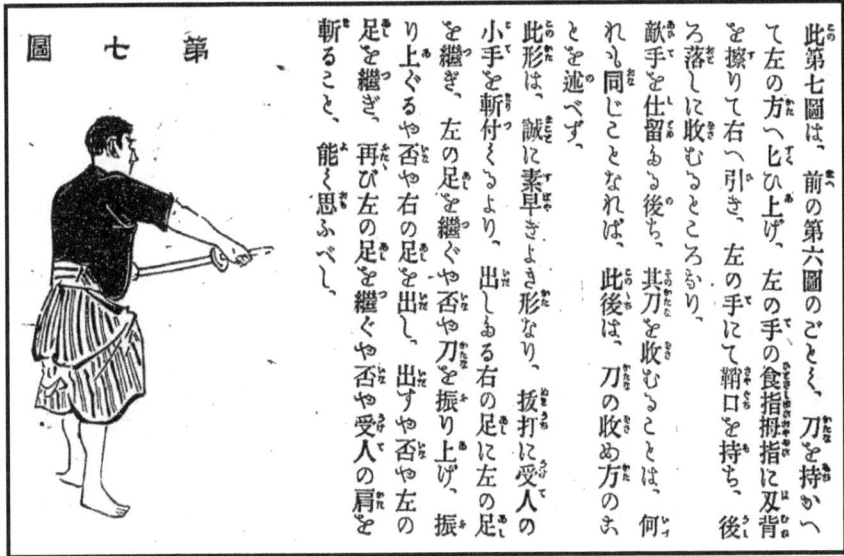

此第七圖は、前の第六圖のごとく、刀を持ちかへ
て左の方へひ上げ、左の手の食指拇指に又背
を擦りて右へ引き、左の手にて鞘口を持ち、後
ろ落しに收むるところるり、
獻手を仕留ある後ち、其刀を收むることは、何に
れも同じことことなれば、此後は、刀の收め方のみ
とを述べず、
此形は、誠に素早きよき形なり、抜打に受人の
小手を斬付くるより、出しるる右の足に左の足
を繼ぎ、左の足を繼ぐや否や刀を振り上げ、振
り上ぐるや否や右の足を出し、出すや否や左の
足を繼ぎ、再び左の足を繼ぐや否や受人の肩を
斬ること、能く思ふべし。

Seventh Illustration

The seventh illustration follows what occurred in the sixth illustration. Rotate your Katana so the blade is up in a scooping motion to your left side. Next, grip the Mune, or back of the blade, with your Hitosashi-yubi, index finger, and Oya-yubi, thumb. The remaining fingers of your left hand hold the opening of the Saya and, as the right hand pulls the blade to your right, the steel slides through the fingers. Then push the Katana into your Saya.

In all of the following techniques, the step after you have taken out your opponent is the Osame Kata, or Way of Sheathing the Sword. As this process is the same every time, it will not be repeated.

This Kata is, as a whole, an extremely fast technique. It begins with a Nuki-uchi, Draw and Cut, to the Opponent's wrist. You then immediately bring your left foot up beside your right, in a movement called Tsugi. The moment your left foot completes the Tsugi, your Katana should be brought up above your head. As soon as the Katana is up, step forward with your right foot. As soon as you step with your right, bring your left foot up beside it. As soon as your left foot is beside your right, cut into the shoulder of your Opponent.

These steps should be considered carefully.

刀を収むるときは前に同じ。

肩を斬下るなり。

刀を振り翳し、まに右の足を引きて左の足に継ぎ、（第五圖のごとく）速に受人の

右の圖のごとく、第四圖のごとく右の足を引きて左の足に継ぎ、斬付けたる刀を引きき、（此時双方右の足を出したる）を視に

第三圖より示すべし、使人は受人の右横腹を抜打に視るを、此試合の初太刀は

は省き、第三圖の斬り付け、（此時双方右の

第一形に示したると同じことなれば、是より

第一は坐禮にて、第二は身搆へして見合ふなり、第二は身搆へして見合ふより後。

○劔術 抜口 第二形

◎ Kenjutsu Nuki-Kuchi, Draw and Cut
Second Kata
Third Illustration

As we have already seen the Za-Rei, or seated bow, in the first illustration, and the Kamae the body should take has already been shown in the second illustration, we shall abbreviate that part and begin from the third illustration.

This Shi-ai, or bout, begins as is shown in the illustration. Without warning, you draw and cut the Migi Yoko-bara 右横腹, or right side, of your Opponent (Note here that both swordsmen have their right foot forward.)

As is shown in illustration four, after cutting, raise your Katana above your head. Pull your right foot back and then pull your left foot beside it. The fourth illustration depicts how the Katana should be held above your head. The fifth illustration shows your next attack as you cut down into the shoulder of the Opponent with Shin-Soku, or divine swiftness.

After this cut, drop back. You then sheathe your Katana as described before.

第四圖

り、能ひ分くべし。
は、抜口は何れも能く似たれど、其うちに變りあ
右の足に繼ぎ、前の第一形に同じ、誠に素早き働きなり、
の足を一足進み近より、神速なる左の足を出して
やう、次の第五圖に見ゆれど、然にあらず、右
是よりは同じ体勢ゆて、受人の肩を斬り下ぐる
翳したる所なり、
を引きて左の足を繼ぎ、神速に刀を上段に振り
の右横腹を斬り付け、其刀を引きさまに右の足
此第四圖は、前の第三圖のごとく、使人が受人

Fourth Illustration

This fourth illustration follows the third illustration. You have cut into the right Yoko-bara of the Opponent. Pull your Katana out while stepping back with your right foot. Then immediately slide your left foot beside it. As your feet come together your Katana should have been whipped up overhead into the Dai-jodan position with Shin-soku, Divine Swiftness.

The next step is to cut down into the shoulder of your opponent from this stance. Though it can't be seen in the fifth illustration, you take one step closer with your right foot, then with Shin-soku, Divine Swiftness, slide your left foot beside your right. You should cut down into the opponent's shoulder the moment your left foot joins your right, or just before. As was shown in the First Kata, the movement must be well and truly fast.

While these Nuki-uchi, Draw and Cut, techniques may resemble one another, there are differences and these must be understood and kept separate in your mind.

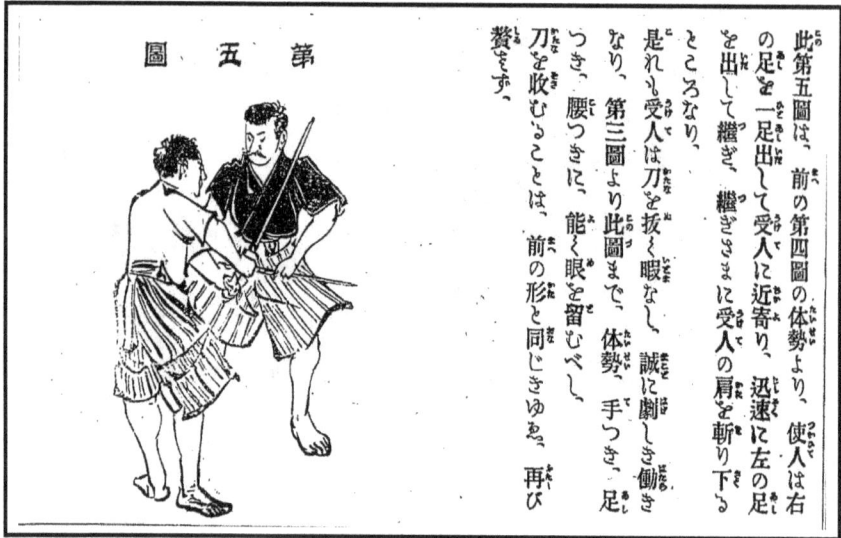

此第五圖は、前の第四圖の體勢より、使人は右の足を一足出して受人に近寄り、迅速に左の足を出して繼ぎ、繼ぎざまに受人の肩を斬り下るところなり、是れも受人は刀を抜く暇なし、誠に劇しき働きなり、第三圖より此圖まで、體勢、手つき、足つき、腰つきに、能く眼を留むべし、刀を收むることは、前の形と同じきゆゑ、再び贅をず。

第五圖

Fifth Illustration

The fifth illustration follows what happened in the fourth illustration. It shows your body positioning after having cut. You take one step forward with your right foot, closing your distance to the Opponent. Then, in a flash, slide your left foot up. The moment your feet come together your sword should cut through his shoulder.

In this technique as well, the Opponent has no chance to draw his Katana due to the absolute ferocity of your movement. Starting from the third illustration your body's position should be scrutinized. Where the hands are. Where the feet are. Where the hips are.

The Katana is sheathed the same way as in the previous Kata, so it will not be reproduced again.

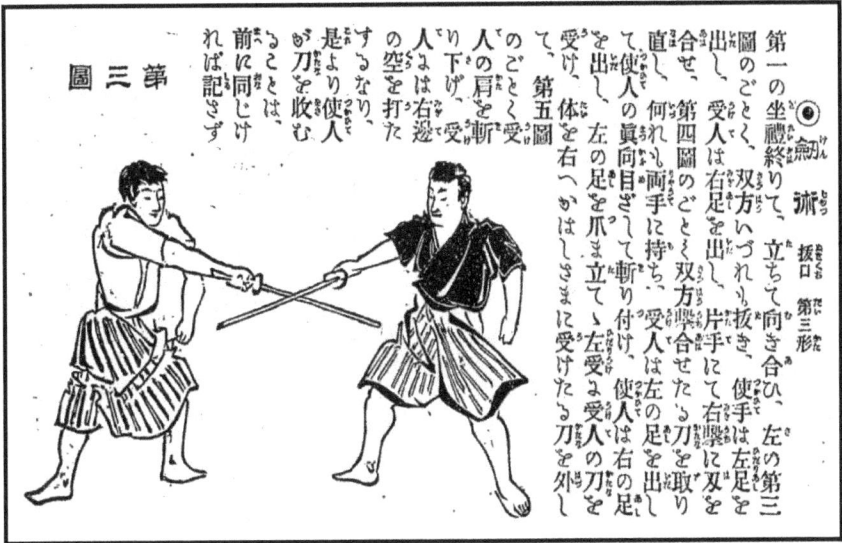

◎ Kenjutsu Nuki-Kuchi, Draw and Cut
Third Kata
<u>Third Illustration</u>

The two combatants stand and face each other after having completed the Za-rei, or seated bow, shown in the first illustration. As shown in the illustration above, both combatants have drawn their sword. You have your left foot out, while the Opponent has his right foot out. You have both swung to the right using a one-handed grip. The blades strike together.

As shown in the Fourth Illustration, the two opponents have dropped back from where the Katana met and are now both holding the Katana in a two-handed grip. The Opponent steps forward with his left foot and, aiming straight at you, cuts down. You step forward with your right foot and allow the heel of your left foot to lift off the ground. This is called Tsuma-dachi 爪ま立ち, poised on the toes position. Block the opponent's cut with 左受 Hidari-uke, Left Block. Twist your body to the right allowing the attack to slide off your sword. Next, as shown in the fifth illustration, cut the Opponent's shoulder. Meanwhile the Opponent's sword cuts empty air on your right side.

The next step is to sheathe your Katana. This is done as described before, so it will not be reproduced.

33

此第四圖は、受人が斬結びたる刀を取り直し、
左の足を出して、両手にて斬て蒐ると、使人は
右の足を出し、左の足を爪ま立て、両手にて左
受え、受人の斬り込む刀を、受け止めたるとこ
ろなり、
是よりは体を右へかはし外して、受人に右の空
を斬らせ、神速に受人の左の肩を斬り下るなり
夫より後は一足引きて刀を収む、前の第一形の
終りの、第六圖第七圖に同じ、
此斬つけたるときの圖は、使人の足ひらきた
れど、直ちに左の足を右の足へ寄せ付け立つ
なり、あれを足を継ぐといふ・

Fourth Illustration

In the previous step, after your swords struck together, the Opponent brought his Katana up into Dai Jodan. Stepping out with his left foot he cuts down on you with a two-handed grip. In response, you step out with your right foot and rise up on the toes of your left foot. Holding the sword with both hands you defend against his cut with a Hidari-uke, left block.

From there the body twist your body to the right, evading, causing the Opponent to slice into the air on your right. With Shin-Soku, Divine Speed, you cut down into the left shoulder of the Opponent.

From there, after stepping back about one foot-span, sheathe your Katana. This Kata ends the same way the previous one did, so the sixth illustration and the seventh illustration are the same.

Note that in the fourth illustration, your feet are shown spread apart as you get ready to cut. However, your next movement will be to slide your left foot beside the right. This movement is referred to as Tsugi.

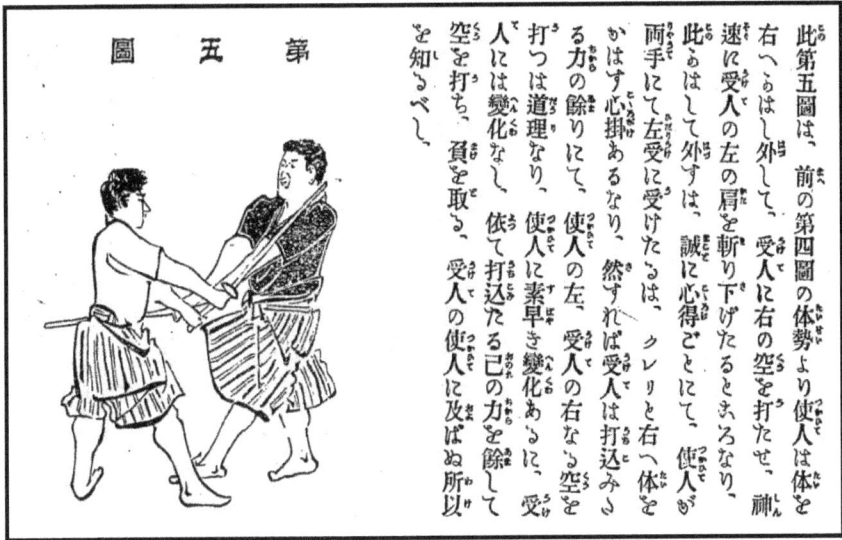

此第五圖は、前の第四圖の體勢より使人は體を右へゐはし外して、受人に右の空を打たせ、神速に受人の左の肩を斬り下げたるとみろなり、此るはして外すは、誠に心得ごとにて、使人が両手にて左受に受けたるは、クレリと右へ體をかはす心掛あるなり、然すれば受人は打込みるる力の餘りにて、受人の右なる空を打つは道理なり、使人の左、受人に素早き變化あるに、受人には變化なし、依つて打込たる已の力を餘して空を打ち、負を取る、受人の使人に及ばぬ所以を知るべし。

Fifth Illustration

The fifth illustration shows how your body position has shifted from the fourth illustration. You twisted your body to the right to avoid the opponent's attack, causing his sword to only cut the air on your right side. Your cut into the shoulder of the Opponent should be done with Shin-Soku, Divine Swiftness.

This evasion of the opponent's cut is a truly important lesson. You must learn how to do a two handed Hidari-uke, Left Block, and then twist your body to the right with a *Kureri!*, the sound of something twisting smoothly away. If done properly, what occurs is that the force of the Opponent's blow will slice through the air on your left, or, from the view of the Opponent, to the right. This is the principle being employed.

In response to your rapid Henka 變化, defensive counter, the Opponent finds himself unable to adapt, and the force of his own cut slices only air, resulting in his defeat.

You should have a firm grasp on why the Opponent is unable to react to your actions.

第一の坐體と、第二の構へとは、何れも同じ事ゆゑ、圖を省く。

第二の構へより試合の初めは、左の第三圖のごとく、受人は上段に構へて撃たんとするを、使人は刀の柄を借りて右の手を掛け、三足出で抜きかけ、受人が斬下ろすを、右の手を一足引きて足をつぎ、第四圖のごとく、（右）の空を打たせ、受人は後へ（右を見る右）の小手を撃ち、右の足を一足受人の左前へ進み、左の足を……神速に刀を取り直し……りるりをののの受ぎて進な下斬肩左人繼め

第三圖

第四形　抜口　術

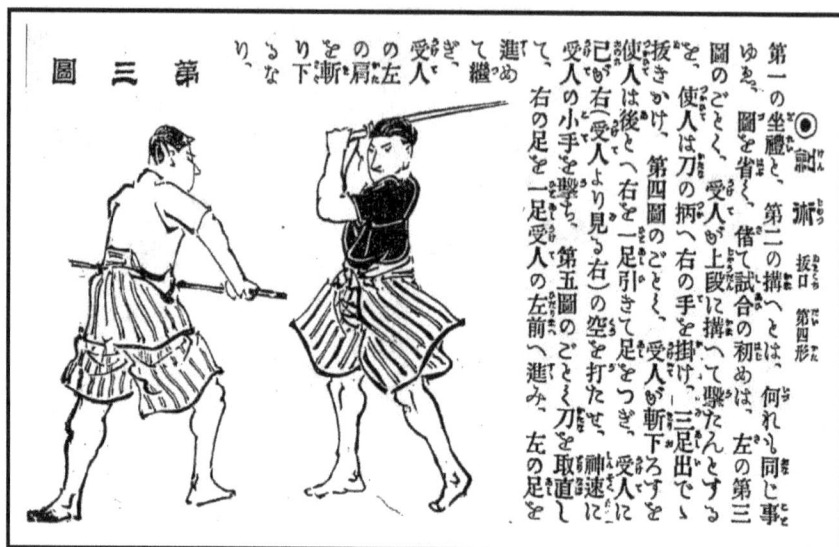

◎ **Kenjutsu Nuki-Kuchi, Draw and Cut**
Fourth Kata
Third Illustration

    Since the Za-rei, Seated Bow, from the first illustration and the Kamae from the second illustration are the same, both illustrations will be omitted.

    So then, the beginning of this Shi-ai, or bout, is as shown in the Third Illustration. The Opponent is in Jodan Kamae preparing to strike down. You have your right hand on the handle of your Katana. When he steps with his honored foot, draw your sword[10]. Then, as is shown in the fourth illustration, when the Opponent cuts, you drop your right foot back one step and bring your feet together. This means the Opponent's cut only slices through the air on your right side (the right from the perspective of the Opponent.)

    With Shin-Soku, divine swiftness, cut the Opponent's wrist. This is shown in the fifth illustration. Then bring your Katana up, reading to strike again. Take one step toward the Opponent's left side with your right foot, then slide your left foot up beside it. Finally, cut down into the Opponent's left shoulder.

---

[10] Omi-ashi "Honored foot" refers (humbly) to someone's foot or leg.

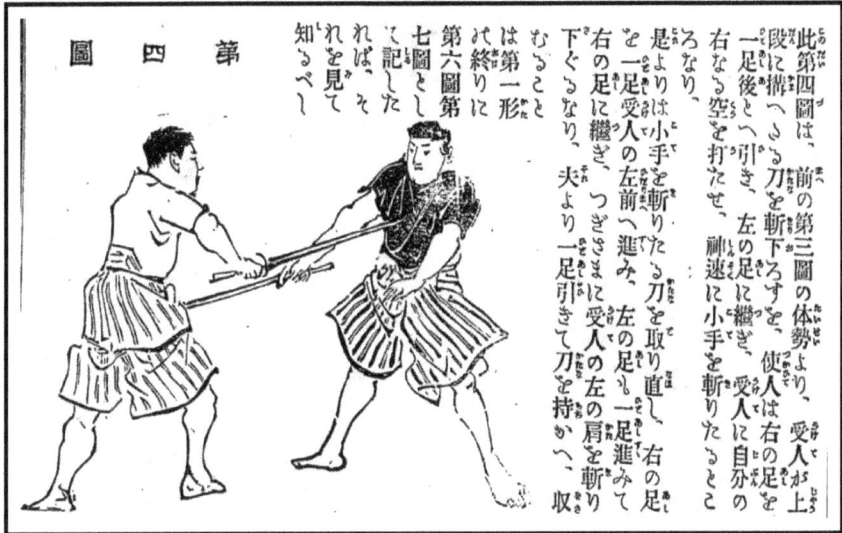

この第四圖は、前の第三圖の体勢より、受人が上段に搆へうる刀を斬下ろすを、一足後へ引き、左の足に繼ぎ、使人は右の足を一足空を打たせ、神速に小手を斬りたるところなり。是よりは、小手を斬りたる刀を取り直し、右の足を一足進みて、左の足を右の足に繼ぎ、つぎさまに受人の左の肩を斬り、夫より一足引きて刀を持かへ、むくろことは第一形にて終りに、第六圖第七圖として記したれば、それを見て知るべし

Fourth Illustration

The fourth illustration follows the position shown in the third illustration. The Opponent, starting from Jodan Kamae cuts down with his Katana. In response you drop your right foot back one step to join it with the left in a Tsugi movement. The Opponent is made to cut through the air to his right, while with Shin-soku swiftness you cut into the opponent's Kote, or wrist.

After cutting his wrist, do a Tori Naoshi 取り直し, meaning bring your sword up and ready for another attack. Take one step forward with your right foot towards the Opponent's left. Your left foot then follows in a Tsugi movement. As soon as your left foot joins your right, cut down into the Opponent's left shoulder.

Following the final cut, step back and rotate the Katana blade over and sheathe. This Kata concludes the same way as the First Kata, thus you can refer to the sixth illustration and the seventh illustration in that technique.

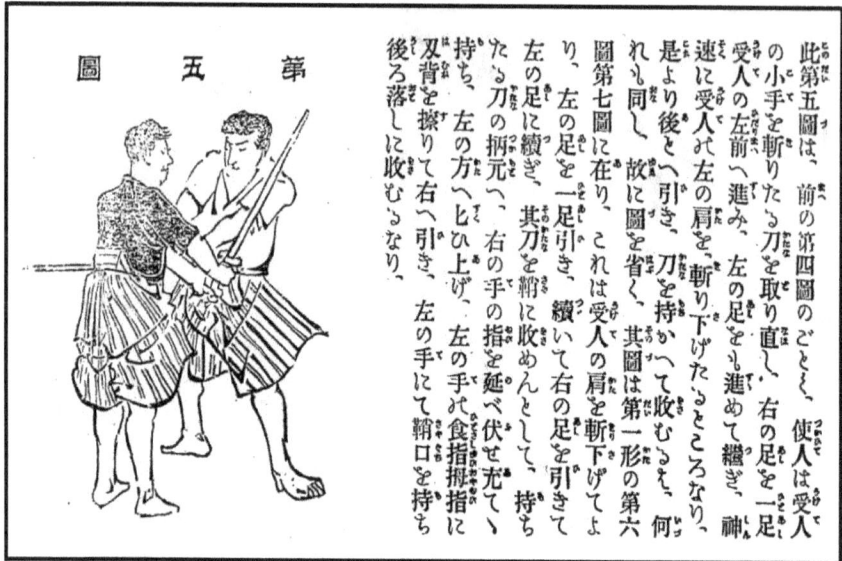

第五圖

此第五圖は、前の第四圖のごとく、使人は受人
の小手を斬りたる刀を取り直し、右の足を一足
受人の左前へ進み、左の足をも進めて繼ぎ、神
速に受人が左の肩を、斬り下げたるところなり、
是より後へ引き、刀を持かへて收むるも、何れ
れも同じ故に圖を省く、其圖は第一形の第六
圖第七圖に在り、これは受人の肩を斬下げてよ
り、左の足を一足引き、續いて右の足を引きて
左の足に續ぎ、其刀を鞘に收めんとして、持ち
たる刀の柄元へ、右の手の指を延べ伏せて、持
ち、左の方へとひ上げ、左の手の食指拇指に
持ち、左の手の食指拇指に
又背を擦りて右へ引き、左の手にて鞘口を持ち
後ろ落しに收むるなり。

Fifth Illustration

The fifth illustration follows what occurred in the fourth illustration. You have cut Kote and then done a Tori Naoshi, bringing your Katana up again ready to attack. You next take one step toward the Opponent's left with your right foot, then slide your left foot up beside it with Shin-soku, Divine Swiftness and cut his left shoulder. You then rotate your Katana so the blade is up and then sheathe your sword. Since this step is the same as before the illustrations will be omitted. The illustrations I refer to are #6 & #7 from the first technique.

After cutting down into the shoulder of the Opponent step back one step, first with your left foot, then with your right. To sheathe your sword, first extend the fingers of your right hand, which are holding the Tsuba-moto of the Katana, should be extended. Then raise the tip of the blade towards your left shoulder as if you are trying to scoop something up with the tip. Hold the back of the sword with the Oya-yubi, thumb, and Hitosashi-yubi, forefinger, of your left hand. Allow the blade to rub them as you pull the sword to your right. The remaining fingers of your left hand hold the end of the Saya as the sword is sheathed.

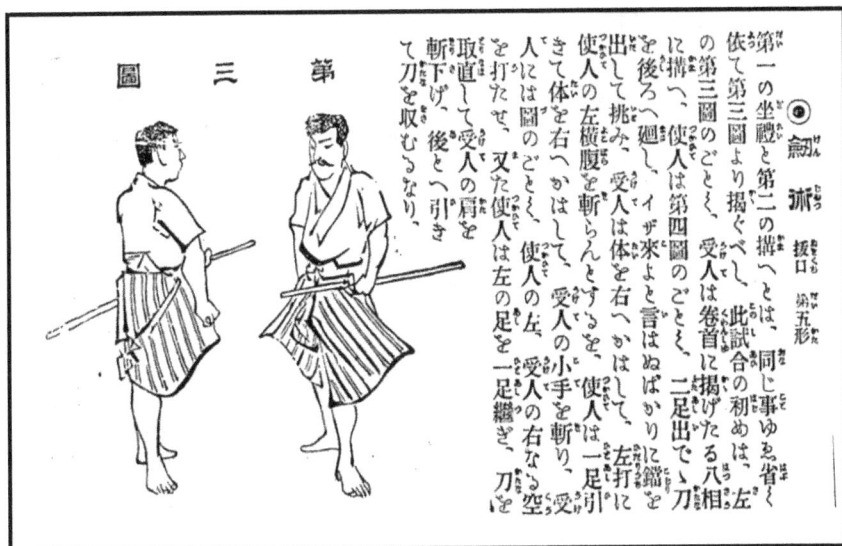

◎ Kenjutsu Nuki-Kuchi, Draw and Cut
Fifth Kata
<u>Third Illustration</u>

As the initial Za-Rei as well as the Kamae are the same as illustrations 1 & 2 from the first technique, they will be omitted here. This Shi-ai, or duel, begins as is shown in the third illustration, above.

As the fourth illustration shows your Opponent goes into Haso Kamae as was described at the beginning of this volume. You have taken one step back with your right foot, and swung your Katana behind. With the Kojiri 鐺, or metal cap on the end of the scabbard, facing the opponent it is as if you are inviting them in and saying, "Come on then!"

Your Opponent is standing with his body turned to the right. He cuts to your left Yoko-bara, or left side of the stomach. In response to this you step back one foot-span with your left foot to remove your body from the attack. You then cut his Kote, or wrist. The Opponent, as shown in the illustration, strikes only the air to the left of you, the right of the Opponent. Next, you bring your left foot up beside your right. Then do a Tori Naoshi, bringing your Katana up again for another strike, and cut the shoulder of the Opponent. From here you drop back and sheathe your Katana.

39

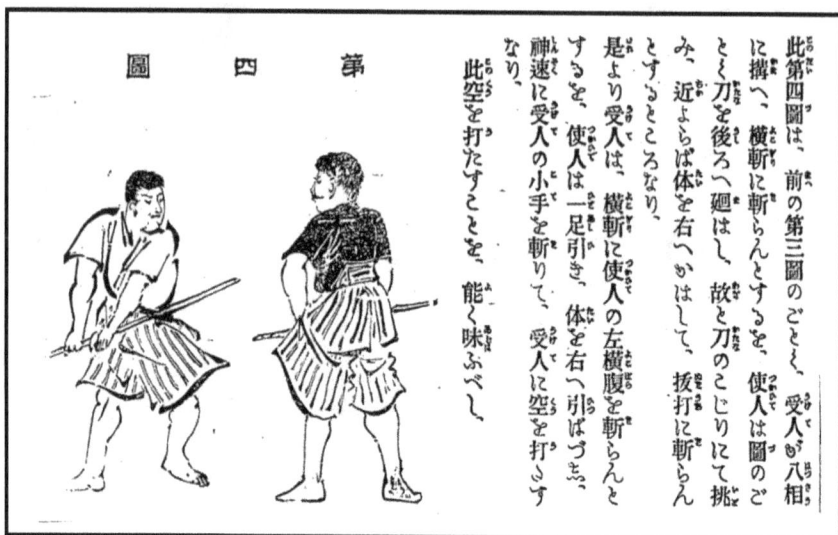

此第四圖は、前の第三圖のごとく、受人が八相
に搆へ、横斬に斬らんとするを、使人は圖のご
とく刀を後ろへ廻はし、故と刀のこじりにて挑
み、近よらば體を右へかはして、抜打に斬らん
とするところなり。
是より受人は、横斬に使人の左横腹を斬らんと
するを、使人は一足引き、體を右へ引ばづき、
神速に受人の小手を斬りて、受人に空を打さす
なり。
此空を打たすことを、能く味ふべし。

Fourth Illustration

This fourth illustration follows what happened in the third, namely the Opponent is in Haso Kamae and is seeking to cut with a Yoko-giri, horizontal cut across your abdomen. You have rotated the handle of your Katana back and are challenging/ threatening/ keeping your opponent at bay with the Kojiri, the metal end of your scabbard. This is shown in the illustration. When the Opponent begins his cut, you step back one pace with your left foot, rotating your body counter-clockwise and do a rapid Nuki-uchi, Draw and Cut.

This illustration shows the moment before your Opponent begins a horizontal cut to the left side of your abdomen. You will respond by dropping back one foot-span, thereby rotating your body counter-clockwise and cutting his wrist with Shin-Soku, Divine Swiftness. Meanwhile your Opponent strikes only air.

The reason your Opponent strikes only air should be considered carefully.

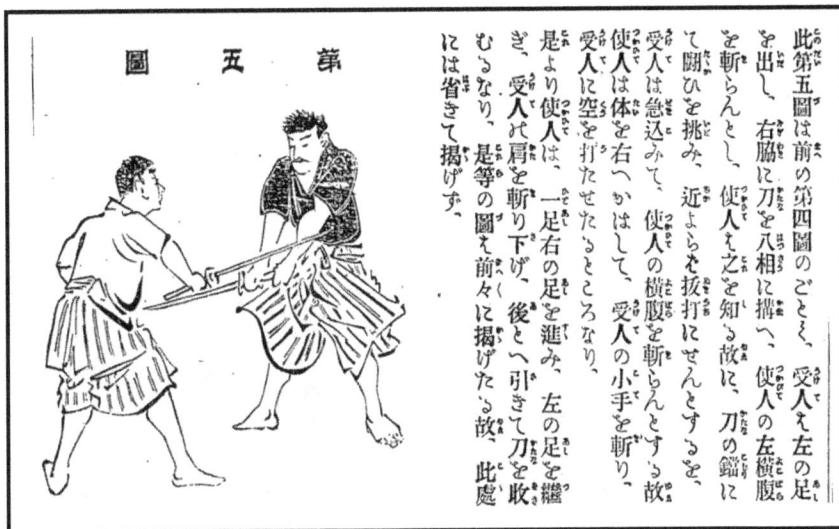

此第五圖は前の第四圖のごとく、受人で左の足
を出し、右脇に刀を八相に搆へ、使人の左横腹
を斬らんとし、使人之を知る故に、刀の鐺に
て鬮ひを挑み、近よらを抜打にせんとするを、
受人は急込みて、使人の横腹を斬らんとする故、
使人は体を右へかはして、受人の小手を斬り、
受人に空を打たせたるところなり。
是より使人は、一足右の足を進み、左の足を繼
ぎ、受人れ肩を斬り下げ、後とへ引きて刀を収
むるなり、是等の圖え前々に揚げたる故、此處
には省きて揚げず。

Fifth Illustration

This fifth illustration follows the preceding illustration four. The Opponent's left foot is forward, and he is holding his Katana along the right side of his body in Haso Kamae. He is looking to cut your left side. You are aware of his intent and are using the Kojiri of your Katana to keep him at bay.

In an effort to close in and strike quickly, the Opponent launches a rapid attack, cutting to your left side. You respond by dropping back one step with your left foot, thereby rotating your body counter-clockwise out of danger. You then cut his Kote while the Opponent is made to strike only air.

From here you step forward with your right foot and slide your left foot up beside it. Bringing the feet together like this is called Tsugi. Finally, you cut down into the Opponent's shoulder.

Take a step back and sheathe your Katana. Since this was presented in previous illustrations, it will be abbreviated and not reprinted.

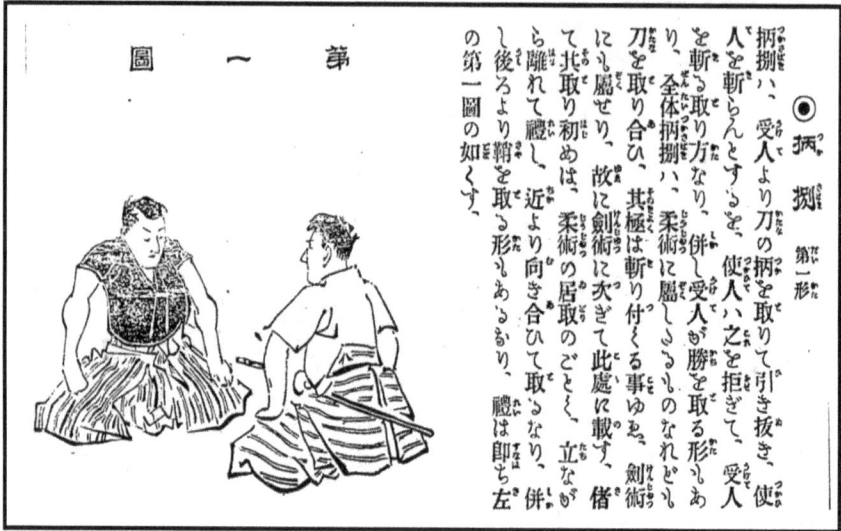

圖　一　第

柄捌、受人より刀の柄を取りて引き抜き、使人
人を斬らんとするを、使人ハ之を拒ぎて、受人
を斬でて取らんとする方なり、併し受人が勝を取る形もあ
刀を取り合ひ、全体柄捌ハ、柔術に屬しるものなれども
に屬せり、故に剣術に次ぎて此處に載す、剣術
て其取り初めは、柔術の居取のごとく、立なり
ら離れて禮し、近より向き合ひて取るなり、禮は即ち左
し後ろより鞘を取る形ちもあるなり、
の第一圖の如くす。

◉柄　捌　第一形　受人

◎　**Tsuka Sabaki,**
　　Defending Against a Grab to Your Sword Handle
First Kata
First Illustration

　　Tsuka Sabaki are techniques where the Opponent attempts to grab the Tsuka, or handle, of your Katana, yank it out and cut you down.　You resists this and it is the Opponent who ends up being cut.　Many think that Tsuka Sabaki techniques are part of Jujutsu, however, as the Katana is the focus of the battle, and it finishes with one person being cut, it is associated with Kenjutsu. This book will classify it as Kenjutsu, a sword art.

　　So then, the technique begins from a Jujutsu style Idori, or seated facing each other.　First, the combatants walk some distance apart from one another and bow. Then, moving close, they drop into a squat.　Note that there are also techniques where the Saya, or scabbard, is grabbed from behind.. The initial position is shown in the illustration above.

偖て禮終れば、左の第二圖のごとく双方向合ひ
て居合腰の胡坐を組み、使人は左の手にて刀の
鯉口を持ち、右の手は拇指を内にして握拳をし
たるを、右の膝に置き、受人も同じく、握拳の
両手を両膝に置く、これは柔術ゆゑ稽古道具を
掛けず、儒袢に長き猿股を穿きたり、之い白き
儒袢を着たるは使人にて、黒き儒袢を着たるは
受人なり、偖て取るはじめは、次の第三圖のご
とく、受人より両手を出して使人の刀の柄を取
知るべし、受人は其技劣るを
るぞ、使人は第四圖のごとく、右の手にて柄頭

第二圖

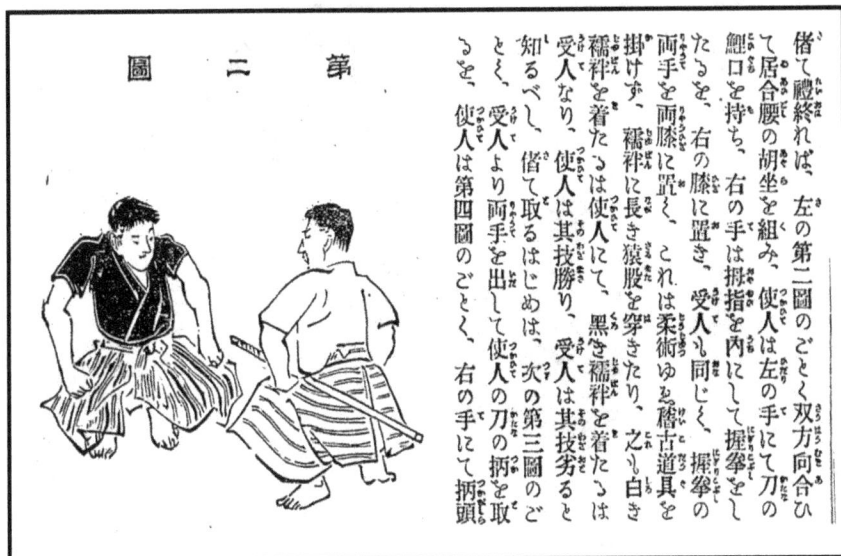

Second Illustration

So then, having finished the Rei, the two face off dropping into an Iai-goshi Agura 居合腰の胡坐, as shown in the illustration above. Your left hand holds the Koi-guchi, or mouth of the scabbard, while your right hand is in a closed fist resting on top of your right knee, with your thumb facing inward. The Opponent is squatting in the same manner, with both hands closed in fists on top of his knees with the thumbs facing in. This starting position originates from Jujutsu Keiko, or Jujutsu training, showing that you have no weapons.

You both wear Juban 儒袢 shirts that have longish sleeves and Sarumata 猿股 "monkey pants" are worn below. The white Juban is worn by you, while the black Juban is worn by the Opponent. Understand that it is you who excels at this technique while the Opponent is rather poor at it.

So then, the first part of this technique is as shown in the third illustration. The Opponent reaches out with both hands grabbing the Tsuka of your Katana. You do as shown in the fourth illustration, taking hold of the Tsuka-gashira with the right hand from below and scooping it up. From here it is as shown in the fifth illustration, you steps out with

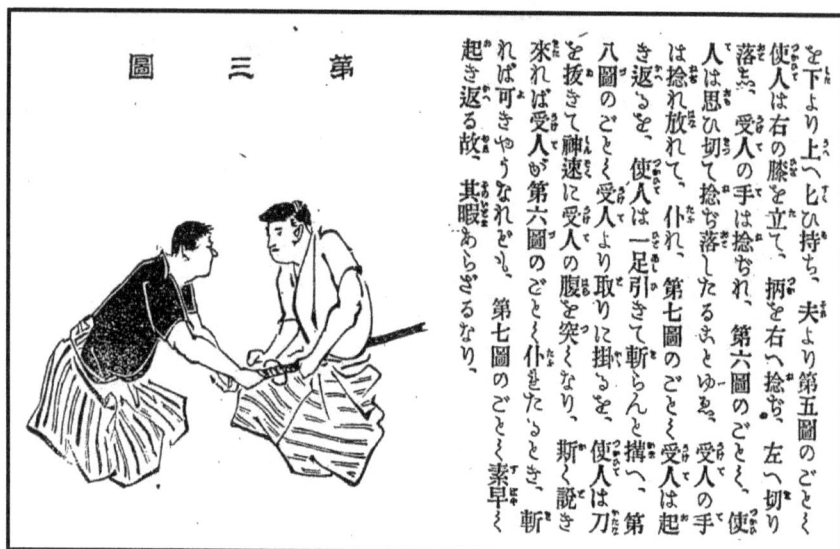

第 三 圖

れ起き返る故、其暇あらざるなり。
れば可きやうなれども、第七圖のごとく素早く斬
來れば受人が第六圖のごとく仆れたるとき、刀
を抜きて神速に受人の腹を突くなり、斯く説き
八圖のごとく受人より取りに掛るを、使人は刀
き返るを、使人は一足引きて斬らんと搆へ、受人は
は捻れ放れて、仆れ、第七圖のごとく、受人の起
人は思ひ切りて捻ち落したるまゝとゆる。受人の手
落ち、受人の手は捻ち落され、第六圖のごとく、
使人は右の膝を立て、柄を右へ捻ぢ、左へ切り
を下より上へと引持ち、夫より第五圖のごとく

Third Illustration

So then, the first part of this technique is as shown in the third illustration. The Opponent reaches out with both hands grabbing the Tsuka of your Katana. You do as shown in the fourth illustration, taking hold of the Tsuka-gashira, pommel, with your right hand from below. You then scoop it up. Next, as shown in the fifth illustration, you step forward with your right foot, bringing your knee upright. Twisting the Tsuka to the right and then suddenly shoving it down to the left causes the hands of the Opponent to be wrenched free.

The sixth illustration shows you twisting and forcing the handle down with all your might, causing the Opponent's hands to release. He is then thrown down and, as shown in the seventh illustration, while attempting to recover you drop back one-step and take a Kamae in order to cut. The eighth illustration depicts you drawing your Katana as the Opponent attempts to grab the Tsuka again. With Shin-Soku, Divine Swiftness, stab straight into his stomach.

At this point a moment should be taken to explain more fully. If your Opponent falls as shown in the sixth illustration, this is a chance to cut and you should take it. However, if he is able to recover quickly, like in the seventh illustration, then there is no chance to strike and end the technique there.

圖 四 第

此第四圖は、前の第三圖のごとく、受人も両手
にて使人の刀の拵を取りゐるを、使人は右の手
にて、拵頭を下より上へ比ひ持ちたるところな
り。
是よりは、次の第五圖のごとく、拵を右へ捻ぢ上げて、左へ切り落さん
とするなり。使人は右の膝
を立て、
捻ぢ放すことは、此仕方を能く熟得すべし。受
人は斯くしらるれば、放さずには居られざるべ
し、併し放せば斬らるゝ故、一揆ねくも放さざる
なり。
此邊りの手つき、腰つき、足つきとも、能く視
るべし。

Fourth Illustration

This fourth illustration follows what happened in the third. The Opponent has grabbed the Tsuka 柄, or handle, of your Katana with both hands. You respond by scooping up the Tsuka-gashira 柄頭, or pommel, from below with your right hand and lifting.

From here, as shown in the following fifth illustration, you bring your right knee up, twist the Tsuka to the right as he brings it up and then rapidly force it down to your left as if you are cutting.

This action, called Neji-hanasu 捻じ放す, or twisting and forcing release, should be trained extensively. Should the Opponent become aware of what is being attempted he will be unlikely to release. If he releases he will be cut so he will struggle mightily to not be thrown off.

You should pay special attention to the placement of the hands, the placement of the hips and the placement of the feet in this scene.

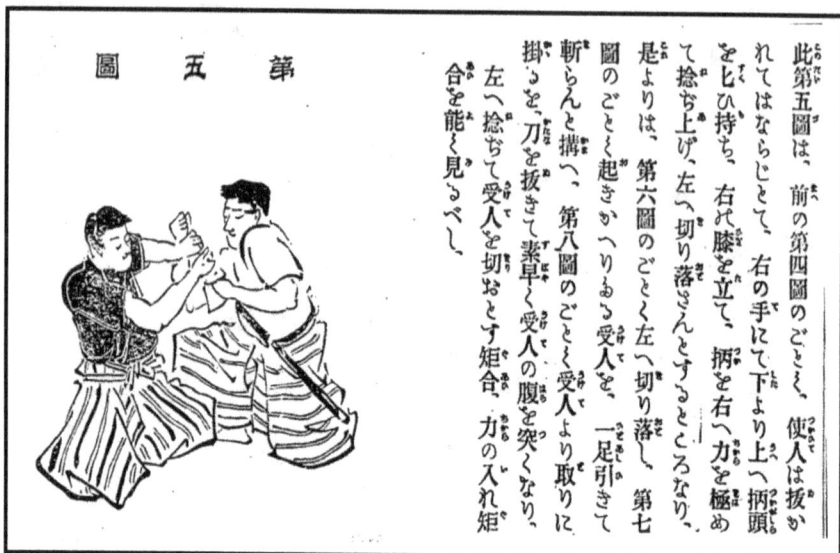

第五圖

此第五圖は、前の第四圖のごとく、使人は抜かれてはならじとて、右の手にて下より上へ柄頭を比ひ持ち、右代膝を立て、柄を右へ力を極めて捻ち上げ、左へ切り落さんとするところなり。是よりは、第六圖のごとく左へ切り落し、第七圖のごとく起きかへりゐる受人を、一足引きて斬らんと搆へ、第八圖のごとく受人より取りに掛るを、刀を抜きて素早く受人の腹を突くなり、左へ捻ちて受人を切おとす矩合、力の入れ矩合を能く見るべし。

Fifth Illustration

This fifth illustration follows what happened in the fourth illustration. In order to prevent your Katana from being drawn from your scabbard, you reach up from below and scoop up the Tsuka-gashira, or pommel. You next bring your right knee up and pour all your strength into twisting the Tsuka up and to the right before forcing it down to the left with a slashing motion.

By looking at the sixth illustration you can clearly see how the dropping slash is done. The Opponent then recovers, as shown in the seventh illustration. In response to this, you drops back one step and prepare to cut. As per the eighth illustration, as the Opponent attempts to re-engage, you rapidly draw your Katana and stab the Opponent in the stomach with a Tsuki, or Thrust.

The illustration above shows how you twist to the right and the sixth illustration shows how the Opponent is dropped down with the slashing motion. The way the power is generated for this defense should be studied thoroughly.

此第六圖は、前の第五圖のごとく、使人が右の
膝を立て、刀の柄を右へ捻ち、左へ切落しむる。
ことゆゑ、受人は仆れたるところなり、
是よりは、次の第七圖のごとく、受人が起き返
るを、使人は一足引きて斬らんと搆へ、第八圖
のごとく受人より取にかゝるを、使人は神速に
刀を抜きて、受人の腹を突くなり、
圖の變轉するところ、体勢、手つき、腰つき、
足つき、能く視るべし。
突きて後ち後とへ引きて刀を收むることは、別
に記さず。

第六圖

Sixth Illustration

The sixth illustration follows what happened in the fifth illustration. You bring your right knee up, twists the handle of your Katana to the right and finally force it violently down your left in a quick slashing motion. Due to this, the Opponent is caused to topple over.

The next step is shown in the following seventh illustration. As the Opponent attempts to right himself, you drop back a step and prepare to cut. The eighth illustration depicts how, as the Opponent attempts to re-engage, you rapidly draws your Katana and stab him in the stomach with a Tsuki, or Thrust.

As the illustrations progress, note carefully how the body position, hand position, positioning of the hips and the positioning of the legs all transition.

What happens following the Tsuki as well as the sheathing of the Katana will not be repeated.

此第七圖は、前の第六圖のごと
く、仆れたる受人が起き返るそ、
使人を一足引きて、斬らんと搆
へるところなり。

Seventh Illustration

Following what occurred in the sixth illustration, this seventh illustration shows the Opponent, having recovered, is now attempting to grab the handle of your Katana again. In response, you have dropped back one step and are now in position to cut again.

Eighth Illustration

In this eighth illustration, the Opponent has recovered and is now attempting to grab hold of the handle of your sword again. In response you draw your Katana with Shin-Soku, Divine Swiftness, and stab the Opponent in the abdomen with a Tsuki, or Thrust.

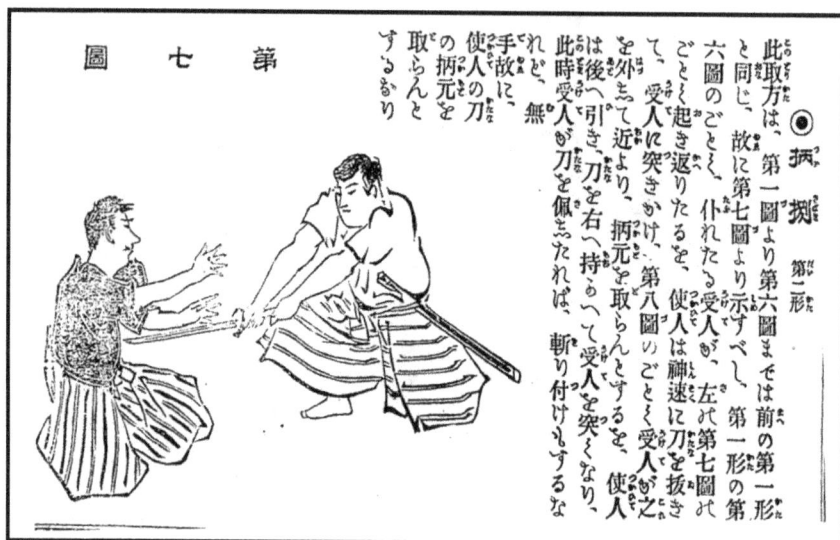

此取方は、第一圖より第六圖までは前の第一
と同じ、故に第七圖より示すべし、第一形の第
六圖のごとく、仆れたる受人が、左だ第七圖より
ごとく起き返りたるを、使人は神速に刀を抜之
て、受人に突きかけ、第八圖のごとく受人を
外よりも近より、柄元を取らんとするを、使人
は後へ引き、刀を右へ持つて受人を突くなり、
此時受人が刀を佩たれば、斬り付けもするな
り、此外に無し。
使人の刀の柄元を
手故に、此時受人が刀を
取らんとするなり。

第七圖

◉ 柄捌 第二形

◎ Tsuka Sabaki,
Defending Against a Grab to Your Sword Handle
Second Kata
Seventh Illustration

Steps one through six of this Kata are identical to the flow in the first Kata so illustrations one through six will be abbreviated and the Kata will be introduced starting from the seventh illustration.

As was shown in the sixth illustration from the first Kata, the Opponent was thrown down, however he recovers and moves to attack again. However, you have drawn your Katana with Shin-Soku, Divine Swiftness, and done a straight thrust at the Opponent.

As shown in the illustration above, however, the Opponent avoids this and moves in to grab the Tsuba-moto, Just Below the Hand Guard. In response to this you drop back, move your sword to the right and do another straight thrust at the Opponent.

In this situation, had the Opponent been wearing a Katana, he would have attempted a cut. Since the Opponent is unarmed he goes for the Tsuba-moto.

圖八第

此第八圖は、前の第七圖のごとく、受人の起き
返りたると、使人は神速に刀を抜きて受人を突
きかけ、受人は之を外をして使人に近より、其柄
元を取らんとするを、圖のごとく使人は後とへ
引き、刀を右へ持ゐて突くところなり、
受人が起きゐへりて後は、此の如く異れど、
受人が仆さるゝまでは異らず。

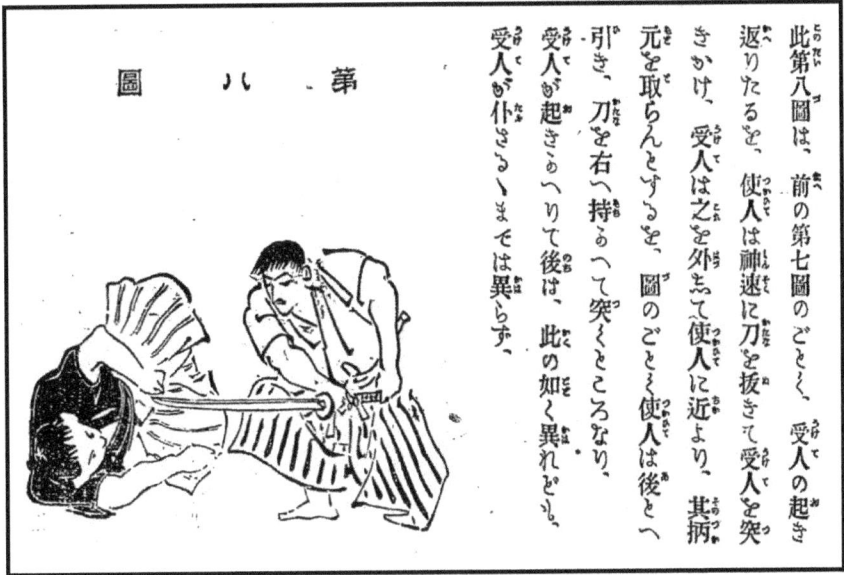

Eighth Illustration

The eighth illustration follows what occurred in the seventh illustration. You draw your Katana with Shin-Soku, Divine Swiftness, and do a Tsuki, Thrust, at the Opponent, who has recovered and is moving to attack. The Opponent dodges this thrust, and moves in close in an attempt to grasp the Tsuka-moto, Just Below the Hand Guard. As is shown in the illustration, you pull back, shifting your sword to the right and then thrusting again.

Though the sequence of events differs after the Opponent recovers from being thrown, what happened up to that point does not alter.

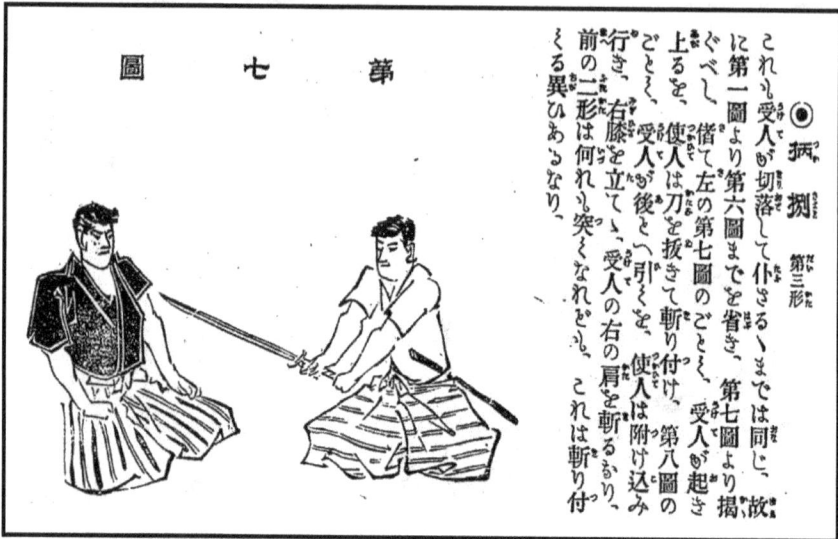

圖七第

◎柄捌　第三形

これも受人が切落して仆さるゝまでは同じ、に第一圖より第六圖までを省き、倩て左の第七圖のごとく、使人は刀を抜きて斬り付け、受人が起きごとく、受人は刀を抜きて斬り付け、使人の起き行き、右膝を立てゝ、受人の右の肩を斬るなり、これは斬り付前の二形は何れも突くなれども、これは斬り付くる異ひあるなり。

◎　**Tsuka Sabaki,**
Defending Against a Grab to Your Sword Handle
Third Kata
<u>Seventh Illustration</u>

For this Kata as well, the first six illustrations will be omitted as it is the same up through the point where the Opponent is thrown down with a Kiri-otoshi. We will begin by looking at the seventh illustration.

So then, as is shown in the seventh illustration the Opponent has righted himself and you has drawn his sword to cut him. As the eighth illustration shows, the Opponent pulls back away from this. In response, you stays with him as he drops back. Raising up his right knee he cuts into the right shoulder of the Opponent. While the previous two Kata ended with a Tsuki, the way of cutting differs here.

第 八 圖

此の第八圖は、前の第七圖のごとく、受人を斬り付けるを、受人は外して後へ引くを、右の膝を立てて、受人の右の肩を斬り込み行きて、右の肩を斬りたるところなり。第一形第二形第三形とも、第六圖までは同じ、第七圖第八圖のみ此の異ひあり。終りたり。劍術の部類は此にて終りたり。但し卷菜斬と土器術は奥に出す、骨法は柔術に屬すれども、刀劍居合は劍を抜き收め、骨法は十手を持つ事ゆゑ、依て、第二卷の骨法居合、第三卷の居合を割、第二卷の骨法居合、第三卷の居合をも視るべし。劍術の關係あり。

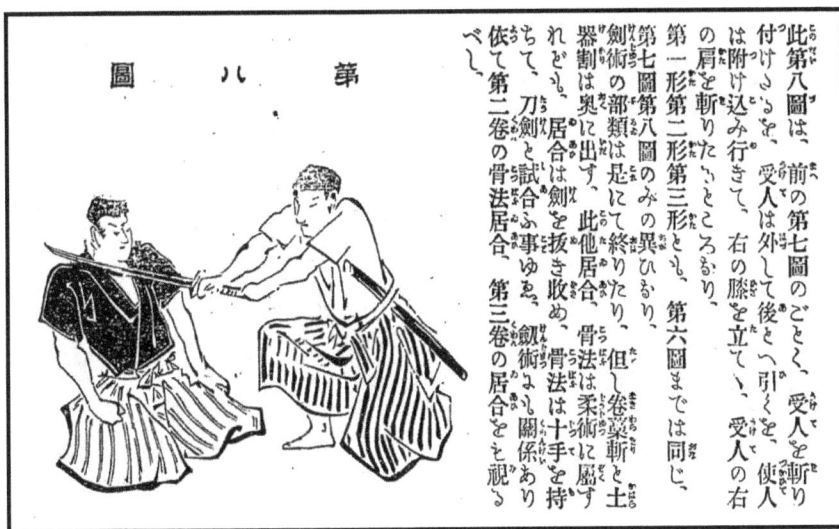

Eighth Illustration

This eighth illustration follows what occurred in the seventh illustration. In order to avoid being cut, the Opponent dodges to the side and back. You responds by standing up on your right foot, bringing your right knee up. This allows you to follow Opponent's movement. You then cut down into his right shoulder.

All three of the Tsuka Sabaki, Defending Against a Grab to Your Sword Handle Techniques, are identical from illustrations 1 ~ 6. They only differ in illustrations 7 & 8.

This brings us to the end of the section on Kenjutsu. That being said, both Maki-wara, Cutting Straw Bales, and Kawara-ke wari, Breaking Earthenware Bowls, will be presented towards the end. Other elements such as Iai, Sword Drawing, and Koppo, Striking the Bones, are classified as part of Jujutsu. This due to the fact that Iai entails the use of the sword and Koppo techniques utilize the Jutte, or Truncheon. These are used in Shi-ai, or competitions, with To-ken, or bladed weapons.

There is a clear connection between the use of the Jutte, or Truncheon, Koppo, or Striking the Bones, and Kenjutsu, or sword fighting. More information on these techniques are in the second volume in this series and one should look to the second volume in this series, which contains information on Koppo and Iai and the third volume, which contains information on Iai Jutsu.

圖三第

此取方は、受人より左の第三圖のごとく、右の手を向ふに、左の手を前にし、使人の偑したる刀の柄を取り、左より引抜きて、抜打に斬らんとするを、使人は、第四圖のごとく、右の手にて下より、受人取りたる、両手の間へ、右の手にて下より、受人取り、左への手は、鞘の鯉口の處を持ち、左へ受人が取りたる手を放させんとき、思ふごとく捻ち廻して、受人を左に切り落し、夫体ごとく、受人を左へ少し左へかはしるは、第五圖のごとく、抜打に受人を斬るなり、此處より第六圖のごとく、抜打に受人を斬るなり、より強く捻ちあれば、前の形のごとく、受

第四形

◎ 捌

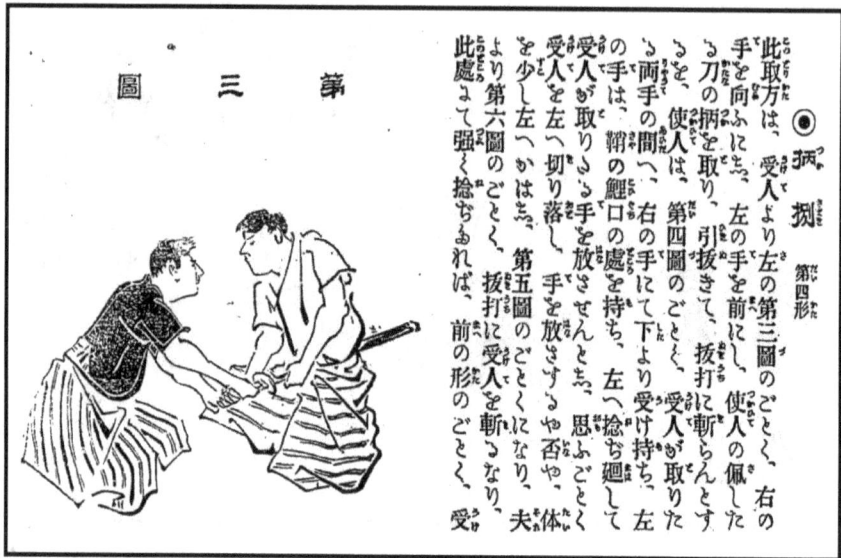

◎ Tsuka Sabaki,
Defending Against a Grab to Your Sword Handle
Fourth Kata[1] Third Illustration

This technique begins as is shown in the third illustration above. The Opponent should be gripping the handle of your Katana as shown, with his right in front of his left hand. In response to his attempt to rapidly yank your Katana out and cut, you do as shown in the fourth illustration. Scoop your right hand up from below to grab between the Opponent's hands on the handle. Your left hand should be holding the Koi-guchi, the opening at the end of your scabbard. Then twist to the left, breaking the Opponent's grip on the handle of your sword. Then do a rapid, powerful Kiri-otoshi, or quick cut and drop motion, throwing your Opponent to the ground.

Getting the Opponent's hands to release can be tricky, so twist your body slightly to the left, as shown in the fifth illustration. From there, as the sixth illustration shows, you finish the Opponent with a Nuki-uchi, Draw and Cut. Note that here, if you twist powerfully,

---

[1] Despite saying "This brings us to the end of the section on Kenjutsu," there is one more technique.

just as in the previous technique, the Opponent will be thrown down and be tumbled by the force of the Kiri-otoshi.

第　四　圖

人は切落されて、倒るゝなれど、輕く捻ちたる手を放る故、仆るゝに至らず、第五圖のごとく、手を放る

左の第四圖は、受人より使人の刀の柄へ両手にて掛けたるを、使人ハ前圖のごとく、左の手を神速に右の手と、受人が握る両手の間へ、仰向けに右の手を入れて、切りおとさんとするところな

取りたる力を入れて、左の方へ捻ち、受人が取りたる両手を放させ、切りおとさんとするところな

是よりは、次の第五圖のごとく、受人の両手を捻ち放すなり。

Fourth Illustration

If, however, your twist is not strong enough, then the opponent will not be toppled, thus you need to have a firm understanding of how to get his hands to release and then throw him down. All this can be understood by looking to the fifth illustration.

The fourth illustration, above, shows the Opponent grabbing the Tsuka, Handle, of your Katana with both hands. You, as was shown in the previous illustration, keep your left hand just at the Koi-guchi. Your right hand moves with Shin-soku, Divine Swiftness, to grip palm up in the space between the Opponent's hands. With this hold in place, squeeze, apply power and twist to the left. The hands of the Opponent are then yanked off with following the Kiri-otoshi, Cut and Drop.

Then, as shown in the fifth illustration, both of the Opponent's hands have been wrenched from the Tsuka.

第五圖

左の第五圖は、前の第四圖のごとき、体勢によって、受人に
使人は思ふごとく、左へ捻ぢて手を放させ、受
人は捻ぢられて、堪へられず、將に仆れんとし
て、蹲止まり、圖のごとく坐したるを、使人は
体を少し左へかはしさまに、右の膝を立て、
尻を上げ、柄を下げ、抜打に受人を斬らんと
するところなり。
能く目を止めて、左の圖を視るべし、受人が両
手をひろげたるは、今放されたるところなり。
夫ほど間のなき瞬間に、使人の体勢の、
で變るは、餘程素早き働きなることを、想ふべ
し。即ち受人は、「ハッ」と思ひ居るところなり

Fifth Illustration

The fifth illustration, above, follows what occurred in the fourth illustration. Through a shift in body position you are able to achieve your intent of causing the Opponent's hands to release by twisting the Tsuka to the left. The Opponent, having had his hands wrenched, is unable to endure it and releases, likely being toppled over in the process. This brings his attack to a screeching halt.

The position of your body, which can be seen clearly in the illustration, has shifted slightly to the left. Your right knee is up with the Saya-jiri, or the butt end of the Saya, raised up while the Tsuka, or handle, is lowered. Here you are completely prepared to execute a Nuki-uchi, Draw and Cut.

You should force your eyes to stop and consider the illustration above. The hands of the Opponent are shown spread apart as they have just been wrenched off. You should understand that your shift to this position has taken place in an almost non-existent, split-second interval. The movement here is so fast the Opponent can only think 「What?」

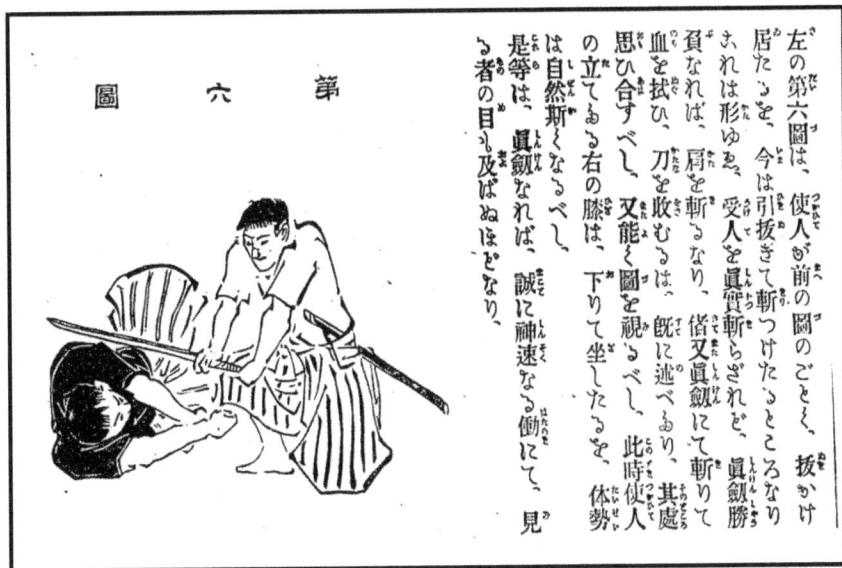

第 六 圖

左の第六圖は、使人を前の圖のごとく、抜かけ居たるを、今は引抜きて斬りつけたるところなり。それは形ゆえ、受人を眞電斬らざれど、眞劍勝負なれば、肩を斬るなり。偕又眞劍にて、斬りて貧なれば、刀を收むるは、既に逃べるあり、其處に血を拭ひ、此時使人思ひ合すべし、又能く圖を視るべし。体勢の立てある右の膝は、下りて坐したるを、は自然斯くなるべし、眞劍なれば、誠に神速なる働にて、見是等は、眞劍なれば、誠に神速なる働にて、見る者の目ら及ばぬほどなり。

Sixth Illustration

The sixth illustration, above, follows what you did in the previous illustration, namely to set yourself up to draw your Katana. Now, we see the moment after you have drawn out his sword and cut.

In reality the Opponent is not cut, however, should this be a situation of Shin-ken-sho-bu 眞釖勝負, or a duel with live blades, it would end with a cut into his shoulder. So then, again, were he to have cut with a Shin-ken, or real sword, you would first wipe off the blood and then sheathe your Katana. These final actions in the Kata have been previously covered so the reader should take the time to recall those elements and examine the relevant illustrations.

At this point your right foot should be forward with your knee up and your left knee is on the ground. Overall the body should be positioned naturally as such. This technique should be done Shin-ken, or seriously and at full speed. If you do it that way, it would be so fast that the technique would hardly register in the eyes of those observing.

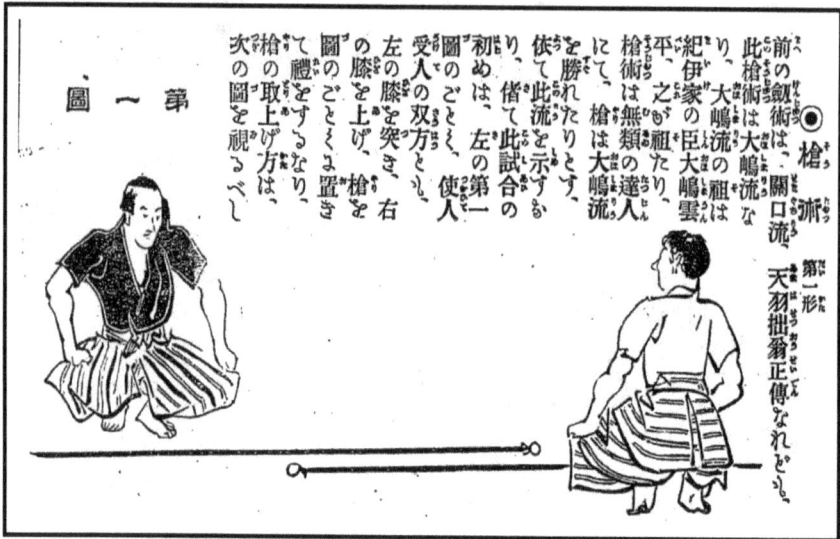

◎ Sojutsu Spear Fighting
First Kata
<u>First Illustration</u>

The previous Kenjutsu was from the direct teachings of Amaha Setsuo of the Sekiguchi School of sword. These Sojutsu 槍術, or Spear Fighting Techniques are from the Oshima School[1]. The founder of Oshima Ryu was a retainer of the Kii Domain named Oshima Unpei (1588-1657.). He is the one who started this school. He was, with regards to Sojutsu, an unparalleled expert. As the spear techniques of the Oshima school are exceptional, they will be presented here.

So then, this Shi-ai, or bout, begins as shown in the first illustration. You, as well as the Opponent, have your left knee planted on the ground, while the right knee is upright. The Yari, or spears, are placed as depicted in the illustration, and from this position you do a bow.

The next illustration will show how to pick up the spear.

---

[1] The Oshima School uses Suyari 素槍 which is a plain spear. It was rather long, about 3.6 meters. While the word for spear in Japanese is Yari, when combined with Jutsu, meaning technique, the word is read as Sojutsu instead of Yari Jutsu.

Second Illustration

The first illustration showed both combatants doing a Rei, or bow of respect. Following that both place their left hand on their left knee. Their right hands go to the Hei, or Shaft of the Spear, and bring it up to rest on their right knees. Both sides lock eyes and work to ensure their Ki-ai, or Fighting Spirit, does not falter.

You should note manner in which the feet are placed.

夫より双方立上り、右の手で槍の刷を持ちた八文字に蹈み、見合ひて互ひに透を狙ひ。足は外る透あ

まゝ立上り、左の手は圖のごとく下げ、

八文字に蹈み、見合ひて互ひに透を狙ひ

突らば突んき、來らば拂はん、とれは何と思居るな

Third Illustration

After that, both sides stand up. The right hand of each continues to hold onto the Hei, or Shaft of the Spear, as they stand up. The left hand hangs down as is shown in the illustration. The feet are planted in a Soto-hachi-Monji, or as the bottom of the character 八 indicates.

The opponents observe each other seeking to find a Suki 透, or Opening, to attack. Both have in mind to launch a Tsuki 突き, or Thrust, should a chance appear. At the same time, they are also both prepared to sweep a Tsuki away should one come at them.

よき足此く夫
、つ視り第左の繰柄れ使に
き、即四のに出に透人
腰ち圖手掛し掛あは
つ素のを受此、り受
き早ご柄體人右を人
、に左と掛を勢手見れ
腰へしけ突及にてに透
つ支、此び、両、あ
き、ふ、両手左り
左手にの手をの
の即きて見

Fourth Illustration

Next, you have found a Suki-ari 透有り, an Opening. You grip the shaft with your left hand and launch thrust at the Opponent. The Opponent rapidly grips the shaft with his left hand, and, using both hands, moves to the left to block. This is what is depicted in the fourth illustration, above.

The positioning of the bodies, the hands, the hips and the legs should be observed.

第五圖

前の第四圖のごとく、受人が神速に使人より突き來る槍を支へ、此圖のごとく落す、されど使人は、次の第六圖のごとく、槍を取直して突き進むなり、突き進みてより後の事は、次の圖を視よ。

Fifth Illustration

As was shown in the previous fourth illustration, the Opponent has blocked your Yari with Shin-Soku, Divine Swiftness. As can be seen in his illustration he then slams it down. However, in the following sixth illustration you rapidly rights his Yari and launches another Tsuki. For the steps after this Tsuki refer to the next illustration.

第　六　圖

り、を突た。突きて勝を取るなり、先には胴を突き、後ち面突き出す槍を、受人より挑進むを、受人は後とへ二足ばかり引き、使人は使人は此第六圖のごとく、槍を取り直して突き

Sixth Illustration

Next, you do as is shown in the sixth illustration. Having returned to your starting stance you are going to attack again with another Tsuki. In response to this the Opponent drops back two steps. You do not allow a chance for the Opponent to sweep away your spear and launch a second strike to Men, the Face, for the win. So, there is a Tsuki to Do, or the Body, first and then this is followed by a Tsuki to Men, the Face.

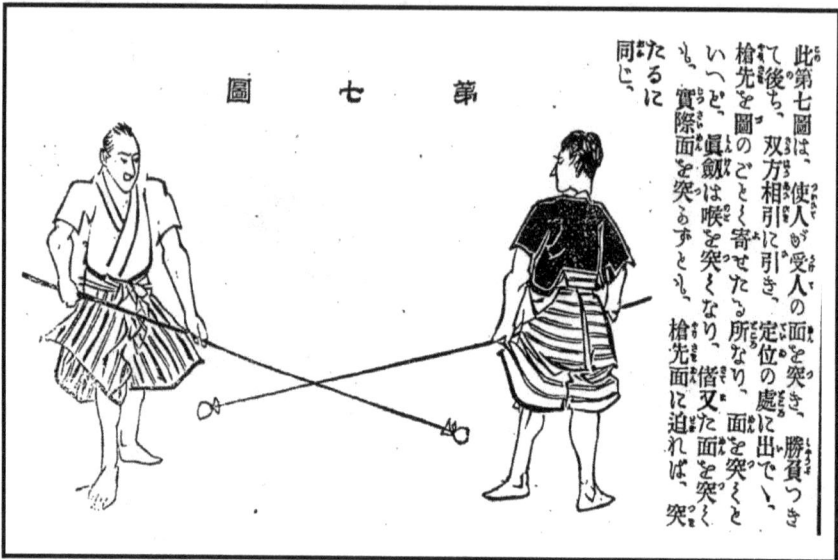

Seventh Illustration

This seventh illustration shows the position after the match has been won with a stab to the Opponent's Men, or Face, by you. The two step back away from each other simultaneously in an Ai-biki, Mutual Withdrawal, movement and position themselves in such a manner as the Yari are crossed as shown in the illustration above.

Though a Tsuki to the face was mentioned, with a Shin-ken, or Real Spear, the Tsuki would be to Nodo 喉, or the throat. Furthermore, the face was not, in fact, struck. Should the end of the spear, draw sufficiently near the face, then it is considered the same as a strike.

第一圖第二圖は、前の第一形に同じ、故に省く

依て第三圖より示すべし、惜て受人は、此第三

圖のごとく、使人の胴を突かんとするを、使人

は右へ掃ひて

次の第

四圖の

ごとく

に落す

なり、

圖　三　第

◎ Sojutsu Spear Fighting
Second Kata
Third Illustration

As what occurs in the first and second illustrations is the same, they will be abbreviated. Therefore we will look at this Kata starting from the third illustration.

The Opponent is attempting to launch a Tsuki to Do, Your Torso, as shown in the third illustration, above. You respond by sweeping this attack to the right and, as shown in the following fourth illustration, forcing his spear down.

Fourth Illustration

In the third illustration your Opponent launches a thrust to your midsection. You respond by rapidly sweeping this attack to the right and forcing his spear down.

Starting from the previous third illustration you should rest your eyes carefully on how you sweeps the spear away. You should focus your attention particularly on the parts of the drawing showing the combination of sweeping and forcing the Yari down, as well as the overall body positioning, hand positioning and the positioning of the hips.

夫より受人は、前の第四圖のごとく、落さるゝ槍を取り、更に使人の面を突かんとするを、使人は此第五圖のごとく、槍先を上て左へはら

ひ、次、圖の第六圖のごとく、り、落すな神速誠なにり、たらきはなるはたらきとなり、拂ひおとすなり、と手で視るべし、つき、拂ひおとすとすべし、視るべし、

Fifth Illustration

From here, following what happened in the previous fourth illustration, the Opponent recovers his spear which you knocked down. He then re-engages with a Tsuki to Men, or a thrust to your face. As shown in the illustration above you raise the Yari-saki 槍 先, or the point of your spear, and sweep it to your left. In the following sixth illustration you force his spear down.

This movement is all done with absolute Shin-soku, Divine Swiftness. Careful attention should be paid to the position of the hands when you execute the Harai-otoshi, Sweep and Drop, forcing your Opponent's spear down. These steps should be considered with care.

Sixth Illustration

This follows the previous fifth illustration. You have swept the Opponent's spear to the side then forced it down. If you were to look back on not the previous fourth illustration, but rather the one before that, then this fairly similar sixth illustration could be omitted. That being said, as there are some small changes in body position in this Kata, it has been included here.

From this point you would do a Tsuki to the Men, which is the same as the sixth illustration from the previous Kata[1].

---

[1] The text says "seventh illustration" however this is probably an error. The fourth illustration of the 3rd spear technique has the clearest picture of the attack to the face.

第　三　圖

な　突　り　附　直　と　　の　四　の　て　挑　右　を　突　人　て　續　落　挑　人　　こ
り　く　面　入　に　く　ご　圖　次　ひ　へ　　　く　面　受　い　し　ひ　よ　れ
　　　　　　　　第　　　　　　　　　　　　り

◎槍術　第三形

第一圖第二圖ハ同じ、左の第三圖ハ、受人ハ左へ使人の胴突突かんとするを、使人ハ左へ受。

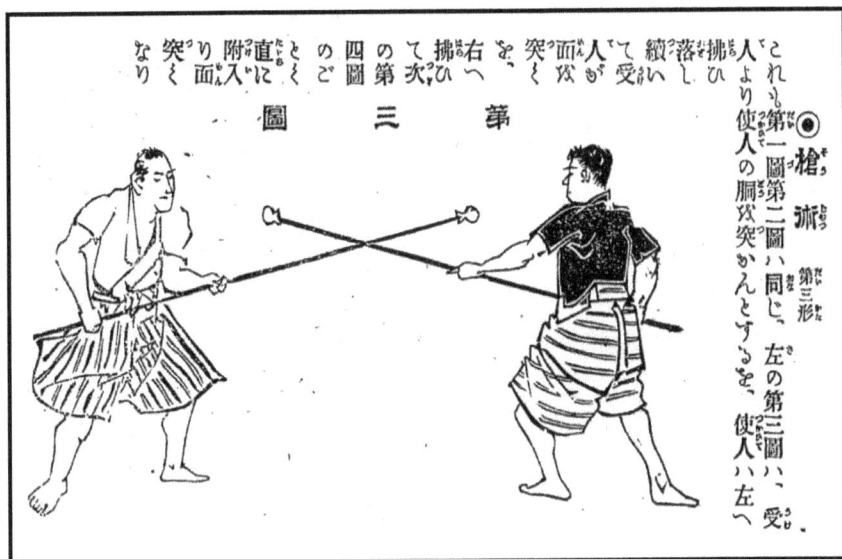

◎ Sojutsu Spear Fighting
Third Kata
<u>Third Illustration</u>

For this Kata as well, the first and second illustrations are the same.

As the illustration above shows, the Opponent thrusts to your midsection with his spear. You defend with a Harai-otoshi, or Sweep and Drop, forcing his spear to the left. Next, your Opponent launches a straight thrust to your face. You sweeps this away to the right and then immediately counterattack with a thrust to the Opponent's face. This attack is shown in the following fourth illustration.

Fourth Illustration

As was shown in the third illustration, you sweep the Opponent's attacks away. The moment he launches his attacks, you sweep the thrust to your midsection to the left, and sweep the attack to your face to the right.

In the next moment you step forward one pace while the Opponent drops back a step. As you are stepping in, simultaneously launch a straight thrust to your Opponent's face.

Since the fifth illustration is the same as the seventh illustration from the first Kata introduced earlier, it will be omitted.

◎ Sojutsu Spear Fighting
Fourth Kata
<u>Fourth Illustration</u>

Since the first illustration and second illustration are the same for this Kata as well, they have been omitted.

In the third illustration the Opponent launches a Tsuki, Straight Thrust, to your Do, or Midsection. You parry this with a Harai-otoshi, Sweep and Drop, defense. At this point the Opponent steps forward one step and you drop back one step. As this does not differ from before, so no illustration will be provided.

Next, the Opponent launches a Tsuki, or Thrust, at your face. You defend against this by bocking it to the right. This is the only difference from before.

The next step is shown in the fourth illustration, above. You advance two steps while the Opponent drops back two steps. Your thrust to the Opponent's face will be shown in the following illustration.

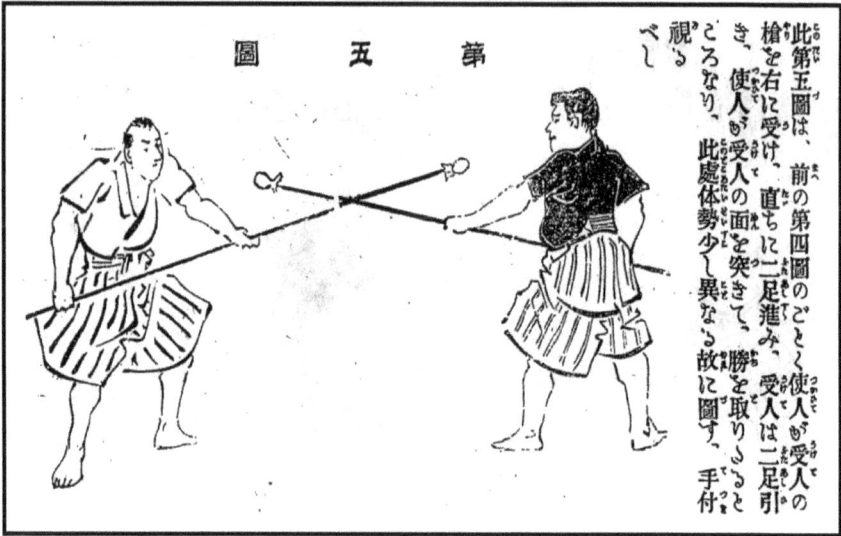

Fifth Illustration

This fifth illustration follows what occurred in the fourth illustration. After you block the Opponent's thrust to the right, you then advance two steps, while the Opponent drops back two steps. You wins with a straight thrust to the face of the Opponent.

As the body position here differs slightly, an illustration has been included. The position of the hands should be observed carefully.

◎ **Sojutsu Spear Fighting**
Fifth Kata
<u>Third Illustration</u>

For this Kata as well, since the first illustration and the second illustration are the same, they will be omitted.

The start of this Shi-ai, or bout, is as shown in this illustration. You ready to launch an attack at your Opponent's face. Seeing you intend to attack, the Opponent thrusts to your face. In response, the following fourth illustration shows how you defend with a Migi-uke, Right Block. You then follow that with a Suri-Otoshi, or scraping your spear down the length of the Opponent's spear and forcing it violently down.

In this third illustration you have provoked your Opponent to enter and attack.

此の第四圖は、前の第三圖のごとき体勢より、受け受け
人が使人の面を突きにかゝるを、使人は右に受け
けて、今や擦り落さんとするところなり、是等
は使人が、前に挑むゝめの槍を出したるとき、
受人より面へ來れば、右へ擦り落さんとの心搆
へはあ
るなり。

Fourth Illustration

The body positioning in this fourth illustration follows what happened in the third illustration. In response to the Opponent launching a straight thrust at your face, you block it to the right. From there you do a Suri-Otoshi 擦り落とし, or scraping your spear down the length of the Opponent's spear and forcing it violently down.

All of this began with you provoking the Opponent with your spear. The moment the Opponent launches a thrust to your face, be ready to block and do a Suri-Otoshi to the right.

第五圖

此第五圖は、前の第四圖のごとく、使人が受人の面を突槍を右へ受けてより、今すり落したるところなり。槍を速く直し取りて、受人は神速より、是より第六の圖のごとく、使人の胴を突きにくる。此、使人が胴を突く時、受人は逆使に右に受くるは、次にるに示す。

Fifth illustration

This fifth illustration follows what happened in the fourth illustration. You have blocked the thrust to your face by the Opponent to the right, and this illustration shows the Suri-Otoshi or scraping your spear down the length of the Opponent's spear and forcing it down.

From here the Opponent recovers his Yari with Shin-Soku, Divine Swiftness and, as is shown in the sixth illustration, attempts a thrust to your Do, or Midsection.

Your Gyaku-Uke, or Reverse Block, to the right will be shown next.

第六圖

Sixth Illustration

This sixth illustration shows how you should be positioned after blocking the Opponent's thrust to your midsection. Your right hand is gripping face down on the end of your spear while your left hand is cupped against the Hei, or Shaft, of the spear facing the direction of the block.

With a Gyaku-dori, Reverse Block, to the left[1], you stop the Opponent's Yari. You first Osae, or Suppressing, his spear, then do a Suri-Otoshi, or scrape down the length of his spear and then force it down.

Understand that this hand positioning is the result of considerable Shuren 修練, or a long period of intense training. The final step is to thrust at the Opponent's face, however since it is the same as the other techniques it will be omitted.

---

[1] The text says "right" but I believe this is an error.

第　三　圖

槍術　第六形

それも第一圖第二圖は、諸形いづれも同じき故に省く、悟て試合は、下の第三圖のごとく、人より使人の胴を突かんとするを、使人は右へ受打り落すなり。此處は打り落したる所なり。

◎　Sojutsu Spear Fighting
Sixth Kata
Third Illustration

 As with all of these Kata as the first and second illustrations are the same so they will be omitted. Thus, this Shi-ai, or match, begins as is shown in the third illustration.

 In response to the Opponent's thrust to your Do, or Midsection, you defend with an Uchi-Otoshi, or strike and force down, to the right.

 This illustration depicts the moment when you, in the white top, are striking with an Uchi-Otoshi.

Fourth Illustration

From there, you launches a Tsuki, or thrust, to the face of the Opponent. The Opponent drops back two steps, which is what is shown in this fourth illustration.

As this point in the Kata, you proceeds forward a step shouting "Ya!" Your thrust to the face is done the same as shown in the seventh illustration from the first Kata, thus it will be omitted[1].

As can be seen here, when striking down his spear with an Uchi-Otoshi, Strike and Drop, or when doing a Harau, or Sweep, a Kakegoe, or Shout, of *Ya! Ya!* should accompany your action[2].

---

[1] Actually the best illustration of the Tsuki to Men is the fourth illustration from the fourth Kata.

[2] The shout of Ya! Ya! Is written with the Kanji for "open" written twice 開々. The Kanji 々 indicates the Kanji before it is repeated.

第五圖

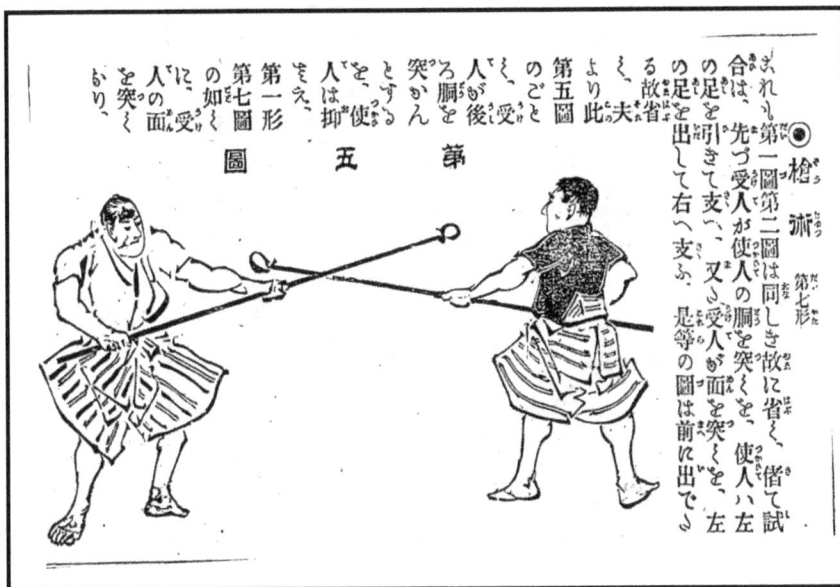

◎ Sojutsu Spear Fighting
Seventh Kata
<u>Fifth Illustration</u>

Since the first illustration and the second illustration are the same in this Kata, they will be abbreviated.

So then, in this Shi-ai the Opponent first launches a straight thrust to Do, your midsection. Step back with your left foot and block. When the Opponent then attacks with a thrust to your face, you respond by stepping out with your left foot and block to the right. These illustrations will be abbreviated as they were shown before.

Here in this fifth illustration the Opponent attacks with a thrust to Ushiro-Do, or to the back of your midsection. In response, you block and, as was shown in the seventh illustration of the first Kata launches a thrust to the face of your Opponent.

◉巻藁斬

刀劍み利き物と鈍き物あり、なまくら刀とあり、然さくといへ斬味に優劣あり。即ち能く斬れる物、又手の内に不鍛錬と鍛錬しあるとあり、其刀の利鈍を、巻藁を斬りて試見るなり。之を試し斬と云ふ、併せ依て刀を買入るとき、其刀の利鈍を、巻藁を斬りて試見るなり。刀を新たに買入るときならずとも、斬習ふ為め斬ることもあるなり、これを斬るには、左に圖を揭ぐるがごとく、第一ニ地上へ土壇といふ物を築き、其上へ米俵の上卷を卷きて、土壇には斬柄を嵌め換へ、之にて斬る菜とし、刀には斬柄を嵌め換へ、之にて斬るなり。依て土壇の築き方、卷藁の製し方、斬柄の事を左に列叙すべし。

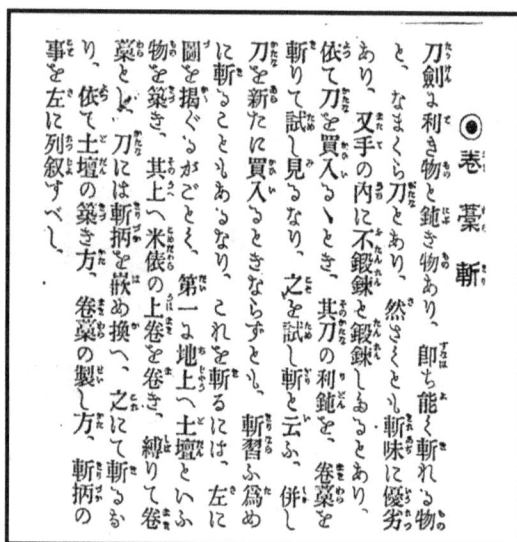

◎ *Maki-wara Kiri* How to Cut Maki-Wara, A Rolled Grass Mat

Amongst bladed weaponry there are those that are sharp and those that are dull. In other words, swords that cut well and Namakura-Gatana, swords that are good for nothing. When considering the purchase of a Katana you need to determine Kiri-aji, the "taste" of the blade or whether it cuts well or not. You must also evaluate the Te-no-uchi, or the handling of the sword. Has it been forged solidly or not? The relative fineness or dullness of the blade can be determined through test-cutting Maki-wara, or rolled up straw mat. This is called Tameshi-Giri, Test Cutting.

Even if you are not contemplating the purchase of a new Katana, cutting in order to learn how to cut should be done. This method is shown in the illustration above.

First of all, a stand referred to as a Do-dan should be built to hold the Maki-wara off the ground. The material that comprises the Maki-wara, the outer wrapper of a rice bale, or a Kome-dawara, is rolled up and tied off thereby making a Maki-wara. The handle of the Katana should be changed to a slightly longer Kiri-zuka, cutting handle, and the actual cutting will be done with that. In the next section the way a stand for the Maki-wara, or Dodan, should be built, the method for making Maki-wara, as well as an explanation of a Kiri-zuka will be addressed in order.

◎土壇築き方の事

土壇は、巻藁を載する築土の臺なり、之に砂の如き石交りても刀の又を損ず、故に土を羽二重の篩にて篩ひ、埴して築くなり、其形容は左圖の如し、併し之を築くは甚だ大厨なり、略にするときは、薪にても、杭にても、右へ二本、左へ二本、何れも前後ぇ打ち、其間ぇ炭の入りたる儘炭俵を挟み、(されば薪二本は炭俵の動かぬやう、留むる為に打つなり、)而して之を土壇に代用し、其上ぇ巻藁を載せて斬るなり、

◎ How a Dodan Should be Constructed

The Dodan is an earthen mound on which the Maki-wara is rested. If the soil used for the Dodan contains sand or stones the blade is like to be damaged. For this reason the soil must first be filtered through a Ha-Buta-e "doubled" sieve. The fine particles that result are then used in the construction of the Dodan. The shape of the Dodan is as shown in the illustration on the following page. Note that this depicts a Dodan that has been painstakingly constructed.

There is also a more abbreviated setup method. Two stakes or even tree branches can be pounded into the ground with two on the left and two on the right. With one set of stakes in front and one in back, wedge a Sumi-dawara, or bale of charcoal, with the charcoal still inside between the two sets of stakes. (When doing this two more branches should be pounded in to keep the Sumi-dawara bales from moving.)[1] This will then act in place of a Dodan and the Maki-wara can be placed atop it for cutting.

---

[1] Brackets are from the original document.

巻藁斬の圖

右に述ぶる土を羽二重へ二重へぶるひにし、練り固めたる刀の萱

物は、巻藁を斬りたる勢にて斬られとも、餘勢に練り固めたる刀の萱

又はこぼれず、炭は殊に此巻藁或は土壇又に障らず、炭俵の手利の萱

利に刀も能く斬るれば、右の如く斬込めども、刀は上へ反るべし。

まで刀も能く斬るるものなり。此巻藁或は土壇代りの手利に、炭俵。

てし亦障らぬものなり。土壇或は土壇代りの手利に、炭俵。

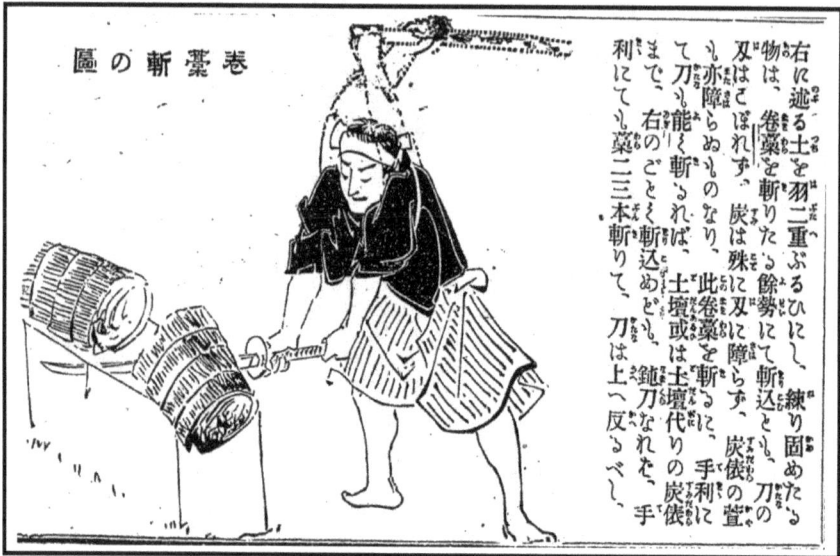

Illustration of Cutting Maki-wara

By sieving the soil and then kneading it into a firm mound, the mound will then absorb the inertia of the cut once the blade passes through the Maki-wara. This method will not chip the blade of your Katana, and the charcoal cause any harm to the blade. In addition, the Kaya-grass 萱[1] wrapping around the Sumi-dawara will also not cause damage.

When cutting Maki-wara like this, if you have become skilled and the Katana is one that cuts well you should have no problem. If you make a Dodan, or the Sumi-dawara that is acting in place of the Dodan, and cut as described above, and the blade is not a Namakura, or Dull Sword, a skilled person should be able to cut the bale two or three times. Each time the Katana should be raised up to the starting position.

---

[1] Kaya is a common grass known by the scientific name *Imperata cylindrical* and the awesome conventional name Japanese bloodgrass.

斬るなり。
斬り、之をも斬り得たれば、横一文字に入れて
を斬り得たれば、竹を俵の中心へ斜めに入れて
を斬り得たれば、二人胴なる二枚を斬り、之を
り順序は、先づ一人胴とさる俵一枚を斬り、之
又骨に代ふゝに竹を以てすることあり、試し斬
と、人一人分の胴とし、二枚を二人分の胴とす
となり、図を見つべし、されば俵一枚巻きたる
て緯り、角結にしては切り、角結にして切りを
米俵の上俵を巻き、三寸ばかり隔てゝ其俵縄に
巻藁は人の胴に代ふるなり、右に云へるごとく
◎巻藁製し方の事

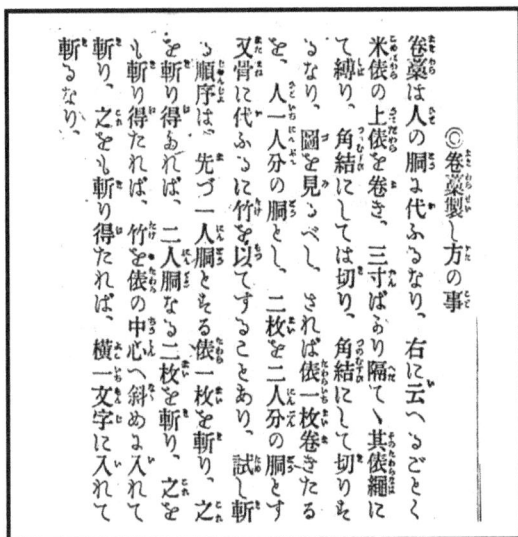

◎ On the Topic of Crafting Maki-wara

The Maki-wara, or rolled grass mat, serves as a substitute for the torso of the human body. As was described previously, the outer wrapping of a rice bale, or the Kome-dawara, is rolled up. Secure the roll by tying it with cord. Spacing the ties out 3 Sun, or about 9 centimeters, and tie each wrapping off with a Tsuno-musubi, or Horned Knot. Tie the first cord, cut the remaining rope, then leave an interval. Tie off each cord with a Horned Knot and then cut off the extra. The illustration can be used for reference.

For refrence, one sheet of Tawara, grass matting, rolled up is about the same thickness as the torso of a single person. Two sheets would be equivalent to the torsos of two people. Further, a piece of bamboo can serve in place of bone.

The proper way in which Tameshi-giri, or test cutting, is done is as follows. First roll up one sheet of grass matting, representing the Do, or torso, of a person and cut it. Should that be successful then two sheets of rolled Tawara, serving as the torsos of two people is cut. Should that too be successful, then a sheet of Tawara with a piece of bamboo at its center should be prepared. Diagonal cuts should then be done. Should these cuts be satisfactory then Yoko Ichi-monji, horizontal cuts, should be done.

斬柄を斬るには、通常の糸巻柄の竹目釘さした
奉藁を斬るには、必ず斬柄と嵌め換へて斬るなり
る物を用ゐず、
通常の柄の儘にて斬れば、柄を損じ、刀を損ず
故なり、斬柄は、前の圖み示すごとく、樫
の木にて、木・口小判形にし、柄袋のごとく、柄頭
柄元にいづれも少し細く、中ほど膨れたる形にて
頭と元とに鐵の締を嵌めて、いづれも中程に寄
せて締め、目釘は鐵目釘と仕替へ、大丈夫にし
て斬るなり、すべて能く注意したるものなり、

◎ On the topic of the Kiri-Zuka or the Cutting Handle

Typically when cutting Maki-wara, an Ito-maki Tsuka, a handle with thread wrapped around it and a Mekugi, peg, made of bamboo are not used. Cutting is always done after removing the standard handle and replacing it with a Kiri-zuka.[1] If you cut with a typical handle it could damage both it and your Katana. This can be seen in the previous illustration.

A piece of Kashi, or evergreen oak, is carved out so that a cross section would resemble the oval shape of a Koban gold coin. It acts somewhat like a Tsuka-bukuro which protects the whole scabbard as well as the handle and hand guard from bad weather and when travelling[2].

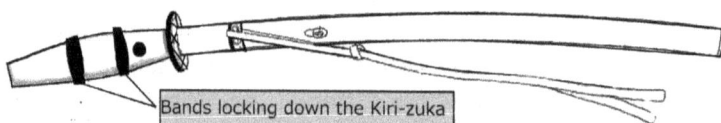

Bands locking down the Kiri-zuka

[1]

[2] Basically a sack that covers the Tsuka and ties off on the other side of the Tsuba. It is said that one of the reasons for the successful assassination of Japanese Chief Minister on 24 March 1860 (known as the 桜田門外の変 Sakuradamon-gai no Hen or The Incident in

The Tsuka-gashira, or the pommel of the Katana, as well as the Tsuka-moto, or the area just below the hand-guard, are somewhat narrower in diameter when compared to a typical handle, while the middle sort of bulges out. Iron rings, like the hoops that go around a barrels, are pushed towards the center, fastening it tight. Finally, an iron Mekugi, or peg, is slotted in to replace the usual one of bamboo and you can now cut without worry.

All of the above procedures should be attended to carefully.

Front of Sakurada Gate) was due to snowy weather. The bodyguards, who were all wearing layers of foul weather gear also were slowed as they struggled to undo the Tsuka-bukuro, sword travel covers, that were affixed to their Katana.

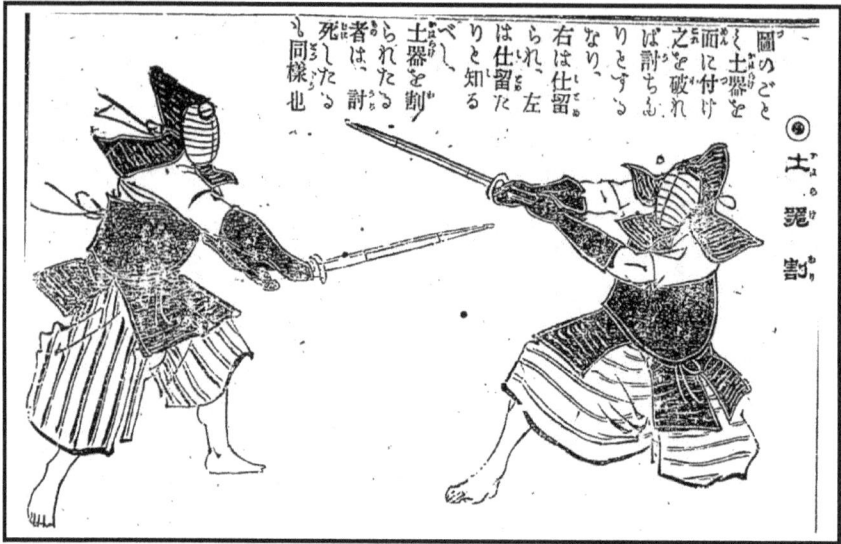

圖のごとく土器を面に付け之を破れば討ちとるなり右は仕留られ左は仕留たりと知る土器を割れたる者は討られたる者は死したる討る同様也

◎ **Kawarake Wari Battle to Split the Earthen Pot**

As shown in the illustration the Kawarake, or simple unglazed earthenware dish, is affixed to the helmet at just the point a Men, or head, strike would happen. Breaking this mean you have won. Understand that the person on the right has been defeated and the person on the left is the winner.

The person whose Kawarake is broken is considered to have died in action.

◎弓術總説

弓術は弓を張り箭を射る術にして日置流伴道雪派の正傳を記す、射習ふ初は巻藁桶を的として射るを定法とす稍や熟したる上は本的に換ふるなり又矢取籠ありて之を一箭づゝ引揚ぐる事なり尚又弓掛あり此弓掛は四ツざしをも可しとす望みある者には三ツざしもあり張弓を壊するに北の方へ擅せ掛くるは惡しく大に心得事なり

◎ Kyujutsu Sosetsu or a General Overview of Archery

Kyujutsu is the art of fitting an arrow to a bow and striking a target. The traditions of the Heiki Ryu[1] as passed down through the Han-Dosetsu Line[2] will be discussed here. When first learning to shoot, a sort of Maki-wara "barrel" is used. When the skills necessary to shoot have become advanced, a person would move on to a Hon-teki or a proper target.

At this stage a Ya-tori Kago or quiver basket is used and arrows are taken one at a time. There is also a Yumi-Kake, or leather glove used when drawing the bow. There are those that prefer a four-fingered Yumi-kake glove, while others prefer a three fingered Yumi-Kake glove. With regards to Hari-Yumi, or stringing of the bow, one should note that doing Hari-Yumi while facing north is considered bad luck.

---

[1] Heki Ryu 日置流 School of Japanese archery was founded by Hekidanjo Masatsugu who lived in the 15th century. This school is known for its walk then shoot style called Katchi-yumi 徒弓 (walk/ground+soldier+bow) or Busha 歩射 (walk+shoot.)

[2] Bankizaemon Katsuyasu（?〜1621）was the son of a Koboshi 小法師 or junior priest at Keninji Temple in Kyoto. His Bugo 武号, or martial arts name, is Dosetsu 道雪.

射る處より的場迄の距離此事

◎射る處より的場迄の距離は張りたる弓の長みを十五回回轉し其距離を定法とす、熟練の上は三十間又は五十間の距離にもするなり

◎的の事

的は人皆知るごとく圓き物なり、此直徑一尺二寸。(曲尺にて)ある物を通常的とす、通常的は直徑一尺二寸あるを定法とするなり、併し大的は直徑六尺とす、此的を射るは熟練したる上の事にて距離も隨て遠く、此他小的或は金銀小的あり前に記すが如く三十間乃至五十間とするなり。

◎箭の早乙の事

始めに射る箭を早箭と謂ひ次に射る箭を乙箭と謂ふ

◎ The Proper Shooting Distance to the Mado or Target

The distance from the place you shoot to the Mado, or Target, is equivalent to the length of the strung bow flipped over and over fifteen times. This is the established distance. When one has become experienced the distance can extend to thirty Ken or fifty Ken[1].

◎ On the Subject of the Mado

The Mado is, as everyone knows, a round thing. The diameter is generally one Shaku and two Sun[2]. The typical size is therefore considered to be one Shaku and two Sun. An O-Mado, or large target, however, can be six Shaku, 180 cm, across. Shooting at this target requires extensive training as the distance is correspondingly far. As was mentioned before a distance of somewhere between thirty Ken and fifty Ken.

---

[1] 間 One Ken is six Shaku. So about 54~90 meters.

[2] One 尺 Shaku is 30.3cm and one 寸 Sun (pronounced "soon") is 3.03cm (so it is 10 Sun to one Shaku).

In addition there are Ko-Mado as well as Kin and Gin, or gold and silver Mado[1].

◎ **On the Subject of the Haya-Oto Arrow**

The first arrow shot is known as the Ha-ya, or former arrow. The second arrow shot is known as the Oto-ya, or the latter arrow[2].

---

[1] 金銀的 Kin-Gin Mado. Gold and Silver Targets are used at a certain stage in archery contests:

Targets 3 Sun, 10 cm, across is covered with gold or silver foil. They are placed on the Azuchi 垜, or mound, in such a way as those shooting see the reflected light. In order to make the overall targets the same size as the normal 1 Shaku 2 Sun targets, leaves are placed in decorative rings around them. Then, beginning from the person with the lowest overall score up to that point in the contest, they shoot one arrow at each target. If one is struck then that target is removed and the person who shot receives it. On the reverse of the target the day and place are written and it is kept as a memento. The arrow is not removed right away, but is removed at the awards ceremony in front of the spectators. If no one strikes one of the gold or silver targets, another round is done until they are hit. From a blog by this guy named Ken:

http://blogs.yahoo.co.jp/kuroken3147/46034267.html

[2] Ha-ya, can be written variously as 甲矢, 兄矢, 早矢

と云へる諺あり
危険なるものなり故に弓張る下には辨慶も居ぬ
弓を張るときには其下に人を覧くべからず甚だ
◎弓に弦を掛け之を張る心得
二手郎ち箭四本の事を四ッ矢と謂ふ
◎四ッ矢の事
の事なり他は推して知るべし
一手と謂ふは箭二本の事にて二手と謂ふは四本
◎箭を一手二手と謂ふ事

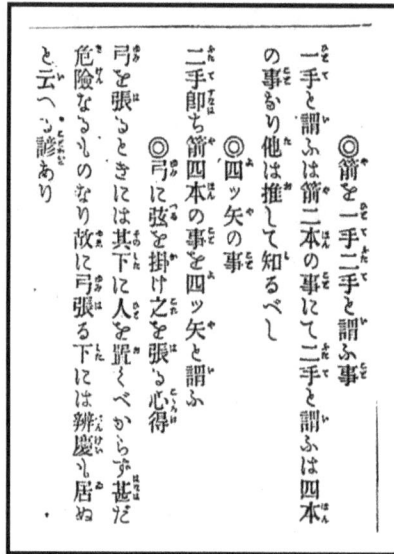

◎ On the Subject of a Hito-te or Futa-te of Arrows

A Hito-te, or a single hand of arrows, refers to shooting two arrows, while a Futa-te, or two hands of arrows, refers to shooting four arrows. Understand that the pattern continues in this fashion.

◎ On the Subject of a Yotsu-Ya of Arrows

Shooting a Futa-te, or two hands of arrows, is referred to as a Yotsu-ya, or a Set of Four Arrows.

◎ Things That Should be Remembered When Stringing a Bow

When stringing a bow, it should never be done with a person standing in front of you as it is extremely dangerous. There is even an expression that goes,

Even the great warrior Benkei won't sit in front of someone stringing a bow [1]

---

[1] 武蔵坊弁慶 Musashibu Benkei (1155–1189,) was a semi-legendary Sohei 僧兵, or Japanese warrior monk, who served Minamoto no Yoshitsune.

◎見分者の事

射前を爲すときには見分者とて見分くる役に當る者あり、射手は此見分者を敬禮するみとなり。小的或は金銀小的を射るときには見分者より望むことあり射手より満ふことあり

◎肩を胆ぐ事
射るときは必ず左の肩を胆ぐ事なり寒きときは又シャツ襦の筒袖の物を下に着て肩の胆ぐべく又稀人の見る前にて肌膚を露はすを厭へば暑き時と雖も夏シャツを用ゐるべし

◎足の踏方の事
立ちて矢を射る正體は必ず外八文字に踏むべし

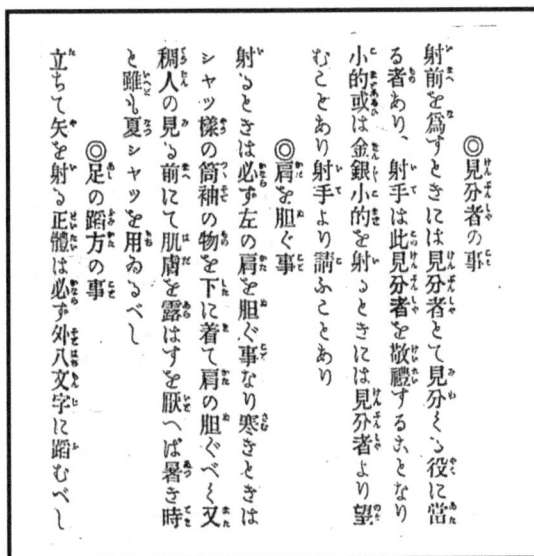

◎ On the Subject of Kenbusha or the Examiner

Before you shoot there is an Examiner whose duty it is to determine whether a hit or a miss has been struck. The Shooter should be utterly respectful to this person. When desiring to shoot at a Ko-mado, Small Target, or a Kin-Gin Ko-Mado, Gold or Silver Target, the Shooter should declare this to the Kenbunsha.

◎ On the Subject of the Uncovering of the Shoulder

When shooting, the clothing that covers the left shoulder is always removed. Should it be particularly cold however, a tight sleeved shirt may be worn. Further, if one does not wish to expose ones flesh when spectators are present, or perhaps in the heat of summer, a summer shirt may be utilized.

◎ On the Subject of the Placing of the Feet

When standing and readying to shoot, your body should always be positioned with the feet like the bottom of a Hachi Monji or the Kanji 八 eight.

弓を握りたる手の指は小指に最も力を入るべし
◎指に力の入れ方の事

弓を握るは難卵一個を握りたる如き心得あるべ
◎弓の握り方の事

矢を射るには弓を持ちたる左の肩を下すべし
◎肩心得の事

的を見定むるは弓と弦との間より見定むべし
◎的見定めの事

弦の引かけは曲尺にて五寸の事
◎弦引かけの寸法の事

箭は目通りより曲尺にて六寸打上ぐべきなり
◎箭の打上げ寸法の事

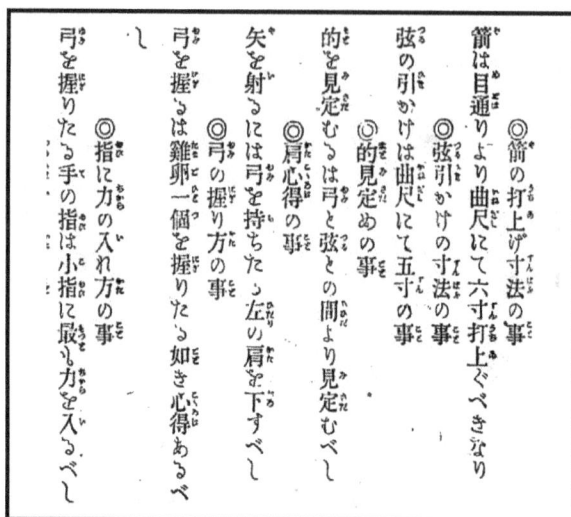

◎ **The Extent to Which the Arrow is Shot Upwards**

The arrow does not fly straight along the line of sight, but rather should be shot upwards about 6 Sun or 19 centimeters.

◎ **The Measurement of the Distance of the String to the Bow**

The string to the bow should be 5 Sun, or 16 centimeters.

◎ **On the Subject of Confirming the Distance to the Mado**

When judging the distance to the target, you should study it while looking between the bow and the bowstring.

◎ **Things You Should Know About the Shoulder**

After shooting, your left arm, holding the bow should drop down.

◎ **On the Subject of Grip the Yumi or Bow**

You should grip the bow as if you were holding a hen's egg.

◎ **On the Subject of How to Put Power in the Fingers**

When drawing, put the most power in your little finger.

弦を引入るゝは右の肩まで入るべし

◎息の張り方の事

引入れの時は息を臍の下へ張り、射放すときには三分の息を殘すべし

◎袴前へ箭の撓せ方の事

四ツ矢を射るとき一手ハ右の手に持ち一手ハ袴の前へ撓せるなり、此撓せ方は矢尻を上にし袴の紐下へ少し斜めに撓せて立てゝかくるなり

◎弓小手の事

弓小手とて革にて造りたるものを拇指に嵌め手に掛けるなり、これは弦にて磨れざる爲めなり

左の圖の右の手に嵌めたり

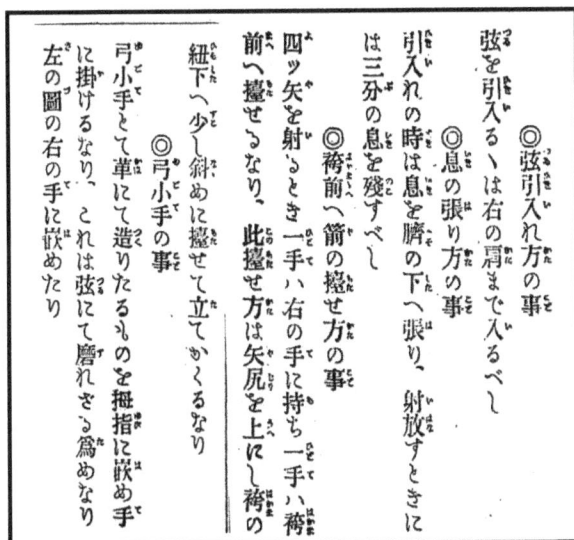

◎ **On the Subject of Drawing Back the Tsuru or Bowstring**

Draw back until it extends all the way to your right shoulder.

◎ **On the Subject of how the Breath Should be Held**

Inhale when drawing the bowstring as if drawing in breath from below the navel. After release, about a third should remain.

◎ **How to Place the Arrows in Front of One's Hakama**

When shooting a Yotsu-te, Four Hands of arrows, the first Hito-te, or two arrows, is taken in the right hand. The other Hito-te is placed, waiting, in front of your Hakama. This Hito-te is planted with the Ya-jiri, or the arrowheads, pointing up and leaning along the seam running down the side of your Hakama.

◎ **On the Subject of Yugote Forearm Guard**

The 弓小手 Yugote is made of leather. The arm is slid in and the loop at the end is hooked over the thumb. It serves to protect against the bowstring scraping cross the forearm [1]. As the illustration on the following page shows, the Yugote is on the left arm.

[1] Also written as 弓籠手. Can be either leather or silk, and are kind of like a snug tube covering used to protect the looser sleeve of the upper Kimono from interfering with the bowstring.

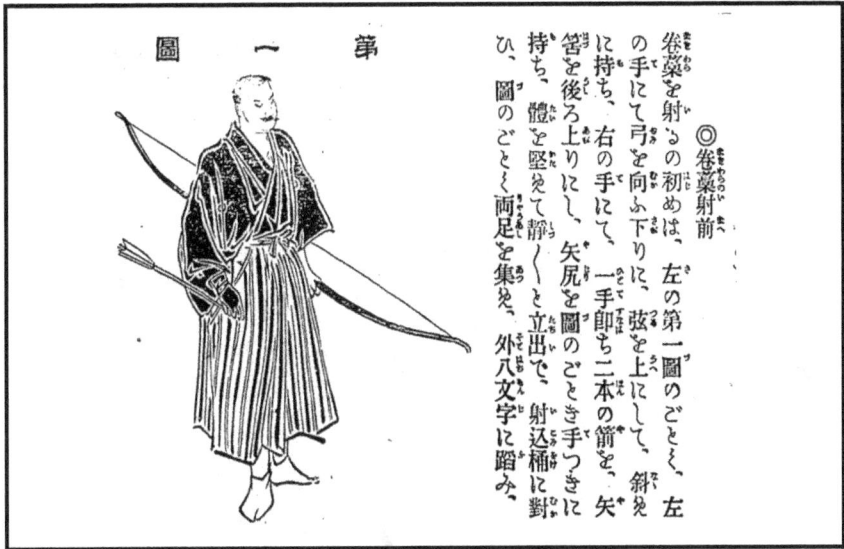

第一圖

◎卷藁射前

卷藁を射るの初めは、左の第一圖のごとく、左の手にて弓を向ふ下りに、弦を上にして、右の手にて、一手卽ち二本の箭を、矢筈を後ろ上りにし、矢尻を圖のごとき手つきに持ち、體を堅えて靜くと立出で、射込桶に對ひ、圖のごとく兩足を集め、外八文字に蹈み。

◎ **Kyujutsu Archery**
First Illustration
◎ **Before Shooting into Maki-wara**

    The first thing to be done when preparing to shoot at Maki-wara is as depicted in the first illustration. The Yumi is held in your left hand, angled down with the Tsuru or bowstring facing upward. The right hand holds a Hito-te of two arrows. The Ya-Hazu, or the nocked end of the arrows, are angled up behind your body with the Ya-jiri, or arrowheads, held as shown in the illustration.

    Your body should be displaying both poise and a profound calmness as you stand before the Ikomi-oke, or the barrel shaped target. Your feet should be gathered together and placed in an outward facing Hachi Monji, or the Kanji for eight 八.

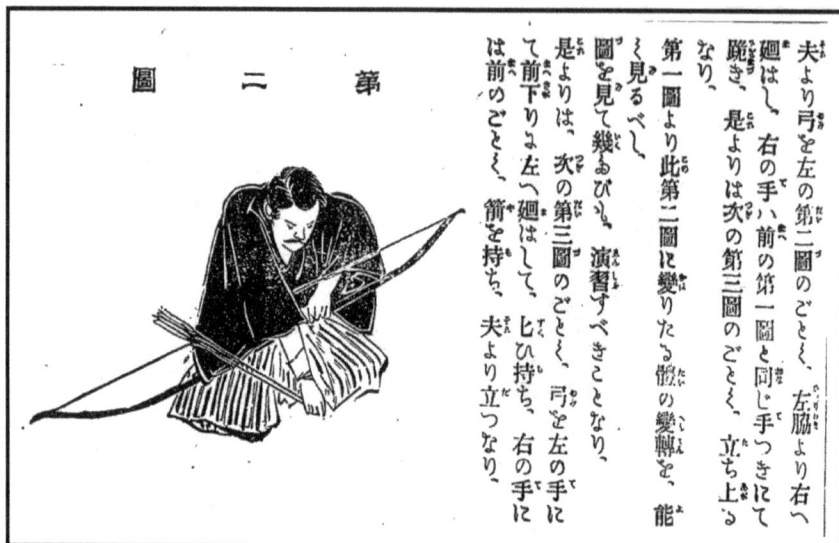

第二圖

夫より弓を左の第二圖のごとく、左脇より右へ
廻はし、右の手は前の第一圖と同じ手つきにて
蹲き、是よりは次の第三圖のごとく、立ち上る
なり、

第一圖より此第二圖に變りたる憾の變輯を、能
く見るべし。

圖を見て幾るびも、演習すべきことなり、
是よりは、次の第三圖のごとく、弓を左の手に
て前下りより左へ廻はして、匕ひ持ち、右の手に
は前のごとく、箭を持ち、夫より立つなり、

Second Illustration

From there shift the bow from under your left arm to a position under your right arm as shown in this second illustration above. You next kneel with the right hand held in the same manner as shown in the first illustration. Following this, you rise up as shown in the following third illustration.

The changes in your body position from the first illustration to the second illustration should be observed carefully. You should refer to these drawings frequently while training to enact this.

From there, as can see in the following third illustration, the bow, held in the left hand with one end down, is swung to your left. The bow is held Sukui-mochi style as if ready to scoop something up, while your right holds the arrows as was described before.

Next, stand up.

第三圖

夫より左の第三圖のごとく、弓を左に手にて第一圖のごとく向は前下りに左へ廻はしとひ持ち、右の手には前のごとくに箭を持、此たびは左の足を向ふへ出し、右の足を少し引き、両足を廣げて立つなり。是よりは又、次の第四圖のごとくに坐して弓を立て、一手の箭を持ちゐる右の手の拇指と食指にて、支へ持つなり。是より下の第七圖に、矢を射はなつ所あり、矢二本とも射はなちて後ち、第八圖のごとく坐するまでに、再び此体勢になるなり、

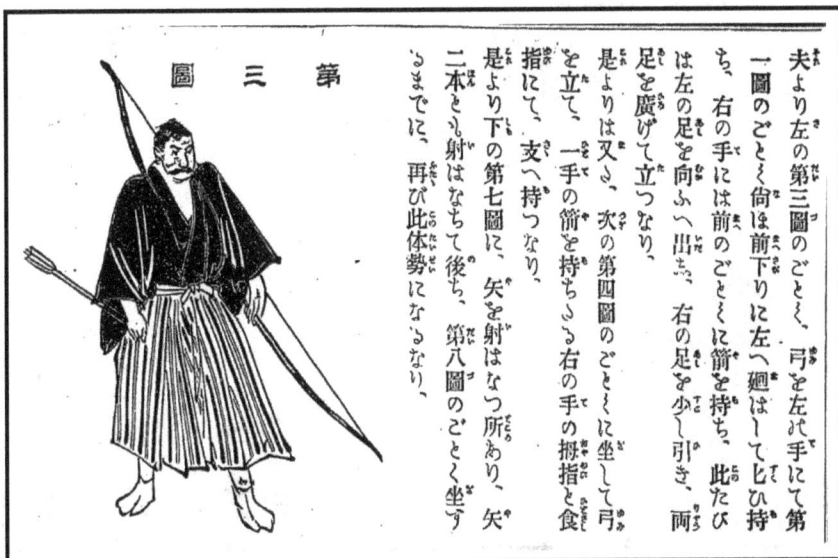

Third Illustration

Next, as can be seen in the third illustration, you have shifted the bow back and are holding it in the same manner as in the first illustration. At this stage, the front of your bow should be angled down. Hold it as if you are readying to scoop something up with the tip. The right hand is as before, holding the arrows.

At this point your left foot is set out aimed down the range, while the right is pulled back slightly. You are standing with both feet set wider apart than before.

The next stage can be seen in the following fourth illustration. You are seated with the bow planted upright. Your right hand holds the Hito-te of arrows, gripping them with the Oya-yubi and the Hitosahi-yubi, or the thumb and forefinger respectively[1].

Skipping down to the seventh illustration, you are preparing to release the arrow. After having fired two arrows, the eighth illustration shows how you sit down again, returning again to this very same position.

---

[1] Written as Oya-yubi 拇指(thumb+finger) and Hitosashi Yubi 食指 (food+finger) respectively.

第四圖

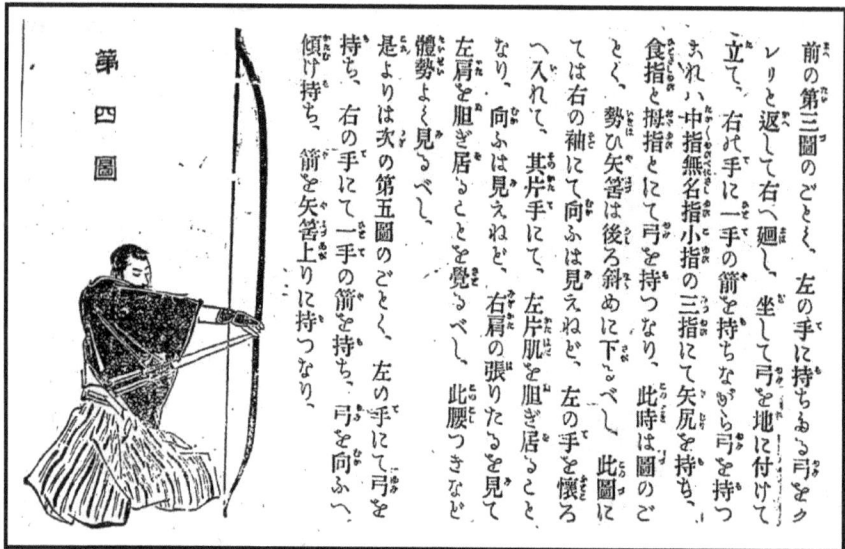

前の第三圖のごとく、左の手に持ちゐる弓を
クルリと返して右へ廻し、坐して弓を地に付けて
立て、右代手に一手の箭を持ちながら弓を持つ
なり、中指無名指小指の三指にて矢尻を持ち、
食指と擬指とにて弓を持つなり、此時は圖のご
とく、勢ひ矢筈は後ろ斜めに下べし、此圖に
ては右の袖にて向ふは見えねど、左の手を懐ろ
へ入れて、其片手にて、
向ふは見えねど、左片肌を胆ぎ居ること
右肩の張りたるを見て
左肩を胆ぎ居ることを覺るべし、此腰つきなど
體勢よく見るべし、
是よりは次の第五圖のごとく、左の手にて弓を
持ち、右の手にて一手の箭を持ち、弓を向ふへ
傾け持ち、箭を矢筈上りに持つなり。

Fourth Illustration

As was shown in the third illustration the left hand that holds
the bow swings it to the right with a smooth Kururi sound. One end
of the Yumi is then rested on the ground, standing it up vertically.
At this point he is holding a Hito-te of two arrows whilst
simultaneously holding the Yumi. This is done by gripping the Ya-
jiri of the arrows with the Naka Yubi, also known as the Takadaka
Yubi, the Mumei-Shi and the Ko-yubi[1]. Meanwhile the Hitosashi-

---

[1] So, though the commonly used word for the middle finger, 中指
Naka-Yubi (literally: the middle finger) is written, above it the
author has given a reading of Takadaka-yubi 高高指 (literally: the
tall, tall finger). This is a variant, a sort of a play on the sound of
Taketaka Yubi 丈高指 (literally the length that is tallest finger).
The next finger is the 無名指 Mumei-Shi or Nanashi-Yubi (literally:
no name finger), which is usually referred to as the ring finger in the
west. The contemporary Japanese use the term 薬指 Kusuri-Yubi
(literally: the medicine finger) as, according to the massive Kojien
Dictionary, it "Was the finger used when mixing medicines." I
found some references to Buddhism as the origin of this, namely the
薬師如来 Yakushi-nyorai or the "Medicine Buddha" who is usually

Yubi and the Oya-Yubi hold the bow. Further, as can be seen in the illustration the Ya-Hazu should, naturally, be facing to the rear and angled downward.

In this illustration only your right sleeve can be seen, the other not being visible. The left hand has been drawn out of the sleeve and to the chest. Thus, the sleeve falls away and the flesh on the left side of your body is exposed. While the other side cannot be seen, one should remember that while the right shoulder is out, the left shoulder is being uncovered. The positioning of the hips and so forth as well as the overall way the body is held should be observed carefully.

From here, as can be seen in the following fifth illustration, your left hand holds the Yumi and the right hand has the Hito-te of arrows. The Yumi is angled slightly down range, while the arrows are held with the Ya-hazu angled upward.

---

shown with a medicine bowl in his left hand. The author, however, has used the reading Kuchibeni-Yubi above the Kanji which means literally "the lipstick finger." Since lipstick was traditionally applied with the same finger as was used for medicine, so in all likelihood this is a stab at comedy.

In review:

Thumb- Oyayubi-拇 or 拇指 or 親指.

Index finger- Hitosashi-Yubi-人差し指 (literally: the point at people finger)　食指 (literally: the point at food finger).

Middle finger- Naka-Yubi, Takadaka-Yubi, Takedaka-Yubi 中指 or 高々指　or 丈高指.

Ring finger- Kusuri-Yubi, Mumei-Shi or Nanashi-yubi 薬指 or 無名指.

Little finger- Koyubi 小指 (literally: the small finger).

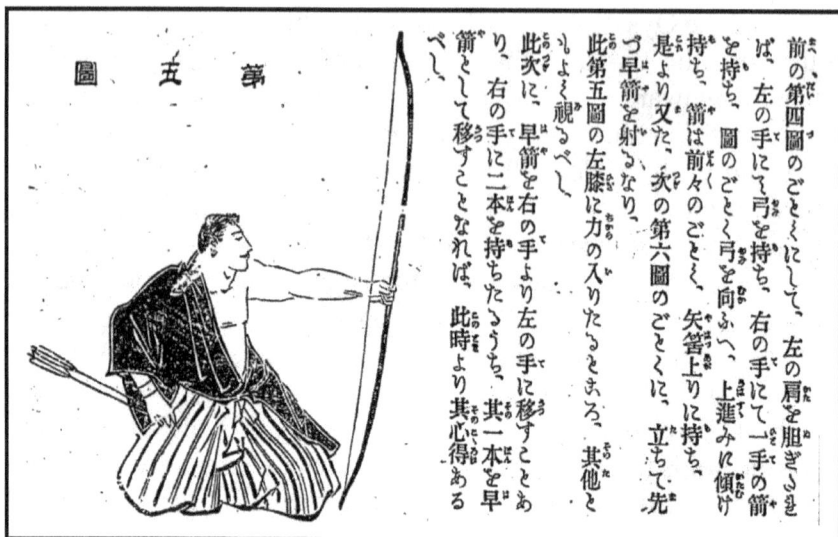

第五圖

前の第四圖のごとくにして、左の肩を胆ぎ\
ば、左の手にて弓を持ち、右の手にて一手の箭\
を持ち、圖のごとく弓を向ふへ、上進みに傾け\
持ち、箭は前々のごとく、矢筈上りに持ち、\
是より又た、次の第六圖のごとくに、立ちて先\
づ早箭を射るなり。\
此第五圖の左膝に力の入りたるときまた、其他を\
よく視るべし。\
此次に、早箭を右の手より左の手に移すこととあ\
り、右の手に二本を持ちたるうち、其一本を早\
箭として移すこととなれば、此時より其心得ある\
べし。

Fifth Illustration

This follows what occurred in the previous fourth illustration. After having removed the clothing covering your left shoulder the Yumi is taken in the left hand. The right hand holds the Hito-te of two arrows. As shown in the illustration the Yumi is held such that the top is forward of the base and overall it is facing down range. The arrows should be held in the manner shown two illustrations ago, with the Ya-hazu, or feathered ends, upward. From there, as the following sixth illustration shows, you stand up and prepare to shoot the Ha-ya, or first arrow. Note everything in this fifth illustration including the fact that you are putting power into your left knee.

Shifting the Ha-ya from the right hand to the left happens next. What needs to be understood here is that of the two arrows held in your right hand, it is the Ha-ya, first arrow, that is being moved.

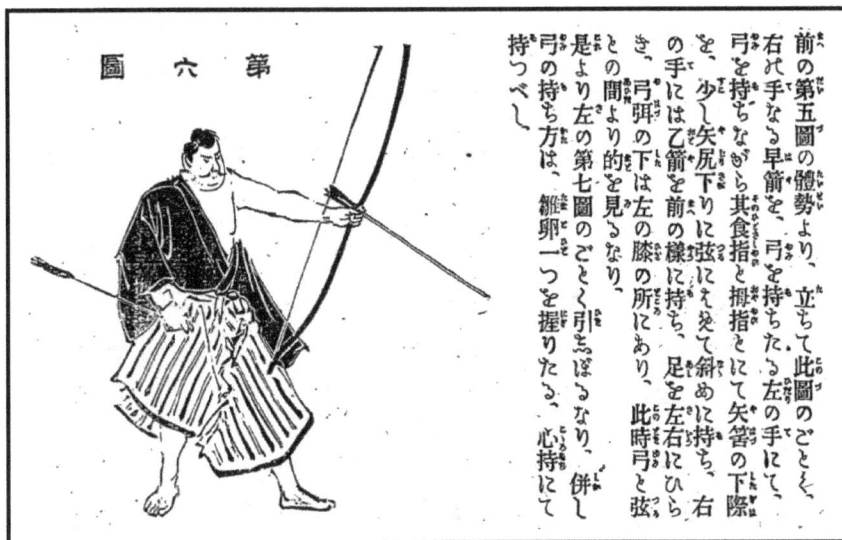

第六圖

弓の持ち方は、雛卵一つを握りたる、心持にて持つべし。
是より左の的を見るなり。弓弾の下は左の膝の所にあり、此時弓と弦と併し、の間より左の第七圖のごとく引きしぼるなり。
の手には乙箭を前の様に持ち、足を左右にひらき、右、
を少し矢尻下りに弦にへて斜めに持ち、
弓を持ちながら其食指と拇指とにて矢筈の下際、
右代手なる早箭を、弓を持ちたる左の手にて、
前の第五圖の體勢より、立ちて此圖のごとく、

Sixth Illustration

Following the position described by the fifth illustration, the sixth illustration shows you standing with the Ha-ya that was previously held in your right hand. You have shifted it to your left hand, which holds the Yumi at the same time.

Your Hitosashi-Yubi, index finger, and the Oya-Yubi, thumb, of the hand holding the Yumi grasp the arrow below where the Ya-hazu meet the shaft. The Ya-jiri, or end of the arrow, is nocked on the bowstring and is held angled slightly downward. Your right hand holds the Oto-ya as before. Your feet are opened up to the left and right and the lower Yu-hazu, or nock where the bowstring is hooked, should be at about the level of the left knee[1]. At this point you should observe the targe in the interval between your bow and the Tsuru, or bowstring.

From here, as shown in the seventh illustration, the bow is drawn. Be aware of the fact that you should grip the Yumi as if you were holding a hen's egg.

---

[1] Written variously as 弓弭, 弓筈 or 弓彇.

第七圖

前の第六圖の體勢より、乙箭を持ちたる右の手
にて、乙矢を持ちながら、弓に番へたる早矢の矢
筈を持ち、左の肩を下し、弓を雞卵を握りたる
心持にて持ち、小指に力を入れ、右の肩まで引
入れ、仲び入り、押手と共に整へて、偕てヒヨ
ーと放して射るなり、即ち前にも逃ふるごとく
引入るときも、息を臍の下へ張り、射放に際には
三分の息を殘すべし、
是より八第三圖のごとき体勢になり、次の第八
圖のごとくに坐するなり、

Seventh Illustration

This follows the position that was taken in the previous sixth illustration. It shows the Oto-ya in your right hand while the left hand is simultaneously grasping the Ya-hazu, nock, of the Ha-ya, first arrow, and the Yumi, or bow. Your left shoulder dips down all the while recalling that the Yumi should be gripped as if you are holding a hen's egg. Power is focused in your Ko-Yubi, or little finger.

You begin to draw back with the right shoulder, pulling back. At the same time, the movement of the hand that pushes should be linked with your shoulder's pull.

In the end your arrow is released with a *Hyo!* smooth whipping sound and the shot is made. Your breath should be held in at a spot below the bellybutton. When the shot is taken, a third of the shooter's breath should remain.

From here your body position returns to that of the third illustration. After that you seat yourself as shown in the following eighth illustration.

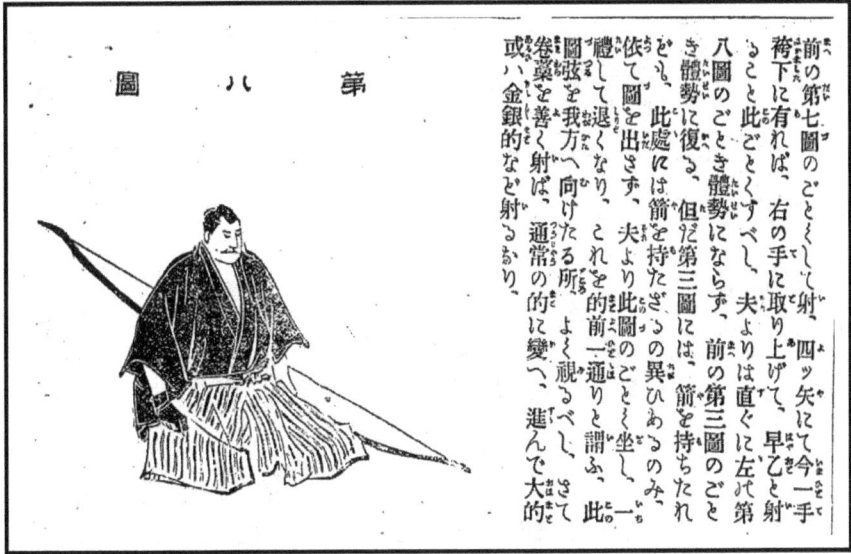

第八圖

前の第七圖のごとくして射
四ツ矢にて今一手
を射るにならば、夫より
は直ちに左第
此。

<u>Eighth illustration</u>

You have finished taking your shot as shown in the previous seventh illustration. If a Yotsu-ya of four arrows is to be shot, then the second Hito-te of two arrows at the bottom edge of your Hakama should be taken up in your right hand.

The entire process of shooting the Ha-ya and Oto-ya arrows should be repeated. Once that has been completed the shooter does not immediately return to the position shown in the eighth illustration, rather you repeat the position detailed in the third illustration. Since the only difference between the third illustration and this stance would proceed the presence of a pair of arrows, that illustration will be abbreviated.

Returning to the matter at hand, you then sit, do a bow and then withdraw. This whole process from start to finish is referred to as Mado-mae Hito-tori, or one full pass at the target[1]. The illustration shows the bowstring facing the shooter. This should be observed carefully. Once having become adept at shooting Maki-wara, one can move to shooting at regular Mado and then finally proceed onto O-Mado, a 1.58 meter in diameter target, the largest, or the Kin-Gin gold and silver Mado.

---

[1] 的前一通 Literally: target + in front of + one + pass.

此的前一通り熟練の上は前に記したるごとく的
塲迄の距離を三十間乃至五十間とし的は六尺直
徑の的を射るなり
右は射手一人として記したり然るに四人或は五
人列び立ちて射ることあり。斯る時第一位の者
射放てば次なる第二位の者搆へて射放ち、第二
位の者射放ては第三位の者搆へて射放ち第四第
五位皆斯くのごとく射人幾人ありとも順次と
れに同じくす此時貴人見あれば一列早矢を射
次に一列乙矢を射て早矢乙矢共に射はをちたれ
ば見分者を前と見て五足後に退き次に又た一
手を射れゝと進みて射處へ直り、前に一手を射た
るごとくし五人射されば五足引きて蹲き弓を左
に持ち弦を我方に向け、禮を爲して退くなり
射前にはつくばひと云ひて蹲いて射る法あり、
立ちて射るにあらず、されど大体に於ては變ら
ことなし
弓は强百發百中すとも妙手と謂ふべからず弱
き弓にて曲射すれば眞の妙手にあらずと器用
に射ることあり夫の揚弓塲にて何丸が百中した
りなど日ふの類なり中りて强らざれば稱せず

Only through intensive training, or Jukuren, in Mado-mae Hito-tori, or one full pass at the target will you be able to, as was previously described, go to the target range, and strike a six Shaku in diameter target from a distance of between thirty and sixty Ken[1].

The text on the previous pages focused on how a single archer would shoot, however there are cases where four or even five archers would line up to shoot at targets. It would proceed from the person in first position, who would fire at the target. The person next in line would then go into Kamae and shoot. Once the second person in line has shot, the third person in line would go into Kamae. The fourth and fifth person in line would follow in the same manner. Thus multiple practitioners would shoot one at a time like a wave.

Should Ki-jin, or nobility, be present the row of archers would first all release the Ha-ya, former arrow, and this would be followed by the whole row shooting the Oto-ya, latter arrow. Once having released both the Ha-ya and Oto-ya arrows the line faces those viewing and steps back five strides. If another Hito-te of two arrows is to be shot, the line would return again to the Ii-dokoro, or shooting point. The next Hito-te of two arrows would be loosed as

---

[1] One 間 Ken is 6 Shaku, about 1.8meters, so 30 Ken would be around 55m and 50 Ken about 91meters to the target.

was detailed before and, having done this, the five shooters would drop back five paces. Each would then kneel with the Yumi held in the left hand, the bowstring facing themselves. Finishing with a bow, they would withdraw. There is a method whereby one kneels before shooting and then shoots from that kneeling position. While this method is not done from a standing position, that is the only aspect that is different from the original.

When speaking of the Yumi, or bow, common expressions like "*Hyaku-hatsu-hyaku-chu,*" or a person who takes a hundred shots and makes a hundred hits, is a marvel!" should not be said. Using a simple Yumi in order to perform trick shots does hardly a true marvel make. Though some may be adept in this manner of shooting at the local Yokyuba[1], or sport shooting range, and can nail any number of bull's eyes, one cannot declare, "He is a marvel!"

---

[1] Starting in the Edo Period, sport archery attractions called Yokyuba 楊弓場 became popular at local festivals. Anyone could try their hand at shooting. The bow was a small, simple affair and when a target was hit, prizes would be awarded. The ladies who retrieved the arrows known as Yaba-onna, or Target-range girls, and worked to draw in male customers. Stands competed to have the prettiest target-range girls. The Yaba-onna eventually morphed into prostitutes and the prizes became a kind of gambling. Police eventually clamped down on the places, and customers drifted off to cheaper drinking establishments so that by the end of the Meiji Era they had all but disappeared.

手練家にも修業が詰めばなれるなるべし
聞えず近よりて驚き一時沮む所ある故か斯る
て空氣に抗してヒュウ〳〵とは言へども遠く
りの砲銃は音より功あれども何分にも音の聞ゆ
あめ會津桑名諸侯以下安心にて落ちたりと云へ
是にて追撃を拒ぎ居たる間に慶喜公はじ
し空中に矢の無き間な
めになりて止まねば如く
序にて左の肌を胆ぎ堤に立ちて差つめ引つめ
矢束を幾個となく射たるに降つゝく雨の足斜
たる矢束百本縺なるを前に置き右に記せる順
を穿きて優然として淀川堤に上り軍卒の持出
二重の小袖を着なもし呂色の大小をさし雪踏
を得す、然る處に會津藩士の某々両人黒羽
西へ〳〵と落ち來るに官軍追撃して無事に落
に其手は官軍に歸順し成算外れて敗軍となり
王山を要害とし其守あるを以て安心したりし
成辰の年伏見鳥羽の戦争の時關東勢は山崎天
を成すものなり。
を沮ますするなど差つめ引つめ矢を射るは大に功
弓も大に功を成す、退軍の時殿りして敵の追撃

Great victories can be had with naught but the Yumi. When one's forces are in retreat, the Shirizori, or rear guard, can use it to thwart pursuing enemy troops. When it is all said and done, great successes were due to the launching of arrows.

During the year of Boshin[1], at the time of the Fushimi-Toba War, the forces of Kanto had made for Yamazaki Tenozan

---

A Meiji or possibly earlier print of a Yaba-onna.

[1] Refers to the year 1868 according to the 干支 Eto, or stems and branches, system of dating.

The Eto is a cycle of sixty terms used for recording days or years that originated in the late second millennium BC in China. Each term in the cycle consists of two Chinese characters, the first representing a term from a cycle of ten known as the Heavenly Stems (天干) and the second from a cycle of twelve known as the Earthly Branches (地支). The first term (甲子) combines the first heavenly stem (甲) with the first earthly branch (子). The second (乙丑) combines the second stem with the second branch. This continues, generating a total of 60 different terms (the least common multiple of ten and twelve), after which the cycle repeats itself. Wikipedia.

The following Boshin years were 1928 and 1988 with the next in 2048.

Mountain[1] thinking to make it their fallback stronghold[2]. They had assumed the Mamori, or lord of that area, would support them. That move was fouled when he returned his allegiance to the Emperor. On the retreat now due to this miscalculation, they fell back to the west and westward again. The government troops were pushing hard and they were unable to make good their retreat. At this point two Samurai from Aizu-han decided to make a stand. Each wore a short sleeved Kuro-ha and wearing Setta[3] leather soled sandals with a set of Ro-iro[4] glossy black Dai-sho, long and short swords at their hip.

These two calmly proceeded to mount the dike holding back the Yodogawa River. They each laid at their feet a bundle of a hundred arrows typically carried by soldiers. The two then, in the order that was described before, uncovered the flesh of their left arm. Rising to standing positions they began to fire off arrow after arrow and these began to fall like a sudden squall of rain on their opponents.

The archers loosed with such rapidity that there was never a

---

[1] South-west of present day Kyoto Station.

[2] 淀藩 Yodo Han, the present day Fushimi area of Kyoto. During the 1868 Battle of Toba-Fushimi, the master of Yodo 稲葉正邦 Inaba Masakuni , famously changed his allegiance from the Shogun to the Imperial forces. Thus he went from 朝敵 Choteki, enemy of the throne, to 朝廷 Chotei, protector of the throne and followed up by refusing to open his gates to the retreating army of the Shogun Yoshinobu. Inaba Masakuni was active in the final years of the Bakufu and worked with Itakura Katsukyo 板倉勝静(kind of a connection here with the story from the first chapter). Even today there are apparently some historical novels that ridicule the Yodo hand for this.

[3] A type of foul weather shoe written 雪駄 or 雪踏. The leather on the bottom of the sandal prevents the feet from getting wet from the ground. You can still buy these at shops for construction workers (and those that like that style) pretty cheaply.

[4] A type of lacquering that results in a mirror like glossy black, with no apparent brush strokes left behind due to the polishing chemicals and oils. Originally the polishing chemical contained powdered deer antlers, but nowadays this is difficult to come by.

time when there was not an arrow in the sky[1]. It is said that due to this barrage the assault was slowed and this allowed, first and foremost, Lord Keiki[2] to fall back in safety, as well as the Lords of Aizu-Han and Kuwana-Han among others.

While rifles and such clearly can have their advantages, they create a terrible racket. Arrows fired from a Yumi emit no sound other than a gentle *Hyu-Hyu* rushing, caused by the resistance of the air. This does not carry far at any rate. When the arrows do strike, they do so suddenly and will cause a fast moving charge to falter. Therefore one must undergo intensive Shugyo, or training, in order to become adept.

---

[1] This anecdote is totally awesome.

[2] Keiki is another reading of Tokugawa Yoshinobu's first name 徳川慶喜. He was the last of the Tokugawa Shoguns, resigning in 1867.

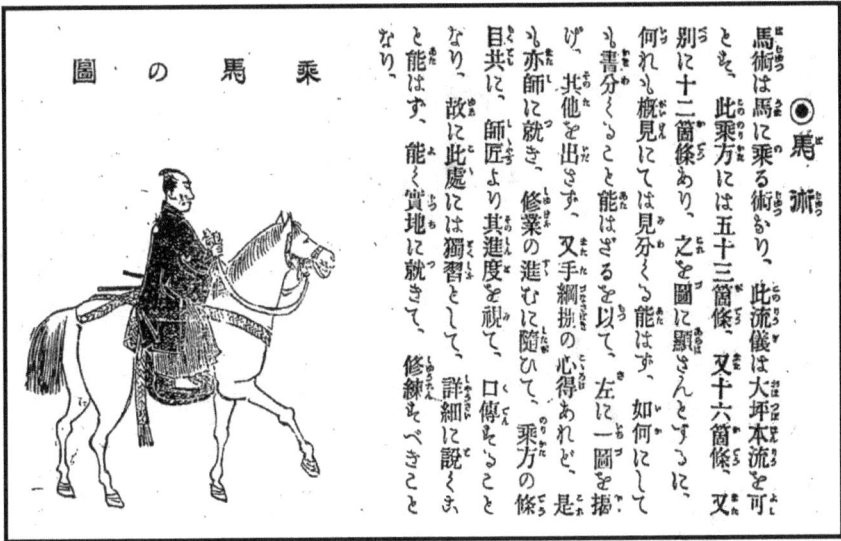

乘馬の圖

◉馬術

馬術は馬に乗る術なり、此流儀は大坪本流を可とし、此乗方には五十三箇條、又十六箇條、又別に十二箇條あり、之を圖に顯さんとするに、何れも概見にては見分くる能はず、如何にして書分くること能はざるを以て、左に一圖を揭げ、其他を出さず、又手綱捌の心得あれど、是亦師に就き、修業の進むに随ひて、乗方の條々も亦師匠より其進度を視て、口傳をること詳細に説くこと目共に、故に此處には獨習として、能くは、能く實地に就きて、修練をすべきこと能はず、能く實地に就きて、修練をすべきことなり。

◎ Bajutsu Equestrian Arts
Illustration of Joba or A Person Riding Upon a Horse

Bajutsu is the art of riding a horse. The Ryugi, or school, that will be introduced here is Otsuba Hon Ryu. It is considered to be of a high standard[1] This method of riding has a total of fifty-three chapters in addition to a sixteen-chapter supplement and an additional manual containing twelve chapters. As illustrations outlining these techniques would not be easily comprehensible and regardless of how much is written it would remain insufficient. Thus other than the single illustration at left, no other will be presented.

Further the Zuna-Sabaki, or the handling of the reins, is also something that can only be learned from an instructor during the course of Shugyo. The chapters dealing with riding are the same as only with a master teacher observing your progress and imparting Kuden, or oral-only transmissions, can one learn. Thus details presented here would only be difficult to interpret. In order to learn

---

[1] The Otsubo School was started by Otsubo Keishu, while Otsubo Hon Ryu 大坪本流 was founded by Saito Sadayasu (1695-1744).

this one should receive instruction at the training ground and drill the basics repeatedly.

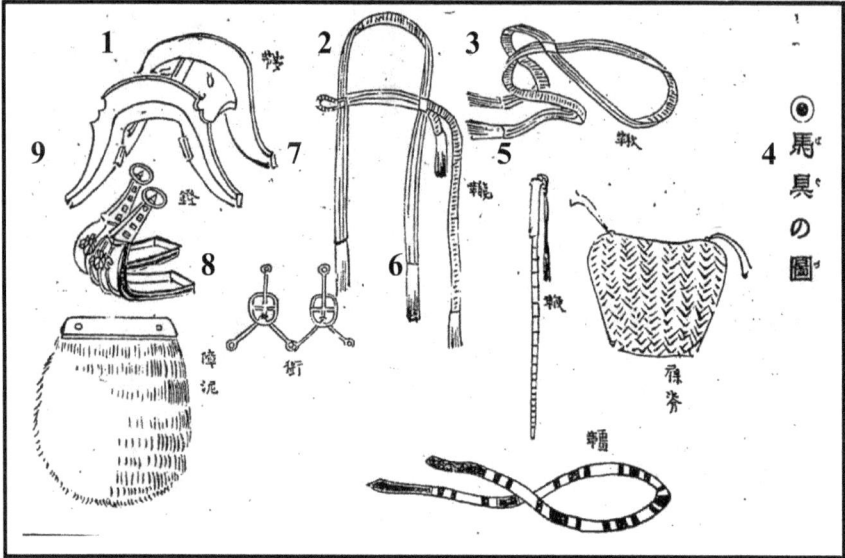

◎　Illustration of Horse Accouterments

1.　鞍 Kura - the saddle
2.　羈　Omogai - headgear
3.　鞦 Shirigai - crupper[1]
4.　鞍下　Kurashita - saddle blanket (Maybe, the Kanji is unreadable)
5.　鞭 Muchi - whip/riding crop
6.　羈 or 羇 or 羈 (Modern Kanji 手綱) Tazuna - reins
7.　轡 Kutsuwa - bit
8.　障泥 Aori - saddle flap
9.　鐙 Abumi - stirrups

---

[1] A crupper is a piece of tack used on horses to keep a saddle, harness or other equipment from sliding forward.

馬具の重なるものは右に圖するがごとし心得べ
きことなり

前に記すがごとく乗馬の術は實地に就き其進度
に隨ひ師より口傳あることにて劍槍柔術のごと
く一定の形あるにあらず、されど馬に乗りて水を
中を行くに就て掌を啓くの一話をなすべし、古
來繪圖などに甲冑を被て軍馬に乗り河或は海を
渉るさまを畫き其記事にも實際馬は人を乗せて
泳ぎたるやうに記しあれど決して斯ることある
にあらず其最も有名なるは源平の頃宇治川の先
陣爭ひに佐々木高綱が梶原景季に向ひ足下の馬
の腹帶緩みたりと曰ひ景季河中馬上にて其腹帶
を締る間に高綱は乗越して對岸に上り先陣した
りとあり此事は斯くあらざりしと思はるる何とな
れば馬は如何に泳ぐとも甲冑を被たる重き物を
乗せ泳ぎうゝものにあらず脊の立つ所なれば斯
くあるべけれど是すら水勢の抵抗に耐へて行く
は困難なり依て實際は深き河を渉るときには馬
え首のみ水上に出してフヽヽと言ひ水を噴く
なり中々畫に書けるやうに飾り總の見ゆるやう
ることは無きなり斯うときには乗る者は馬の

The important elements of Bagu, or horse riding implements, are recorded in the illustration on the previous page. You should use those illustrations to familiarize yourself with those tools.

As was recorded before, Joba no Jutsu, or the art of horseback riding, can only be learned at an actual training place, with Kuden, oral instruction, from an instructor as they observe your progress. This is wholly unlike Ken-So-Ju Jutsu, or the arts of the sword, the spear and unarmed combat, where there are Kata, or fixed sets of pre-determined attacks and defenses. Here I would like to offer a story and a bit of an insight into riding a horse in water.

Old paintings often contain depictions of Gunba, or war horses, wearing armor and swimming across rivers or in the ocean. The notations on these pictures also indicate that riders were actually mounted atop the horses as they swam. This is, however, not at all realistic. The most famous of these episodes is perhaps one that took place during the Genpei Era of the 12th century.

At the Uji River, just outside Kyoto, two warriors, Sasaki Takatsuna[1] and Ojihara Kagesue[2] were competing to be the first of the vanguard to make contact with the enemy forces. The former cautioned the latter that the chest strap of his horse was loose. In the span of time it took Kagesue to tighten his saddle strap while atop his horse in the river, Takatsuna had already reached the opposite side of the river and had engaged the enemy.

The above depiction is completely without merit. The reason is, no matter how great a swimmer a horse may be, if it is burdened with the weight of armour, it becomes impossible for it to swim. If the water is not covering the back of the horse it may be possible to traverse a body of water. In the midst of a flowing river staying atop ones mount would be no easy task as the risk of being swept away by the current would make the crossing difficult. The fact of the matter is that horses, when crossing deep water, have only their heads above water, breathing through their noses with a *Fu-Fu-*sound as waterspouts out.

One is not like to find a realistic painting of this hung up on somebody's wall.

---

[1] 佐々木高綱 (1160 –1214). A Samurai in the Genpei War, which was between the Minamoto and Taira Clans. This tale of Takatsuna racing Kagesue across the River Uji occurred during the 1184 Battle of Uji. He was on the Emperor's Minamoto no Yoritomo's (源 頼 朝 1147 –1199) white horse. Yoritomo was the founder and the first Shogun of the Kamakura Shogunate. Image from Wikipedia.

[2] 梶原景季 (1162 - 1200) A samurai in service to the Minamoto Clan during the Genpei War. He was mounted on the Emperor Yoritomo's black horse. I was unable to determine why they had the Emperor's horses. Some kind of bet?

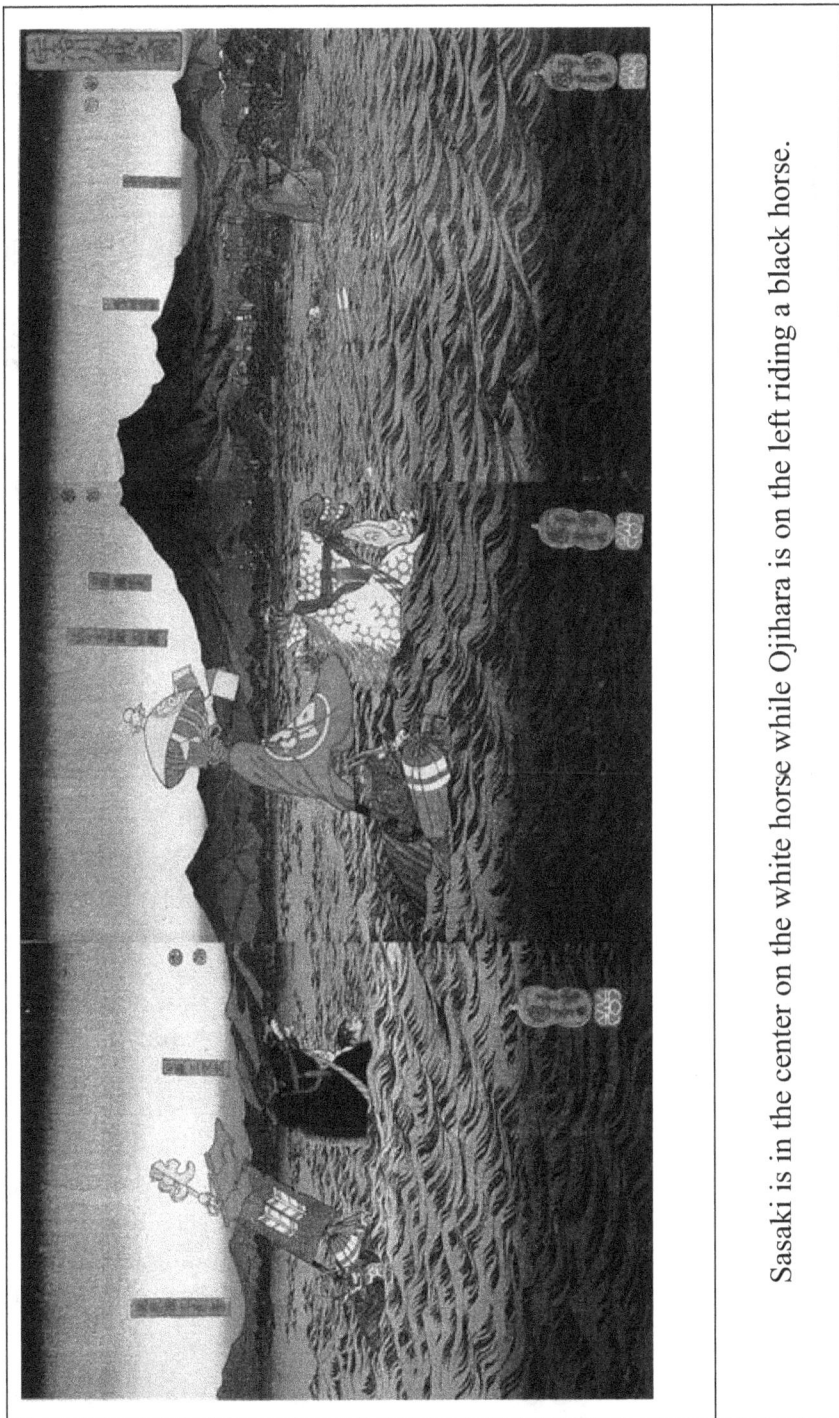

Sasaki is in the center on the white horse while Ojihara is on the left riding a black horse.

口を収り已に共に水中に入り馬と共に泳き渡く春の立つ處に到りて脊に乗ることなり、然るに河の中流にて景季も腹帯を締めらるゝ答もなし又高綱後より腹帯の綾みたるを見ることを能はず景季も亦後ろより高綱何と曰ふとうも之に應ず暇はあらざるべし今若し師に就かざる器用の乗人ありて是等の事を信じて深水を渉らば誠に危険なり是れ大に心得事なり右の話は河故に如何にしてか渉りしなるべし今一つ明智左馬介光春ぶ近江の湖水を渉りて辛崎に行きたる繪圖あり、而ども其雲龍を描きたる陣羽織は風に飜りて勇威凛々たる状あり河にてすら右に逃うごとくなるに湖水を乗わたることは万々無きことなり、若し然あらば光春の體し大に水中に沈み入り馬は困みて水面へ首のみ出して水を噴たるゝなるべし、尚々信ぜられぬとなりさて今は兵科の中に騎兵あり又西洋鞍に乗るの妙術あらん。兎に角に馬は實地に就きて其善き所に随ひ學ぶべし前の馬具の圖に鞭を圖したれども今も多く革製の西洋鞭を用ゐ陸軍にては靴に拍車を附て打つ

The way to swim with a horse is as follows: the rider grabs the horse by the mouth and swims through the water alongside the horse. In shallow water, when the back of the horse rises above the surface, the rider can then remount.

In the midst of a flowing river, the Samurai Kagesue would hardly have been able to tighten the chest strap of his horse, just as it is equally unlikely Takatsuna would have been able to determine the chest strap was loose while following behind him. Further, it is even less plausible that Kagesue would have been in a state of mind to hear what he was saying much less respond to whatever Takatsuna said to him.

When considering all that has just been relayed, if you were to choose *not* to enter as a student under a master-teacher and, instead, deem yourself competent and, believing the above tale to be true, attempt to cross deep water in the same fashion, know that it would be extremely dangerous.

There should be no doubt with regards to this point. The abovementioned discussion was in regards to rivers which can, invariably at some point or other, be crossed. Now then, we have the painting of Akechi-Samano-Mitsuharu[1] who crossed through the

---

[1] Akechi-Samano-Mitsuharu 明智左馬助秀満 (1536 - 1582) was a retainer of Akechi Mitsuhide under the warlord Oda Nobunaga.

114

lake waters of Omi on his way to Karazaki[1]. Indeed, in this very scene the Un-Ryu, or dragon cloud motif, drawn on the platoon Haori is fluttering proudly and bravely in the breeze with a *Rin-Rin* sound. While with a river it may be possible, but crossing through the waters of a lake in such a fashion is hardly conceivable. In reality, if such a thing were to be done, Mitsuharu's body would be submerged in the water and his horse would be struggling mightily with just its head above the surface of the water, puffing a spray of water up in the air. All the more reason to disbelieve the original depiction.

Amongst the branches of the army there is, of course, the Kihei 騎兵, or cavalry, who excel at the use of the western style saddle. In the end, if you seek to learn equestrian arts, you must receive instruction at a facility that teaches such arts and learn horsemanship at a pace the teacher deems suitable for you.

Amongst the Bagu or horse fittings presented in the previous illustration, the riding crop is of western design and the majority of them are made of leather. The army tends to use Hakusha 拍車,or spurs, attached to their shoes to urge their horses on.

Akechi Mitsuharu actually led the attack on Honno-ji where Nobunaga was forced to commit suicide. He became a legend for his rapid crossing of Lake Biwa and this scene is often depecited in artworks, one of which is on page 115.

[1] The waters of Omi 近江 refers to Lake Biwa, the largest lake in Japan located in what is present day Shiga Prefecture. 辛崎 Karazaki is the area on the opposite shore.

Painting by Utagawa Toyonobu, 1883.

◎ **Suiei-Jutsu**
The Art of Swimming

Since Suiei-jutsu, or the art of swimming, also falls under the auspices of martial arts techniques, only an outline of this art will be presented. As with the other Bugei, or martial arts, that are done on the ground you needs to be under the tutelage of a master. Should one not be available, then learn from an experienced student. Though all the illustrations presented are illustrations of people in the water, you should not enter the water and attempt to learn them on your own.

Recently a method has been developed where your body is suspended in the water in two places by specially crafted Obi or belts. These allow you to float while your body becomes accustomed to exercising in water. It is important to understand that swimming, as with any exercise that takes place in the water, if one has no experience one therefore has no understanding of Mizu no Kokoro 水の心, or *the heart of the water*. Thus, before you enter the water you must be under the supervision of an experienced practitioner before any of what follows be attempted.

First, you should find a river with a relatively slow moving current. Ideally you should seek out a spot close to the riverbank where your feet can brush across a pebbled bottom. A muddy bottom is dangerous. You should firmly grip an Uki-bukuro, or floatation bladder, or perhaps fasten a Tarai, or wooden basin, to a board.[48] Utilizing one of these items begin your training in the swimming arts.

After having become accustomed to moving in the water and absorbed knowledge of *the heart of the water* to a degree, the next step is to enter the water together with an experienced student. Upon finding an appropriate location, a rope would be attached to the Shoshinsha 初心者, or beginner. The senior student would then hold the end of the rope, while still in the boat and give oral instructions.

万一の危險を免れんが爲に學ぶものなるが故也
を冷す爲にては無く水中にて技を慰むにあらず
らず又永く水中に在るべからず、水泳は畢竟身
されば前にも述べたるごとく空腹の時は水に入
は關節の水に浸りて冷きるよりも起るものなり、
あらず此コブラガヘリは重に空腹より起るか又
を妨げて溺れ沈み一命をも失ふゆゑ注意せずば
水中にてはコブラガヘリと云ふ事起り為に運動
ことも出來れど上達の後ならでは能はず
險なり依りて是等に注意すべし是等の物を取除る
纏ふことあり、身体の自由を害するゆゑ危
漸く熟して水に入り泳ぐとき水草などの手足に
する為めなり
り壓す性あれども体中に空氣を多くし身を輕く
を下腹におとしつけて入るべし、是れ水は下よ
而して水に入る時には充分に空氣を吸ひ込み心
水に入るは宜しからず、又早朝は惡しゝ
寒又は頭痛する時、暑き時身を一旦冷さずして
心得べし空腹なる時、食後、疲勞したる時、惡。
借て水中に入りて宜しからぬ時あれば先づ之を
求むる熟練者と共に水中ゝ入りて習ふなり

After having become accustomed to moving in the water and having absorbed *the heart of the water* to a degree, the next step is to enter the water with the experienced student together. Through this, one's desire for further learning can be achieved.

---

[48] I was unable to find images of either of these. The Ukibukuro seems to be an inflatable device like a life preserver, while the Tarai on a board is like an upside down bucket that would trap air, thus floating.

So then, there are in fact times when it is inadvisable to enter the water and you should make yourself aware of these. On an empty stomach, after eating, if one is excessively fatigued, when feeling chilled, cold or with a headache. When it is hot out, suddenly chilling the body by entering the water is inadvisable. Further, swimming early in the morning is also not recommended.

When you have at last reached an advanced level and you enter the water to swim, be aware that Mizu-kusa, or water plants, can catch on your hands and feet. These can rob the body of freedom of movement and thus should be considered dangerous. Take care in an area with water plants. Though clearly you could remove these obstructions, however when you have reached the level of Jo-tatsu, or highly experienced, it will no longer matter.

While in the midst of swimming a thing called Kobura Gaeri 腓返,[49] or a cramp in the calf muscles, can occur. Proper exercises should be done to prevent this least one drown and sink to the bottom, losing your life. You should pay attention to this. This Kobura Gaeri typically manifests itself in the stomach or when water infiltrates the joints chilling them. Thus, as was mentioned before, do not enter the water on an empty stomach and you should not swim for long durations in the water. Finally, when swimming your body will certainly cool down all the way to your core. Therefore the techniques you learn are not simply for amusement, but rather to protect your life in case of an emergency.

---

[49] Komura refers to the calf muscle and Gaeri means return. Together the term means cramping or spasms 痙攣, or Keiren, somewhere on the body.

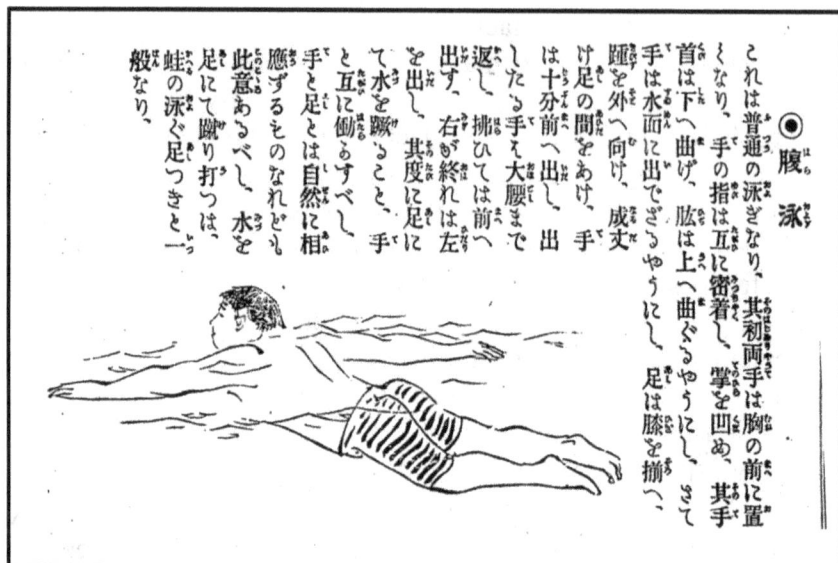

◉ 腹泳

これは普通の泳ぎなり、其初両手は胸の前に置くなり、手の指は互に密着し、掌を凹め、其手の指は下へ曲げ、肱は上へ曲ぐるやうにし、さて首は水面に出でざるやうにし、足は膝を揃へ、踵を外へ向け、成丈け足の間をあけ、手は十分前へ出し、出した手え大腿まで挑ひては前へ返し、右も終れば左に其度に足に出す、其度に足に出し、水を蹴ること、手と足とは自然に相応ずるものなれども、手と足とは互に傾ふすべし、此意あるべし、水を足にて蹴り打つは、蛙の泳ぐ足つきと一般なり、

◎ **Hara Oyogi**

This is the basic stroke for swimming. The first position is with both arms out in front of your chest. The fingers are squeezed together and the Te-no-hira, or palms of the hands, are cupped. The wrist is bent down and the elbow is bent slightly up. When swimming, your hands should not break the surface of the water. Your knees are together with your heels facing upward. Spread the legs apart as far as you can while bringing your arms forward in a full stretch. The outstretched hand should be brought all the way back down the length of your body, while the hand that has previously swept back is brought forward. If the right is finished then the left is moved forward. At this point the kicking out of the legs and the hand and arm movements should be in unison. This Shizen, or natural, cooperation between the arms and legs should be taken to heart.

The way you are kicking your legs closely resembles that of a frog swimming.

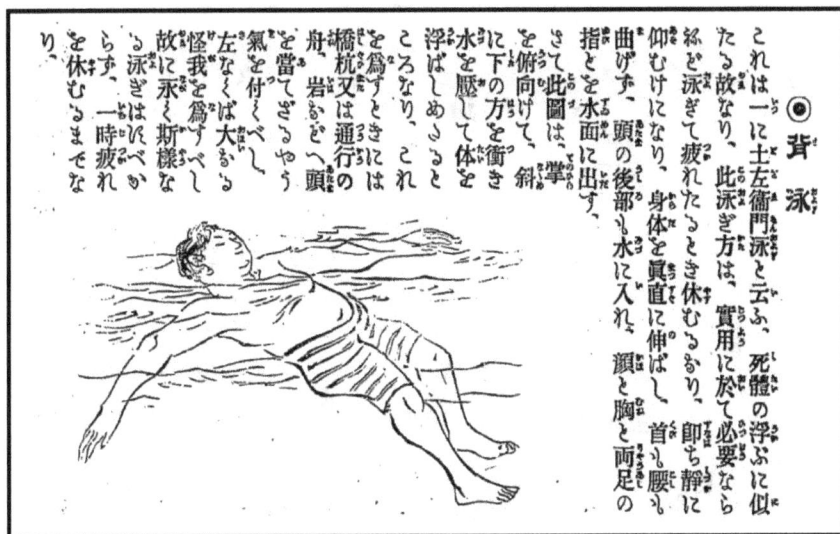

◎背泳

これは一に土左衛門泳と云ふ、死體の浮ぶに似たる故なり、此泳ぎ方は、實用に於て必要ならねど泳ぎて疲れたるとき休むるなり、即ち静に仰むけになり、身体を真直に伸ばし、頭と腰の曲げず、頭の後部も水に入れ、顔と胸と両足の指とを水面に出す。

さて此圖は、掌を俯して向けて水に壓すとき、これを為すときは、これ浮ばしめ浮ぶところなり。橋杭岩などへ頭舟杭又は通行のを當てざるやう氣を付くべし。左なく大なる怪我を為すべし。故に泳ぐべきは怪我を承はらぬ様に、左の泳ぎは大なるらぬ泳ぎは斯様なる。一時疲れりを休むるまでなり。

◎ Se Oyogi Backstroke

This is also known as the Dozaemon 土左衛門 float, since it resembles how a dead body floats in the water.[50] This stroke is used when you become too tired from swimming and you need to rest while still in the water. The method consists of resting in a face up position with the body extended straight out. Your head and hips are kept straight and the back of the head is in the water. Your face, chest and the toes of both feet are breaking through the surface of the water.

So then, this illustration shows the Te-no-hira, or palms, facing downward. When thrust diagonally down into the water they will serve to help float the body. When in this position you should be careful your head does not knock against foundation columns of bridges, passing boats or rocks.

You should not swim continuously for a long time, but rather, if you becomes tired, take a rest.

---

[50] In the Kyoho 享保 (1716-1735) a Sumo wrestler named Narisekawa Dozaemon 成瀬川土左衛門 was very fat and had very pale skin, so people began to say that bloated bodies found in the river were "all white and swollen like Dozaemon."

◉足泳

これを立泳と云ふ、餘ほど熟練せざれば、此
泳ぎ方は出來ず、即ち身体を收束して、重点を
一處へ集め、身体の平均を取るなり、而して泳
ぎ行くときは、手を動かさず、足のみにて泳ぐ
なり、故に足泳と云ぬなり、又歩くやうなるを以て
歩泳とも云ぬなり、此始え、前に少し傾くを可
しとす、但し足のみにて泳ぐは、水を蹴りて行
くなり、
此泳ぎ方は、諸の泳ぎの中にて、一段優美なる
泳ぎなり、躰の平均を取りて、浮き泳ぐことゆ
を、又静かなり、泳ぎに慣れたる者は、誠に容
易に出來得ることなり、

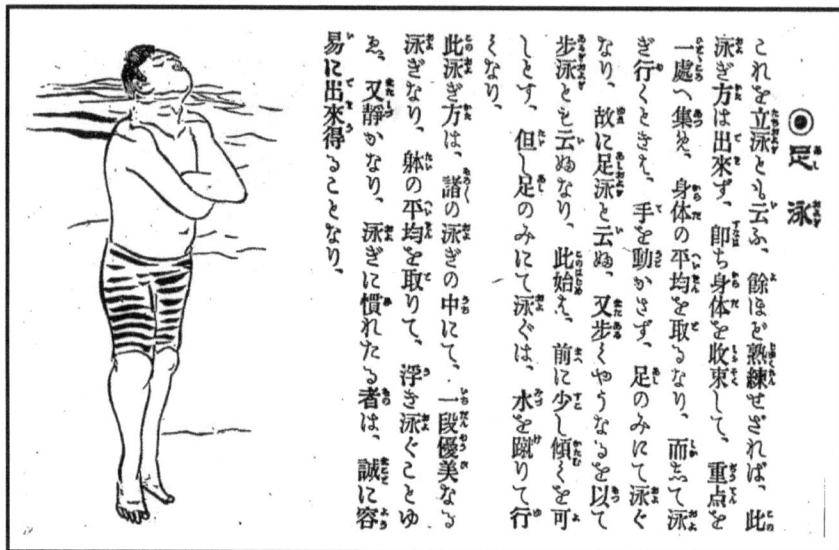

◎ Ashi Oyogi Treading Water

This is also known as Tachi Oyogi 立泳 or "standing swimming," commonly known as treading water. Without extensive training this manner of swimming is all but impossible. Your body must, in a word, be fully adapted to the water with all your weight focused on one point and the body balanced overall.

Note that in this style of swimming the arms do not move. It is only the legs that are working. For this reason, it is known as Ashi Oyogi, or leg swimming. Further, as it resembles a walking motion it is also referred to as Aruki Oyogi, or waking swimming.

Initially, it is best to have your weight slightly forward. Be that as it may, this method of swimming uses naught but the legs, thus you must learn to kick your way through the water. This is probably the most elegant and graceful way to swim. Balancing the body and doing a kind of floating swim. Further this style of swimming makes no noise. A person who has become skilled at is able to do it without the slightest difficulty.

武藝全書上卷終　出すべし。ごとく手を前へ切るには、なれども、方へ所なり。は通常のごとく泳ぎ。甲図は浮みたる所に在て乙図は易なり。泳ぐには川上より川下へ行く。体を斜めなりに沈むより下になり。首を下の方に向けて沈むに最も深く沈む。又、体を斜めに水の方へ突く少しむときは足にて沈むくは水をつくこれは水入とも云　◎潜泳

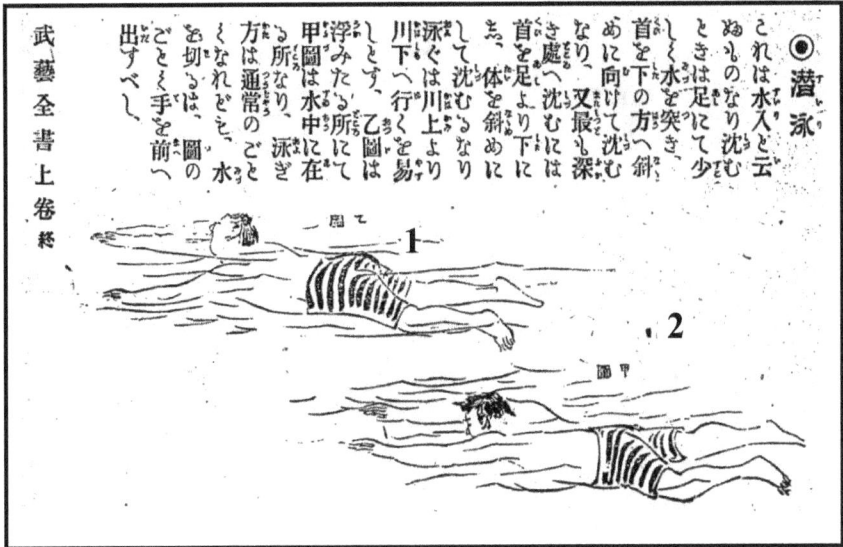

図乙　図甲

◎ Su-iri Entering the Water

1. Oto no Zu- The Primary Illustration
2. Ko no Zu- The Secondary Illustration

This is referred to as Sui-iri, or entering the water. When submerging the feet strike slightly at the surface of the water and the head is angled diagonally downward, pushing one underwater. At the bottommost point of the dive the head is below the level of the feet. The body is angled downward as it sinks. Swimming from upriver to downriver is the easiest.

The Oto-zu at the top shows the position when surfacing while the Ko-zu depicts the position when below the water. the method of swimming is normal, thought when breaking the surface of the water the hands are extended forward as shown in the illustration.

The Complete Martial Arts of Japan
Part One of Three
End
Printed on July Fifteenth of the 31st Year of Meiji 1898

The
Complete Martial Arts of Japan
Volume Two

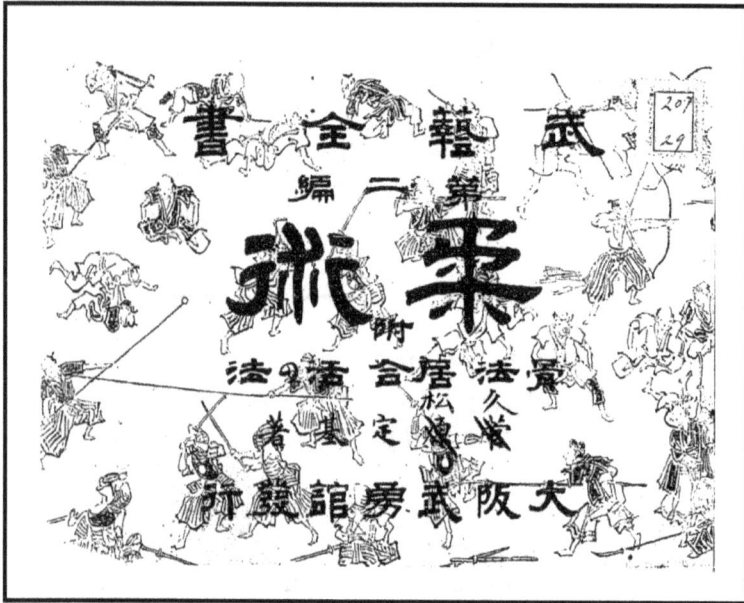

柔術：Jujutsu

Published 1898

By Sadamoto Sugawara

Illustrated by Fujita Shiun
Translated by Eric Shahan

1898 Advertisement for
The Complete Martial Arts of Japan: Jujutsu

This book introduces many Jujutsu techniques including, seated, standing, mid-level, drawing close, seated drawing close and separated. In addition there is also a sections on Koppo (used for restraining people) striking points, resuscitation points, resuscitation, and sword drawing.

The Complete Martial Arts of Japan: Jujutsu is intended to help people conduct training on their own, without a teacher. This is achieved through detailed illustrations and explanations. Descriptions of how to conduct training as well as what the person doing the technique should be doing and what the person receiving the technique should be doing has been explained in detail. It is as if a teacher is right there with you!

The lessons in this book are the direct teachings of Ameha Setsuo of the Sekiguchi School of martial arts. This is an unparalleled chance to learn directly from this great teacher, and truly a volume to be studied carefully.

Table of Contents

Jujutsu is the Mother and Father of the Six Martial Arts		
Shin-Gi, or Truth and Falsehood, in Jujutsu		
How Jujutsu Practitioners Can Escape Danger		
How Jujutsu is a Shapeless System for Defending the Body		
Jujutsu Keiko is Good Exercise and Good for Your Health		
On the Topic of Beginning Jujutsu		
The Most Effective Places to Grab		
The Most Effective Places to Hit		
The Most Effective Places to Strike With a Tsuki		
The Most Effective Places to Kick		
The Most Effective Places to Land a Blow		
The Most Effective Places to Focus One's Weight		
Common Expressions Used in Jujutsu		
Iidori	First Kata	Illustrations 1 ~ 6
Iidori	Second Kata	Illustrations 3 ~ 6
Iidori	Third Kata	Illustrations 3 ~ 8
Tachi Ai	First Kata	Illustrations 1 ~ 4

目錄擧

○居合 二形 自第一圖至第六圖 八十八
○活の入れ方 八十七
○急處活之圖 八十六
○中身急所之圖 八十
○捕縛器 八十七
○全 第一形 自第二圖至第五圖 八十六
○全 第二形 自第二圖至第六圖 八十七
○骨法 一形 自第二圖至第六圖 八十二
○離れ形 一形 自第三圖至第六圖 七十七
○居要門 一形 自第二圖至第八圖 七十六
○要門 第三形 自第二圖至第九圖 七十二
○全 第二形 自第二圖至第六圖 六十六
○全 第三形 自第二圖至第八圖 六十一
○中段 第一形 自第二圖至第六圖 四十一
○同 第三形 自第二圖至第八圖 廿九
○同 第二形 自第二圖至第四圖 廿八

Intro

自叙

予少壮嗜武技。以當時在士籍。雖必不得不修之。抑亦性也。常謂武是護國之器。雖鎖國之世然矣。況坤與邦國林立。争輸贏之今日乎。果哉知武之護國器。欲學之者。日増月盛焉。恂可賀也。夫柔術者。古来謂六藝之父母。學武技者。必也先始于此。顧得順次之正者乎。是以序少壮所修之柔術諸形。圖之解之。使目下少壮者得窺其一斑。竊謂不無爲國家少補。今也解常職。真草荼之士也。雖然不可不報國恩萬一。是則予素志也。此書公行尚有採用爲國器養成之一助。何喜如之。起稿非私計。出愛國熱意。覧者請憫焉炎吐露微衷。以爲序

明治戊戌春三月

浪速處士 菅原定基撰

I was born into a Bushi house and thus from a very young age I studied Budo. Budo is a tool that exists to protect the nation. However, recently in the world today people expressing interest in Budo are not to be found. While it is true that Japan is a country closed to outsiders however within our own nation the various states are not unified and lack central control. Should you truly seek to do all that you can for your country, think of embarking again on the path of Budo.

The techniques contained within Jujutsu have, from days long past, been considered to be the parents of the Rikugei, the six military arts. Those that seek to study Budo must first learn how to protect. Were you to look to the people who lived in the past you would find just that. As a youth they would learn to find Mu, or nothingness, through Jujutsu and would then draw what they had learned so that it could be further analyzed. Further, those even younger would steal what they could of this learning. All this was done to make oneself a better patriot.

As for myself, I have already retired from the world and become just another person in society, but should trouble come to this land I would surely seek to do all that I could for my country. This is my fervent belief.

I hope that through this book I am able to offer assistance to those who seek to be of use to their country. This is in no way for my own self-gratification but rather a representation of the passion I hold for my country. What do you think? Do those reading this passage desire to do as I have described?

This was written while thinking of my county, while I was worrying over my country.

Written in Spring of the 31st Year of Meiji 1898
by
Nami wa sho shi or Citizen of the Lands of Osaka :
Sugawara Sadamoto[51]

---

[51] My deepest thanks to Manaka "Unsui" Sensei, Kancho of the Jinenkan, for his assistance with the difficult Kanbun, Chinese style writing, in this section.

已の力にて已も投られ或は伏せらるゝなり此書
力を利用し而して勝ちを取るの術なり即ち敵は
遭ふとも其剛力の力を柔かに受け術を以て敵の
柔術なるものは力の劣る者已に勝る剛力の者に
〇柔術に眞偽ある事
ありて自ら妙手となると謂ふて可なり
り即ち弓を挽くにも馬に乘るにも劍を撃つにも
槍を使ふにも砲を發つにも銃を發つにも
を道に入るの門として先づ之を心得べきことな
と知るべし、されば武藝を學ばんとする者は之
術基本と爲りて六科の武藝の各を産み出すもの
科の諸藝を謂ふなり斯く父母と云ふからには此
云へり、六藝とは弓、馬、劍、槍、砲、銃此六
助と爲るものなり故に武術に於て六藝の父母と
柔術は都て武藝の基本と爲り又事を決斷するの
〇柔術は武術六藝の父母なる事

関口流柔術天羽拙翁正傳
菅原定基著
藤田慧雪画

武藝全書
中之卷
柔術

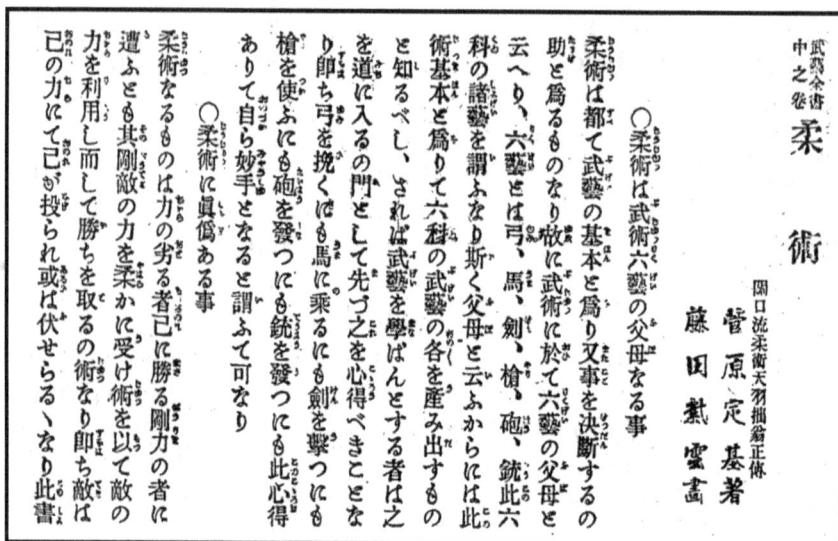

◎ Jujutsu is the Mother and Father of the Six Martial Arts

Jujutsu is the mother and father of the Riku Gei, or the Six Martial Arts. Jujutsu contains the fundamentals of all the martial arts. Since it helps to develop Ketsu-dan, or decision making abilities, it is known as the Fubo 父母 or mother and father.

The Six Martial Arts are as follows:

弓 Yumi - the bow,
馬 Uma - the horse,
劍 Ken - the sword,
槍 Yari - the spear,
砲 Ho - the cannon,
銃 Ju - the rifle.

You should be aware that the reason Jujutsu is referred to as the mother and father is because the Fundamentals of Jujutsu form the base that all other martial arts derive from. Thus it is said that those that wish to enter through the Mon 門, or the gate, of martial arts training and embark on a path of studying the way of the warrior should first obtain knowledge of Jujutsu. In other words, it doesn't matter if your goal is to become an archer, study the equestrian arts, learn the sword, the spear, or shoot a cannon or rifle, knowledge of Jujutsu will allow you to become expert.

に示す諸形の中にも特に愛門を見れば自ら術の
妙即ち力劣れる者も力勝れる者に勝つの理を知
るを得べし例へば十七八の處女も肚士に投げ伏
せするの不思議ならぬを悟り得べし小説本など
に武者修行する者が幾人も靺ては投げ靺ては伏
せすると書けるも強ち其武士に怪力あるにあら
ず實は此術に長けたるなり此等を眞の柔術とす
然るに之を誤り柔術と稱へながら術といふもの
は無くて力づくにて取合ひ勝負を決する流儀あ
り之を偽と謂ふも可なり斯のごとくなれば力の
強き者は必ず力の弱き者に勝ち、力の弱き者は
必ず力の強き者に頁くる事にて術とは謂ふべか
らず即ち力くらべにて角力に似たるものなり相
撲にすら四十八手ありと聞く、少しは術あるな
るべし然るに柔術と云ひて力くらべするは此相
撲にだも如かずと謂ふて可ならん柔術は柔の字
に眼を着くべし剛になりては誤なり此術を
誤りたるものは決して術にてはあらねと假に剛術
と名づけて眞傳を守る者は嗤ふなり本帯を見て
能々此差別を識るべし
〇柔術の心得ある者は不意の危難を

◎ Shin-Gi 眞偽, or Truth and Falsehood, in Jujutsu

Jujutsu is perhaps best described as a set of techniques that allow you, a person of inferior physical strength to, when faced with a person of exceptional strength, achieve victory by responding flexibly to rigid power. Then these techniques allow you to utilize your adversary's own strength to achieve victory. In other words, your opponent is being thrown by his own power and possibly even being laid flat out.

For example, you should know that a maiden [young girl] of seventeen or eighteen years of age throwing a full grown man down flat on his back is in no way mysterious. Novels and so forth contain depictions of those on Musha Shugyo, or on the path of intense martial arts training, fighting numerous people at the same time. If the hero is able to take hold of them, they are rapidly thrown to the ground. The reality is that such Samurai are not in possession of some great supernatural strength, rather it is testament to the strength of their *technique*. These books claim to portray true Jujutsu. Truth be told, calling the techniques told in those stories Jujutsu is an error. Jujutsu is not a system whereby Shobu 勝負, or winning or losing, between two opponents is decided by strength alone. Jujutsu is about technique.

The reason the above is false is that, were it to be true, then a person of great physical *strength* would invariably win against a person of weaker strength, and persons of weaker physical strength will always lose against those with greater strength. If this is the case then it can hardly be said to be about *technique*. Then Jujutsu would be nothing but a test of strength, like two Sumo wrestlers.

Many have perhaps heard of the *Forty-eight Hands of Sumo*, and thus there is some element of technique within the Sumo style of wrestling[52]. However, when compared to Jujutsu, it is fair to say that Sumo is more of a test of strength. One should focus on the Kanji Ju 柔 in the word Jujutsu which means soft and flexible. Turning it into Go 剛, meaning hard or rigid, would be an error. Jujutsu is a Shin-jutsu 眞術, or True Set of Techniques, and applying it mistakenly as described above will only result in a Jujutsu that we should perhaps label as Gojutsu 剛術, Rigid Technique. This last will no doubt cause those following the true way of Jujutsu teachings to laugh.

◎ Those Versed in Jujutsu Are Able to Get Away When Faced With an Unexpected Danger

If you are knowledgeable in Jujutsu and suddenly come under attack by multiple adversaries, then fleeing is the only option. You can make use of any natural obstructions that may be around. You may be able to leap over some, or in the case of trees or bamboo, you can scale up them. Perhaps even the bamboo itself can be used to successfully traverse swampy areas. Thus, in some of these cases a direct confrontation does not even take place.

----

[52] *Forty-eight Hands of Sumo* or 四十八手 The Shi-ju-ha-Te. Originating in the 14th century. The number 48 seems to indicate "many" rather than a specific nuber. By the end of the Edo Era Sumo had over 300 techniques, including newer ones and ones that had different names for the same technique. In 1955 the Japan Sumo Federation established 70 techniques, however this was later expanded to 82.

を勉めざるべからず将た尚武の時節にもあれば
るときは何を以て免れん其時こそ此柔術の心得
ありて可なるものなり尚又少壮の人は必ず兵役
きものなり万一にも途中にて危難に遭はんとす
差一本を差したれとも今は固腰なり誠に便りな
のにあらず昔は平人にても旅行には旅差とて脇
ず仕込杖或は短銃を持つ者ありても人各持つ
を取扱ふは夫々の掛り官にて平人は何をも携へ
防ぐは此柔術に限るなり、而して洋剣、砲、銃を
込杖、短銃等を用ゐる、凶器を持たずして敵を
熟れか用ゐるざるを得ず、今は洋剣、砲、銃、仕
太刀、刀、脇差、匕首、手裏剣、弓、大砲、銃
凶器を携帯せざるを得ず昔ならば槍、薙刀、剣
柔術を除くの他凡そ敵を拒ぎて我身を護るには

○柔術は無形の護身器なる事

時のみならず
も越ゆることを得るものなり敵と勝負を決する
り竹などゝの抗め得らるゝ物は其末を執りて河沼
得ず逃るゝ時諸の障害物を飛越い又は竹木に登
柔術を心得たる者は不意に多勢に襲はれ止むを
を免かるゝを得る事

◎   Jujutsu is a Shapeless System for Defending the Body

If one were to take Jujutsu out of the equation, then to protect yourself against adversaries you would have to resort to carrying weapons. In the past you had to make use of one or more of the following weapons:

槍 Yari - the spear
薙刀 Naginata - the halberd
劍 Ken - a western style sword
太刀 Tachi - a large sword
刀 Katana - a Japanese style sword
脇差 Wakizashi - the short sword
匕首・懐劍 Kaiken - a dagger kept inside the front of the shirt
手裏劍 Shuriken - throwing spikes
弓 Yumi - the bow
大砲 Taiho - the cannon
鉄砲 Teppo - the rifle

Nowadays there are western swords, cannons, rifles as well as Shi-komi Tsue 仕込杖, or walking sticks with swords concealed inside, and things like small pistols. Should you not carry a lethal weapon on your person then Jujutsu is the only thing that remains for self-defense against assailants.

Things like western swords, cannon and rifles should be left to specialists. Average people most likely go about unarmed and even if you were to find someone who carries a sword concealed in a walking stick or a pistol, this is hardly the norm and would not represent most people. In the past, when travelling people would sometimes take a single Wakizashi, short sword, as a Tabizashi 旅差, travel knife, for "on the road protection" but these days most people go around Maru-goshi 圓腰, "nothing about the waist" which means "unarmed." Such people have absolutely no mechanism for self-defense.

If the unthinkable occurs and they encounter danger along the way, by what means will they escape? It is in this very situation that Jujutsu comes into play. These days it is not a given that youths will have served time in the military. Should time and opportunity present themselves, one should strengthen your spirit by sharpening your martial arts ability.

武藝を研ぎて心丈夫に爲し置くべきなり
○柔術の稽古をすれば善き運動どな
りて衛生に益ある事

常に胃病を患ふる者などは運動の足らざる故な
り之を兔れんが爲にとて適度の運動を爲すこと
は誰も知りたる事にて體操と云ふものもあれと
此稽古も亦顔る運動には善きものなり

○柔術初手の事

柔術の取はじめは先づ眉間を打ちかゝるを或は
片手或は両手にて敵の胸なる襟を取るか又は後
より抱きつきて襟を取るか又は腕首或は二の腕
を取るかなり、但し左右の両手にて襟を取ると
きには右の手を上にし左の手を下にするなり此。
他拂捌きとて敵の刀を奪はんには必ず其柄を両
手にて取るなり足等を爲す前両手共空手の時或
は片手の空手の時には必ず拇を内にして握拳を
爲し居るべし又初め身搆への時の胡坐は必ず居
合腰に胡坐をかき立ちて身搆へる時には足を外

○取る所の要處

八文字に踏むべし

喉、胸、肩、肱、二の腕、腕首、

◎ Doing Jujutsu Training is Good Exercise and Pays
Healthy Dividends

Typically, those that suffer from ailments of the stomach and
such, tend to do exercise in insufficient amounts and therefore use
that as a reason to avoid such training. But just like the 体操 Taiso
exercises that everyone knows so well, if this Keiko is done your
athletic ability will surely improve.[53]

---

[53] The Department of Education invited an American doctor to
develop a Karutaiso 軽体操, or light gymnastics program, using
Tetsuarei 鉄亜鈴, or dumbbells, Kyukan 球竿, or a pole with a
weight on each end, and Konbo 棍棒, a kind of weighted club, in
1878. These are all shown in the illustration on the following page.
The Radio Exercise program, or Rajio Taiso ラジオ体操, began in
1928 to commemorate Emperor Hirohito's coronation. After being
briefly banned in post-WW2 Japan, it re-emerged and is now done
in local parks in the mornings in summertime and before sports
festivals at schools.

Illustration of Elementary School Physical Fitness
小学生徒体操之図 By Yoshu Shuen 楊洲周延画, 1886

◎ On the Topic of Beginning Jujutsu

Jujutsu techniques often begin with a strike to Miken 眉間, or between the eyebrows. Another possibility is to grab the adversary's Eri 襟, or Collar, with either one or both hands. Also, you can grab both lapels from behind, seize the wrists or take the Ni-no Ude 二の腕, or the forearm.[54]

Be aware that when grabbing hold of the collar on both sides, your right hand should grip high and your left hand should grip low. Also, when doing Tsuka Sabaki 柄捌き, or techniques that involve the enemy attempting to steal your sword by the handle, it is essential that you try and take the handle with both hands. Before any of this begins be aware that even if both hands are Karate, or empty, your Oya Yubi 拇, or thumb, should always be tucked in when making a fist.[55] This applies even if you have one hand empty. In addition, when going into the initial Agura 胡坐, which in this case is a position consists of both the knees and toes touching the ground with your buttocks on top of your heels, be sure to first drop into Iai-Goshi 居合腰, or a squat, before lowering your knees. When standing, your feet should be planted like the bottom of a Hachi-monji 八文字, or the bottom of the Kanji for eight 八.

---

54 Nowadays the term Ni-no Ude refers to the bicep, however this volume seems to indicate that it is the forearm. Contemporary dictionaries list it as "from the shoulder to the elbow" a Japanese-Portuguese dictionary from 1603 日葡辞書 *Nippo Jissho Vocabulário da Língua do Japão*, defined it as *from elbow to wrist.*

55

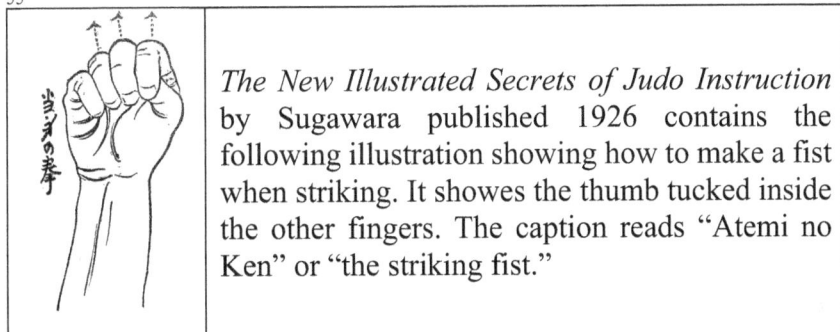

The New Illustrated Secrets of Judo Instruction by Sugawara published 1926 contains the following illustration showing how to make a fist when striking. It showes the thumb tucked inside the other fingers. The caption reads "Atemi no Ken" or "the striking fist."

○打つ所の要處
眉間、

○突く所の要處
喉、睪丸、

○蹴る所の要處
喉、睪丸、

○中てる所の要處
睪丸、

○掛くる所の要處
肋三枚、睪丸、

○柔術の通語
坐するときは膝、立てるときは足、
取伏せ、引倒す前には必ず此心得あるべし、

一本
これは一試合の事を云ふ、
使人
これは技の勝れたる方の人なり、
受人
これは技の劣りたる方の人なり、
此書の畫に白き襦袢を着たるは使人にて黒き
襦袢を着たるは受人なり、受人は又單に受共
云、

此他、打つ、受る、取る、掛る、外す、切る、
拂ふ、蹴込む、上る、引く、押す、伏る、投る、
投け、中る等あり、是等をも記臆すべし、

◎ The Most Effective Places to Grab
喉 Nodo - The Throat
腕 Ude - The Arm
肩 Kata - The Shoulder
肱 Hiji - The Elbow
二の腕 Ni no Ude - The Forearm
腕首 Ude Kubi - The Wrist

◎ The Most Effective Place to Hit
眉間 Miken - Between the Eyebrows

◎ The Most Effective Places to Strike With a Punch
喉 Nodo- The Throat, 睪丸 Kogan [Kintama] - The Groin [The Testicles]

◎ The Most Effective Places to Kick
睪丸 Kogan [Kintama] - The Groin [The Testicles]

◎ The Most Effective Places to Land a Blow
肋三枚 Abara San-mai - The Third Rib from the top on the left
睪丸 Kogan [Kintama] - The Groin [The Testicles]

◎ The Most Effective Places to Focus Your Weight

When seated, on the knees. When standing, on the feet. Before knocking your opponent over or pulling him down, be sure to reaffirm this concept in your mind.

◎ Common Expressions Used in Jujutsu

Ippon - This is how a single Shi-ai or bout is counted.

Tsukai-te - This is the person whose technique is superior.

Uke-te - This is the person whose technique is inferior.

Throughout this document the person wearing the white 襦袢 Juban, or shirt, is *you*, while the person in the black Juban is the *Opponent*. The Opponent will also sometimes be referred to simply as "the Uke."

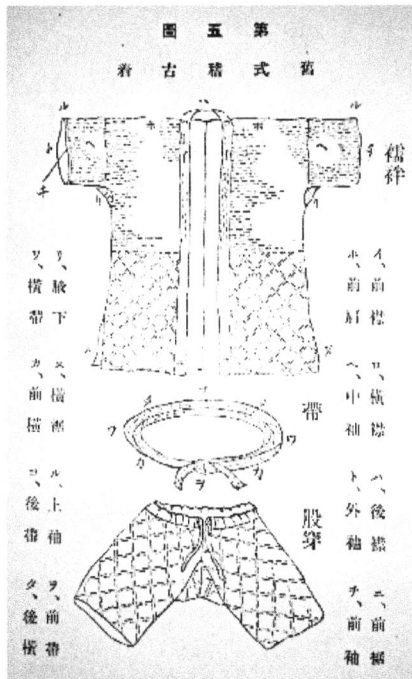

Translator's note:

The above illustration is from *The New Illustrated Secrets of Judo Instruction* by Sugawara published 1926. I have included it to show the type of training clothing worn. It says *Old Style Keiko or Training Uniform*. The top is called Juban. The belt is Obi. The shorts are called Mata-haki.

◎ **In addition, the following terms should be memorized:**

打つ Utsu	-	a Strike
受る Ukeru	-	to receive or block
取る Toru	-	to take hold of
掛る Kakeru	-	to place upon
外す Hazusu	-	to release
切る Kiru	-	to cut or pull away in a sharp motion
拂う Harau	-	to sweep away or sweep at
蹴込む Keri-komu	-	to kick in
上る Ageru	-	to rise up
引く Hiku	-	to pull
押す Osu	-	to push
伏る Fuseru	-	to lay flat out
投る Nageru	-	to throw
投げ Nage	-	a throw
中てる等あり Ateru-Toari	–	attacking vital points

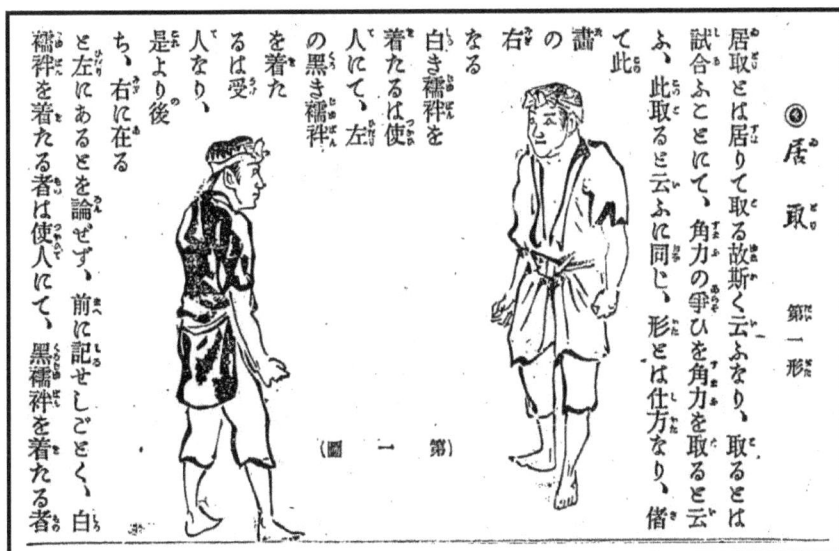

居取とは居りて取る故斯く云ふなり、取るとは
試合ふことにて、角力の爭ひを角力を取ると云
ふ、此取ると云ふに同じ、形とは仕方なり、偖
右の畫て此
なる
白き襦袢を
着たるは使
人にて、左
の黒き襦袢
を着た
る人なり、
是より後
人なり、
ち、右に在る
と左にあるとを論ぜず、前に記せしごとく、白
襦袢を着たる者は使人にて、黒襦袢を着たる者

◎ 居取 第一形

◎ Iidori Seated Technique
First Kata
First Illustration

The name Iidori is given because one practitioner takes hold of the other while seated. When we speak of the word Toru 取る, in this case, it means "to engage in a bout." A battle of strength is referred to as *Sumo wo Toru*, or "taking Sumo,"[56] and we are using the word Toru in the same manner here. The term 形 Kata refers to the way something is done.

So then, in this document the person on the right wearing the white Juban is you. You are the one applying the technique, and the person wearing the black Juban is the Opponent, or the one who is receiving the technique. From here on the phrase "the one on the right" or "the one on the left" will not be used. As was written before, understand that the person wearing the white Juban is you and that the black Juban is worn by the Opponent.

---

[56] Here the Kanji 角力 Kakuryoku, or comparing strength, is used with the reading Sumo above it. Even in contemporary Japan Sumo is referred to as 角界 Kakuaki or the "world of Sumo."

141

は受人と知るべし、此稽古は、袴を着くること
もあれど正式は通常の物より長き、圖の如き猿
股引を穿くなり、袴の時にても、必ず猿股引を
穿く、これは睪丸を蹴られぬやうに、要心をす
るなり、偖て取る初めは双方の間を六尺隔て、
立ち、前

に述べた
手を、右
の第一圖の
ごとくに、下
挵を内に
して握拳

にしたる
るごとく、
足を外
け、

八文字に蹈
みて立ながら一禮し、右の第三圖のごとく、徐々
々と近より、此處にては双方の間を六寸明け、
通常の胡坐にては無く、居合腰に胡坐を組み、
両手を膝に置き、互に透を見合ひ、一方より手
を出すなり、此時手を出すには、前方より手を

(圖 貳 第)

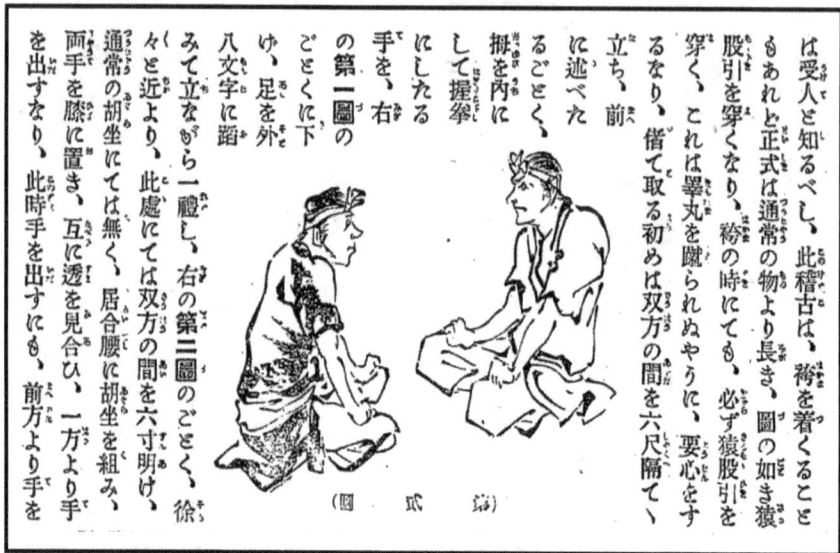

Second Illustration

Though seeing people train in Hakama skirts is common, the official way is to wear normal clothes that are just a bit longer. As can be seen in the illustration, the combatants are both wearing Saru-mata-biki 猿股引, or "monkey thigh" trousers. Even those that train in a Hakama always wear Saru-mata-biki underneath. This is to ensure that you are not kicked in 睪丸 Kogan (Kintama), or The Groin (The Testicles).

So then, at the beginning you stand about 6 Shaku, or 1.5 meters, apart. Your hands should be in fists with the thumb tucked in inside, as was described before. Your arms should hang at your sides as shown in the first illustration on the previous page. Plant your feet as if they were making the bottom of a Hachi-monji, or Kanji for eight 八. Then a Rei, or bow is done.

As can be seen here in the second illustration above, the two opponents gradually approach each other until they are roughly 6 Sun, or about 18 centimeters apart. They lower themselves down, but the legs do not go into a regular cross-legged Agura 胡坐 sitting position. Rather each person goes first into Iai-goshi 居合腰, or a squat, and then to a Agura sitting style, but with just the knees and toes on the ground.

廣げず、献の襟なり腕なりへ近づきて廣げ、神速に取り摑み、或は取り握るなり、蓋にあらはせば、第二圖第三圖第四圖と變形するの間、縱やかに見ゆれど、實際は伏せるまでの間、神速にて、見物人の眼も及ばぬくらゐなり、偖て此取はじめは、下の第三圖のごとく黒を右の手にて使人の眉間を打てか、るを、使人は左の手にて受け、同時に受人の右手の二の腕を右の手にて取る、此時使人の右の膝は、少し上る氣味あり、受人は變らず、夫より使人は、次の第四圖のごとく、神速に右の膝を立て、左膝を突き同時に受人の右の手を上げ、次に第五圖のごとく、使人は受人の受け止めたる手の手首を返し、受人

(第 三 圖)

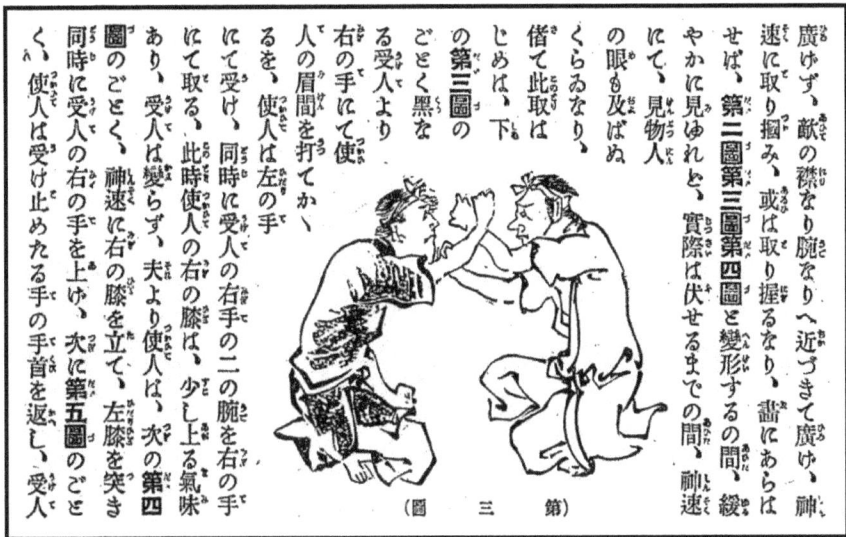

Third Illustration

The hands of both combatants are placed on the knees as they each look for a Suki 透, or opening, in the defenses of the other. If they see a chance, one of them will engage by reaching out with their hands. When engaging with the hands do not attempt to reach out for the opponent with only the hands. Whether you are going for the collar or the arms, first move your body towards the opponent *and then* grab or take hold of the spot.

If put into pictures and writing then the progression between the second illustration, the third illustration and the fourth illustration can be viewed leisurely. The reality is that the movement, up to the point at which the opponent has been thrown flat, has occurred with Shin-soku, or Divine Speed. This means it is so fast as to hardly register in the eye of any observer that happens to be there.

So then, this Tori, or match, begins as shown in the third illustration above. The Opponent, wearing black, strikes to Miken, or between your eyebrows. You respond with a Hidari Uke, or block with your left hand. At the same time, you take hold of his right Ni-no Ude, or the bicep, with your right hand. At this point your right knee of is beginning to rise slightly, while the Opponent's position remains unchanged. From there you do as shown in the following fourth illustration.

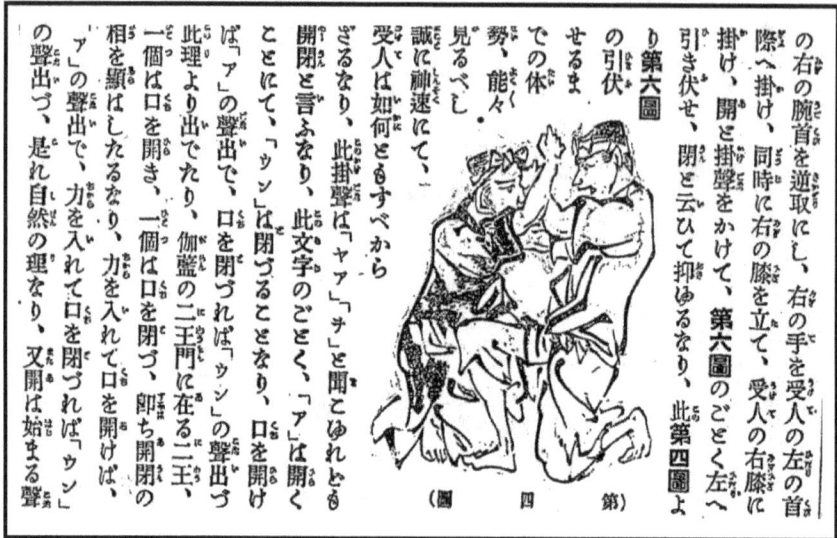

の右の腕首を逆取にし、右の手で受人の左の首
際へ掛け、同時に右の膝を立て、受人の右膝に
掛け、開と掛聲をかけて、第六圖のごとく左へ
引き伏せ、閉と云ひて抑ゆるなり、此第四圖よ
り
第六圖
の引伏
せるま
での体
勢、能々
見るべし
誠に神速にて、一
受人は如何とすべから
ざるなり、此掛聲は「ヤァ」「チ」と聞こゆれども
開閉と言ふなり、此文字のごとく、「ア」は開く
ことにて、「ウン」は閉づることとなり、口を開け
ば「ア」の聲出で、口を閉づれば「ウン」の聲出づ
此理より出でたり、伽藍の二王門に在る二王、
一個は口を開き、一個は口を閉づ、即ち開閉の
相を顕はしたるなり、力を入れて口を閉づれば、
「ア」の聲出で、力を入れて口を閉づれば、「ウン」
の聲出づ、是れ自然の理なり、又開は始まる聲

(第 四 圖)

Fourth Illustration

Bring your right knee is brought up with Shin-soku, Divine Swiftness, and press your left knee down. At the same time, you raise the Opponent's right arm up. As the following fifth illustration shows, after blocking the original strike, you rotate your left wrist around to grab the Opponent's wrist from the inside. With your right hand grab the left side of his neck where it meets the shoulder. At the same time, stand up and step forward with your right foot so it is beside the Opponent's right knee.

With a Kake-goe of "Ah!" you throw him down as shown in the sixth illustration. You should press the Opponent down firmly while shouting "Un!" You should carefully observe the body positioning shown in the illustrations 4 ~ 6. This technique should be executed with absolute Shin-soku, Divine Swiftness. The Opponent must be unable to counter in any way.

While you might hear Kake-goe that sound like "Yaa!" or "Chi!" the proper ones are, "Ah!" and "Un!" As the Kanji dictate, "Ah!" is Hiraku 開く, or to open, while "Un!" is Tojiru 閉じる, or to close. When your mouth opens your voice should come out as an "Ah!". When you close your mouth, you should emit a sound like "Un!" The origin of this can be found in the Ni-o 仁王, or guardian figures that protect the Ni-o Mon 仁王門, or the protective gate, at a Garan

伽藍, or large Buddhist temple. One of these figures has its mouth open, the other has it closed. This, in other words, represents the dual "Ah-Un," or open-closed, which is written as 開閉 in Kanji. Putting power in and opening the mouth results in an "Ah" being voiced, while putting power in while the mouth is closed results in an "Un" sound being emitted. This principal is quite natural. [57]

Translator's Note:
The Kongorikishi on display in front of Todai temple in Nara. Left is Misshaku Kongo 密迹金剛 on the right is Naraen Kongo 那羅延金剛. By Ogawa Kazuma 小川一真 from Photographs of Carvings 彫刻写真帖 1888.

---

[57] These two statues are referred to as the 金剛力士 Kongorikishi or "the Sumo wrestlers forged in steel." Misshaku Kongo has his mouth open uttering the first letter of the Sanskrit alphabet "Ah." The other is Naraen Kongo who has his mouth closed and is saying "Un." These two sounds represent the beginning and end of all things. The sounds themselves are known as the Ah!-gyo 阿形 and Un!-gyo 吽形. People are said to be born with their mouths open saying "Ah" and die with their mouths closed saying "Un."

にて、閉は終る聲なり、先づ閉と言ひて、閉と
は此らず、されば閉と言ひてよりは、閉と言ふ
まで、閉の餘聲は人には聞にねども、氣は續き
ありて、閉と言ひて其聲止むるものなり、都て伏
せる時と投げるときは、此掛聲を掛けることに
て、此他眉間を打つ時、肋を中てるときは、睾
丸
を蹴るとき、都て力を入
るときは、自然
り、然
る故
に此聲出づる
に、受け止む
るとき、拒ぐと
き、閉の聲出る
も當然の事なり、これ
も此柔術に限らず、押すときは開と言ひ、
すときは、閉と言ひ、剣術にても、押返
此掛聲は有る事なり、僖て、此第六圖のごとく
伏せたれば、使人は受人の襟を右の手にて取り

（第　六　圖）

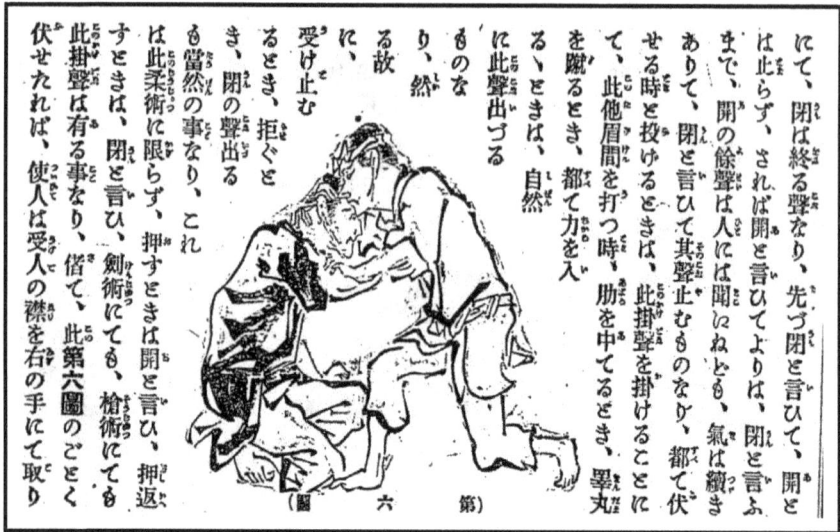

Fifth Illustration [58]

Further, "Ah!" is the vocalization of something beginning while "Un!" is the sound to signify the end. Neither begin with "Un!" nor end with "Ah!" In other words, one should not think of it solely as saying "Ah!" or saying "Un!" but rather it is a continuous sound.

To those observing, the entire duration of the "Ah!" cannot be heard, your Ki, or fighting spirit, continues to flow through to the end when the "Un!" sound ends. Throughout the time the opponent is falling onto his face, throughout the time you are throwing him, this Kake-goe should be continued.

In addition, you should use Kake-goe when punching to Mi-ken, between the eyes, when striking to the ribs or when kicking to 睾丸
Kintama   The Testicles
Kogan, or The Groin. Anytime you are putting power into an attack you should shout a Kake-goe.

Therefore, it follows quite naturally that when blocking an attack from the Uke or repelling the opponent, a "Un!" sound should be clearly emitted. This is not limited only to the Jujutsu of which we speak. When pressing the adversary, say "Ah!," when persisting in an attack an "Un!" is voiced. It doesn't matter if you training with the sword or with the spear, know that these Kake-goe are used.

---

[58] The illustration is labeled "sixth," but this is likely a misprint.

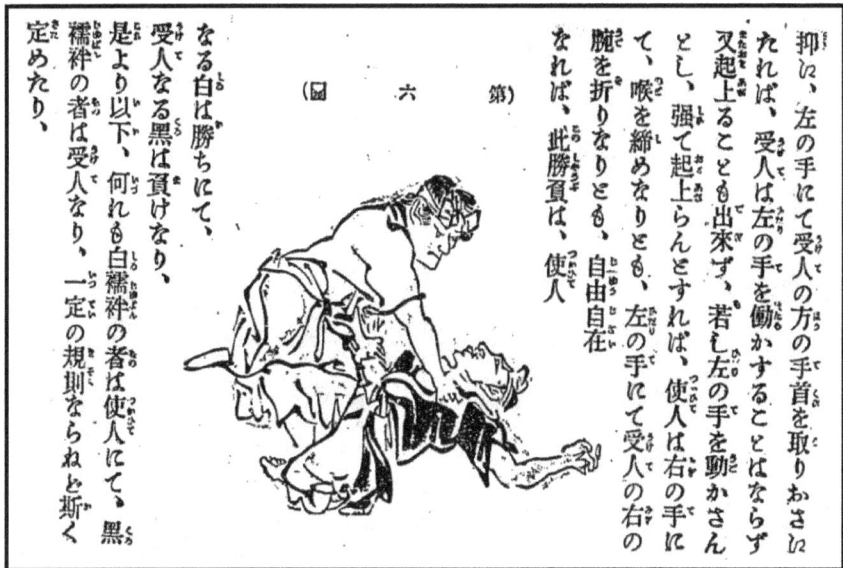

（第 六 図）

抑に、左の手にて受人の方の手首を取りおさゝれ
ば、受人は左の手を働かすることはならず
又起上ることも出來ず、若し左の手を働かさん
とし、強て起上らんとすれば、使人は右の手に
て、喉を締めなりとも、左の手にて受人の右の
腕を折りなりとも、自由自在
なれば、此勝負は、使人
定めたり、
糯袢の者は受人なり、一定の規則ならねと斯く
是より以下、何れも白糯袢の者は使人にて、黒
受人なる黒は貧けなり、
なる白は勝ちにて、

Sixth Illustration

So then, after throwing the Opponent down flat on his back as shown in the illustration above, you should be holding down his collar with your right hand. If you have a firm hold with your left hand on the opponent's right wrist, then he should be unable to move it. In addition, he would be unable to rise.

If the Opponent attempts to resist with his left hand, or tries to force his way up you can either do a Shime 締め, or Choke, to 喉 Nodo, the throat, with your right hand or break the Opponent's right arm with your left arm[59]. If all of this is done properly then one is in a situation of Jiyu-Jizai 自由自在, or in total control and possessing total freedom of action. Thus, it is you in white who is the winner and the Opponent in black is defeated.

From this point on, the person in the white Juban is you and the person in the black Juban is the Opponent. This is not a rule per se, but it will remain constant throughout.

---

[59] I presume this means by using your left hand to bend your Opponent's right arm with your left knee.

Overview of the First Idori Kata

1	2

3	4

5	6

◉居取

第二形

これは前の第一形の反にて、右と左の異ひある
のみなり、第一の立ちて禮すると、第二の胡坐
を組みて身搆へするとは、同じ事ゆゑ記さず、
左のごとく、第三圖より掲ぐべし、其取はじめ

（第　三　圖）

は第三圖のごと
く受人が左の手
にて使人の眉間を打ちか
へるを、使人は右の手にて之を受け止め、同時
に左の手にて受人の左の二の腕を取り、次には
神速に次の第四圖のごとく、左の膝を立て、右
の膝を突き、同時に受人の左の手を上げ、夫よ
り又神速に、第五圖のごとく使人は受け止めた

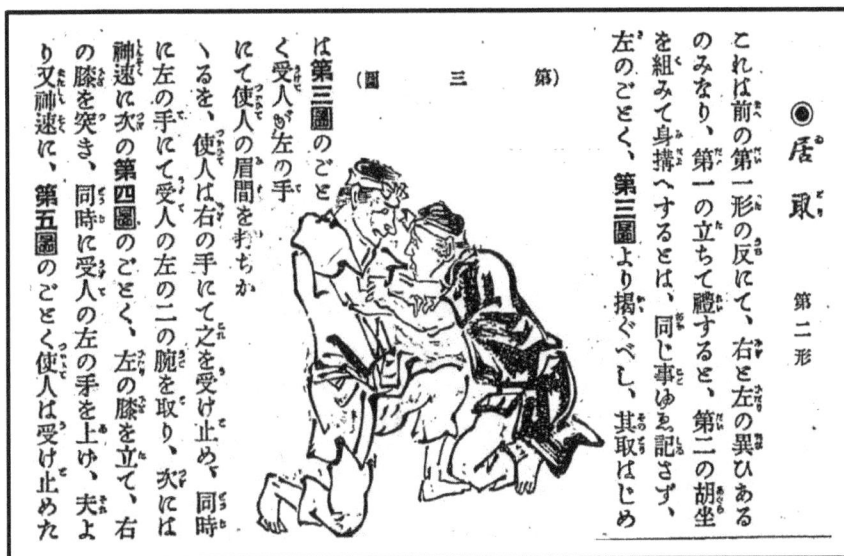

Iidori   Seated Technique
Second Kata[60]
Third Illustration

In contrast to the previous first Kata, this one uses the left instead of the right. Otherwise the first and second illustrations are the same. For that reason, the illustrations showing the initial standing Rei and one showing both combatants seated in Agura style Kamae will not be reproduced. We will begin with the movement as shown in the third illustration, above.

The beginning of this Tori, or match, begins as can be seen in the third illustration. The Opponent punches with the left hand to Miken, or the area between your eyebrows. In response to this, you block with your right hand. At the same time, you grab his Ni-no Ude or, or bicep, with your left hand. Next, move as depicted in the fourth illustration. With Shin-soku swiftness you raise left knee up while you plant your right knee on the ground. At the same time, lift the Opponent's left arm.

---

[60] In an error that tormented me for no small amount of time, all the pictures for this Kata were printed backwards. They are properly displayed now. Seriously, I thought I was gonna lose my mind.

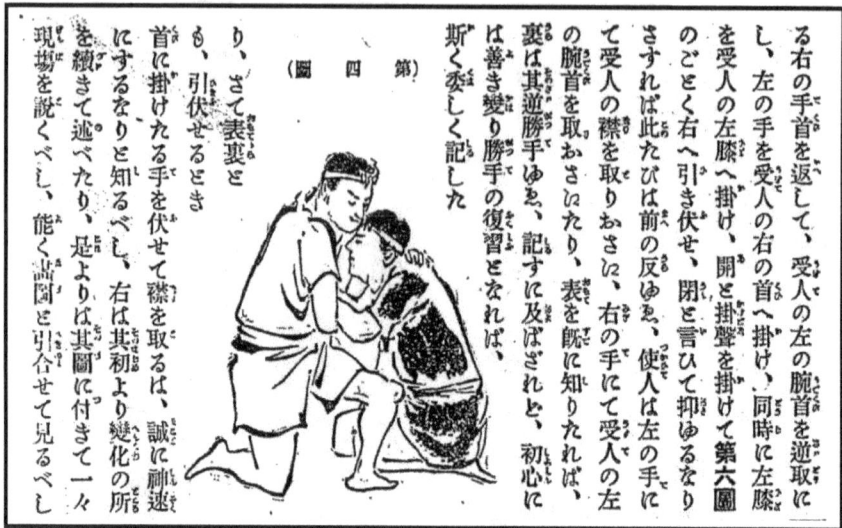

（第 四 圖）

る右の手首を返して、受人の左の腕首を逆取に
し、左の手を受人の右の首へ掛け、同時に左膝
を受人の左膝へ掛け、開と掛聲を掛けて第六圖
のごとく右へ引き伏せ、閉と言ひて抑ゆるなり
さすれば此たびは前の反ゆえ、使人は左の手に
て受人の襟を取りあさに、右の手にて受人の左
の腕首を取りあさいたり、表を既に知りたれば、
裏は其逆勝手ゆえ、記すに及ばざれど、初心に
は善き變り勝手の復習となれば、
斯く委しく記した

り、さて表裏と
も、引伏せるとき
首に掛けたる手を伏せて襟を取るは、誠に神速
にするなりと知るべし、右は其初より變化の所
を續きて逑べたり、是よりは其圖に付きて一々
現場を説くべし、能く高圖と引合せて見るべし

Fourth Illustration

Following this you do what is shown in the illustration above with Shin-soku, Divine Swiftness. You have blocked the Opponent's left punch with your right hand. Twist that wrist around and grab the inside of the Opponent's wrist in a Gyaku-tori 逆捕 movement. Your left hand grabs the right side of the Opponent's neck, while simultaneously your left foot is planted in front of your Opponent's the left knee.

With a Kake-goe of "Ah!" throw the Opponent flat on his back to the right. This is shown in the sixth illustration. An "Un!" is voiced you 抑え Osae, or force the Opponent down. If you execute this technique as described, then, in contrast to the previous Kata, your left hand is holding his collar and your right hand is suppressing the left wrist of the Opponent.

When it is all said and done, if one understands the Omote 表, or Outer version of a technique, then the Ura 裏, or Inner version of the technique, is r simply the same technique on the other side.[61] For this reason, while it is not essential to reproduce the remainder of this Kata, it would no doubt serve to re-enforce how the Kata

---

61 Omote and Ura can also be the "obverse and reverse."

progresses. Therefore for the benefit of Shoshin Sha 初心者, or beginners, it shall thus be described in detail.

So then, be aware with both the Omote and the Ura that when throwing the Opponent down on his back with a Hikifuse 引伏せ, or yank down flat on the ground, the hand gripping at the neck should move with absolute Shin-soku, Divine Swiftness, to his collar.

In the above passage the progression of the technique has been explained. I recommend that you talk with someone at a training facility in and then compare that with what you learned from just looking at the drawings.

転ばぬやうに、重心を取らずばあらず
るも肝要なれど、自分の体に透のなきやう、又
因に云ふ利處を摑み、利處を打ち、利處を中て
など、総て體勢を能く見るべし、
後とへ敷されたるところ、手の掛り矩合、腰つき
の膝を突きて脚を

（第　五　圖）

てたるところ、右
へ引伏せんとするところなり、圖の左の膝を立
今や開と掛聲をかけて、次の第六圖のごとく右
時に神速に密と左の膝を受人の左の膝へ掛け、
同時に左の手を受人の右の首ぎはへ掛け、又同
首を密と返して、受人の左の腕首を逆取にし、
を打ちかゝりたるを、使人は受け止めたる右の手
左の第五圖は、受人が最初に左の手にて、眉間

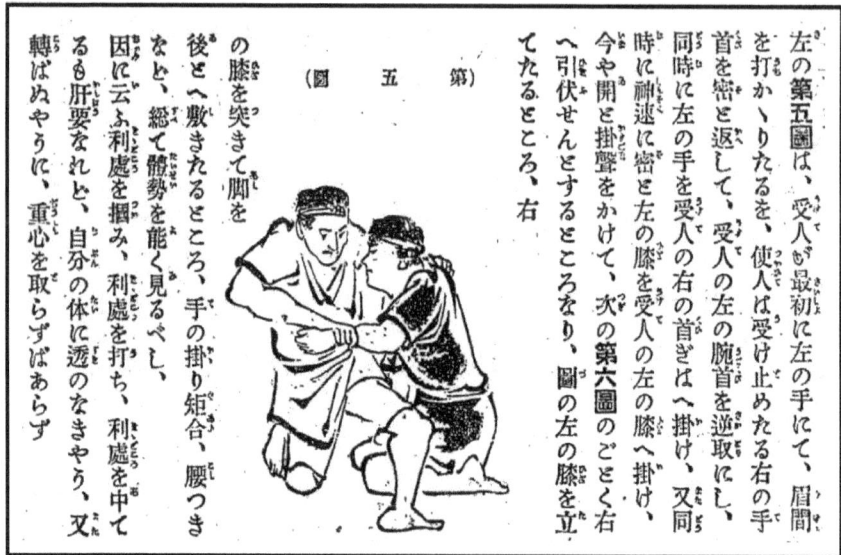

Fifth Illustration

The fifth illustration above shows how the Opponent beginning the technique with a strike with his left fist to Miken, the spot between your eyebrows. You respond to this with an Uke-tome, or a Block and Stop, with your right hand. You then deftly twist your wrist around and grab the inside of the Opponent's left wrist in an Gyaku-tori. At the same time your left hand grabs the right side of his neck, where it joins the shoulder. In the same moment you are also bringing your left knee up and plant your left foot in front of the Opponent's left knee with Shin-soku, Divine Swiftness. At this point, shout a Kake-goe of "Ah!" Next pull the Opponent down to the right and onto his back.

All the points shown in this illustration, including the positioning of your left knee and leg, your knee planted on the ground with the other leg along the ground behind, the way the hands are positioned, the way the hips are positioned and the overall posture, should be observed carefully. To put things another way, it is essential that you use Kiki-dokoro 利處, or pressure points. Endeavor to grab, strike and otherwise make use of these vital points. Finally, eliminate all openings in your own defenses and keep your Jushin 重心, or center of gravity, from being taken.

左の第六圖は、前の使人より受人の左の腕首を
逆取にし、左の手を受人の右の首際へ掛け、又
左の膝を受人の左の膝へ掛けて、掛譬かけて右
へ引伏せ、閉と言ひて抑へ、是れは
左の手にて、受人の襟を取抑に、右の手にて受
人の左の腕首を取抑にたり、是れ亦た受人が、
強て右の手を動かさん

（第 六 圖）

とし、体を起上ら
んとせば、使人は左
の手にて、受人の喉を締め
なりとも、右の手にて受人の左の腕を折りなり
とも自在に爲し侍べし、依して使人は、勝負勝ち
にして、受人は負けなり、

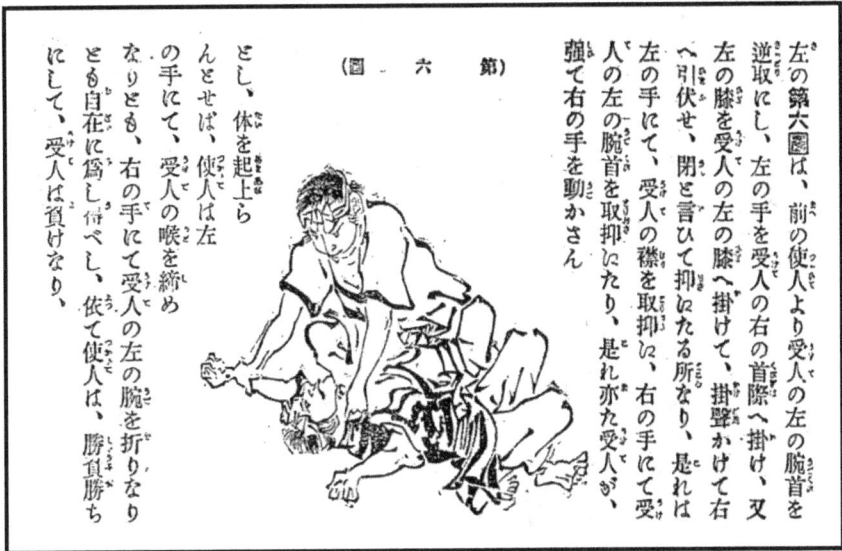

Sixth Illustration

The sixth illustration above depicts what occurred after you have taken hold of the Opponent's left wrist from the inside, in a Gyaku-tori move. You have also grabbed where the right side of his neck meets his shoulder with your left hand.

From there your left knee comes up and you plant your left foot in front of the left knee of your Opponent. Shouting a Kake-goe you pull the Opponent down to the right and onto his back with a Hiki-fuse. As you force the Opponent down shout an "Un!" Be sure your left hand is pushing down while holding his Eri, or collar. Your right hand is holding down his left wrist.

If at this point the Opponent were to try and resist with his right hand or rise up, you can twist off his windpipe with your left hand. Another response is to use your right arm to break his left arm. You should have complete control in this situation.

Thus it is you who wins this bout and the Opponent that loses.

Translator's Note:
Here is the entire sequence as originally presented in the book, clockwise from the top left:

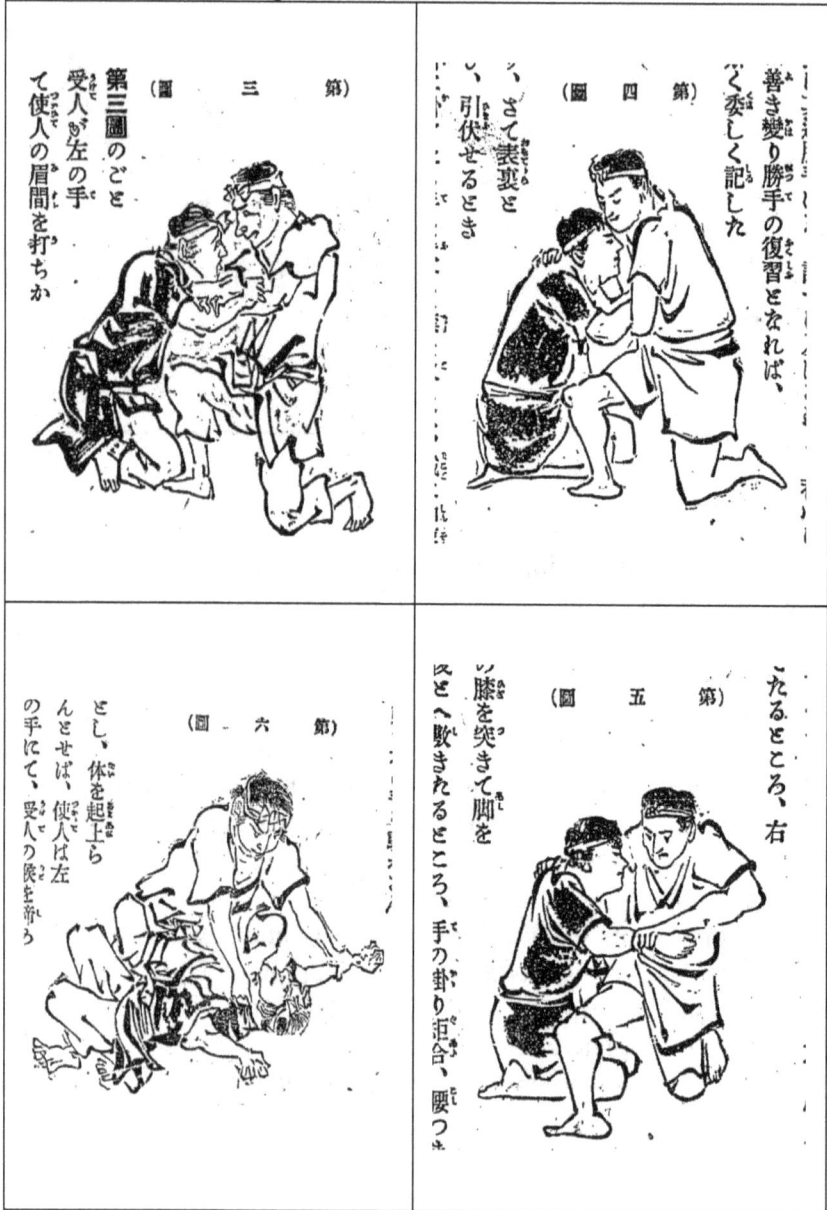

（第　三　圖）

第三圖のごと
受人を左の手
て使人の眉間を打ちか

（第　四　圖）

善き變り勝手の復習とをれば、
く委しく記した
さて表裏と、
引伏せるとき、

（第　六　圖）

とし、体を起上ら
んとせば、使人は左
の手にて、受人の後を祈う

（第　五　圖）

たるところ、右
膝を突きて脚を
とへ敷きれるところ、手の掛り迫合、腰つき

Overview of the Second Idori Kata

1	2
3	4
5	6

◎居取　第三形

これも第一の立體、第二の近寄りたる身搆への圖は略す、依て第三圖より掲ぐべし、此取はじめは、眉間を打たず、左の第三圖のごとく、つ受人より両手にて使人の襟を取るなり、此受人の取りたる

手つきを能く見るべし、巻首にも記せしごとく、右の手を上にし、左の手を下にしたるを、此時使人は神速に左の手にて受人の襟を逆取に取るなれど、手の込みたるところを一圖に書きては解り兼ぬるゆゑ、开は次の第四圖に示すべし、又心を込めて両手の取り方を示し

(第　三　圖)

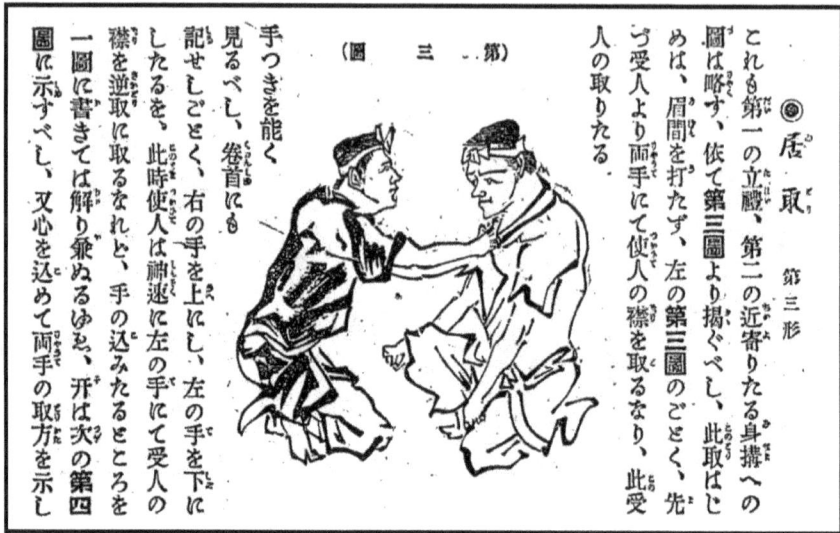

Iidori Seated Technique
Third Kata
<u>Third Illustration</u>

The illustrations that proceed this one, showing the initial standing Rei and the following approach and entering of Kamae, will be abbreviated. We will begin by looking at the third illustration. This Tori 取, or match, does not begin with a strike to Miken, but rather starts as shown in the third illustration shown above.

The Opponent reaches out with both hands to grip your Eri, or collar, on the left and right. The way the hands of the Opponent are positioned should be observed carefully. His right hand should be higher and the left hand should be lower, as was discussed in the beginning of this volume.

In response to being grabbed, you react with Shin-soku 神速, Divine Swiftness, to grasp your Opponent's collar with your left hand. As showing all of this in a single illustration would prove difficult, your reaction to being attacked will be shown in the following fourth illustration.

Take care to note that this is demonstrating a committed attack.

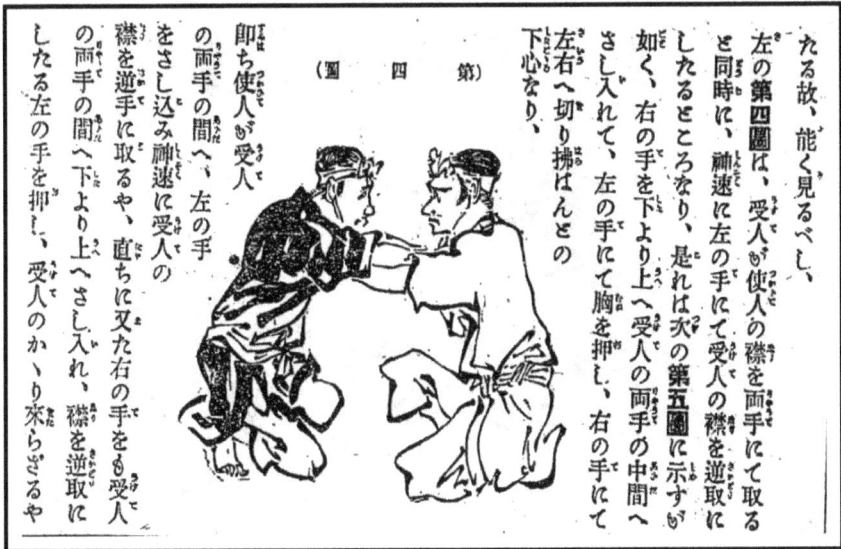

（第 四 圖）

Fourth Illustration

The fourth illustration above shows the Opponent grabbing both sides of the Eri, or collar, in a two-handed grip. At the same time you, with Shin-soku, Divine Swiftness, grab the Opponent's collar with your left hand.

The movement following this is shown in the fifth illustration. Raise your right arm up from below into the space between his arms. You then push on his Mune 胸, or chest, with your left hand. Understand that the Shita-gokoro 下心, or underlying plan, is to set up for a sharp left and right sweeping motion with your right hand.

In other words, you have slipped your left hand between the opponent's arms with Shin-soku swiftness and grabbed hold of his collar. In the next moment, your right hand moves up from below into the space between the two hands gripping your collar. Your left gripping his collar pushes in order to defend against the pressure of the Opponent's attack. This serves to prevent the Opponent from entering in.

157

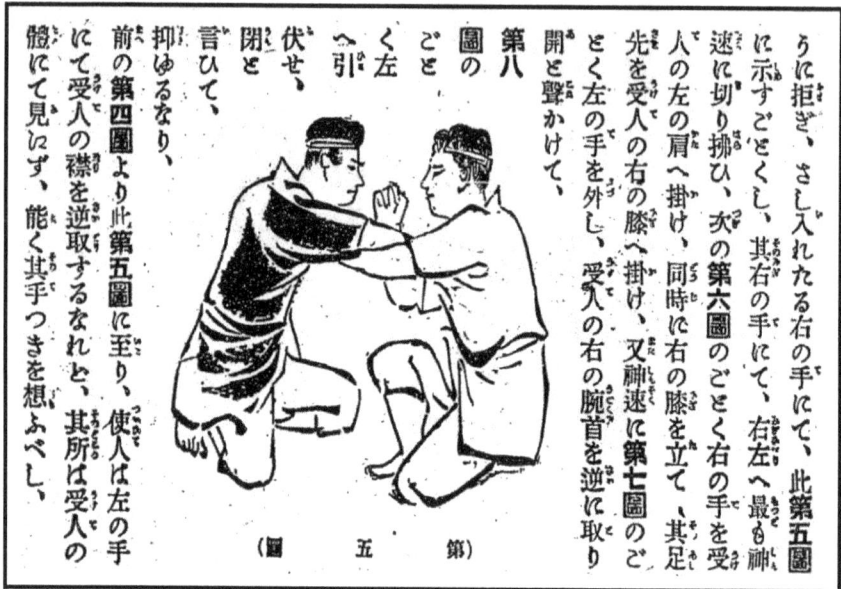

うに拒ぎ、さし入れたる右の手にて、此第五圏
に示すごとくし、其右の手にて、右左へ最も神
速に切り抛ひ、次の第六圏のごとく右の手を受
人の左の肩へ掛け、同時に右の膝を立て、其足
先を受人の右の膝へ掛け、又神速に第七圏のご
とく左の手を外し、受人の右の腕首を逆に取り
開と聲かけて、

第八
圏の
ごと
く左
へ引
伏せ、
閉と
言ひて、
抑ゆるなり、
前の第四圏より此第五圏に至り、使人は左の手
にて受人の襟を逆取するなれど、其所は受人の
體にて見ねず、能く其手つきを想ふべし、

(第 五 圖)

Fifth Illustration

Your right hand, which has slipped in between the opponent's arms, next does as shown in the illustration above. You do a left-right Kiri-hari 切り払い, or a sharp sweeping motion to either side, with your right arm using as much Shin-soku, Divine Swiftness, as can be mustered.

As shown in the following sixth illustration, your right hand next grabs the Opponent's left shoulder while you simultaneously step forward with your right foot. Plant your right foot in front of the Opponent's right knee. Further, with Shin-soku, Divine Swiftness, release with your left hand and take hold of the Opponent's right wrist. This is shown in the seventh illustration.

Pull the Opponent down with a Kake-goe of "Ah!" This is shown in the eighth illustration. Push him firmly onto the ground with an "Un!"

Beginning from the previous fourth illustration up through this fifth illustration, your left hand of has continued to grip the Eri of the Opponent in a Gyaku-tori. This is not easy to see as the Opponent's body is in the way. You should clearly envision how this hand is positioned.

此第六圖は、前の圖に示すがごとく、右の手を
受人の兩手の間へ下よりさし入れ、左の手にて
受人の胸を押しつゝ、受人の兩手を右と左へ切
り挬ふや否や、直ちに其手を受人の左の肩へ掛
け、同時に右の膝を立て、
其足先を受人の右の
膝へ掛けたるところなり。

(第　六　圖)

これは次の第七
圖に示す所の働きを爲
し、引伏せんとする下心なり、是等は碁を打つ
とき、二目も三目も先の手を知りて、此次は何
うする、其次は何うすると、目算するなり、此
目算は、誠に肝要なり、將棊には利處へ打つ駒
あり、碁にも亦此心得あり、其のごとく心得あ
るべきことなり。

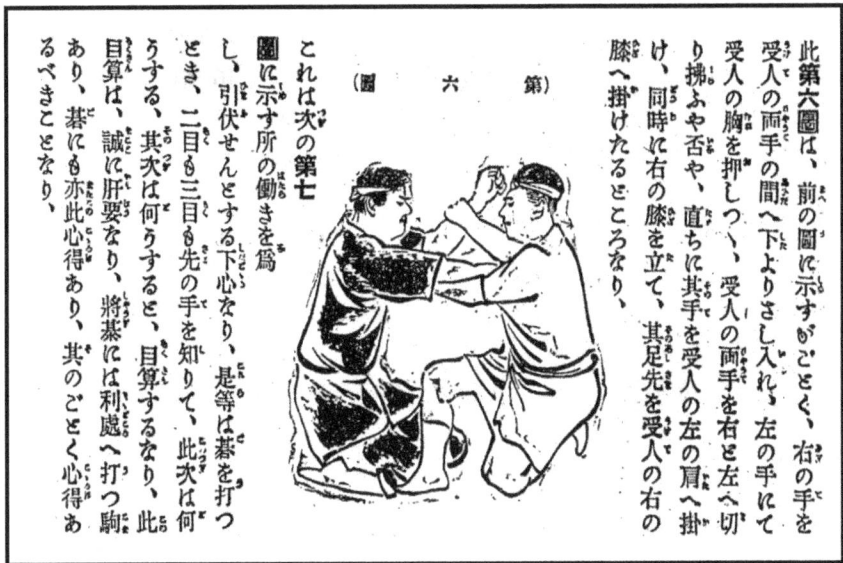

Sixth Illustration

This sixth illustration follows the movement begun in the previous illustration. You move your right hand up and slip it between the space of the Opponent's arms. Meanwhile, your left hand continues to push on the Mune, or chest. As soon as your right hand has done a sharp sweeping cut to the left and right arms of the Opponent, that hand then immediately goes to his left shoulder. At the same time bring your right knee up and plant your right foot in front of his right knee.

All of this is the Shita-gokoro 下心, or set up, for the movement that begins in the seventh illustration. You are setting up to do a 引伏せ Hiki-fuse, or an action to pull the opponent down flat on his back.

This set up is very similar to when one is playing the game of 碁 Go[62]. When a player is placing pieces, or "striking the board" as

---

[62] Go, or Igo as it is sometimes called, originated 2500 years ago in China. With regards to placing stones:
Clacking a stone against another stone, the board, or the table or floor is also discouraged. However, it is permissible to emphasize

it is known, that person is already conscious of where the 二目 Futa-moku, or the second stone, and the 三目 Mitsu-moku, or the third stone will be placed. This is known as the Saki-no-te wo Shiru 先の手を知る, when one has already calculated what to do next and what will occur after that.

This kind of calculating is absolutely essential to Jujutsu. In 将棋 Shogi[63], or Japanese Chess, one places the 駒 Koma, or pieces, in a manner which will reap the greatest benefit, in a Kiki-dokoro[64]. This logic applies to Go as well.

You should endeavor to keep this aspect in mind.

---

dramatic moves by striking the board more firmly than normal, thus producing a sharp clack. Wikipedia.

[63] Originating in India in the 6th century, was brought first to China and then Japan sometime in the 10th to 12th centuries. Shogi in its present form was played as early as the 16th century.

According to *The Chess Variant Pages*:

Perhaps the enduring popularity of Shogi can be attributed to its "drop rule." It was the first chess variant wherein captured pieces could be returned to the board to be used as one's own. David Pritchard credits the drop rule to the practice of 16th century mercenaries who switched loyalties when captured—no doubt as an alternative to execution.

[64] A Kiki-dokoro is a spot likely to cause the most damage, in both a game and when striking an opponent.

此の第七圖は、使人が受人の襟を取りたる左の手
を外し、外すや否や直ちに受人の右の腕首を逆
に取り、開と掛聲を掛けて、左へ引伏せんとす
るところなり、此外すや否や、神速に受人の右
の腕首を逆に取るなどは、全く手練にあること
なれば、平素能くこれに慣れ置かず
ばあらず、柔術の

（第　七　圖）

舉手は、離れさう
でも離れず、恰もトリモ
チの着たる如く、付まはりて離れぬやうにす
誠に不思議に思はる程なり、能く注意の行届
きたるものと謂ふべし、これも斯く來れば
くすると前以て一手も二手も先に用意すること
にて、敵手を求めて手の握り矩合の一部分をも
取り習ふべし、

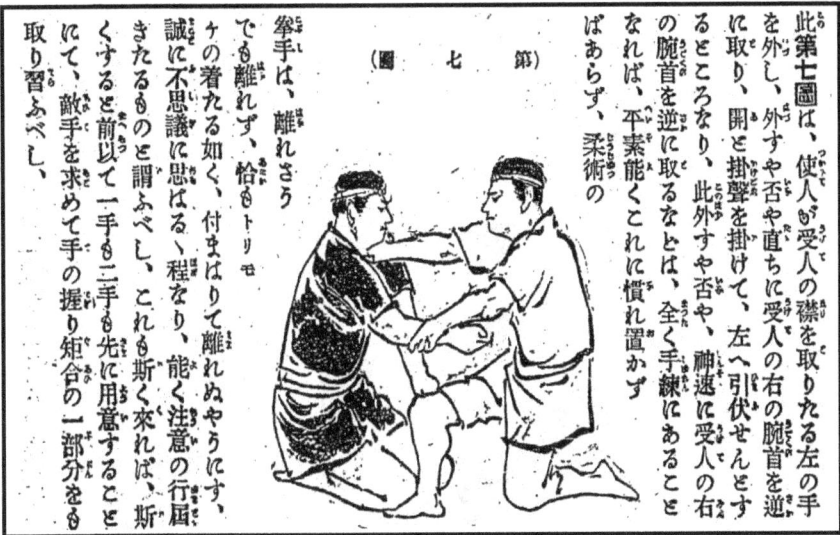

Seventh Illustration

This seventh illustration shows your positioning after you have knocked the Opponent's left hand off your collar. You then immediately seize his right wrist with your left hand from the outside. With a Kake-goe, or shout, of "Ah!" you do a left Hiki-fuse, meaning the Opponent is pulled down to the left, flat on his back.

Knocking his hand away and then immediately grabbing the right wrist with Shin-soku, Divine Swiftness is something that requires a great deal of dexterity. You cannot hope to become proficient in this Jujutsu technique without drilling it repeatedly over a long period of time.

The way Jujutsu is employed here interesting. At first, it seems to be in order to gain distance from the opponent, yet this is not the case. This action is only serving to facilitate *the appearance of trying to gain distance*. Speaking in this manner is bound to make one think Jujutsu is all very mysterious. However, this concept should be thought of as describing a person who is very thorough in their preparedness. If the opponent decides to launch an attack, then a prepared set of movements, first *this* then *that*, has already been readied. The attacker should also train thoroughly in his role. Specifically, the way he seeks to grab the lapels should also be trained.

此第八圖は、前の第七圖の体勢より開と言ひて
左へ引き伏せ、閉と言ひて抑ねたるところなり
是れも右の手にて受人の襟を取り、左の手にて
受人の右腕首を取りたれば、其腕を折りなりと
も、喉を締めぬなりとも自由なれば、受人は起上
ること能はず、使人は勝ちにて、受人は負けな
り、此圖を見るべし、
使人はいつにても相
手を伏せたるときは、
片膝を突き、片足を投
出し蹈張る、諸形いづれも同じこ
となり、これは閉と言ひたるとき、投出したる
足先に力入り、蹈ばることとなり、

（第 八 圖）

Eighth Illustration

The body positioning in this eighth illustration continues from where the seventh illustration ended. With a Kake-goe of "Ah!" you pull him down flat on his back in a Hiki-fuse. Here you can see where the Osae, or suppression, with an "Un!" sound is done.

This illustration shows how your right hand grips the Opponent's Eri, while your left hand has seized the Opponent's right wrist. You are in complete control in this final position. Should the Opponent resist, you can break the right arm or do a Shime, or strangle, to the throat. The Opponent is unable to rise, thus you are the winner and the Opponent is the loser.

You should note in this illustration that whenever you have toppled the Opponent one knee is planted on the ground, while the foot of the other leg is thrown out and planted firmly. All of the Kata are the same in this regard. You should put power into that foot as it goes out and is planted firmly with a "Un!"

Translator's Note: The illustration as it was printed:

Overview of the Third Idori Kata

1	2
3	**4**
5	**6**
7	**8**

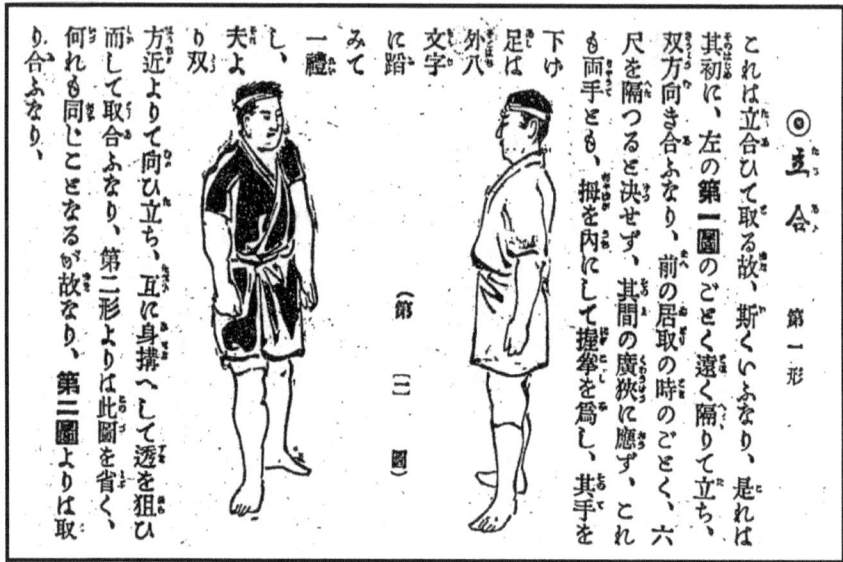

◎立合
第一形

これは立合ひて取る故、斯くいふなり、其初に、左の第一圖のごとく遠く隔りて立ち、是れは雙方向き合ふなり、前の居取の時のごとく、六尺を隔つると決せず、其間の廣狹に應ず、これも兩手とも、拇を內にして握拳を爲し、其手を下げ、足は外八文字に蹈て一體みてによ、夫れ雙方近よりて向ひ立ち、互に身搆へして透を狙ひ而して取合ふなり、第二形よりは此圖を省く、何れも同じことなる故なり、第二圖よりは取り合ふなり。

◎ Tachi-ai Standing Bout
First Kata
First Illustration

The reason this is called Tachi-ai 立合, or Standing-bout, is because you engage your opponent from a standing position. This Kata begins as is shown in the first illustration above. You and your Opponent stand some distance apart and both turn to face each other. Unlike in the previous Iidori techniques standing 6 Shaku, or180 centimeters apart, is not necessary. The distance separating you and your Opponent should reflect the room's relative spaciousness or lack thereof.

The hands should be held in fists with the thumbs tucked inside. The arms hang at the sides of the body. The feet are placed like the bottom of a Hachimonji, or the Kanji for eight 八.

After first doing a Rei, or bow, you begin to approach one another maintaining this Kamae as you look for a Suki 透き, or opening, in the other's defenses.

Starting from the second Kata, this illustration will be abbreviated. The reason for this is that it is identical in every case, therefore each Tori-ai, or start of combat, will begin from the second illustration.

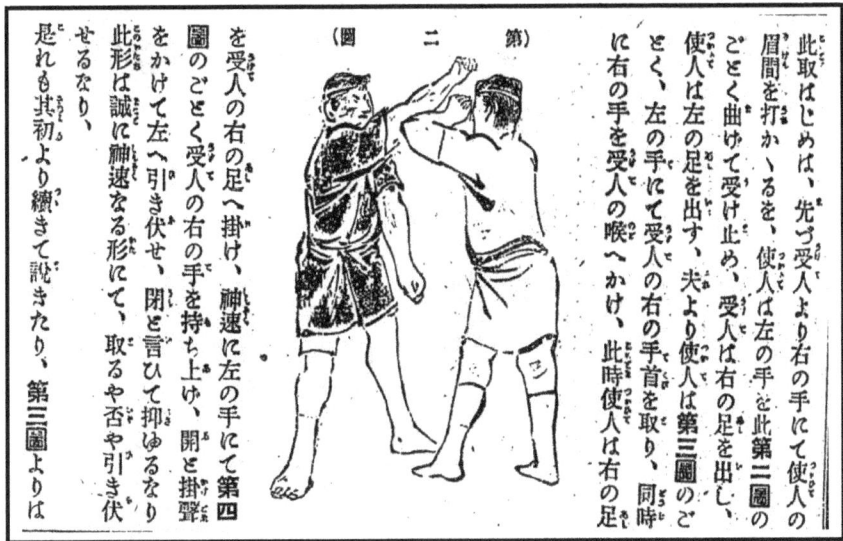

此取はじめは、先づ受人より右の手にて使人の
眉間を打かゝるを、使人は左の手を此第二圖の
ごとく曲げて受け止め、受人は右の足を出し、
使人は左の足を出す、夫より使人は第三圖のご
とく、左の手にて受人の右の手首を取り、同時
に右の手を受人の喉へかけ、此時使人は右の足

を受人の右の足へ掛け、神速に左の手にて第四
圖のごとく受人の右の手を持ち上げ、閉と掛聲
をかけて左へ引き伏せ、閉と言ひて抑ゆるなり
此形は誠に神速なる形にて、取るや否や引き伏
せるなり、
是れも其初より續きて説きたり、第三圖よりは

Second Illustration

This bout begins with your Opponent punching with his right fist to Miken 眉間, or between the eyebrows. In response you an Uke-tome 受け止め, or Block and Stop, with your left arm bent. This is shown in the second illustration. Your Opponent steps forward with his right foot out while you step forward with your left foot.

Next, you do as shown in the third illustration, namely sieze the Opponent's right wrist with your left hand and simultaniously grab Nodo 喉, or his throat, with your right hand. Then place your right foot beside the Opponent's right foot and, with Shin-soku, Divine Swiftness, do as demonstrated in the fourth illustration.

As you raise the Opponent's right hand, shout a Kake-goe of "Ah!" You then pull him down flat on his back in a Hiki-fuse, Pull and Flatten. Push down on the Opponent with an "Un!"

This Kata is one that must be done as fast as possible. Within a moment of beginning this Tori, or bout, the Hiki-fuse should hae been completed.

Starting on the following page the technique will be explained from the beginning and the essential points of each illustration will be discussed.

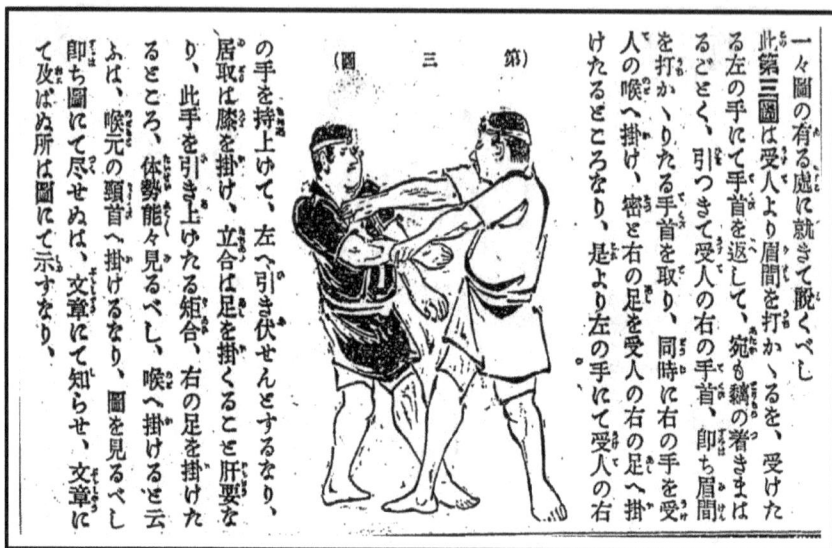

の手を持上げて、左へ引き伏せんとするなり、居取は膝を掛け、立合は足を掛くること肝要なり、此手を引き上げたる矩合、右の足を掛けたるところ、体勢能々見るべし、喉へ掛けたるふは、喉元の頸首へ掛けるなり、圖を見るべし即ち圖にて尽せねば、文章にて知らせ、文章にて及ばぬ所は圖にて示すなり、

一々圖の有る處に就さて脱くべし此第三圖は受人より眉間を打かゝるを、受けた左の手にて手首を返して、宛も鵜の着きまはるごとく、引つきて受人の右の手首、即ち眉間を打かゝりたる手首を取り、同時に右の手を受人の喉へ掛け、密と右の足を受人の右の足へ掛けたるところなり、是より左の手にて受人の右

Third Illustration

The illustration above shows what happens after you block the Opponent's punch to Miken, the Spot Between Your Eyebrows. Your left wrist rotates around to grasp the right wrist firmly as if it has been coated with Tori-mochi 鳥黐.[65] In other words, you grabbed the wrist of the hand that just punched to your eyebrows. At the same time, grab the Opponent's throat with your right hand and place your right foot deftly by his right foot.

Next, use your left hand to raise his right hand and then pull him down flat on his back in a Hiki-fuse. In Iidori, Seated Techniques, the knees that are the Kanyo 肝要, or essential point. In Tachi-ai, however, the Kanyo is the placement of the feet.

You should carefully study how your hand is brought up, the placement your right foot, as well as the overall body positioning. When I say "grabbing the throat" this indicates you should seize the windpipe at the base of the throat. Refer to the illustration. Things that the illustration cannot capture are relayed in the text. Similarly, things that the text does not adequately describe are contained in the illustrations.

---

[65] Tori-mochi, or Birdlime, is a natural adhesive that when spread on branches can trap birds.

此第四圖は左へ引き伏せたるところなり、斯く
使人が左の手にて受人の右の手首を取り、右の
手を喉くびへ掛け、右の足を掛けたれば、引き
伏すべき準備は整ひたり、其上に左の手にて其
右の手を引き上げたれば、伏せらるゝ筈なり、
術といふものは、
實に妙なるものなり、

（第 四 圖）

偖て斯く伏せたれば、
使人は右の手にて喉を
締めなりとも左の手に
て受人の右の腕を折りなりとも自由自在なり、
依て使人は勝ち、受人は負なり、卷首にも逃べ
たるごとく、使人は勝りたる者、受人は劣りた
る者と知るべし、

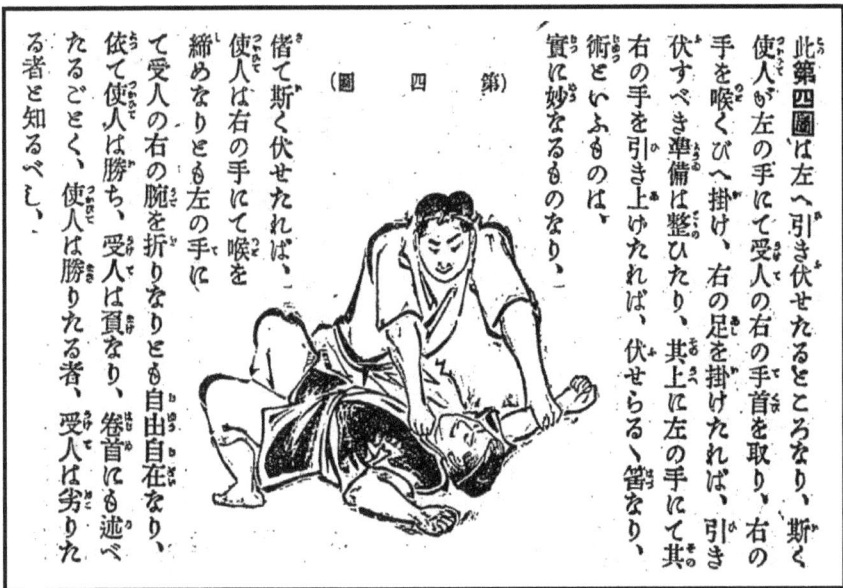

Fourth Illustration

The fourth illustration, above, shows how the Hiki-fuse, Pull and Flatten, to the left is done in this technique. As can be clearly seen, your left hand grips the right wrist of the Opponent, while your right hand is gripping where the throat meets the base of the neck. If you place your right foot has been placed properly then the preparation for the Hiki-fuse are ready. At this point all that is required is to lift his right hand up with your left, which will cause him to topple. As the saying goes,

Jutsu to iu mono wa, Jutsu ni Myo naru mono nari.
"These things called techniques can, in reality,
be quite curious things indeed."

So then, having brought the opponent down on his back, you have achieved a state of Ji-yu Ji-zai 自由自在, or having both total control and freedom of movement, as your right hand on his windpipe can do a Shime, or choke, and your left hand can break the right arm of the Opponent.

Thus it is you who wins and the Opponent who is defeated. As was mentioned at the beginning of this volume you are the one skilled and the Opponent is the one lacking. You should keep this distinction in mind.

Overview of the First Tachi-ai Kata

1	2
3	4

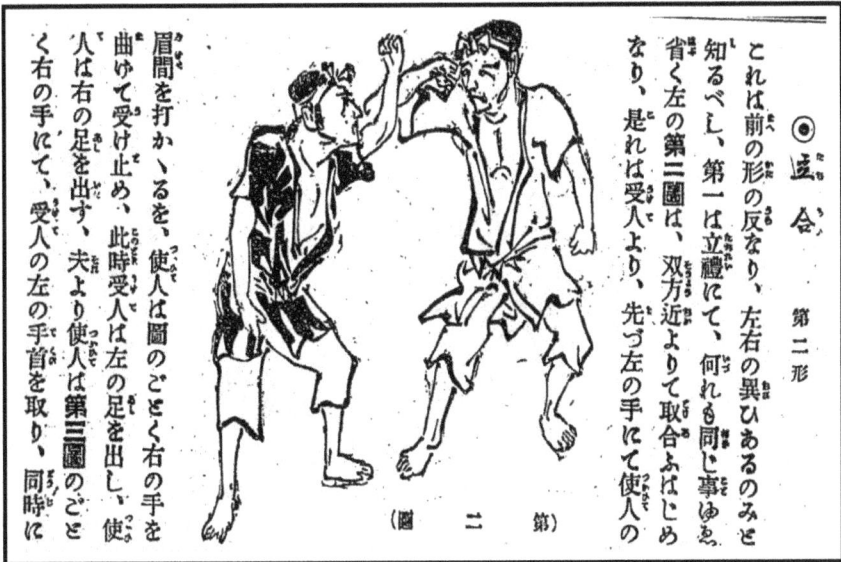

眉間を打かゝるを、使人は圖のごとく右の手を曲げて受け止め、此時受人は左の足を出し、使人は右の足を出す、夫より使人は第三圖のごとく右の手にて、受人の左の手首を取り、同時に

これは前の形の反なり、左右の異ひあるのみと知るべし、第一は立礼にて、何れも同じ事ゆえ、省く左の第二圖は、双方近よりて取合よはじめなり、是れは受人より、先づ左の手にて使人の

◎ 匠合　第二形

(第 二 圖)

◎ Tachi-ai   Standing Bout
Second Kata
<u>Second Illustration</u>

This Kata is the Ura, or the same technique but starting with a strike from the opposite hand. However, understand the only difference is the switch from the right side to the left. As the first illustration with the initial standing Rei, or bow honoring your opponent, is the same for all of the Kata it will be abbreviated.

The second illustration, above, shows the two combatants approaching and beginning the Tori-ai, or bout. It starts with the Opponent striking to Miken, or between your eyebrows, with his left fist. You respond as shown in the illustration. You do an Uke-tome, or Block and Stop, by raising your right arm and bending it as shown. At this point the Opponent has stepped forward with his left foot while you have stepped forward with your right foot.

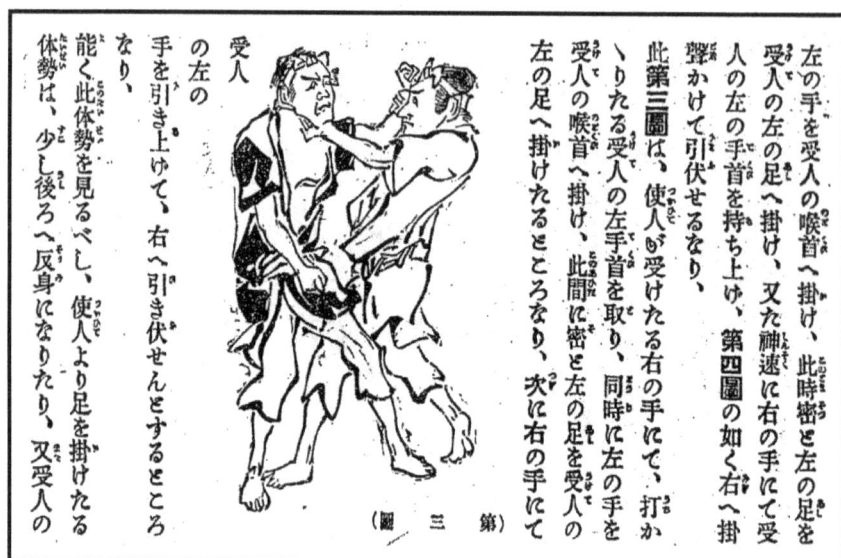

左の手を受人の喉首へ掛け、此時密と左の足を
受人の左の足へ掛け、又た神速に右の手にて受
人の左の手首を持ち上げ、第四圖の如く右へ掛
聲かけて引伏せるなり、

此第三圖は、使人が受けたる右の手にて、打か
ゝりたる受人の左手首を取り、同時に左の手を
受人の喉首へ掛け、此間に密と左の足を受人の
左の足へ掛けたるところなり、次に右の手にて

受人
の左の
手を引き上げて、右へ引き伏せんとするところ
なり、
能く此体勢を見るべし、使人より足を掛けたる
体勢は、少し後ろへ反身になりたり、又受人の

(第 三 圖)

Third Illustration

From there you move as shown in the third illustration, with your right hand seizing the Opponent's left wrist, while at the same time your left hand goes to the Opponent's Nodo, or Throat.

Step deftly with your left foot and plant it snugly against the Opponent's left foot. At the same time, raise his right hand up with your left using Shin-soku, or Divine Swiftness. As shown in the fourth illustration, with a Kake-goe, or Shout, the Opponent is pulled down flat on his back in a Hiki-fuse.

The Taisei 体勢, or Body Positioning, shown in the third illustration should be studied carefully. When you place your leg against the opponent's leg, note that you are leaning back slightly. Though the right hand of the Opponent is free, you have seized his left wrist as well as his throat. This will make it difficult for the Opponent to do anything.

右の手は空きてあれど、左の胴首を取られ、喉
へ手を掛けられたれば、奈何ともしがたきなり
此第四圖は、前の体勢より、開と掛聲を掛けて
右へ引き伏せ、閉と言ひて抑にたるところなり
使人の体にて制然とは見ぬざれとも、使人は左
の手にて受人の襟を取り、右の手にて受人の左
の手を取りたり、斯くすれば、左の手にて受人
の喉をしむるとも、右の手にて受人の左の手を
折るとも自由なり、故に使人は勝ちにて、受人
は負けなり。
此体勢亦た能く見るべし、総て斯る
体勢を見るは、前の体勢を能く心に
想び浮べて、
斯くすれば、成
くなる理合なり、此
程腕首を取りたるは此
了簡なり、足を掛けたるは
此積りにてありしなりと、能く合點すべきこと
なり。

（第 四 圖）

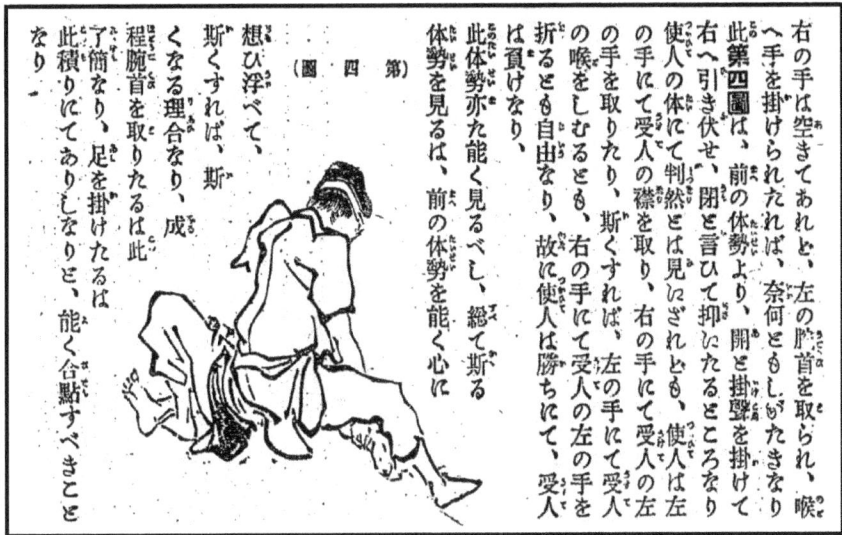

Fourth Illustration

This fourth illustration follows the Taisei 体勢, or Body Positioning, shown previously. With a Kake-goe, or Shout, of "Ah!" you do a Hiki-fuse, pulling the Opponent down flat on his back to your right. Press down on him with a Kake-goe of "Un!"

In the above illustration it is hard to see what your hands are doing. You have gripped the Opponent's Eri, or Collar, with your left hand. Your right hand has control over his left hand. In this situation you have complete freedom to either strangle off the Opponent's windpipe with your left hand or to break his left arm with your right. Thus you are the winner and the Opponent has been defeated.

The Taisei, or body positioning, showing the end of the Kata should also be observed carefully. As a general rule, when looking at the Taisei, call to mind the body positioning from the previous drawings. By doing this you will be able to visualize and understand the underlying logic behind the movements that make up this technique. Thus you should go over it in your head like this:

"I understand, the reason for taking the wrist is thus… My foot was planted against the Opponent's in order to facilitate that, which then leads to the next step."

It is important to realize how all the parts fit together.

Overview of the Second Tachi-ai Kata

1	2

3	4

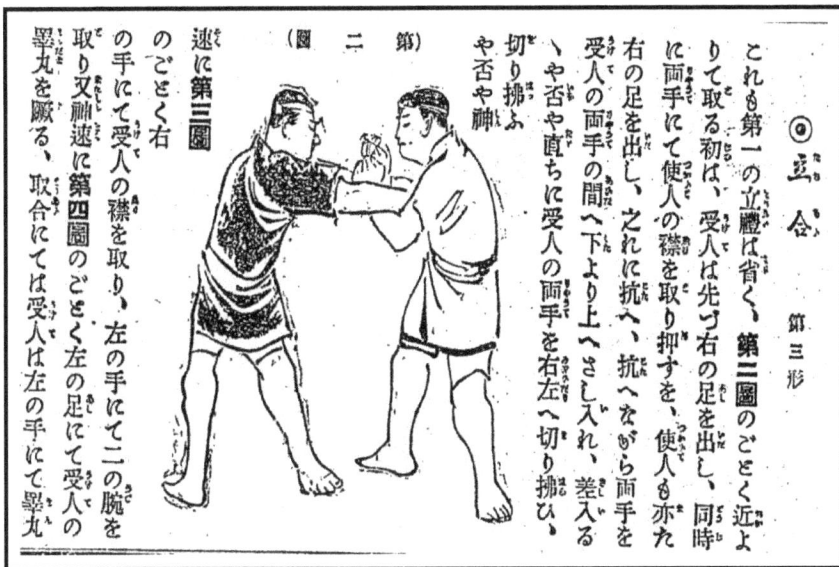

これも第一の立體は省く、第二圖のごとく近よ
りて取る初は、受人は先づ右の足を出し、同時
に両手にて使人の襟を取り押すを、使人も亦た
右の足を出し、之れに抗へ、抗へながら両手を
受人の両手の間へ下より上へさし入れ、差入る
や否や直ちに受人の両手を右左へ切り拂ひ、
や否や神
切り拂ふ

速に第三圖
のごとく右
の手にて受人の襟を取り、左の手にて二の腕を
取り又神速に第四圖のごとく左右の足にて受人の
翠丸を蹴る、取合にては受人は左の手にて翠丸

(第 二 圖)

◎ Tachi-ai Standing Bout
Third Kata
<u>Second Illustration</u>

In this Kata as well the initial standing Rei, or bow honoring your opponent, will be omitted. As pictured in the second illustration, this bout, or Tori, begins with the two opponents drawing close.

First, the Opponent steps forward with his right foot and grabs hold of your left and right lapels. You also take one step with your right foot. This is part of your response. You also move your hands up, slipping them between the hands of the Opponent.

The moment your hands are in position, do a Kiri-Harai 切り拂い, or a sharp, left and right sweeping motion.

The moment the sweeping strike is finished, you grab his collar with your right hand using Shin-soku, Divine Swiftness, as shown in the third illustration on the next page. Your left hand seizes the Opponent's right Ni-no Ude, or forearm.[66] Then, again with Shin-

---

66 Nowadays, Ni-no Ude (literally "part two of the arm") refers to the bicep. The illustrations, however, clearly show the Tsukai-te holding the forearm. This could be a mistake by the illustrator,

soku swiftness, do as shown in the fourth illustration. Kick the Opponent in the groin with your left foot.

In this Tori-ai, or match, the Opponent covers his Tama, or testicles, with his left hand. During an actual match, know that he would have been knocked out by this blow[67].

---

however the 1603 edition of 日葡辞書 *The Nippo Jisho* (literally the "Japanese–Portuguese Dictionary") compiled by Jesuit Missionaries records that the portion from the shoulder to the elbow is "ichi no ude" or "part one of the arm" while from the elbow down is "part two."

67 Kogan 睾丸 is the more scientific name for testicles. Kintama 金玉 is more along the lines of "the family jewels" as the Kanji are literally gold + ball. The author also uses the Kanji 睾丸蹴り Kogan Keri, or kick to the testicles, with the reading Tama Keri which is the cruder "kick in the balls." While not included in this volume another related term is *So wa Iaka no Kintama* そうは烏賊の金玉 meaning "It isn't going to happen any more than you can find a squid's balls."

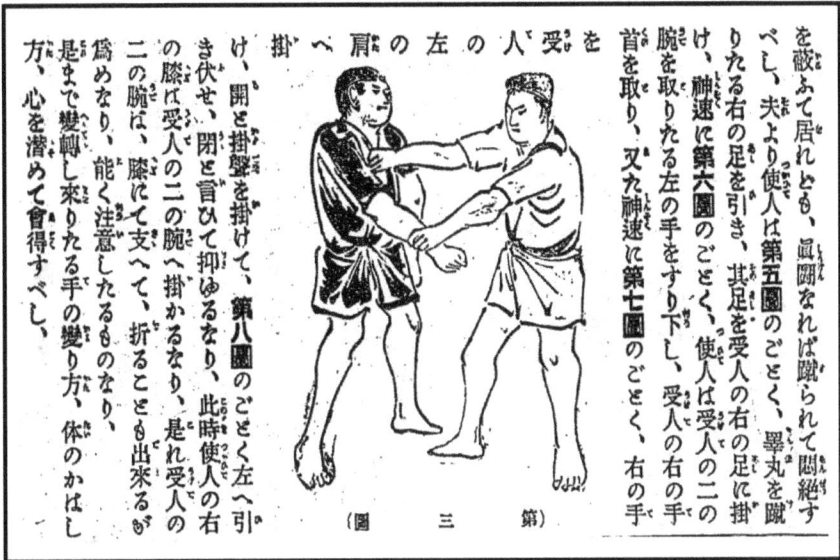

（第 三 圖）

Third Illustration

After kicking to his groin, you do as shown in the fifth illustration. Pull the right leg that you have just kicked with back. Next, hook that leg against the outside of the Opponent's right leg. Next we have illustration six. Slide your left hand down from the Opponent's forearm to his wrist with Shin-soku, Divine Swiftness. This movement is known as Suri-oroshi 揩り下ろし, or sliding the hand down without breaking contact.

The seventh illustration demonstrates how you place your right hand on his left shoulder with Shin-soku swiftness. With a Kake-goe of "Ah!" do a Hiki-fuse, Pull and Flatten. This is shown in the eighth illustration. Press him down with a Kake-goe of "Un!" At this point your right knee should be pushing down on the Opponent's Ni-no Ude, or forearm.

Note that the forearm, or Ni-no Ude, of the Opponent could be broken by the knee that is holding it down, so great care should be taken when training.

The various transitions and movements your hands go through as well as how your body moves and how it is positioned should be thoroughly studied and absorbed.

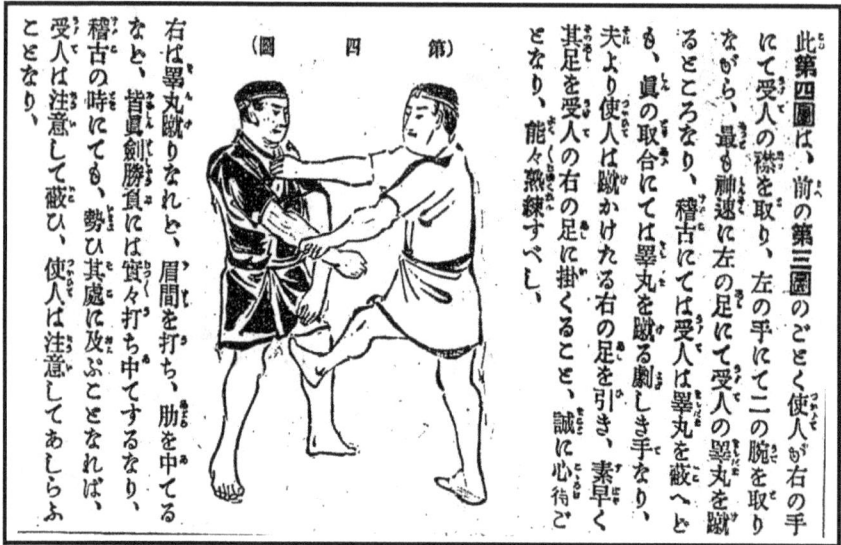

（第 四 圖）

此第四圖は、前の第三圖のごとく使人が右の手
にて受人の襟を取り、左の手にて二の腕を取り
ながら、最も神速に左の足にて受人の睾丸を蹴
るところなり、稽古にては受人は睾丸を蔽へと
も、眞の取合にては睾丸を蹴る劇しき手なり、
夫より使人は蹴かけたる右の足を引き、素早く
其足を受人の右の足に掛くること、誠に心待ご
となり、能々熟練すべし。

右は睾丸蹴りなれど、眉間を打ち、肋を中てる
など、皆眞劍勝負には實々打ち中てするなり、
稽古の時にても、勢ひ其處に及ぶこととなれば、
受人は注意して蔽ひ、使人は注意してあしらふ
ことなり、

Fourth Illustration

This fourth illustration follows what was demonstrated in the third illustration. Initially, you took hold of the Opponent's collar with your right hand and his forearm with your left hand. You then Kicked with unparalleled, Shin-soku, Divine Swiftness, to the Opponent's groin. During Keiko 稽古, or Training, the Opponent will protect his Kogan 睾丸, or testicles. However, if this were a real bout, the kick to Kintama 金玉, or the balls, would be an extremely powerful blow.

From there you draw back the right leg that kicked and rapidly places it snugly against the right leg of the Opponent. All of this requires a comprehensive understanding of Jujutsu and thus should be extensively, *extensively* trained.

In actual combat situation, or Shin-ken Shobu 眞劍勝負, all the strikes described above, such as the kick to Kogan 睾丸, or the groin, the punch to Miken 眉間, or between the eyes and punching to Abara 肋, or the ribs, would be done with full power precisely in the spot described. When doing Keiko 稽古, or training, attacks should be done at a high level of intensity, however the Opponent should take care to protect his vitals and you should maintain control at all times.

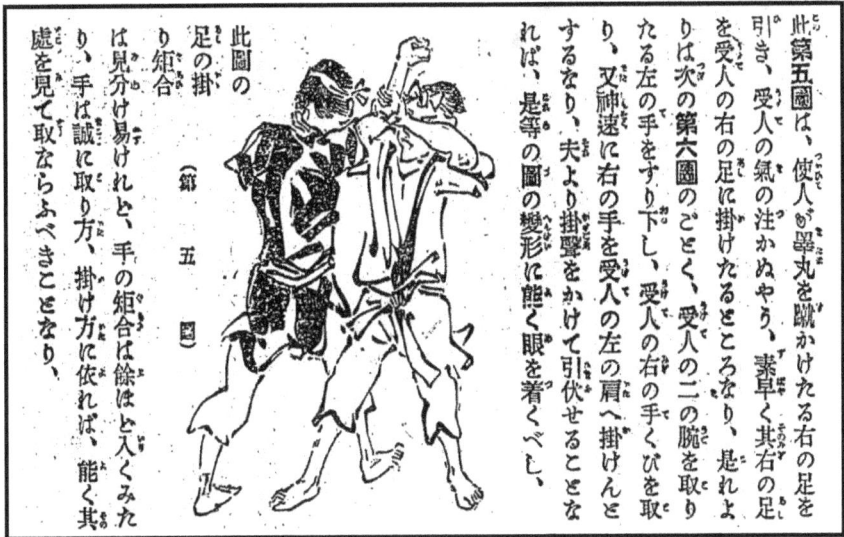

此第五圖は、使人が睾丸を蹴かけたる右の足を引き、受人の氣の注かぬやう、素早く其右の足を受人の右の足に掛けたるところなり、是れより次の第六圖のごとく、受人の二の腕を取りたる左の手をすり下し、受人の右の手くびを取り、又神速に右の手を受人の左の肩へ掛けんとするなり、夫より掛撃をかけて引伏せることとなれば、是等の圖の變形に能く眼を着くべし、

此圖の足の掛り矩合〔第五圖〕は見分け易けれど、手の矩合は餘ほど入くみたり、手は誠に取り方、掛け方に依れば、能く其處を見て取ならふべきことなり、

Fifth Illustration

This fifth illustration shows you positioning your right leg against the outside of the Opponent's right leg after kicking to his groin. You should move quickly as not to draw the attention of the Opponent.

From there the Kata proceeds to the sixth illustration where your left hand, which is holding the Opponent's forearm, slips down to grasp his right wrist. This action is known as Suri-oroshi, or sliding the hand down without breaking contact.

Again, with Shin-soku, Divine Swiftness, your right hand seizes the Opponent's left shoulder. From there, with a Kake-goe, you pull him down flat on his back. You should carefully observe the way the body positions change in the illustrations.

Though the illustration above clearly shows how your right leg is positioned, the way you right hand is placed is not. Consider carefully where and how your right hand should grab. Train this aspect extensively.

此第六圖は、使人より受人の二の腕を取りたる左の手を摺りおろし、受人の右の手首を取りたるところなり、是れよりは次の第七圖のごとく右の手を受人の左の肩へ掛くるなり、偖て第七圖第八圖と、掛聲をかけて引伏せるところ、能く心を注ぐべし、

（第六圖）

せではならぬものなり、せずばあらず、其前の二三の變化は、誠に素早くるとかする、其うちにも投るとか伏せ神速にせずばあらず、其うちにも投るとか伏せ何事にても歪みありてはならねと、殊に柔術は

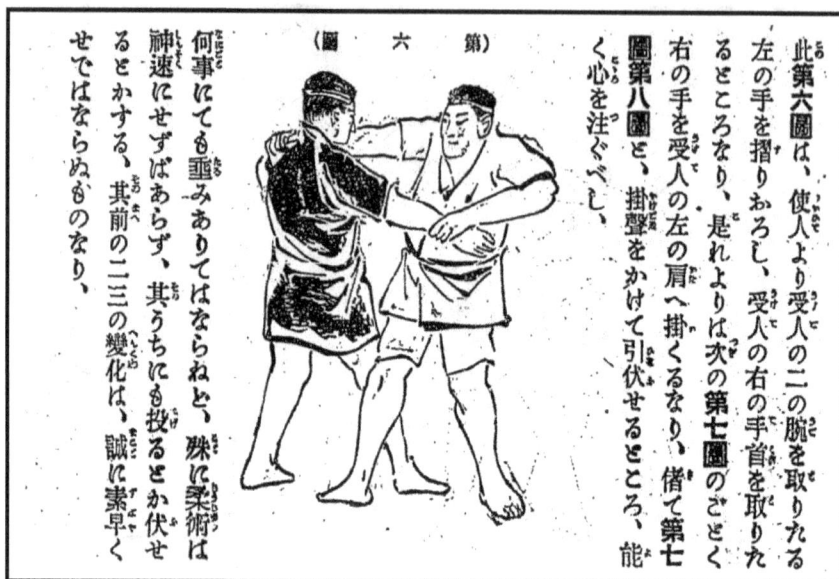

Sixth Illustration

The sixth illustration shows how your left hand, which has taken the Opponent's forearm, slides down to grip his right wrist. From there, as shown in the following seventh illustration, your right hand grabs the Opponent's left shoulder. Finally, the Kake-goe, Shout, and Hiki-fuse, Pull and Flatten, shown in the eighth illustration should be studied with great care.

There should be no sloppiness at any point during this technique. Keep in mind that,

In Jujutsu there are no elements done without Shin-soku, Divine Swiftness.

As you proceed through the steps of a technique, it doesn't matter if you are trying to throw or pull the Opponent down, the two or three moves that proceed it must be executed with upmost speed.

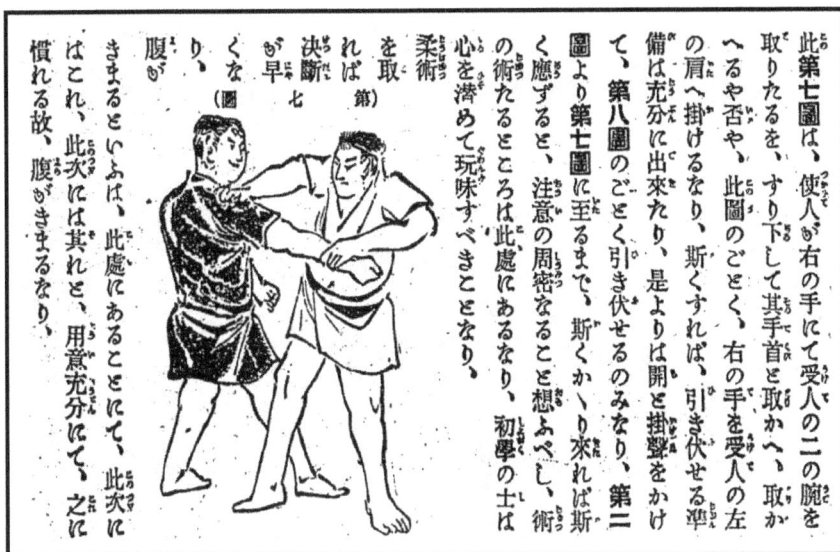

此第七圖は、使人が右の手にて受人の二の腕を取りたるを、すり下して其手首と取りかへ取かへるや否や、此圖のごとく、右の手を受人の左の肩へ掛けるなり、斯くすれば、引き伏せる準備は充分に出來たり、是よりは開と掛聲をかけて、第八圖のごとく引き伏せるのみなり、第二圖より第七圖に至るまで、斯くかゝり來れば斯く應ずると、注意の周密なること想ふべし、術の術たるところは此處にあるなり、初學の士は心を潛めて玩味すべきことなり。

柔術（第七圖）を取れば、決斷力が早くなり、くなり、腹がきまるといへば、此處にあることにて、此次にはこれ、此次には其れと、用意充分にて、之に慣れる故、腹がきまるなり、

Seventh Illustration

The seventh illustration, above, shows how your right hand has slid down from the Opponent's forearm to his wrist. The moment you do that, your right hand grabs the Opponent's left shoulder.[68] If this is done then all the preparations necessary topple the Opponent. From there, with a Kake-goe of "Ah!" pull him down flat on his back as shown in the eighth illustration.

Looking again at the sequence of movements that began in the second illustration and proceeded on to the seventh illustration, as the opponent has attacked first, you had no choice but to respond. You must have total concentration in order to carry out this technique. This is the essence of technique. Those individuals who may be new to training should take this advice to heart. Doing Jujutsu improves your Ketsudan-ryoku 決斷力, or decision making ability, as well as Hara ga Kimaru 腹が決まる, or making gut decisions. "First I will do this, then here and after this comes that…"

As you become used to making decisions in this fashion you will become able to make decisions based on instinct.

---

[68] Up until now your hand has grabbed the left shoulder, but both the illustration and the text say/show the right shoulder.

此第八圖は、前の第七圖の體勢より肘と掛擊を
かけて、左へ引き伏せ、閉と言ひて抑ひたると
ころなり、使人の右の膝の受人の二の腕へ掛か
りたる、注意の周密なること、誠に驚くべし、
斯くすれば、使人は受人を右の手にて喉を締め
なりとも、左の手にて受人の右の腕を膝に支へ
て折りなりとも、何れとも自由に爲し得べし、
即ち使人は勝ちにて、受人は負けなり。

人を伏せ押ゆるにても、通例にては利處を外す
ことあり、柔術の心得あれば抜目はなし、人
々心得おくべきことな
り、

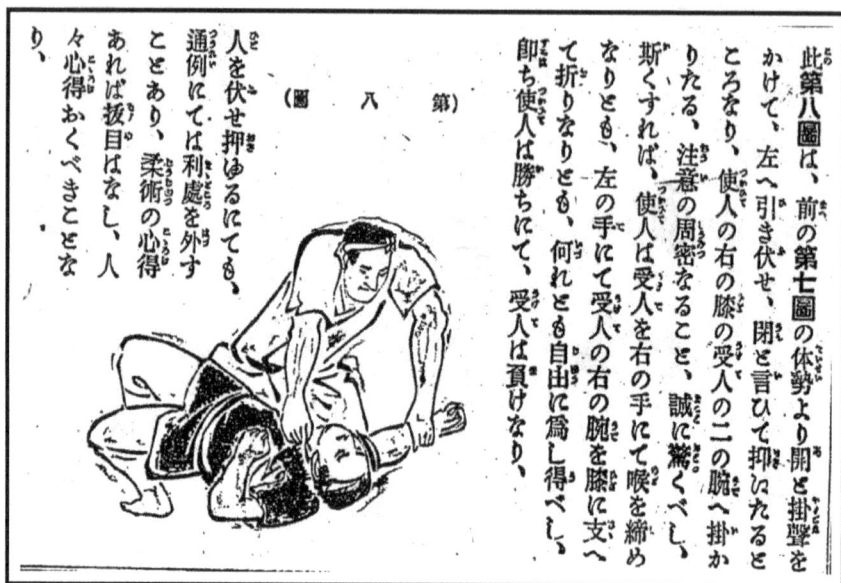

(第 八 圖)

Eighth Illustration

This eighth illustration follows the Taisei, or Body Positioning, from the previous seventh illustration. With a Kake-goe of "Ah!" pull the Opponent down flack on his back. Then press down on him with an exclamation of "Un!" Your right knee should be placed against the Opponent's Ni-no Ude, or Forearm.

If you are meticulous in your application of this technique, it will result in your adversary being caught completely off guard. Thus you are in total control and can choke off the Opponent's windpipe with your right hand while your left hand can break the Opponent's right arm, since it is braced against your right knee. You should be free to perform either of these actions.

In other words you is the victor and the Opponent is the loser. Typically, during training, when dragging someone down and holding them you avoid vital areas. In a real application of Jujutsu, however, understand that you do not refrain from attacking these points. People should make themselves aware of this concept.

These vital areas are known collectively as Kiki-dokoro 利處, literally a "useful" or "effective" point on the body.

Overview of the Third Tachi-ai Kata

1	2

3	4

5	6

7	8

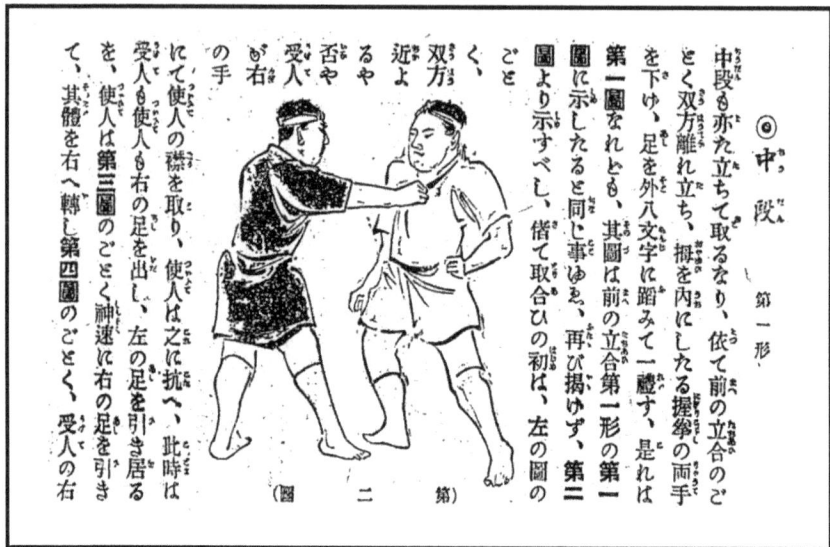

（図　二　第）

◎中段

第一形

中段も亦た立ちて取るなり、依て前の立合のごとく双方離れ立ち、拇を内にしたる握拳の両手を下げ、足を外八文字に蹈みて一礼す、是れは第一圖なれども、其圖は前の立合第一形の第一圖に示したると同じ事ゆゑ、再び揭げず、第二圖より示すべし、偕も取合ひの初は、左の圖の

ごとく、双方近よるや否や受人が右の手にて使人の襟を取り、使人は之に抗へ、此時は受人も使人も右の足を出し、左の足を引き居るを、使人は第三圖のごとく神速に右の足を引きて、其體を右へ轉し第四圖のごとく、受人の右

◎ Chudan Mid-Level Techniques
First Kata
Second Illustration

The Chudan, or Mid-Level Techniques, are also done from a standing position, therefore they begin the same way as the previous techniques. The two combatants stand with their arms hanging at their sides. Their hands are in fists with the thumbs tucked in. Their feet are planted like the bottom of the Kanji for eight, Hachi 八. You and your Opponent do a Rei 禮, or Bow of Respect, to each other. This is all depicted in the first illustration but, as it is the same as the first illustration from the first kata of Tachi-ai, it will not be reproduced again. The technique will therefore begin from the second illustration.

So then, this Tori-ai 取合, or bout, begins as shown in the second illustration above. As soon as the distance between the two lessens, the Opponent grabs your collar with his right hand and you resist this. At this point both combatants have their right foot out, with the left pulled back.

Then with Shin-soku, Divine Swiftness, step back with your right foot. Simultaneously, twist your body to the right, seize his right wrist with your right hand and lift it up. This is shown in the fourth illustration.

の手首を、右の手にて取り上げ、次の第五圖の
ごとく、左の手にて受人の右の二の腕を取り、
素早く右の足を受人の右の足に掛け、右の手の
肱にて受人の右の肋三枚を中て、又た第六圖の
ごとく素早く手首を取りたる手を逆に持ちかへ、
右の手を受人の左の肩へ掛け、開と掛聲をかけ
て左へ引き伏せ、閉と言ひて抑ゆるなり、稽古

の時には、肋三
枚を中てる眞似
するのみなれ共、
るなり、稽古の時、受人は使人より肋を中てる
眞似をしられたるときは、眞に中てられたるも
のと思ふべし、

眞の勝負には眞實肋を中て
られたるときは、眞に中てられたるも

（第　三　圖）

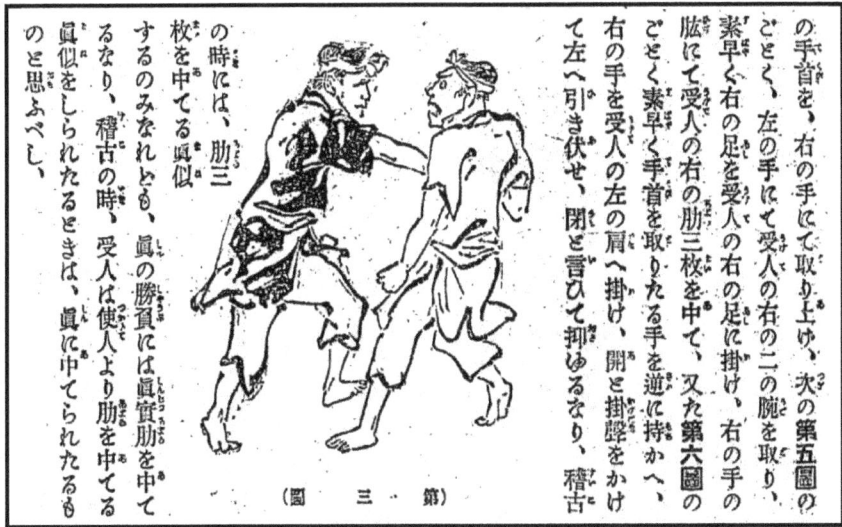

Third Illustration

As shown in the fifth illustration, you next grab his Migi Ni-no Ude, or Right Forearm, with your left hand. You then rapidly plant your right leg up against the Opponent's right leg. Your right Hiji 肱, or Elbow, is then free to strike to Abara San-mai 肋三枚, or the Third Rib From the Top,[69] on the right hand side.

Then, as shown in the sixth illustration, you reverse your left hand so you are gripping the Opponent's right wrist from the outside. Your right hand seizes the Opponent's left shoulder. With a Kake-goe of "Ah!" the opponent is pulled down flat on his back. Force him down with a shout of "Un!"

When training this technique, the strike to Abara San-mai is only pantomimed. In a real combat the strike to the ribs would be full force. During training the Opponent should reacts as if being struck. Consider the destructive effect of this strike.

---

[69] I could only find references to this vital point with regards to hunting bears: *You only get one shot at a bear and you better aim for Abara San-mai, as the heart is there. If you miss, the bear will get you.*

此第四圖は、使人が體を右へかはして、神速に受人の右の手首を、右の手にて取上げたるとろなり、是れよりは、手首を取りたる右の手の下手なる、其同じ右手の二の腕と取りて、に素早く右の足を受人の右の足へ掛け、是れにて引き伏せる準備を爲じ、偕て右の手の肱にて

（第四圖）

受人の右の肋三枚を中て、中てるや否や手首を取りたる手を逆に持ちかへ、右の手を受人の左の肩へかけて伏せるの、劇しき働きをするなり前の第三圖にては、使人は受人より右の手にて襟を取らる、此圖の右の手にて受人の右の手首

Fourth Illustration

As the fourth illustration shows you have shifted your body to the right and, with Shin-soku, Divine Swiftness, seized the Opponent's right hand and forced it up. You can see the moment his right arm has been forced up. Next you switch hands, grabbing his right forearm with your left hand. At the same time, rapidly step forward with your right leg and place it against the right leg of the Opponent. This completes your set-up for the final Hiki-fuse, Pull and Flatten.

Strike with your right Hiji 肱, or Elbow, to Abara San-mai, or the Third Rib, of the Opponent. The moment after your elbow crashes into his rib, the left hand switches its grip from the inside of the forearm to the outside of the right wrist. Your right hand seizes the Opponent's left shoulder. You then pull him down. All of this movement is extremely forceful and intense.

Earlier, in the third illustration, the Opponent grabbed hold of your collar, with his right hand. The illustration on this page shows you taking hold of the Opponent's right wrist and breaking his hold on your collar and forcing it upward.

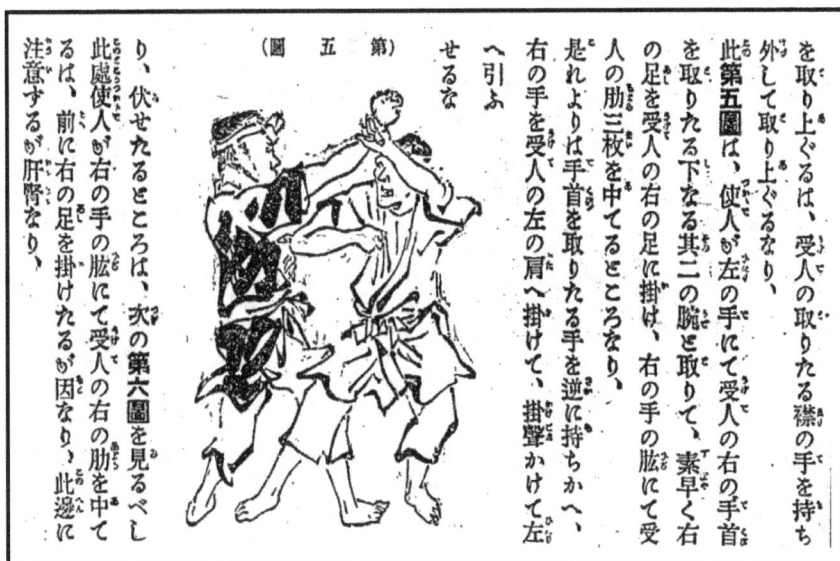

（第五圖）

を取り上ぐるは、受人の取りたる襟の手を持ち外して取り上ぐるなり、此第五圖は、使人が左の手にて受人の右の手首を取りたる下なる其二の腕と取りて、素早く右の足を受人の右の足に掛け、右の手の肱にて受人の肋三枚を中てるところなり、是れよりは手首を取りたる手を逆に持ちかへ、右の手を受人の左の肩へ掛けて、掛聲かけて左へ引ふせるな

り、伏せたるところは、次の第六圖を見るべし此處使人が右の手の肱にて受人の右の肋を中てるは、前に右の足を掛けたるが因なり、此邊に注意するが肝腎なり、

Fifth Illustration

This fifth illustration shows how you take hold of the Ni-no Ude, Forearm, just above his wrist, with your left hand. At the same time, you have stepped forward rapidly with your right leg and placed it against the Opponent's right leg. You then strike with your elbow to his ribs.

From here the hand that has the forearm switches its grip around and takes his wrist while your right hand seizes his left shoulder. With a Kake-goe, or Shout, the Opponent is pulled down to the left with a Hiki-fuse, Pull and Flatten. Refer to the sixth illustration for the scene of the Opponent after he has been pulled flat on his back.

The illustration above shows how your right elbow is striking the Opponent's ribs on his right side. Before that, however, pay attention to the fact that your right leg must be placed before this strike. This is essential.

此第六圖は、使人が受人の右なる肋三枚を、右の肱にて中てるや否や、素早く手首を取りたる手を逆に持ちかへ、右の手を受人の左の肩へ掛け、闕と掛聲をかけ、左へ引き伏せ、閉と言ひて抑にたるところなり、斯くすれば、使人は受人の腕を折りなりとも、喉を締めなりとも、自在にすることを得、故に使人は勝ちにて、受手は頁けなり、此處手の取り方を示したれば、能く見るべし、手の取方は誠に肝要なり、柔術取人の拳の中には、万斤の力ありと謂ふも可なり、俳し實地は力のみにあらず、精神の籠りあるなり、

（第　六　圖）

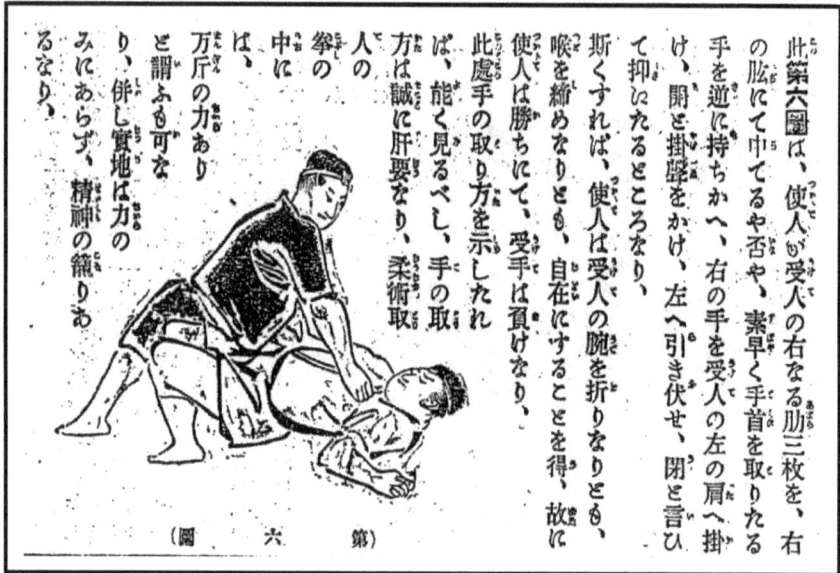

Sixth Illustration

This sixth illustration shows what happens after you struck his ribs with your elbow. Your left hand switches from holding the Opponent's forearm on the inside to holding his wrist on the outside. Seize his left shoulder with your right hand and with a Kake-goe, or Shout, of "Ah!" pull him down to the left. As you press him into the ground shout a Kake-goe of "Un!"

Thus as you have Jizai 自在, or Complete Control, to either break the Opponent's arm or strangle off his windpipe. Thus, you are the winner and the Opponent has lost. The way in which the hands are positioned should be studied carefully as this is the fundamental point of this technique.

There is a saying about Jujutsu that describes its teachings as containing *Mankin no Chikara* 万斤の力, or the power of ten thousand axes. In reality, this is not referring only to physical power but also about the Seishin 精神, or Spiritual, energy that is required.

186

Overview of the First Chudan Kata

1	2
3	4
5	6

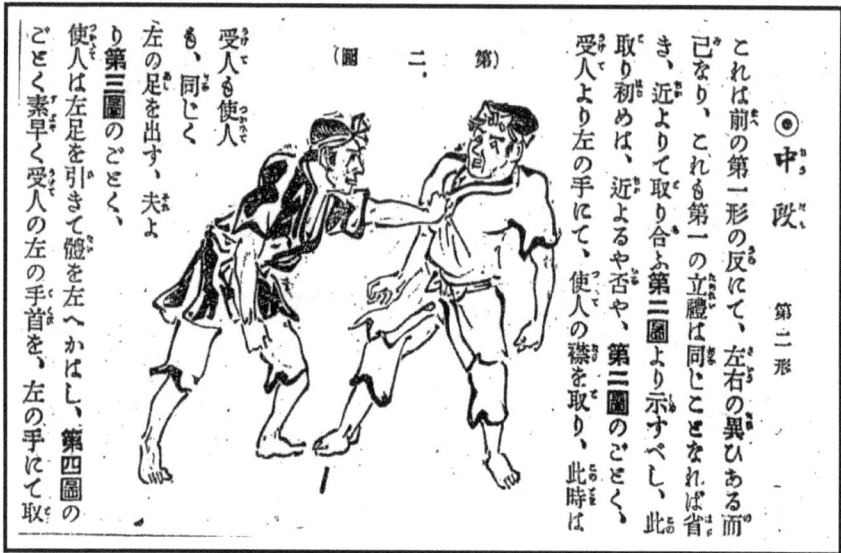

◎ 中段

第二形

これは前の第一形の反にて、左右の異ひある而已なり、これも第一の立體は同じことなれば省き、近よりて取り合ふ第二圖より示すべし、此取り初めは、近よるや否や、第二圖より左の手にて、使人の襟を取り、此時は受人より左の手にて、使人の襟を取り、第三圖のごとく、り第三圖のごとく、夫よ左の足を出す、夫よも、同じく受人も使人使人は左足を引きて體を左へかはし、第四圖のごとく素早く受人の左の手首を、左の手にて取

（第二圖）

◎ **Chudan Mid-Level Techniques**
Second Kata
<u>Second Illustration</u>

This is the Ura, or the Reverse, of the first technique. This means the technique is the same except the left and right are reversed. It begins with the Opponent grabbing you with his left hand instead of his right. As the first drawing depicting the Rei, or Bow of Respect, is the same it will be omitted. The technique will begin with the second illustration above.

The second illustration shows that as soon as the opponents draw close, the Opponent seizes your Eri, or Collar, with his left hand. At this point, both combatants step with the left foot. The Opponent steps forward and you step back.

Next, the third illustration shows how you have stepped back with your left foot and twisted your body to the left. Then, as the fourth illustration shows, you rapidly force the Opponent's left wrist up with your left hand.

若し此一手外るれば、能く注意して記臆しおく べし、
こと能はず、能く注意して記臆しおくべし、
手首を左の手にて、取り上げんとする下心なり
次の第四圖に示すがごとく、素早く受人の左の
ろなり、是れは
かはしたるとこ

（第 三 圖）

左の第三圖は、使人が左足を引きて、休を左へ
せ、閉と言ひて抑ゆるなり、
右の肩へ掛け、開と掛聲をかけて、右へ引きのせ
取りたる手を、逆に持ちかへ、左の手を受人の
枚を中て、又た第六圖のごとく、素早く手首を
左の足に掛け、左の手の脇にて、受人の左脇三
の左の二の腕を取り、素早く左の足を、受人の
り上げ、次の第五圖のごとく、右の手にて受人

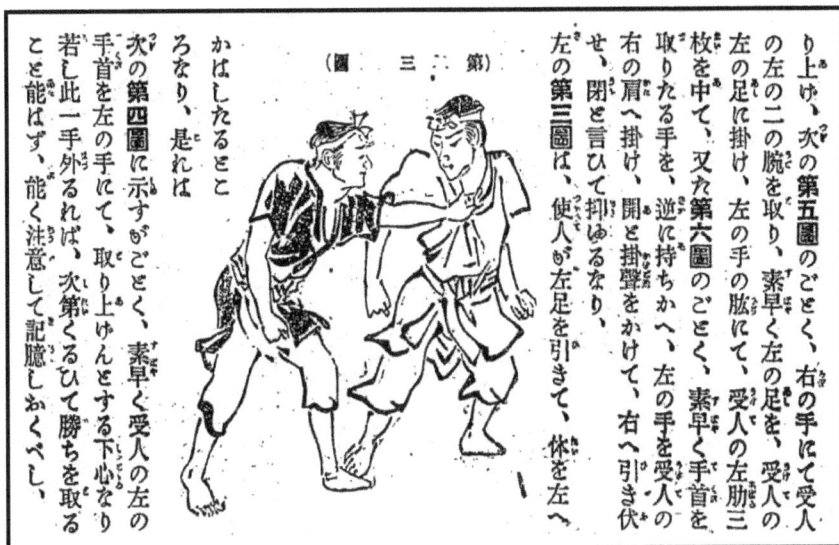

Third Illustration

The fifth illustration shows how you seize the Opponent's left Ni-no Ude, or Forearm, with your right hand. Next, your left leg moves rapidly against the Opponent's left leg. Then slam your left elbow into the Opponent's left Abara San-mai, or Third Rib from the Top.

Further, as the sixth illustration depicts, your right hand switches its grip from the inside to the outside and you seize the Opponent's right shoulder with your left hand. With a Kake-goe, or Shout, of "Ah!" you pull the Opponent flat on his back to your right. Once on the ground you press him down with a Kake-goe of "Un!"

This third illustration shows how you step back with your left foot and twist your body to the left. In the following fourth illustration, you rapidly take hold of his left wrist. This serves as Shita-gokoro 下心, or Set-up, for yanking his hand off and forcing it up. Should this Itte 一手, or Move in a Game, fail then things will begin to unravel and the chances of winning will plummet. This should be carefully committed to memory[70].

---

[70] 一手 Itte, literally "one hand," is used when referring to moves in games like chess or Igo, but also to military or political moves.

此第四圖は、前の第三圖のごとく、素早く左の
足を引きて、体を左へかはすや否や、受人の左
の手首を、左の手にて取上げたるところなり、
是れよりは次の第五圖のごとく、右の手にて受
人の左の二の腕を取り、素早く左の足を受人の
左の足へ掛けんとす。
夫より後ちは、左の手の肱にて、受人の左肋三
枚を中て、第六圖のごとく、素早く手首を取り
たる手を、逆に持ちかへ、左の手を受人の右の
肩へ掛けて、右の方へ引き伏せるなり。

此圖にては、使人の右の足
かゝりて無けれど、向ふへ出でたるところ肝要
にて、次の圖のごとく、体をかはして左を掛く
るに妙をり。

(第　四　圖)

Fourth Illustration

This fourth illustration follows what occurred in the third illustration. You step back with your left foot and twist your body to the left. seize the Opponent's left wrist and force it up.

Next, the following fifth illustration shows how your right hand takes hold of the Opponent's left forearm. Step forward rapidly and plant your left leg against the left leg of the Opponent. Next, strike the Opponent's ribs on his left side with your left elbow. The following sixth illustration shows how your right hand switches from gripping the forearm to the wrist, at the same time your left hand seizes the Opponent's right shoulder.

In this illustration your right leg is out in front. This is essential at this point. However, note the subtle move that occurs in the following illustration where you twist your body to the left as your left leg is pressed against the opponent's leg.

此に至るまでに、已に透のありたる故なり。斯くなれば、受人は引伏せられましとすれとも、能はず、伏せらる、は当然の理合なり此に至るまでに、已に透のありたる故なり。誠に神速にすべきことなり。手を受人の右の肩へかけ、右へ引き伏せるなり人の手首を取りたる、手を逆に持ちかへ、左の是れより後ちは、次の第六圖のごとく、既に受つるところなり。け、又た左の手の肱にて、受人の左脇三枚を中の腕を取り、素早く左の足を受人の左の足に掛を取り上けながら、右の手にて受人の左の二此第五圖は、使人が左の手にて受人の左の手首

(圖 五 第)

Fifth Illustration

You have forced the Opponent's left wrist up with your left hand and, as this fifth illustration shows, seized his left forearm with your right hand. After that, you rapidly placed your left leg against the Opponent's left leg.

The next step will be to strike to Abara San-mai, or the Third Rib, on the Opponent's left side with your left elbow. The technique continues in the sixth illustration.

You have switched your grip and now hold the outside of the Opponent's left wrist with your right hand. Your left hand grips Opponent's right shoulder. You use that to pull him down to your right. These movements should all be done with absolute Shin-soku, or Divine Swiftness.

Given all the set-up you have done, to say that the Opponent would not be yanked to the ground would be wholly inconceivable. There is a rock-solid reason for this. It is because there was a clear Suki 透, or opening, available.

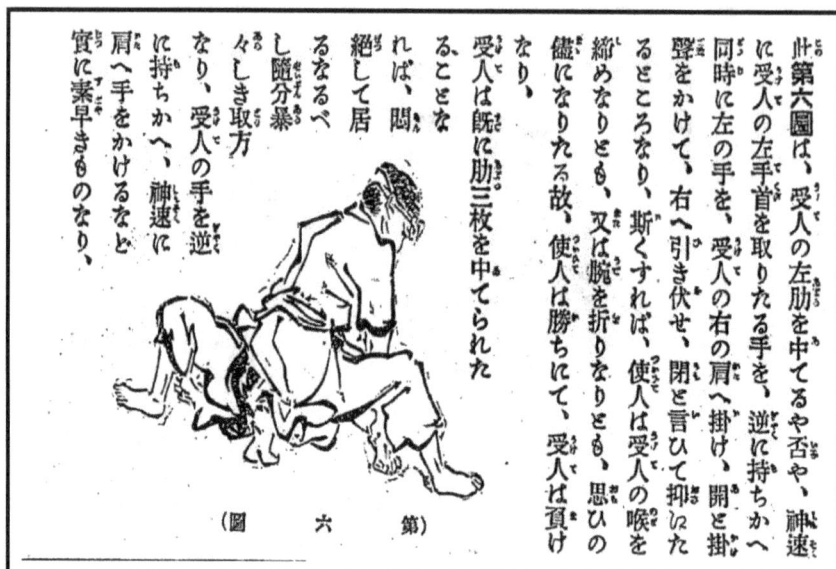

此第六圖は、受人の左肋を中てるや否や、神速に受人の左乎首を取りたる手を、逆に持ちかへ同時に左の手を、受人の右の肩へ掛け、開と掛聲をかけて、右へ引き伏せ、閉と言ひて抑へたるところなり、斯くすれば、使人は受人の喉を締めなりとも、又は腕を折りなりとも、思ひの儘になり得る故、使人は勝ちにて、受人は頁け なり、受人は既に肋三枚を中てられたることな るなるべし隨分暴々しき方れば、悶絶して居なり、受人の手を逆に持ちかへ、神速に肩へ手をかけるなど實に素早きものなり、

（第　六　圖）

Sixth Illustration

The sixth illustration shows the scene after you have struck the Opponent's ribs on his left side with your left elbow. You then reverse your grip on the Opponent's left wrist and, simultaneously, seize his right shoulder with your left hand. With a Kake-goe of "Ah!" he is pulled down to the right in a Hiki-fuse, Pull and Flatten. Once on the ground, you force him down hard with a Kake-goe of "Un!"

Now, as shown above, you can either choke the Opponent with a Shime 締, or choke, or you can break his arm. Since you have either option available, you are deemed the winner while the Opponent has been defeated. As the Opponent has been dealt a rather severe strike to the ribs, be aware that this technique is very intense.

Be aware that both when you are switching your grip on the Opponent's arm, as well as when you are seizing his shoulder, the movements should all be done with Shin-soku, Divine Swiftness.

Overview of the Second Chudan Kata

1	2
3	4
5	6

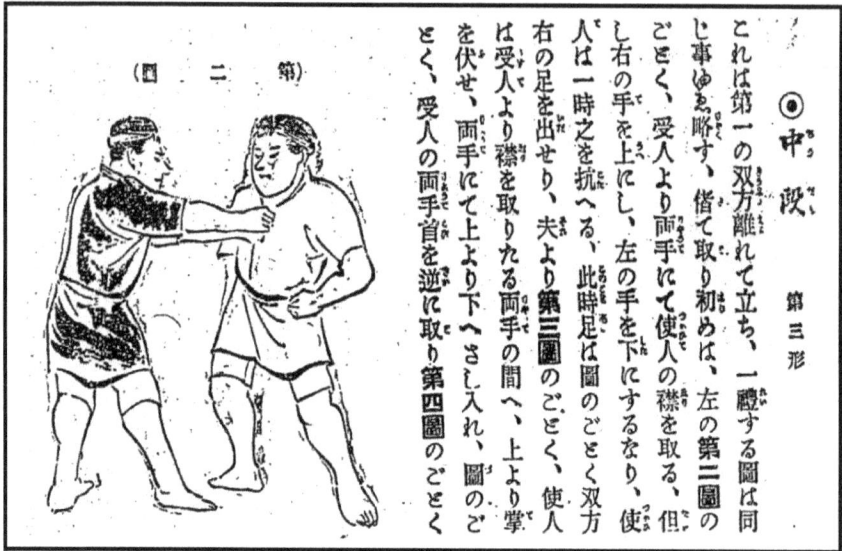

とく、受人の両手首を逆に取り第四圖のごとく
を伏せ、両手にて上より下へさし入れ、圖のご
は受人より襟を取りたる両手の間へ、上より掌
右の足を出せり、夫より第三圖のごとく、使人
人は一時之を抗へる、此時足は圖のごとく双方
し右の手を上にし、左の手を下にするなり、使
ごとく、受人より両手にて使人の襟を取る、但
じ事ゆゑ略す、偖て取り初めは、左の第二圖の
これは第一の双方離れて立ち、一體する圖は同

◉ 中段、

第三形

◎ Chudan Mid-Level Techniques
Third Kata
__Second Illustration__

As the illustration depicting the opponents across from each other and doing a standing Rei 禮, or Bow, is identical to the first Kata, it will be omitted.

So then, the beginning of this Tori, or Bout, begins as shown in the second illustration above. The Opponent grabs you collar with both hands. Note here that his right hand is gripping higher while his left hand is gripping lower. You resist this for a moment. At this point in the Kata, both combatants have their right foot forward.

The movement continues as can be seen in the third illustration, on the next page. Raise your hands up and insert them between your Opponent's arms from above. As he holds your collar, push both of your hands in from above. Then, as the illustration dictates, take both of the Opponent's wrists in a Gyaku-waza 逆技, or a Reverse Joint Lock.

The fourth illustration show how you force the Opponent's hands off your collar and rotate them out with a Kureri クレリ, or the sound of something rotating smoothly.

クレリと返して受人の両手を外し、取り上げ、其機みに、素早く受人の睾丸を第五圖のごとくに蹴るを、受人は素早く体を左へかはし、使人は第六圖のごとく、両手にて受人の両肱を持ち同時に右の足を受人の右の足へ掛け、夫より使

人は、左の手にて、受人の右手の肱を外より持ちたるを、とく内より外へ持ちかへ、同時に肱を持ちたる右の手を離し、神速に受人の左の肩へ掛け、開くと掛聲をかけて右へ引き伏せ、第八圖のごとく閉と言ひて抑ゆるなり、これも伏せるときには左の肩へ掛けたる手にて、受人の襟を素早く取るなり、

(第 三 圖)

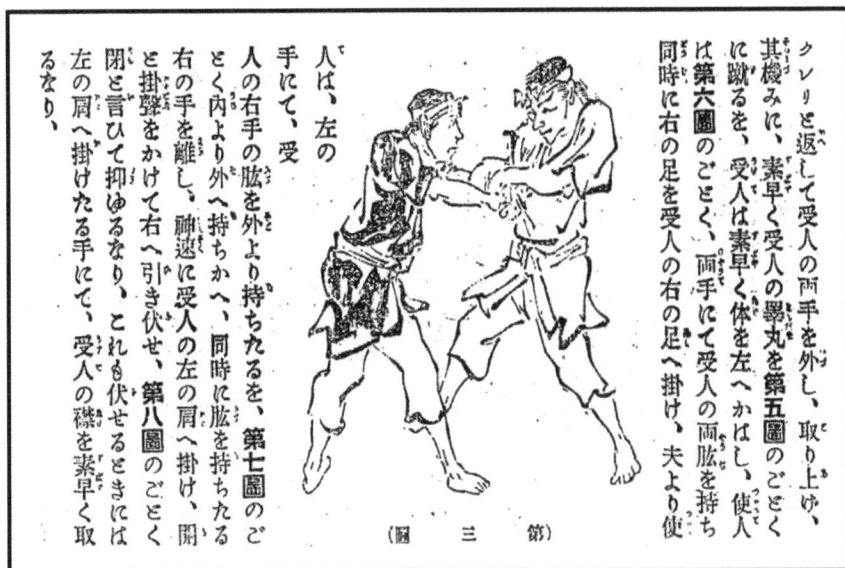

Third Illustration

Using this opening you have created, you swiftly kick the Opponent in Kogan 睾丸, or testicles. This is shown in the fifth illustration. The Opponent avoids this by rapidly moving his body to the left. Then, as the sixth illustration depicts, you seize the Opponent's elbows and, at the same time, placing plant your right leg against his right leg.

From there your left hand switches from an outside grip on the elbow to an inside hold on the wrist. This is shown in the seventh illustration. At the same time, release his left elbow with your right hand and with Shin-soku, Divine Swiftness, seize the opponent's left shoulder.

With a Kake-goe of "Ah!" pull the Opponent is pulled down to the right in a Hiki-fuse, Pull and Flatten. You then press him into the ground with a Kake-goe of "Un!" This is shown in the eighth illustration.

To help pull him down your left hand, which is on his shoulder, should grabs his collar beside his neck.

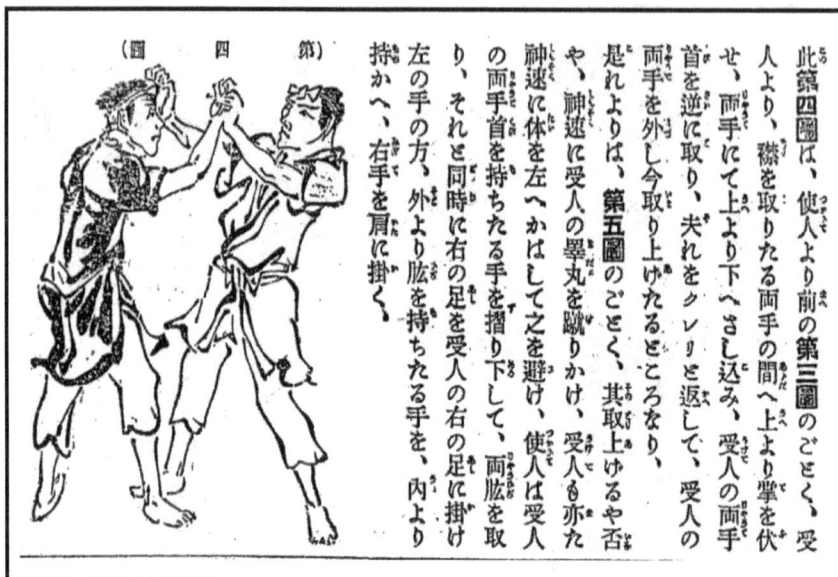

此第四圖は、使人より前の第三圖のごとく、受
人より、襟を取りたる両手の間へ上より掌を伏
せ、両手にて上より下へさし込み、受人の両手
首を逆に取り、夫れをクレリと返して、受人の
両手を外し今取り上げたるところなり、

是れよりは、第五圖のごとく、其取上ゆるや否
や、神速に受人の睪丸を蹴りかけ、受人も亦た
神速に体を左へかはして之を避け、使人は受人
の両手首を持ちたる手を摺り下して、両肱を取
り、それと同時に右の足を受人の右の足に掛け
左の手の方、外より肱を持ちたる手を、内より
持かへ、右手を肩に掛く。

Fourth Illustration

This fourth illustration continues from where the previous third illustration ended. The Opponent's hands are gripping your collar. You slip your hands in-between them from above.
Push both hands in and grab the Opponent's hands in a Gyaku-waza, or a Reverse Joint Lock. Next, rotate his wrists outward with a smooth Kureri twisting sound. This forces the hands of the Opponent off your collar and up into the air.

The following fifth illustration shows how you kick with Shin-soku swiftness to the Kogan, or Testicles, of the Opponent as soon as you wrench his hands free of your collar. The Opponent, in turn, avoids this by shifting his body to the left with Shin-soku, Divine Swiftness. With both hands do a Suri-oroshi 擦り下し, or Sliding Down, action to seize both elbows. Simultaneously, move your right leg against the right leg of the Opponent. Switch your left hand from an outside grab on the elbow to an inside grab while your right hand releases the Opponent's elbow to seize his shoulder.

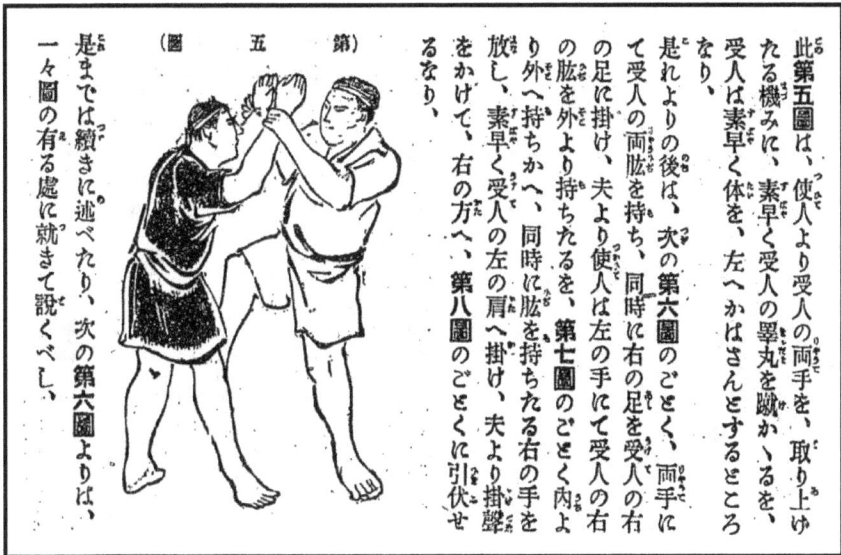

（第　五　圖）

此第五圖は、使人より受人の両手を、取り上げたる機みに、素早く受人の睾丸を蹴かゝるを、受人は素早く体を、左へかはさんとするところなり、

是れよりの後は、次の第六圖のごとく、両手にて受人の両肱を持ち、同時に右の足を受人の右の足に掛け、夫より使人は左の手にて受人の右の肱を外より持ちたるを、第七圖のごとく内より外へ持ちかへ、同時に肱を持ちたる右の手を放し、素早く受人の左の肩へ掛け、夫より掛聲をかけて、右の方へ、第八圖のごとくに引伏せるなり、

是までは續きに述べたり。次の第六圖よりは、一々圖の有る處に就きて説くべし、

Fifth Illustration

The fifth illustration above shows how you use the opening created by forcing both the Opponent's arms up to kick to his groin. The Opponent evades this by rapidly shifting his body to the left.

The next step can be seen in the sixth illustration. Seize the Opponent's elbows and, simultaneously, place your right leg against the right leg of the Opponent.

Next, switch your left hand from an outside grip on the Opponent's right elbow to, as shown in the seventh illustration, an inside grip on his wrist. At the same time, your right hand releases his left elbow and rapidly seizes the Opponent's left shoulder.

The following eighth illustration shows how you pull the Opponent down with a Hiki-fuse, Pull and Flatten. You do a Kakegoe, or Shout, as you do this.

Starting with the following sixth illustration the remaining illustrations will focus on details regarding how this technique should be done.

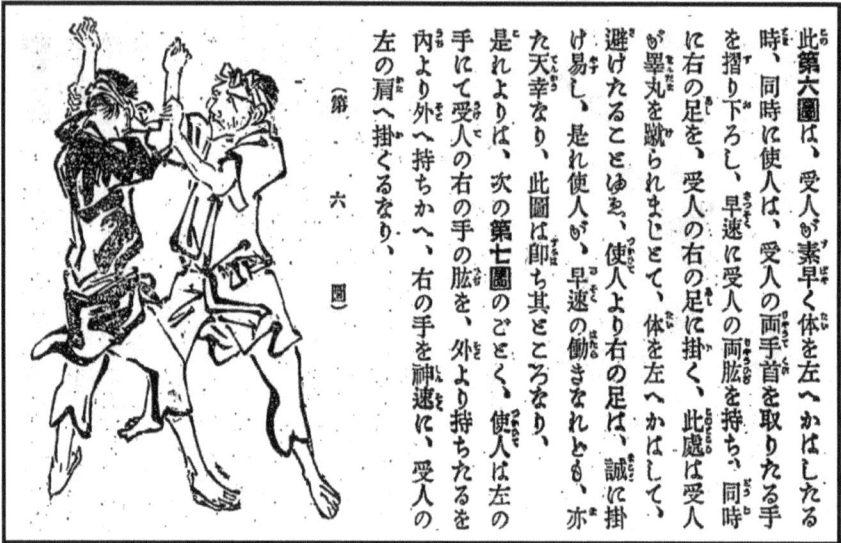

此第六圖は、受人が素早く体を左へかはしたる
時、同時に使人は、受人の両手首を取りたる手
を摺り下ろし、早速に受人の両肱を持ち、同時
に右の足を、受人の右の足に掛く、此處は受人
が睾丸を蹴られまじとて、体を左へかはして、
避けたることゆゑ、使人より右の足は、誠に掛
け易し、是れ使人が、早速の働きなれと、亦
た天幸なり、此圖は即ち其ところなり、
是れよりは、次の第七圖のごとく、使人は左の
手にて受人の右の手の肱を、外より持ちたるを
内より外へ持ちかへ、右の手を神速に、受人の
左の肩へ掛くるなり、

（第

六

圖）

Sixth Illustration

This sixth illustration shows the Opponent shifting his body rapidly to the left. At the same time you do a Suri Oroshi 摺り下ろし, sliding your hands down from his wrists to his elbows without breaking contact. Simultaneously, place your right leg against the Opponent's right leg.

Since your Opponent has dodged to the left to avoid your kick to his groin, you can position your leg against his without any undue effort. The speed with which you execute these movements should be as if you were receiving divine instructions. This is what this illustration depicts.

The movement continues in the seventh illustration. You switch your left hand around from an outside grip on his elbow to an inside grip while your right hand goes to his left shoulder with Shin-soku, Divine Swiftness.

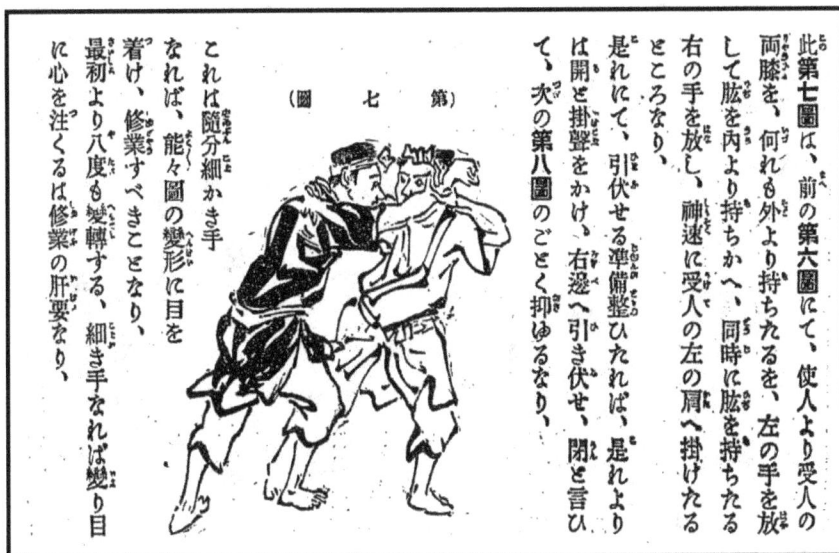

此第七圖は、前の第六圖にて、使人より受人の
両膝を、何れも外より持ちたるを、左の手を放
して脇を内より持ちかへ、同時に脇を持ちたる
右の手を放し、神速に受人の左の肩へ掛けたる
ところなり、
是れにて、引伏せる準備整ひたれば、是れより
は開と掛聲をかけ、右邊へ引き伏せ、閉と言ひ
て、次の第八圖のごとく抑ゆるなり、

これは随分細かき手
なれば、能々圖の變形に目を
着け、修業すべきことなり、
最初より八度も變轉する、細き手なれば變り目
に心を注くるは修業の肝要なり。

Seventh Illustration

The seventh illustration follows what occurred in the preceding sixth illustration. You are holding both of the Opponent's elbows[71] from the outside. Release your left hand and then grab his wrist from the inside. At the same time your right hand releases its hold on his left elbow and seizes the Opponent's left shoulder.

Having reached this point, all the preparations for the Hiki-fuse have been completed. With a Kake-goe of "Ah!" you yank the Opponent down to your right onto his back. Shove him into the ground with an "Un!" This is shown in the following eighth illustration.

It will take time to become experienced at the various details presented in this technique. Thus the changes that occur from one illustration to the next should be scrutinized and extensive Shugyo, or intensive focused training, should be done. Starting from the beginning, there are eight transitions.

If you wish to become adept at this, pouring one's attention into these changes and conducing Shugyo in each aspect is essential.

---

[71] The text actually says that he "has hold of both knees" but that is clearly a misprint.

此第八圖は、前の第七圖の体勢より開と掛撃を
かけて右へ引き伏せ、閉と言ひて抑ふたるとと
ろなり、第七圖にて使人より受人の肱を、内よ
り持ちかへたるは、引伏せるとき、力を強く利
かせんが爲めなり、外より肱を持ちたる儘、引
き伏せも出來得るならんが、夫れにては逆手に
して、充分力の利きめは無し、縦し引き伏せ得
るとも、力づくにて引き伏せ得たるなり、是れを
術とは謂ふべからず、誠に感ずべきとにて、
術といふものは、能く注意したるものなり、誤
りの剛術
にて、此
邊の抜け
目あるべ
し、柔術
の柔術た
る所、又
九行届き
たる所を
知るべし

（第　八　圖）

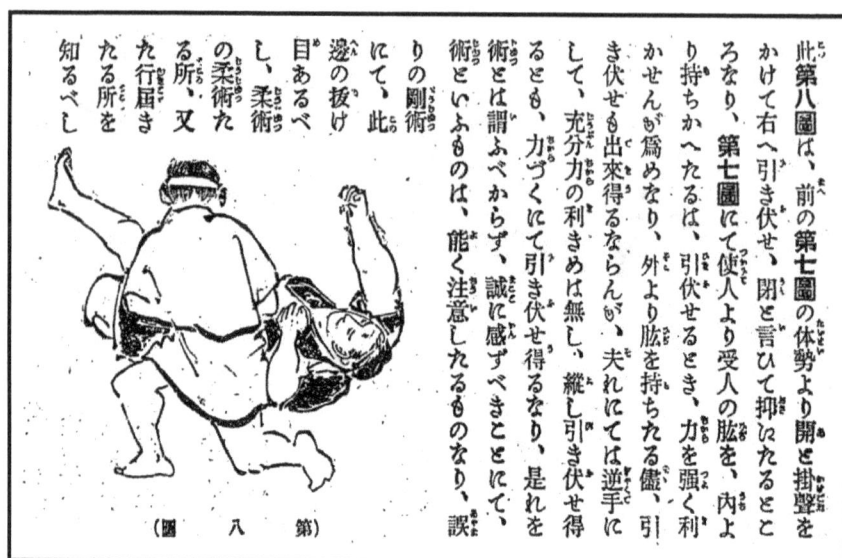

Eighth Illustration

The eighth illustration continues the movement set up in the previous seventh illustration. With a Kake-goe of "Ah!" the Opponent is pulled down onto his back on your right side. Push him into the ground with Kake-goe of "Un!"

The seventh illustration describes how your left hand switches from an outside grip on the Opponent's elbow to an inside grip on his wrist. This allows the pull in the Hiki-fuse, Pull and Flatten, to be more powerful and therefore more effective. While the Opponent can certainly be pulled down with the hand on the outside of the elbow however, as your hand would then not be ideally placed, it would prove difficult to put sufficient power into the pull.

Even if you are able to pull him down from that position, it would rely on power alone, thus this action could not be said to be "Jutsu," or Technique. You should endeavor to be sensitive and aware to whether you are using technique or just power.

Being alert and not allowing "Go-Jutsu 剛術" or techniques relying only on strength, to slip in is an essential point. Know that you should be vigilant regarding how you define Jujutsu when doing Jujutsu and to be consistent in your application.

Overview of the Third Chudan Kata

1	2

3	4

5	6

7	8

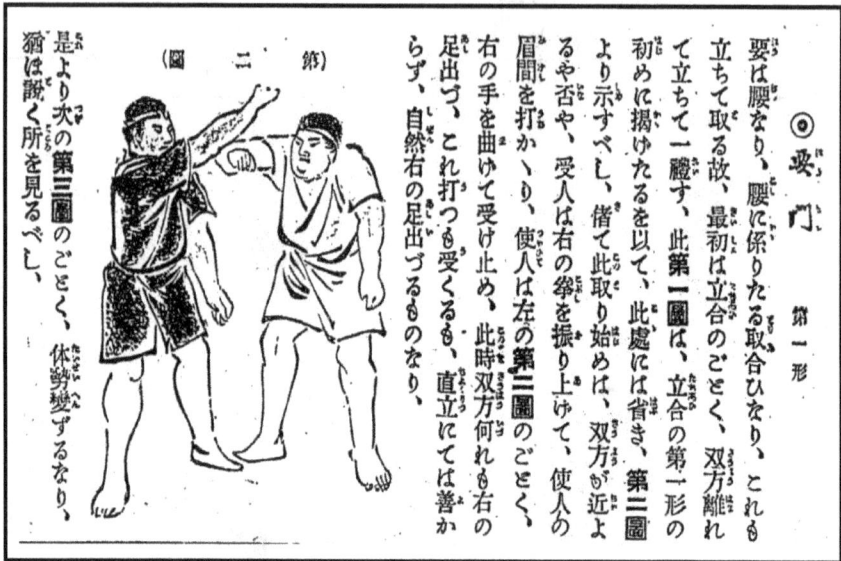

（第　二　圖）

◎要門

第一形

要は腰なり、腰に係りたる取合ひなり、これも立ちて取る故、最初は立合のごとく、双方離れて立ちて一體づ、此第一圖は、立合の第一形の初めに掲げたるを以て、此處には省き、第二圖より示すべし、偖て此取り始めは、双方が近よるや否や、受人は右の拳を振り上げて、使人の眉間を打かへり、使人は左の第二圖のごとく、右の手を曲げて受け止め、此時双方何れも右の足出づ、これ打つも受くるも、直立にては善か足出づるものなり、自然右の足出づるものなり、是より次の第三圖のごとく、猶は説く所を見るべし、体勢變ずるなり、

◎ Yoh Mon Fundamental Technique
First Kata Second Illustration

The essential point is in the hips. The Yoh 要 in the title is the Kanji for "essential" and the Kanji for "hips," or Koshi 腰, contains the Kanji 要 as part of its shape, thus *the hips are essential*. The following matches all focus on the importance of the hips.

These techniques also begin from a standing position with both combatants doing Rei, or Bow of respect. As the first illustration would only repeat what was presented in the first Taichi-ai Kata it will not be reproduced. We will begin from the second illustration.

This bout begins with both combatants approaching each other. As soon as they close in, the Opponent punches with his right fist, aiming to strike Miken, between your eyebrows.

You respond as shown above with a right Uke-tome, Block and Strike, with your arm bent. At this point both combatants have their right foot forward. This is regardless of whether they are striking or blocking. Strictly speaking this is not because it is better, rather it is because it is natural that the right foot should move out first.

The next movements are shown in the third illustration. There will be changes in Taisei 体勢, or body position, that will occur. From here on carefully note the changes that are explained.

夫より此第三圖の ごとく、使人は受人の右手の
二の腕を、左の手にて取る、此時双方互ひに少
し後と へ足を引く、故に圖の足開けたり、斯る
細密の處にも眼を著くべし、次に第四圖のごと
く、使人は神速に受人の左肋三枚を、右の手に
て突くを、受人は然うはさせじと體を引き、肋
を左の手にて蔽ふ、夫より使人は、第五圖のご
とく右の手にて受人の

（第 三 圖）

右の肱を取
り、左の手を放して素早く其手を受人の頸に掛
け、これと同時に右の足を受人の右の足に掛
け、其體勢にて使人は體を受人の後背へ移し、足を
左右に踏みかへ、第七圖のごとく、右の手にて
受人の後ろ襟を持ち、左の手にて帯を持ち、夫

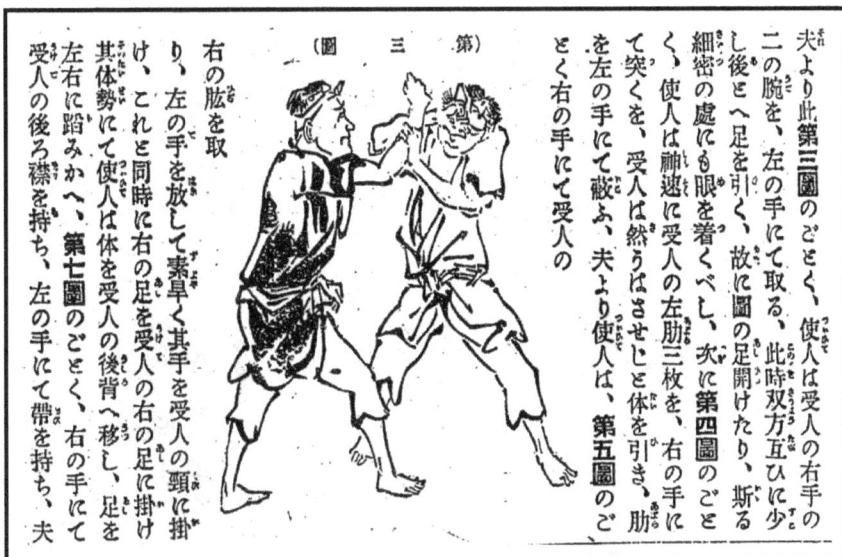

Third Illustration

The Kata continues as shown in the third illustration. You seize the Opponent's right Ni-no Ude, or forearm, with your left hand. As you can see in the illustration, both combatants have widened their stances. It is essential that you pay attention to these small details.

The following fourth illustration shows how you punch the Opponent with Shin-soku, Divine Swiftness, in his left Abara San-mai, or the third rib from the top, on the left-hand side.[72] The Opponent naturally recoils away from this by protecting his ribs with his left hand.

From there you continue as shown in the fifth illustration. Take hold of the Opponent's right elbow with your right hand. Your left hand lets go of the forearm and rapidly seizes where the Opponent's neck meets his shoulder. At the same time, you step forward with your right leg and place it against the right leg of the Opponent. This is shown in the sixth illustration. Next, do a cross step with your left foot and move behind the Opponent. The right leg is then on the right and the left leg on the left.

---

[72] The text says "left side," however this is likely a printing error.

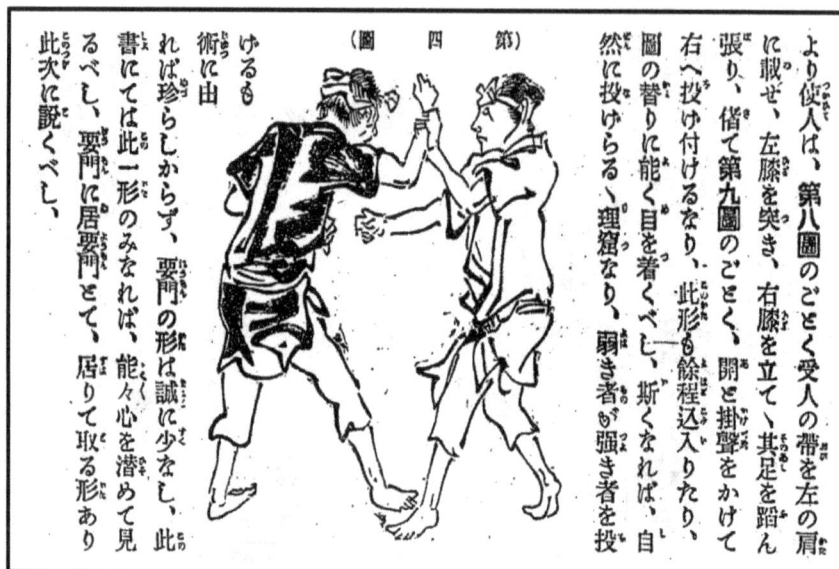

此次に説くべし、
るべし、要門に居要門とて、居りて取る形あり
書にては此一形のみなれば、能く心を潜めて見
れば珍らしからず、要門の形は誠に少をし、此
術に由
げるも

（第　四　圖）

然に投げらる〻理窟なり、弱き者も強き者を投
圖の替りに能く目を着くべし、斯くなれば、自
右へ投げ付けるなり、此形も餘程込入りたり、
張り、偕て第九圖のごとく、開と掛聲をかけて
に戴せ、左膝を突き、右膝を立て〻其足を踏ん
より使人は、第八圖のごとく受人の帯を左の肩

Fourth Illustration

The movement continues in the seventh illustration. Next, your right hand seizes the Opponent's Eri, or collar, from behind and your left hand grips his Obi, or Belt.

The next movement is shown in the eighth illustration. You load his Obi onto your left shoulder drop onto your left knee. Focus your balance on your right knee which is kept upright.

Then, as the ninth drawing illustrates, with a Kake-goe of "Ah!" you throw the Opponent down to your right in a Nage-Tsuke 投げ 付け, or Throw Down Hard.

This Kata is fairly complicated all around with many different elements crammed in. The progression of the illustrations should be observed carefully and with attention. If this is done, you will be able to throw the opponent quite naturally. Since you are using Jujutsu, it is a wholly unremarkable feat that a weaker opponent can throw a stronger one.

Kata that come under the heading of Yoh Mon, are rather scarce. Indeed, in this document only a single Yoh Mon technique will be presented. Every aspect of it should be thoroughly taken to heart.

The next technique will be a seated one called Ii Yoh Mon. It has some similarities to this Yoh Mon technique.

り、開と聲かけて、受人を右へ投げ付けるなり。
左の膝を突き、右の膝を立てゝ、其足を踏んば
第八圖のごとく、受人の帯を左の肩へ載せ、
足を踏みかへ、又た第七圖のごとく、右の手に
の後ろへ移し、右の足を右へ、左の足を左へと
是れよりは、使人は第六圖のごとく、体を受人
右の足を、受人の右の足へ掛けれるところなり
居たる左の手にて、受人の頸を抑さい、同時に
手にて、受人の右平の脇を取り、同じ腕を取り
此第五圖は、前の第四圖に、肋を突きたる右の

Fifth Illustration

This fifth illustration picks up where the fourth illustration leaves off. Your right hand, which has just struck the ribs of the Opponent, now seizes his right elbow. Your left hand releases the forearm of that same right arm and then takes a firm hold of where the neck of the Opponent meets his shoulder. At the same time step forward with your right leg and place it against the right leg of the Opponent.

From this point you move as depicted in the sixth illustration, slipping your body behind the Opponent's. You next step with your left leg switching your legs so that you end up with your left leg on your left and right leg on your right.

What follows is as shown in the seventh illustration. Your right hand takes hold of the Opponent's Eri, or Collar, while your left grabs his Obi, or Belt.

The next movement is shown in the eighth illustration where you load the Opponent's Obi onto your left shoulder. Plant your left knee on the ground while keeping your right knee upright. Keeping your balance on your right leg, throw the Opponent with a Nage-Tsuke, Throw Down Hard. You should shout a Kake-goe of "Ah!" as you do this.

り目に、能く目を認むべし、此こと肝要なり。
取初めより投げまで、變化の處々、即ち圖の變
示す、此一形は、中々手の込入れたる取方なり、
右へ投げけるなり、投げられたる所は、第九圖に
を突き、右の膝を立て、其足を蹈んばり夫より
圖のごとく、受人の帶を左の肩に載せ、左の膝
頸に掛け、左の手を受人の帶に掛け、次に第八
是れよりは、第七圖のごとく、右の手を受人の

（第　六　圖）

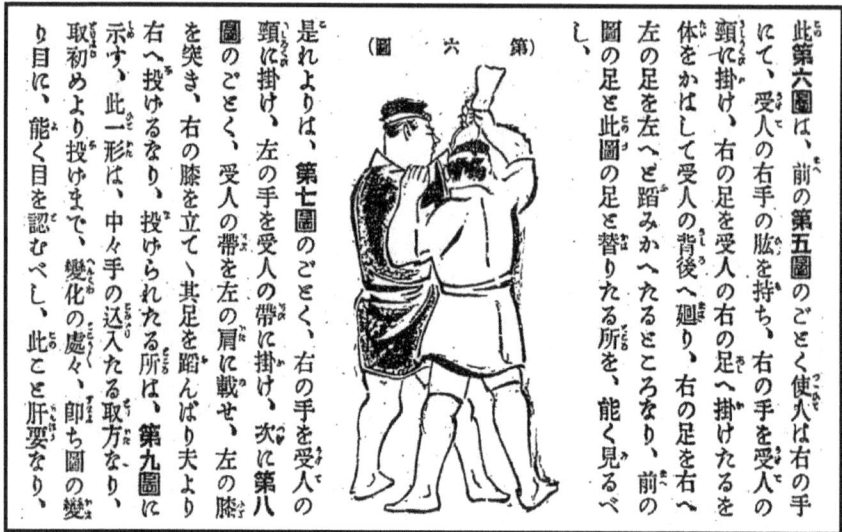

し、
圖の足と此圖の足と替りたる所を、能く見る
左の足を左へど蹈みかへたるところなり、前の
体をかはして受人の背後へ廻り、右の足を右へ
頸に掛け、右の足を受人の右の足へ掛けたるを
にて、受人の右手の肱を持ち、右の手を受人の
此第六圖は、前の第五圖のごとく使人は右の手

Sixth Illustration

The movement in the sixth illustration follows what happened in the fifth illustration.

You seize the Opponent's right elbow while your left hand goes to where the neck meets the shoulder. Step forward with your right foot and place it against his right leg. This is the set-up for moving behind the Opponent. The illustration above shows your positioning after you move behind him. Great care should be taken when noting the difference between the way in which the legs are positioned in the previous illustration versus how they are placed now.

The next movement is shown in the seventh illustration. Your right hand seizes the collar at the back of the Opponent's neck, while your left hand reaches down to grab his belt.

The technique proceeds in the following eighth illustration. Load the Opponent's Obi onto your left shoulder and plant your left knee is planted on the ground. Keep your right knee upright and focus your balance there. Next, you will throw to the right. The throw is shown in the ninth illustration.

This technique is very involved since it has a surprising number of small steps layered atop one another. You should carefully note how the hands and body move from one illustration to the next. This is the essential point.

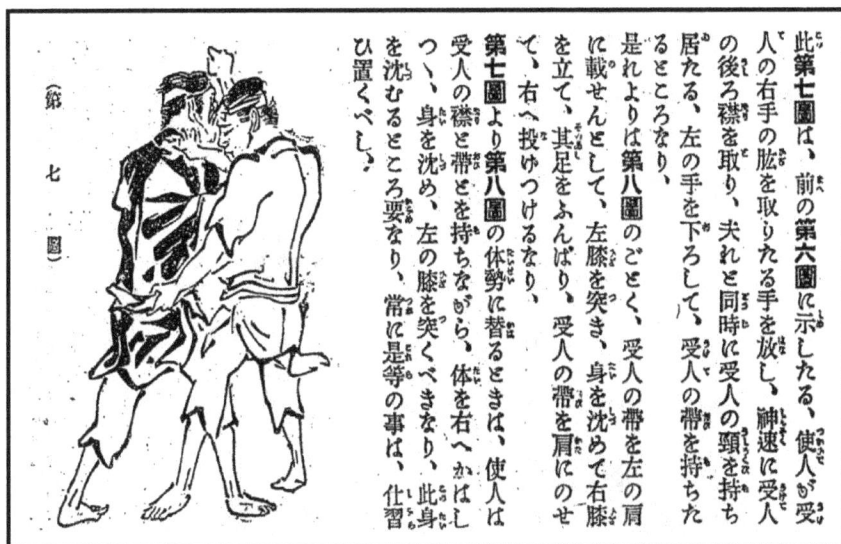

此第七圖は、前の第六圖に示したる、使人が受人の右手の肱を取りたる手を放し、神速に受人の後ろ襟を取り、夫れと同時に受人の頸を持ち居たる、左の手を下ろして、受人の帯を持ちたるところなり、

是れよりは第八圖のごとく、受人の帯を左の肩に載せんとして、左膝を突き、身を沈めて右膝を立て、其足をふんばり、受人の帯を肩にのせて、右へ投げつけるなり、

第七圖より第八圖の体勢に替るときは、使人は受人の襟と帯とを持ちながら、体を右へかはしつ、身を沈め、左の膝を突くべきなり、此身を沈むるところ要なり、常に是等の事は、仕習ひ置くべし。

（第七圖）

Seventh Illustration

The movement in the sixth illustration continues in the seventh above. You release the Opponent's right elbow and seize the back of the Opponent's collar with your right-hand using Shin-soku, Divine Swiftness. At the same time, your left hand drops from where it is holding the neck down to the belt.

The next movement is shown in the eighth illustration. In order to load the Opponent onto your shoulder with his belt, allow your body to sink down and plant your left knee on the ground. Keep your right knee up and focus your balance there. Lift the Opponent's Obi onto your shoulder and throw him to your right.

There are two major changes in Tai-sei 体勢, or Body Positioning, that occur from the seventh illustration to the eight illustration. The first is that your body, and thereby his mass, sinks down as you plant your left knee on the ground.

The second is how you twist your body to the right while keeping a grip on the Opponent's collar and belt. This sinking of the body is a Kaname 要, or Fundamental, of Jujutsu.

These points should all be trained extensively.

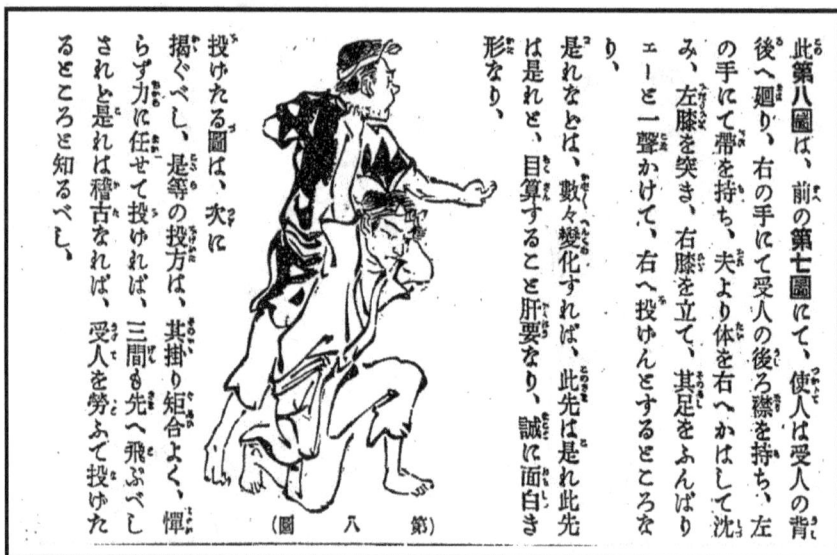

此第八圖は、前の第七圖にて、使人は受人の背
後へ廻り、右の手にて受人の後ろ襟を持ち、左
の手にて帯を持ち、夫より体を右へかはして沈
み、左膝を突き、右膝を立て、其足をふんばり
エーと一撃かけて、右へ投けんとするところを
り、
是れなとは、数々変化すれば、此先は是れ此先
は是れと、目算することに肝要なり、誠に面白き
形なり、

投けたる図は、次に
揚ぐべし、是等の投方は、其掛り矩合よく、憚
らず力に任せて投ければ、三間も先へ飛ぶべし
されと是れば稽古なれば、受人を労ふて投けた
るところと知るべし、

Eighth Illustration

The movements in the eight illustration continue from where seventh illustration leaves off.

You have rotated around behind the Opponent. Your right hand holds of the back of the Opponent's collar, while your left hand takes hold of his belt. Next, rotate your body to the right and sink down. Plant your left knee on the ground while keeping your right knee upright. Your balance should be centered on your right leg. With a single shout of "Eh!" you throw him down to your right.

There are a multitude of transitions in this technique. You should think, "After *this* comes *that*. Following *that* is *this*."

Developing a sense for what the next move will be is absolutely essential. This is a Kanyo 肝要, or Fundamental. This technique is extremely interesting all around.

The illustration depicting the throw will be presented next. If you set-up the Nage-kata, or method of throwing, as described in this book, and you do it without hesitation, the strength of this movement will cause the Opponent to fly nearly 3 Ken 間, or 5 meters. As this is clearly training, the Opponent is fully aware that he will be thrown.

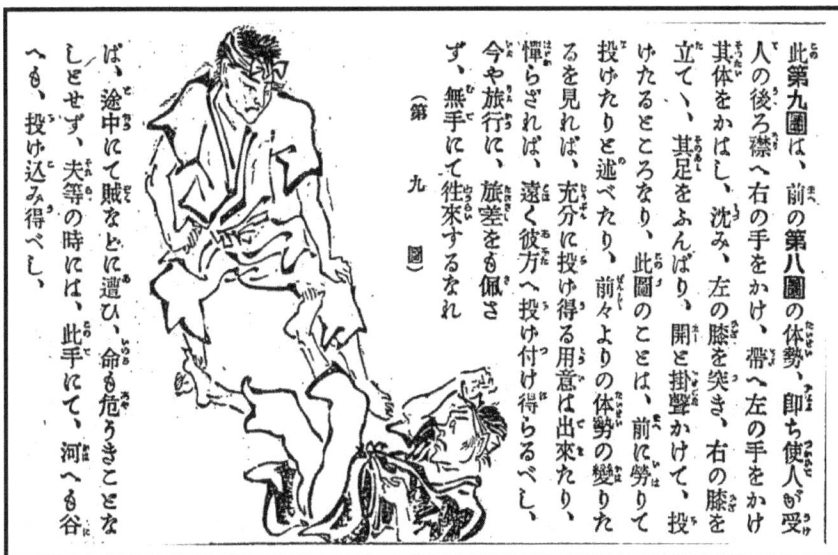

此第九圖は、前の第八圖の体勢、即ち使人が受
人の後ろ襟へ右の手をかけ、帯へ左の手をかけ
其体をかはし、沈み、左の膝を突き、右の膝を
立て、其足をふんばり、開と掛聲かけて、投
けたるところなり、此圖のことは、前に勞りて
投けたりと述べたり、前々よりの体勢の變りた
るを見れば、充分に投け得る用意は出來たり、
懼らされば、遠く彼方へ投け付け得らるべし、
今や旅行に、旅差をも佩さ
ず、無手にて徃來するなれ

（第九圖）

ば、途中にて賊などに遭ひ、命も危うきことな
しとせず、夫等の時には、此手にて、河へも谷
へも、投け込み得べし、

Ninth Illustration

The ninth illustration, above, follows the Taisei 体勢, or Body Positioning, from the previous eighth illustration.

You have gripped the Opponent's collar with your right hand while your left hand has hooked into the Opponent's belt. Twisting your body you sink onto your left knee keeping your right knee upright. Your balance should be focused on your right leg as you throw with a Kake-goe of "Ah!"

If we were to look at movements, starting from two illustrations back, it is plain that there has been sufficient preparation to make a proper throw. As long as there is no hesitation you could throw him all the way to where you are sitting now!

These days most people travel about unarmed, not even bothering to carry a Tabizashi 旅差, or "travel dagger" for protection. Should you be set upon by thieves, your life would not be in danger since you know Jujutsu. You would be able to, through these methods, throw them down into the river or valley.

Overview of Yoh Mon

1	2

3	4

5	6	7

8	9

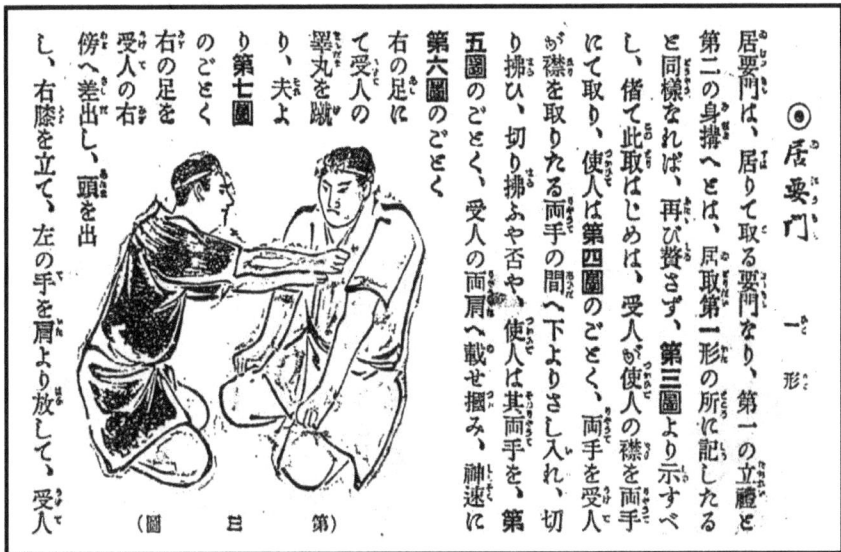

居要門は、居りて取る要門なり、第一の立體と
第二の身搆へとは、尻取第一形の所に記したる
と同樣なれば、再び贅さず、第三圖より示すべ
し、偖て此取はじめは、受人が使人の襟を両手
にて取り、使人は第四圖のごとく、両手を受人
が襟を取りたる両手の間へ下よりさし入れ、切
り拂ひ、切り拂ふや否や使人は其両手を、第
五圖のごとく、受人の両肩へ載せ摑み、神速に
第六圖のごとく
右の足にて受人の睾丸を蹴り、夫よ
り第七圖
のごとく
右の足を受人の右
傍へ差出し、頭を出
し、右膝を立て、左の手を肩より放して、受人

（第 三 圖）

◎居要門

一
形

Ii Yoh Mon Seated Fundamentals Technique
One Kata
<u>Third Illustration</u>

Ii Yoh Mon is the seated version of the previous technique. As the illustrations depicting the initial standing bow and the following starting position, are the same as in the first Kata they will not be included again. The Kata will be presented starting from the third illustration.

So then, this technique begins with the Opponent seizing your collar in a two handed grip. You respond as shown in the fourth illustration. Slip your hands up from below, between the Opponent's hands which are gripping your collar. Next, do a Kiri-Harai 切り拂い, or a sharp sweeping motion back and forth, then immediately after the Kiri-Harai, reach out and seize his shoulders. This is shown in the fifth illustration.

With Shin-soku, Divine Swiftness, kick the Opponent in Kinteki, the Golden Target, or the groin. This is shown in the sixth illustration.

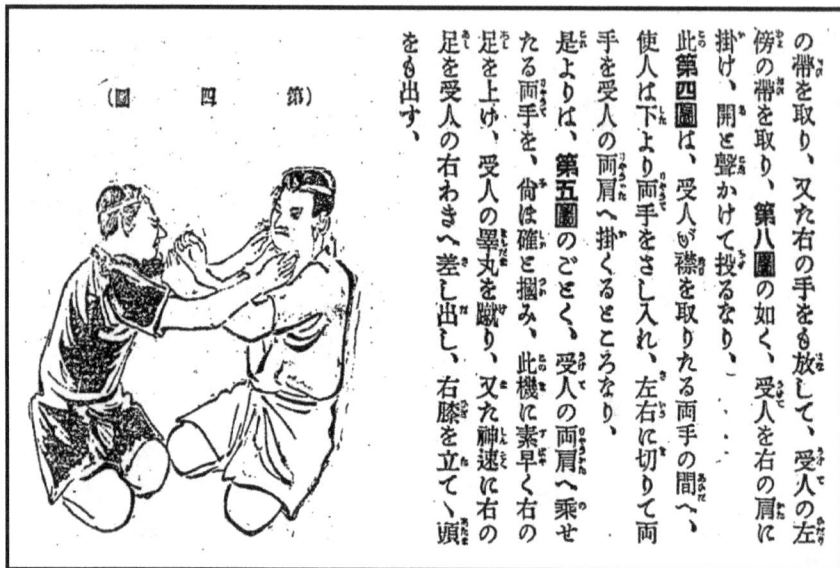

の帯を取り、又た右の手をも放して、受人の左
傍の帯を取り、第八圖の如く、受人を右の肩に
掛け、開と聲かけて投るなり、
此第四圖は、受人が襟を取りたる両手の間へ、
使人は下より両手をさし入れ、左右に切りて両
手を受人の両肩へ掛くるところなり、
是よりは、第五圖のごとく、受人の両肩へ乘せ
たる両手を、尚は確と掴み、此機に素早く右の
足を上げ、受人の睾丸を蹴り、又た神速に右の
足を受人の右わきへ差し出し、右膝を立て、頽
をも出す、

Fourth Illustration

After you kick to the Opponent's groin you plant your right foot beside his right leg. This is shown in the seventh illustration
Lean your head forward and down as you put your weight on your right foot. Release the Opponent's shoulder with your left hand and grab his belt on the right side. You then let go with the right hand and grab the Opponent's belt on his left side.

As can be seen in the eighth illustration, you load the Opponent onto your right shoulder and with a Kake-goe of "Ah!" you throw him.

The fourth illustration, above, shows how you slipped your hands up from below in between the Opponent's arms. You knock his hands off your collar with a Kiri-Harai 切り拂い, Cut and Sweep, attack. You then seize his shoulders.

Gripping his shoulders firmly, the next movement is shown in the fifth illustration. You are now set up for the kick and you shoot your right foot out to strike the Opponent's Kinteki, the Golden Target or groin. After the kick, you follow this up by placing that same right foot with Shin-soku, Divine Swiftness, against his right leg.

此第五圖は、前の第四圖のごとく、受人の両手
を切りはらひ、直ちに共両手を、受人の両肩へ
掛けたるを、確と摑みたるところなり、
是れよりは、使人は右の足を上げて受人の睾丸
を蹴り、右の足を受人の右の傍へさし出し、又
受人の帯を取り、續いて右の手にて左わきの帯
たる其處へ頭を出し、右の膝を立て、左の手にて
受人の帯を取り、夫より受人を右の肩にかけ、
をも取り、開と聲を
かけて投るなり、睾丸を蹴る所は、圖に出さね
ど、右の足を受人の右の傍へさし出したるは、

第六圖の
ごとく、
頭を出し
膝を立て
、、受人
の帯を取
りたる所
は、第七
圖のごとく、投た
る所は第八圖のごとし、

(第　五　圖)

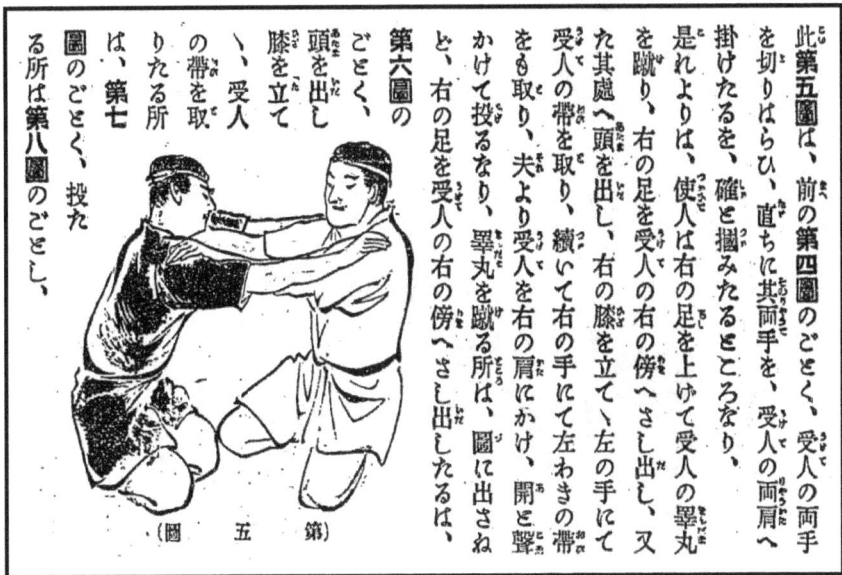

Fifth Illustration

The movement in this fifth illustration is a continuation of the movement from the fourth illustration. The Opponent's hands have been knocked away with the sweeping Kiri-Harai strike and, following that, they both firmly grip the shoulders of the Opponent. Next, you kick to Kinteki, the Golden Target.

After that, plant your right foot beside the Opponent's right leg. Shift your weight onto your right foot and lean your head forward. Your left hand slips down to grab the Opponent's belt. Following that, your right hand takes hold his belt on his left side.

Next, you load the Opponent onto your right shoulder and, with a Kake-goe of "Ah!" you throw him.

While an illustration depicting the kick to the groin will not be presented, the sixth illustration shows how your right foot should placed beside the Opponent's right leg.

The way your head leans forward, the way your weight is shifted onto your knee and your hands taking the Opponent's belt are all presented in the seventh illustration. The throw is shown in the eighth illustration.

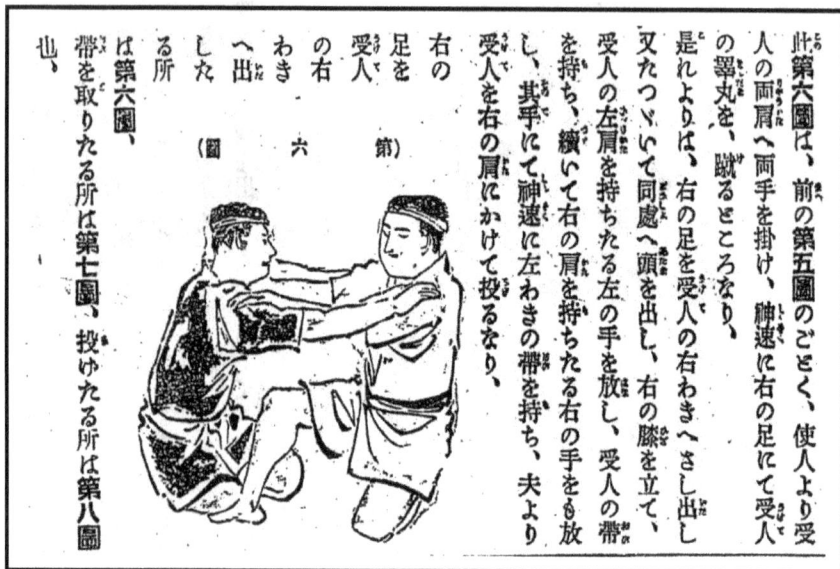

此第六圖は、前の第五圖のごとく、使人より受人の両肩へ両手を掛け、神速に右の足にて受人の翠丸を、蹴るところなり、是れよりは、右の足を受人の右わきへさし出し又たつゞいて同處へ頭を出し、右の膝を立て、受人の左肩を持ちたる左の手を放し、續いて右の肩を持ちたる右の手をも放し、其手にて神速に左わきの帯を持ち、夫より受人を右の肩にかけて投るなり、受人の足を受人の右のわきの右へ出したる所を第六圖、帯を取りたる所は第七圖、投げたる所は第八圖也。

(第 六 圖)

Sixth Illustration

This sixth illustration follows what occurred in the previous fifth illustration. You have seized the Opponent's shoulders, then with Shin-soku, Divine Swiftness, you kick him in Kinteki with your right foot. Next, you plant your right foot beside the Opponent's right leg.

Next, you lean your head forward you shift your weight onto your right knee. Your left hand, which has been holding the Opponent's right shoulder, releases to grab his Obi, or belt. After that your right hand, that has been gripping the Opponent's other shoulder, releases and he moves it with Shin-soku swiftness to the Obi on his left. From there, you lift the Opponent up onto your right shoulder and throw.

The way your right foot is positioned against the Opponent's right leg is depicted in this sixth illustration. The way you grab his Obi, or Belt, is shown in the seventh illustration. The throw is shown in the eighth illustration.

此第七圖は、使人が右の足を、受人の右わきへ
差し出し、續きて頭を出し、右膝を立て受人の
左の肩を持ちたる左の手を放し、其手にて受人
の帶を取り、又受人の右の肩を持ちたる手を放
し、其手にて受人の左わきの帶を取り、偖て受
人を右の肩にかけ、開と聲かけて投んとすると
ころなり、投げれる圖は此次に揭ぐ、
使人が右の足を受人の右わきへ出し、又つゞい
て頭を出し、膝を立て、肩を持ちたる手を放し
素早く帶を取り、又た左わきの帶を取り、右の
肩へ掛くるまで、神速にせずばあらず、此神速
にすることは、神速にせずばあらず、此神速
度々取りて

(第 七 圖)

熟練するなり、

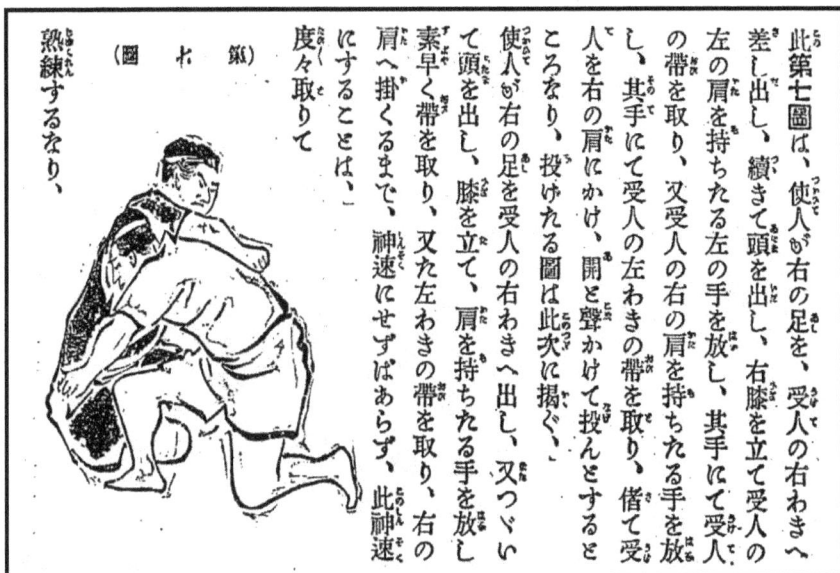

Seventh Illustration

The seventh illustrations shows how you have placed your right foot beside the Opponent's right leg. Next, you lean your head forward and shift your weight onto your right foot. Your left hand, which has been holding onto his right shoulder, releases and slips down to the belt. After that your right hand that is holding the Opponent's left shoulder lets go and seizes his belt on his left side.

Following this, load the Opponent onto your right shoulder and with a shout of "Ah!" throw him. The drawing that shows this throw will be presented next.

Your right foot goes up against the Opponent's right leg. The next step in this technique is to lean your head forward and shift your body weight onto your right foot. One hand holding the shoulder releases and rapidly grabs the Obi. Next the other hand takes the Obi on the left side and the Opponent is loaded up onto your right shoulder.

None what has been described can be done without Shin-soku, Divine Speed. Achieving this level of speed is a gradual process that requires Jukuren 熟練, a long period of extensive training.

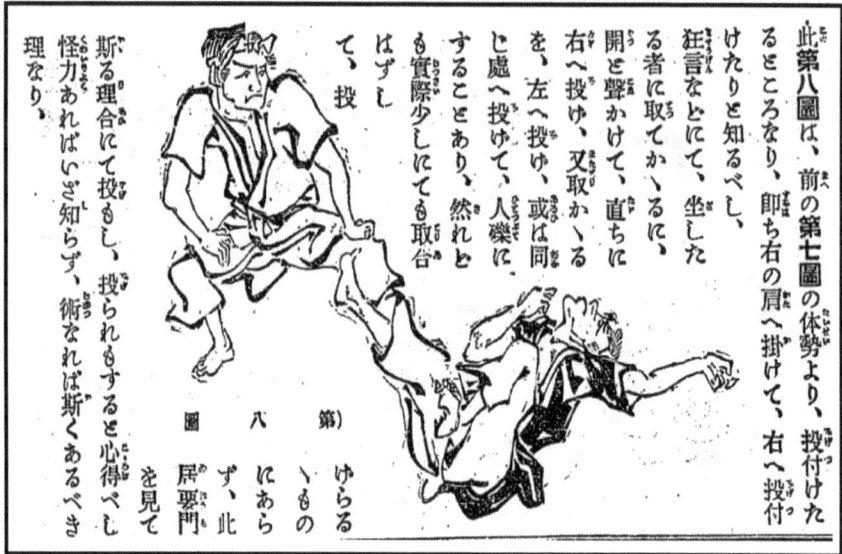

此第八圖は、前の第七圖の体勢より、投付けた
るところなり、即ち右の肩へ掛けて、右へ投付
けたりと知るべし、
狂言などして、坐した
る者に取てかゝるに、
開と聲かけて、直ちに
右へ投げ、又取かゝる
を、左へ投げ、或は同
じ處へ投げて、人樂に
することあり、然れと
も實際少しにても取合
はずし
て、投
　　　　　けらる
　　　　　ゝもの
　　　　　にあら
　　　　　ず、此
　　　　　居要門
　　　　　を見て
斯る理合にて投もし、投られもすると心得べし
怪力あればいざ知らず、術なれば斯くあるべき
理なり、

（第 八 圖）

Eighth Illustration

The Taisei, or body positioning, shown in this eighth illustration follows the movement shown in the seventh illustration.   The drawing above shows the situation after you completed the throw. In other words, the position after the opponent has been loaded up onto your right shoulder and hurled to the right.

The whole scene is like a person enthralled during a Kyogen 狂言, a comical play performed in the intermissions of the more serious Noh plays. When the performers shout "Ah!" he is thrown to the right. When caught up in the story again he is thrown to the left. Or, maybe, he is thrown back from whence he came. Flicked around like a human pebble!

In the end, however, you must understand that being just a little bit off in your movement will mean not being able to achieve a throw. In this Ii Yoh Mon technique the principle itself has been thrown at you. To become able to throw you must absorb this knowledge.
As the saying goes,

Thinking ferocious strength will lead to victory is an error, but if you are using Jutsu (technique) you must understand the underlying principles.

Overview of Ii Yoh Mon

1	2
3	**4**
5	**6**
7	**8**

離れ形は、立ちて離れて取るなり、第一の立體
は、立合第一形の處に記したると同じ、故に省
く、偕て近よりて取はじむるは、左の第二圖の
ごとく、受人より使人の襟を、両手にて取り、
三足押すを、使人は三足引きて抗め、夫より使

人は第三圖のごとく、受人
がゑりを取りたる両手の間へ、掌を伏せて両手
を上より逆にさし入れ、受人の両腕首を取りて
クレリと獪し上げ、第四圖のごとく、拇をかけ
て痛め、神速に左の足にて、睪丸を蹴り、夫よ
り第五圖のごとく、手を上ゲなゞら、左の足を

(第 二 圖)

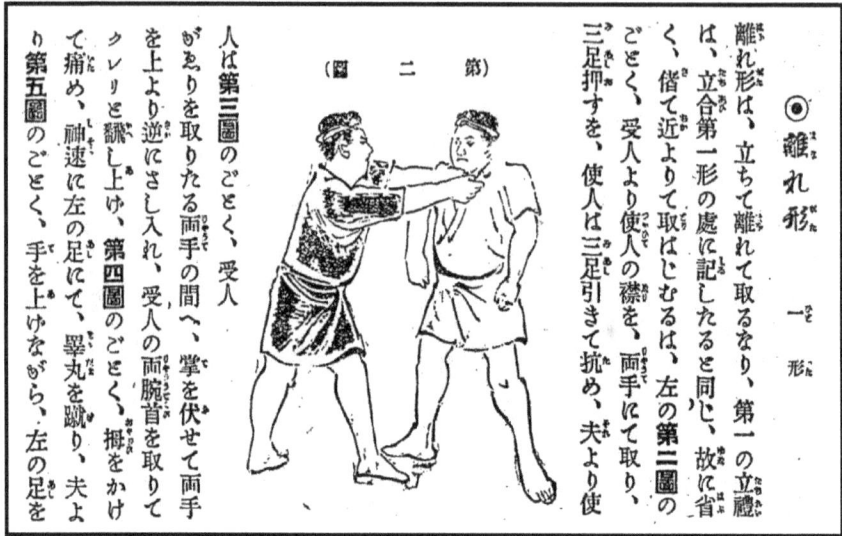

◎ Hanare Gata Standing Apart Techniques
One Kata
Second Illustration

Hanare Gata 離れ形 describes a technique that begins with an attack by one standing opponent against another. The initial standing Rei was shown in the first Tachi-ai technique and therefore it will not be repeated.

So then, this bout begins as shown in the second illustration above. The attack beings with the Opponent grabbing hold of your collar with both hands. Pushing forward the Opponent forces you back three steps, and you drop back three steps.

From there you respond as shown in the third illustration. You places the palms of both hands on top his wrists, which are holding your collar. Pushing down and in from above you forces both of the Opponent's wrist off and with a Kureri クレリ, smooth rotating sound, you twists them up into the air.

As the fourth illustration shows, both Oya-yubi 拇, or Thumbs, are used to apply painful pressure. [73] With Shin-soku, Divine Swiftness, you kick him in Kinteki, the Golden Target, or groin.

---

[73] The Kanji for Oya-yubi contains the elements "hand + mother."

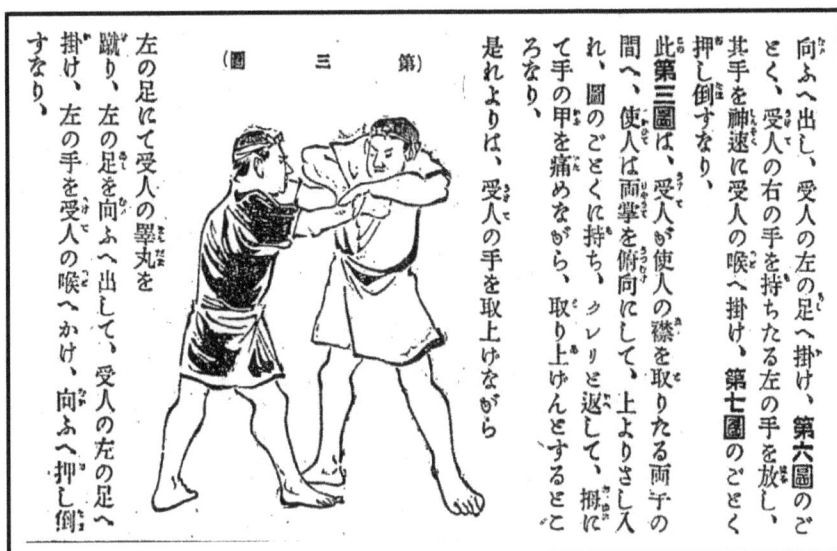

（第 三 圖）

向ふへ出し、受人の左の足へ掛け、第六圖のごとく、受人の右の手を持ちたる左の手を放し、其手を神速に受人の喉へ掛け、第七圖のごとく押し倒すなり、

此第三圖は、受人が使人の襟を取りたる両手の間へ、使人は両掌を俯向にして、上よりさし入れ、圖のごとくに持ち、クレリと返して、捌にて手の甲を痛めながら、取り上げんとするところなり、

是れよりは、受人の手を取上げながら

左の足にて受人の睪丸を蹴り、左の足を向ふへ出して、受人の左の足へ掛け、左の手を受人の喉へかけ、向ふへ押し倒すなり、

Third Illustration

The technique continues in the fifth illustration.

After raising both hands, step forward with your left leg and plant it against the Opponent's left leg. Next, release your grip on the Opponent's right hand, and with Shin-soku, Divine Swiftness seize his Nodo 喉, or Windpipe, with your left hand. The sixth illustration shows the Oshi-taoshi 押し倒し, or Push Down[74].

The third illustration above shows how you reach up and place your palms face down between the Opponent's arms. Grip as shown above. Next you twist his hands up and out with a smooth Kureri sound. Both Oya-yubi, or Thumbs, should press painfully into the back of the palms as you bring his hands up.

As soon as you bring his hands up, kick the Opponent in Kinteki, the Golden Target, or groin, with your left foot. After kicking, plant your left leg against his left leg. Seize the Opponent's throat with your left hand. Then force him violently down with an Oshi-taoshi, Push Down.

---

[74] The passage says "seventh illustration," but the last drawing is the 6th and the book does not appear to have a missing page.

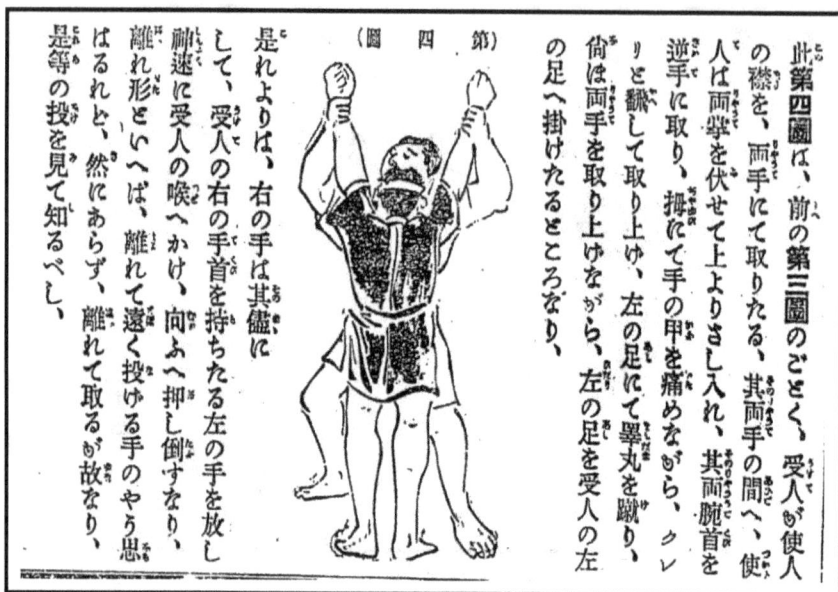

（第　四　圖）

此第四圖は、前の第三圖のごとく、受人が使人の襟を、兩手にて取りたる、其兩手の間へ、使人は兩拳を伏せて上よりさし入れ、其兩腕首を逆手に取り、拇にて手の甲を痛めながら、クレリと飜して取り上げ、左の足にて睾丸を蹴り、尚は兩手を取り上げながら、左の足を受人の左の足へ掛けたるところなり、是れよりは、右の手は其儘にして、受人の右の手首を持ちたる左の手を放し神速に受人の喉へかけ、向ふへ押し倒すなり、離れ形といへば、離れて遠く投げる手のやう思はるれど、然にあらず、離れて取るが故なり、是等の投を見て知るべし、

Fourth Illustration

The movement in this fourth illustration follows the third illustration. The Opponent grabs your collar with both hands. You respond by raising your hands and placing your palms against his wrists, pushing in between his hands. Then, seize both hands in a Gyaku-te, or Reverse Joint Lock. Your Oya-yubi 拇指, or Thumbs, should be pressing painfully into the back of his hands as you rotate his wrists out and up in a one smooth motion. You then kick with your left foot to Kinteki, the Golden Target, groin.

Next, while keeping both his hands up in the air, plant your left leg against the Opponent's left leg. Then, while keeping your grip with your right hand, release your left hand and seize the Opponent's windpipe with Shin-soku, Divine Swiftness. You then shove the Opponent down violently with an Oshi-taoshi, Push Down.

This is an Hanare-kata, a technique where the combatants are standing apart. Thinking of this as a method to throw someone a great distance would be a mistake. It is a technique that begins with someone attempting to take hold of you. All parts of this technique should be viewed carefully.

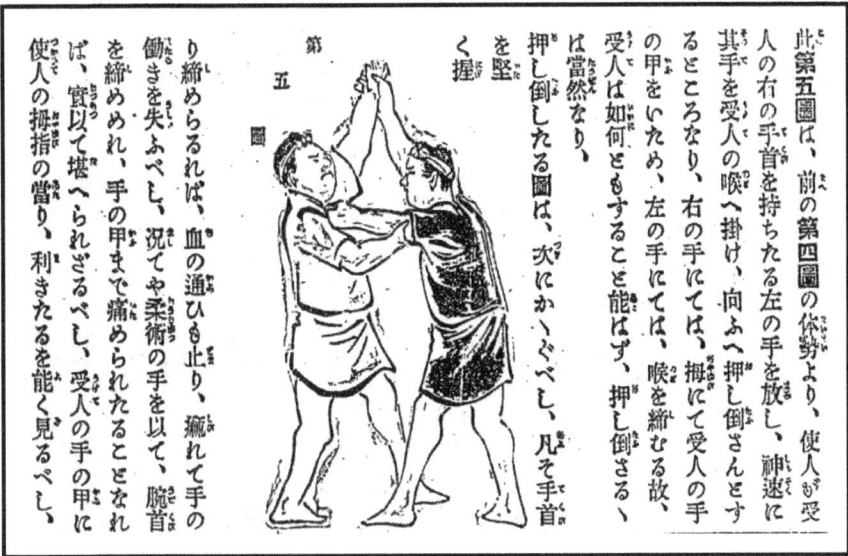

此第五圖は、前の第四圖の體勢より、使人が受人の右の手首を持ちたる左の手を放し、神速に其手を受人の喉へ掛け、向ふへ押し倒さんとするところなり、右の手にては、搦にて受人の手の甲をいため、左の手にては、喉を締むる故、受人は如何ともすること能はず、押し倒さるは當然なり。

押し倒したる圖は、次にかへぐべし、凡そ手首を堅く握り締められば、血の通ひも止り、癲れて手の働きを失ふべし、況てや柔術の手を以て、腕首を締めれば、手の甲まで痛められたることなれば、實以て堪へられざるべし、受人の手の甲に使人の拇指の當り、利きたるを能く見るべし。

Fifth Illustration

The Taisei, or Body Positioning, in the fifth illustration follows the fourth illustration.[75]

Release your grip on the Opponent's right wrist with your left hand and seize his windpipe with Shin-soku, Divine Swiftness. From there you shove him down onto his back with an Oshi-taoshi, Push Down.

The use your right Oya-yubi, or Thumb, to press into the back of the Opponent's hand. Thus, as your left hand is squeezing the Opponent's throat, he is completely unable to do anything. You will have no trouble shoving him down on his back from this position.

You can see how the take-down is done by looking at the illustration on the following page. If you grip his wrist with enough strength, blood will cease to flow to it, rendering it numb and useless. If you seize his elbow in the same way and it would cause pain all the way down to the back of the hand. It would be so painful, your Opponent would not be able to endure it. Be sure to carefully observe how you press your thumb into the backs of his hands.

---

[75] Both the 5th & 6th images were printed backwards. I have corrected them. This illustration has you in a black shirt instead of a white.

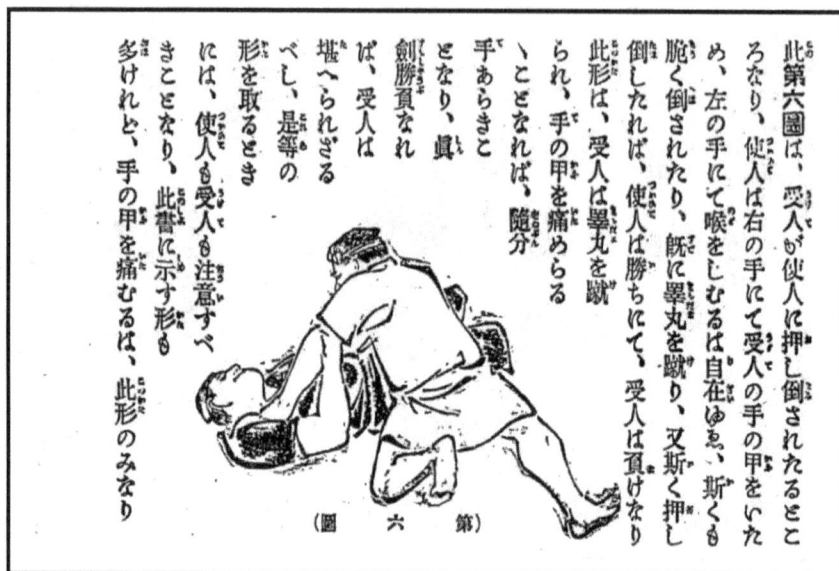

此第六圖は、受人が使人に押し倒されたるとろなり、使人は右の手にて受人の手の甲をいため、左の手にて喉をしむるは自在ゆゑ、斯くも脆く倒されたり、既に睾丸を蹴り、又斯く押し倒したれば、使人は勝ちにて、受人は頂けなり此形は、受人は睾丸を蹴られ、手の甲を痛めらゝことなれば、随分手あらきことゝなり、眞剣勝負なれば、受人は堪へられざるべし、是等の形を取るときには、使人も受人も注意すべきことゝなり、此書に示す形も多けれど、手の甲を痛むるは、此形のみなり

(第　六　圖)

Sixth Illustration

This sixth illustration shows your position after you have thrown the Opponent. Your right hand is applying painful pressure to the back of the Opponent's hand. At the same time, your left hand is squeezing off his windpipe. Therefore you have complete control and freedom of action. Even if your throw is not particularly hard, recall that you kicked him in Kinteki, the Golden Target. In conclusion, since he has been toppled, you are the winner and the Opponent has lost.

In this Kata, as the Opponent is kicked in Kinteki, the Golden Target, or groin, and painful pressure is applied to the back of his hand, this is a very rough technique indeed.

In the event this was Shinken Shobu 真剣勝負, or a Real Fight, the Opponent would be wholly unable to bear such agony. When conducting training in this Kata, both you as well as the Opponent should exercise caution.

Though many techniques are presented in this document, this is the sole one to contain the application of painful pressure to the back of the hand.

Overview of the Hanare Gata

1	2
3	4
5	6

骨法は、捕縛の所爲なり、これも柔術の中にて立ちて取る、第一の双方離れて立つは、立合第一形の處に記したると同じ、故に第一圖を省き第二圖、即ち近よりて取はじむる所より記すべし、其取はじめは、左の第二圖のごとく、使人より受人の右手首を、左の手にて取り上げ、使人は第三圖のごとく、右の足を受人の右の足に附け右手に持ちたる十手にて肩、二の腕、腕首を、圖のごとく一、二、三と打ち、夫より使人は、第四圖のごとく、左の手にて、受人の右の手首

◎骨法　第一形

第二圖

Koppo Bone Manipulation
First Kata
<u>Second Illustration</u>

Koppo 骨法, or Bone Manipulation, is the science of restraining people. The two Kanji that form the word literally stand for *the bones of the body* 骨 combined with *rule* 法.

When doing Koppo techniques, they begin the same way as standing Jujutsu techniques do. Both combatants begin standing apart. Since this initial stage where the combatants stand apart before beginning is the same as in the first Tachi-ai technique, the first illustration will be abbreviated. The technique will begin from the second illustration with both opponents drawing close and engaging.

The first attack is shown in the second illustration above. You seize the Opponent's right wrist with your left hand and raise it up. Next, as shown in the third illustration, step forward with your right foot and place your leg against his right leg. Use the Jutte 十手, or Truncheon, in your right hand to strike in quick succession to Kata 肩, the Shoulder, Ni-no Ude 二の腕, the Forearm and Ude-kubi 腕首, or the wrist. This is a quick a one, two, three action. This is shown in the illustration.

Translator's note

The techniques in this volume utilize the Jutte (also pronounced Jitte), a short shaft of metal with an "L" shaped hook to capture swords or parts of the body i.e. the wrist. Sword breakers were common weapons in all nations. They emerged in Japan in the Muromachi Era in the 14th C. Later in the Edo Era a variation of the Hana-neji, or short rod used to pull cattle (and criminals) around by the nose, came into use. Koppo/Jujutsu techniques using the shorter Jutte likely emerged in this time period. It became the de-facto weapon of non-samurai officials. It even miniaturized into a decorative symbol of authority wielded by police, firefighters, official inspectors and community leaders. As there is no Kagi 鉤, or hook, at the base of the Jutte shown in this volume a simplified Hana-neji truncheon is what seems to be employed in these techniques.

The photograph on this page shows some of the variety of shape and size apparent in Edo through Meiji Era Jutte. The Jutte courtesy of the Nathan Wood collection.

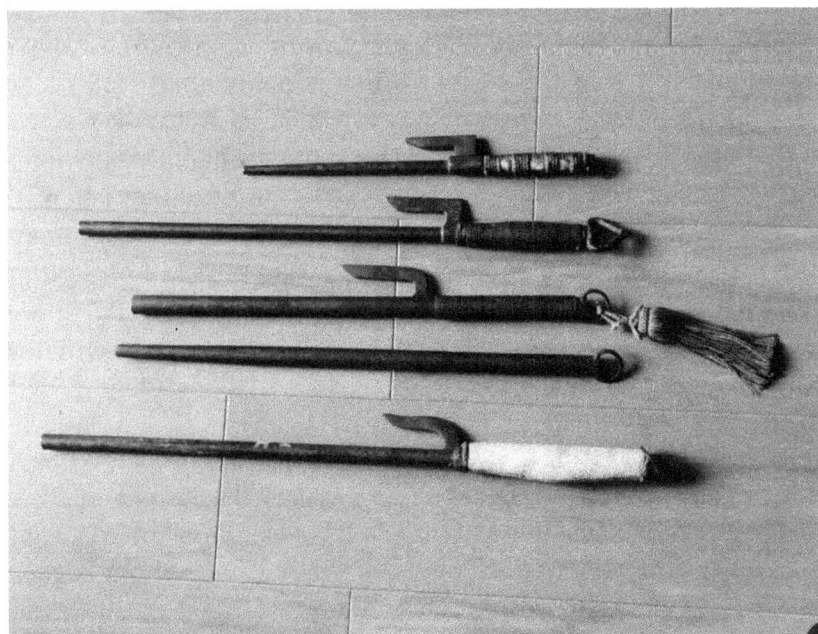

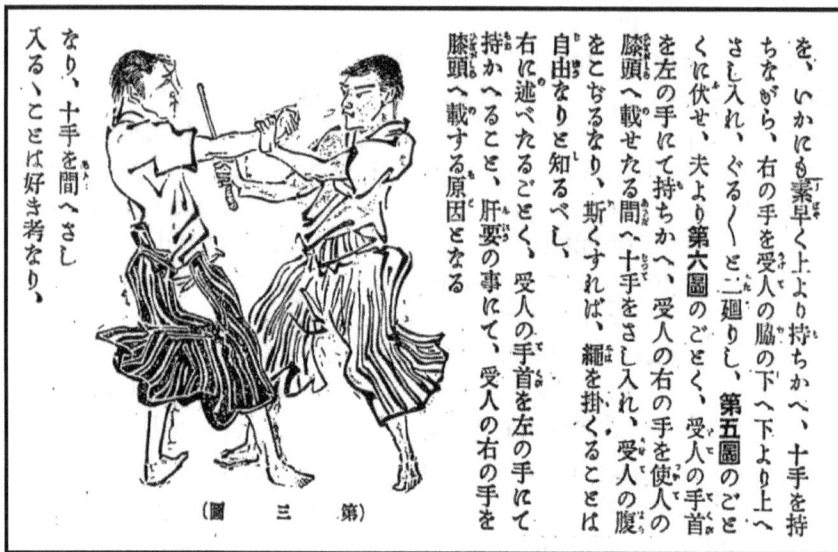

なり、十手を間へさし
入ることは好き考なり、

を、いかにも素早く上より持ちかへ、十手を持
ちながら、右の手を受人の脇の下へ下より上へ
さし入れ、ぐるぐると二廻りし、**第五圖**のごと
くに伏せ、夫より**第六圖**のごとく、受人の手首
を左の手にて持ちかへ、受人の右の手を使人の
膝頭へ載せたる間へ、十手をさし入れ、受人の腹
をこぢるなり、斯くすれば、繩を掛くることは
自由なりと知るべし。
右に逑べたるごとく、受人の手首を左の手にて
持かへること、肝要の事にて、受人の右の手を
膝頭へ載する原因となる

(第 三 圖)

Third Illustration

Your next move is shown in the fourth illustration on the following page. The hand holding the Opponent's right wrist reverses its grip in a flash from below to a grip from above. Meanwhile slip your right hand, which is holding the Jutte, under the Opponent's right armpit. Wrap your arm around his with a Guru-guru ぐるぐる, or sound of something smoothly entwining. Then, take the Opponent down as shown in the fifth illustration.

After that, reverse your grip with your left hand so you hold his right wrist the other way. This is shown in the sixth illustration. You then pull his right wrist against your kneecap. The Jutte is threaded in the space under his right arm and into his midsection. If done properly it is clear you will be in complete control and able to secure your Opponent with rope.

As was described above, the point where your left hand switches its grip on the Opponent's wrist is the Kanyo 肝要, or Fundamental Point, of this technique. It is also important to keep in mind that the bracing of the Opponent's right hand on your kneecap serves as the set up for inserting the Jutte.

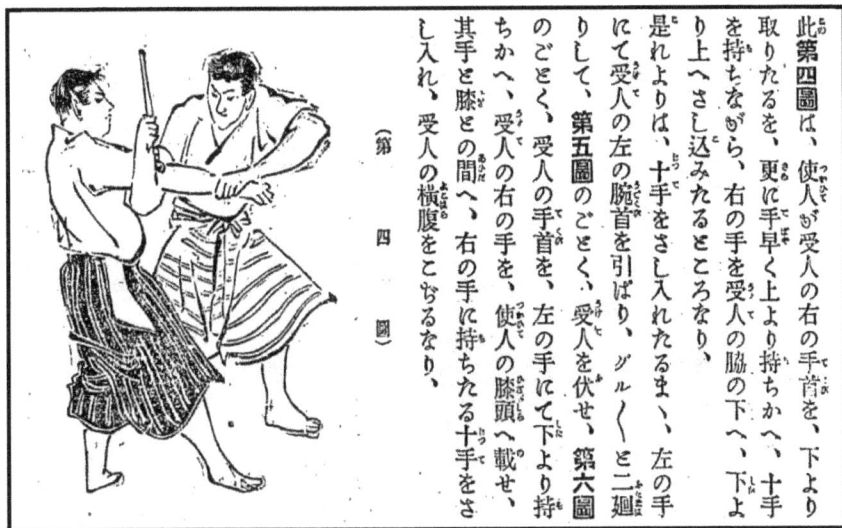

此第四圖は、使人が受人の右の手首を、下より
取りたるを、更に手早く上より持ちかへ、十手
を持ちながら、右の手を受人の脇の下へ、下よ
り上へさし込みたるところなり、
是れよりは、十手をさし入れたるまゝ、左の手
にて受人の左の腕首を引ばり、グルグルと二廻
りして、第五圖のごとく、受人を伏せ、第六圖
のごとく、受人の手首を、左の手にて下より持
ちかへ、受人の右の手を、使人の膝頭へ載せ、
其手と膝との間へ、右の手に持ちたる十手をさ
し入れ、受人の横腹をこぢるなり、

（第　四　圖）

Fourth Illustration

This fourth illustration shows your position after you have switched your left hand on the Opponent's right wrist from a grip from below to a grip from above. This should be done in a rapid movement. Your right hand, which is holding the Jutte, slips under the Opponent's armpit and scoops up.

With the Jutte threaded under his arm, pull the Opponent's right wrist with your left hand. Wrap your right arm holding the Jutte around his arm with a Guru-guru ぐるぐる entwining sound. You next pull the Opponent down as shown in the fifth illustration.

The illustration above shows how you have switched your grip on the Opponent's right wrist from under to over. After you pull him down rest the Opponent's right hand on your kneecap. Finally, slip your Jutte in between his right arm and your knee and into his midsection.

を、中てずに斯くするなり、　し、されど、罪の定らざる者を捕縛することゆ　右の脇腹をこぢることは、肋三枚を中てる帆近　十手をさし入れ、受人の脇腹をこぢるなり、　の間へ、右の手に持ちたる　膝の上へ載せ、其手と膝と　の右の手を、使人の　より持ちかへ、受人

（第五圖）

首を、左の手にて下　是れよりは受人の手　と二廻りして八受人を伏せざるところなり、　し入れ、其左の手首を引ばりながら、グルグル　手を持ちながら、受人の脇の下へ下より上へ差　の左の手首を、左の手にて取り、右の手にて十　此第五圖は、前の第四圖のごとく、使人が受人

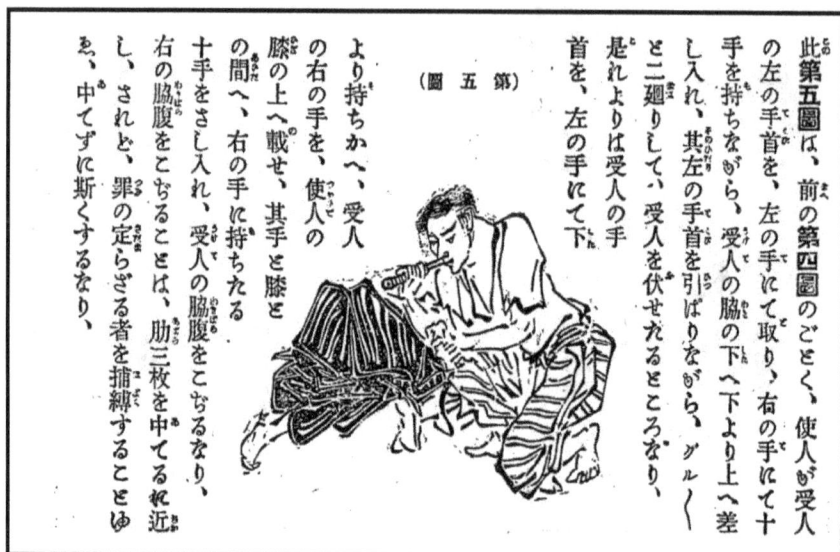

Fifth Illustration

This fifth illustration follows what occurred in the fourth illustration. You hold the Opponent's right wrist with your left hand. Your right hand, which is holding the Jutte, slips under the Opponent's armpit. With the left hand pulling on the Opponent's right wrist the hand holding the Jutte encircles back upon itself with a Guru-guru ぐるぐる wrapping sound. The Opponent is then pulled to the ground.

The fourth illustration shows your left hand, which is holding the Opponent's wrist, switches its grip so that it is holding not from below, but from above.

After you take him down pull that wrist onto your kneecap. Slip the Jutte, held in your right hand, in the space between his right arm and your knee. Then press into the side of the Opponent's stomach.

Though you are forcing the Jutte into the right side of his stomach, you are not pressing into the vital point Abara San Mai 肋三枚, or the third rib from the top. The reason is because this person has not yet been determined to be a criminal, thus that spot should be avoided.

此第六圖は、前の第五圖のごとく、グルヽ廻
して、伏せるや否や、受人の手首を、左の手に
て下より持ちかへ、受人の右の手を、已れが膝
へのせ、其受人の右の手を、自分の膝との間へ
右の手に持ちたる十手をさし入れ、受人の脇腹
を、こぢたるところなり、是れにて使人は勝ち
受人は負けなり、此使人を捕吏とし、受人を罪
人とすれば、斯くせし上は縄をかくること容易
なり、

骨法は首尾よく、捕縛
するが主意なれば、

同じ柔術のうちにも、
勞はる所あり、

（第 六 圖）

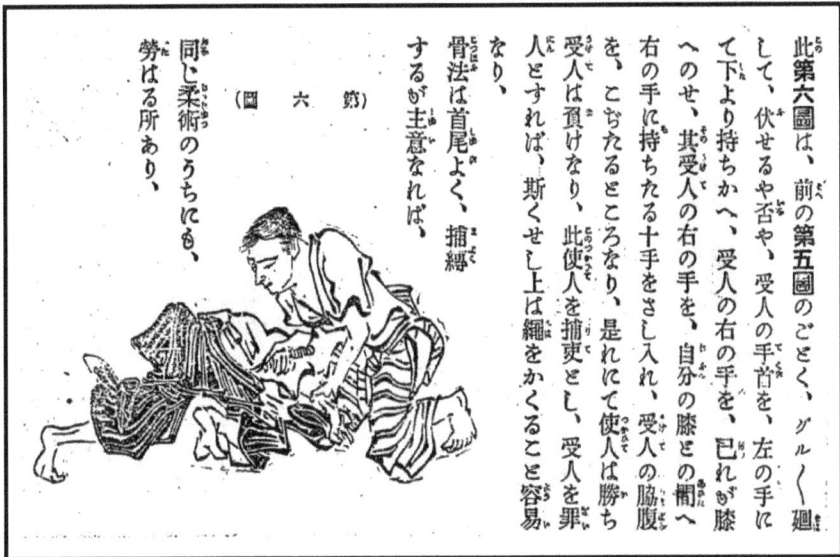

Sixth Illustration

The sixth illustration shows your positioning after you have wrapped up the Opponent's right arm with your Jutte in a Guru-guru wrapping sound and pulled him down. This was shown in the fifth illustration.

The set-up for this was done before when you switched the way your left hand gripped the Opponent. Your hand switches from an under-grip to an over-grip. After you pull him down you place his right hand onto your kneecap. The Jutte, held in your right hand, is then slipped in between that hand and your right knee to dig into the Opponent's midsection.

Thus you have won and the Opponent has lost. If you were the Torei-te 捕り手, or the official, and the Opponent the criminal, then the latter could easily be tied up.

The Koppo 骨法 technique shown here is completely effective in response to this kind of attack. The principals are clear from stem to stern. The main guiding principle here is to restrain the opponent. If you pay attention, you can find the same techniques within Jujutsu.

Overview of Koppo First Kata

1	2

3	4

5

6

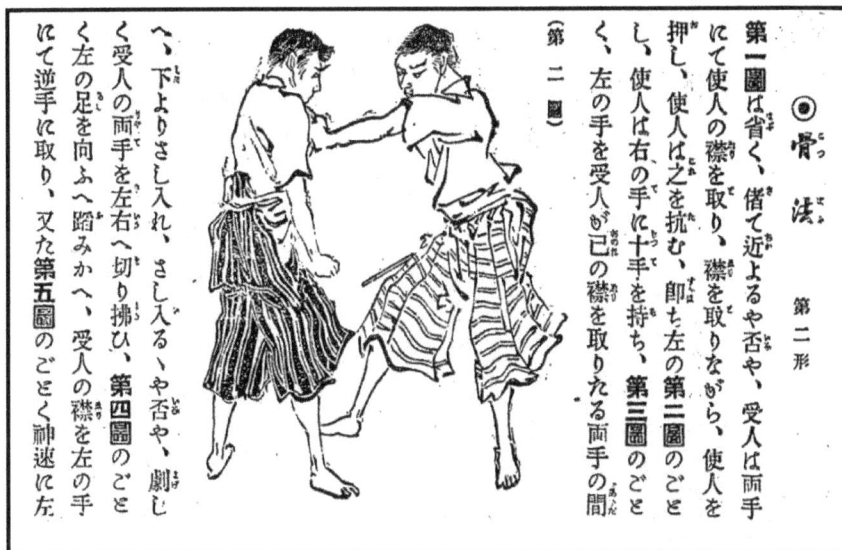

◎ **Koppo Bone Manipulation**
Second Kata
<u>Second Illustration</u>

The first illustration will be abbreviated. As the distance between the combatants closes, the Opponent grabs your collar with both hands.[76] As soon as he takes hold with both hands he pushes you. You resist this as you hold a Jutte in your right hand.

As the third illustration shows, you slip your left hand between the Opponent's arms, which are holding your collar. As soon as your hand is between them, do a Kiri-Harai 切拂い, or sharp, quick sweeping strike to the left and right. This will knock the Opponent's arms free.

Next, step forward with your left foot and grab the Opponent's collar with your left hand and twist. This is shown in the fourth illustration. Then, as shown in the fifth illustration, with Shin-soku, Divine Swiftness, your left hand releases his collar and grabs his right forearm. Strike the Chikara Kobu 力瘤, or Bicep, of his right arm. The force of this blow will render that arm useless.

---

[76] The illustration shows you, on the right, grabbing the Opponent's collar. The description indicates the first move is the Opponent grabbing your collar with both hands.

の手にて、受人の右の二の腕を取りかへ、右の
手にて、十手にて、其手の力瘤の處を打ち取り
たる手を外させ、第六圖のごとく、受人の左手
首を取り、右の手に持ちたる十手にて、左の脇
三枚へ中てるなり、

此第三圖は、前の第二圖のごとく、受人が使人
の襟を取りたる其兩手の間へ、使人は右の手に
て十手を持ち、左の手のみを下よりさし入れ、
劇しく左右へ切拂はんとするところなり、

（第三圖）

是れよりは、思ひのごとく切り拂ひ、次の第四
圖のごとく、左の足を向ふへ踏みかへ、次の第四
襟を逆手に取り、又素早く、左の手にて受人の
の二の腕を取りかへ、右の手の十手にて、
の處を打つなり、

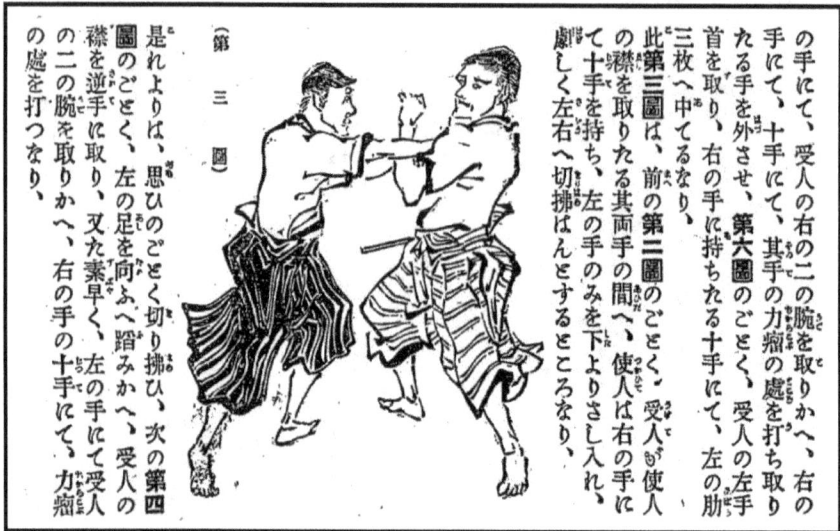

Third Illustration

The sixth illustration shows you holding the Opponent's left wrist and striking Abara San-mai 肋三枚 on his left side with the Jutte in your right hand.

The third illustration on this page follows what occurred in the second illustration. With a Jutte in your right hand you slip your left arm between the Opponent's hands holding your collar. You then do a violent Kiri-Harai, sweeping the arms of the Opponent away by striking to the left and right with your forearm. This Kiri-Harai should be done with full power.

Having struck and swept his arms forcefully aside, the next step is shown in the fourth illustration. You step forward with your left leg while taking hold of the Opponent's collar with your left hand and twist. You then release with your left hand and grab his left Ni-no Ude, or Forearm. Strike his right Chikara Kobu, or Bicep, with the Jutte held in your right hand.[77]

---

[77] The Kanji are "strength + protuberance," referring to the front of the bicep.

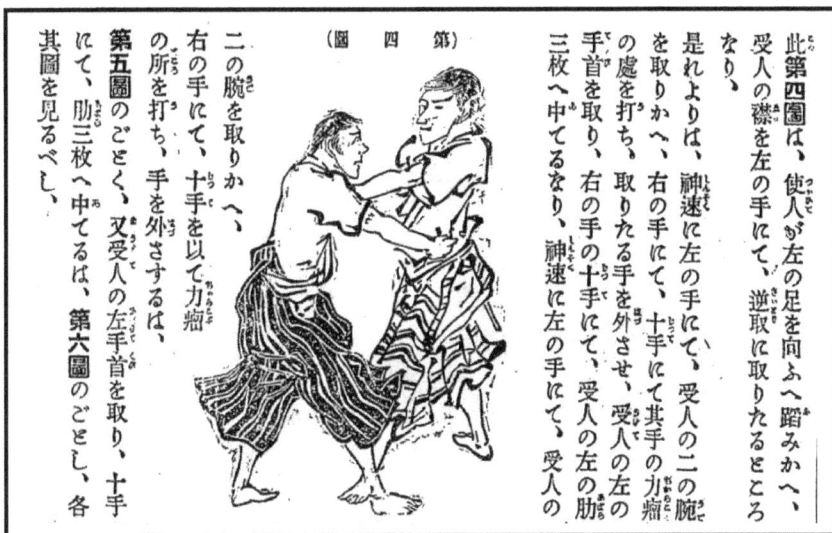

（第四圖）

此第四圖は、使人が左の足を向ふへ踏みかへ、受人の襟を左の手にて、逆取に取りたるところなり。是れよりは、神速に左の手にて、受人の二の腕を取りかへ、右の手にて、十手にて其手の刀癇の處を打ち、取りたる手を外させ、受人の左の手首を取り、右の手の十手にて、受人の左の肋三枚へ中てるなり。神速に左の手にて、受人の二の腕を取りかへ、右の手にて、十手を以て力癇の所を打ち、手を外さするは、第五圖のごとく、又受人の左手首を取り、十手にて、肋三枚へ中てるは、第六圖のごとし、各其圖を見るべし。

Fourth Illustration

This fourth illustration shows how you step forward with your left foot and seize the Opponent's collar with your left hand and twist. You then move your left hand from his collar to his right forearm, with Shin-soku swiftness. Your right hand, armed with the Jutte, then strikes the Chikara Kobu of the Opponent's right arm. This effectively puts that arm out of commission.

Next, you seize the Opponent's left wrist. Strike the third rib from the top on his left side with the Jutte, which is in your right hand.

The fifth and sixth illustrations show how your left hand moves from his collar to his forearm with Shin-soku, Divine Swiftness. You can also see how to strike the Chikara Kobu, with the Jutte in your right hand. This strike causes that arm to become useless.

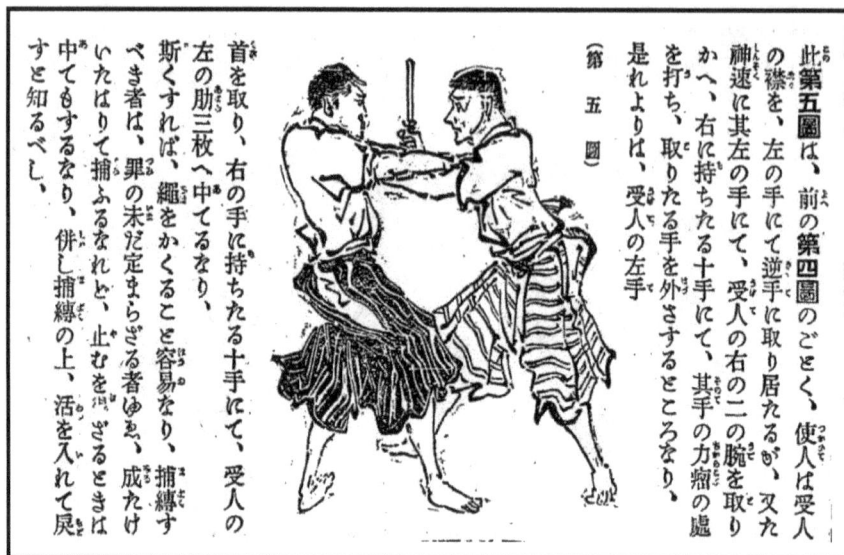

首を取り、右の手に持ちたる十手にて、受人の
左の脇三枚へ中てるなり、
斯くすれば、繩をかくること容易なり、捕縛す
べき者は、罪の末だ定まらざる者ゆゑ、成たけ
いたはりて捕ふるなれど、止むを得ざるときは
中てもするなり、併し捕縛の上、活を入れて戻
すと知るべし、

此の第五圖は、前の第四圖のごとく、使人は受人
の襟を、左の手にて逆手に取り居たるが、又た
神速に其左の手にて、受人の右の二の腕を取り
かへ、右に持ちたる十手にて、其手の力瘤の處
を打ち、取りたる手を外さするところなり、
是れよりは、受人の左手

（第五圖）

Fifth Illustration

This fifth illustration follows what happened in the fourth illustration. You initially grabbed the opponent's collar with your left hand, but this release and with Shin-soku, Divine Swiftness, seize his right forearm. Your right hand, armed with the Jutte, strikes to the point known as the Chikara Kobu, or the bicep. This renders the Opponent's right arm useless.

After that you grab the Opponent's left wrist and you strike with the Jutte to Abara San-mai, or the third rib from the top, on his left side. If this is done correctly, then binding the opponent up with rope will not result in any undue hardship.

As the person who has been restrained has not yet been convicted of any crime, or even of being a criminal, care should be used when taking him into custody. If he put up a fight, then strikes would be done more forcibly. However, if the person loses consciousness anytime during this process you should administer Katsu wo ire 活を入れ, or Resuscitation.[78]

---

[78] This Katsu wo ire 活を入れ method of resuscitation is discussed at the end of this volume.

此第六圖は、使人が受人の左手首を取り、右の
手に持ちたる十手にて、受人の左の肋三枚へ中
てたるところなり。
肋を中てたれば、氣絶すれとも、罪人なれば縄
をかけたる後ち、直に活を入れて戻すことを得
たとへば賊と見たるものなれば、餘程手ごわき
者なり、其初め受人が、両手にて使人の襟を取
り、使人を押す所より、使人が受人の両手の間
へ、十手をさし入れ、烈しく其手を左右へ切り
拂ひ、左の足を向ふへ蹈かへ、受人の襟を逆手
に取るなと、能く心を潜めて思ふべし、而して
此左の足を、向ふへ蹈かゆるは、就中肝要の事
なるを知るべし。

（第
六
圖）

Sixth Illustration

As the above sixth illustration shows, you have taken hold of the Opponent's left wrist and you are striking Abara San-mai 肋三枚, or the third rib from the top, on his left hand side with the Jutte in your right hand.

If you strike a person in the ribs with sufficient force it can cause them to pass out from the pain. Even if your adversary is a confirmed criminal, or Zai-nin 罪人, after tying him up with rope you should immediately perform Katsu-wo-ire, or Resuscitation, in order to revive them.

That being said, if you sense from the very beginning your opponent is a tough customer the first move will be different. In such cases, as soon as the Opponent grabs your collar with both hands and begins to push, slide your Jutte between his arms instead of your left arm. Then do a Kiri-Harai, or a violent sweeping motion, with the Jutte to knock his hands free.

The sequence of actions starting from when you step toward the opponent with your left foot and grab his collar with your left hand and so forth should be studied until his has been absorbed and ingrained into your body and mind. Stepping out with your left foot toward the opponent is the Kanyo 肝要, or Critical Move, of this Kata.

Overview of the Koppo Second Kata

1	2
3	4
5	6

両手にて十手を受人の両手の間へ下よりさし入
て使人の襟を取るを、使人は第四圖のごとく、
即ち第二圖の、夫より受人は第三圖のごとく、両手に
は後へ引く

ごとし、
（圖 二 第）

るを受入
を打か
にて受人の眉間
て近よるや否や、使人は右の手に持ちたる十手
立禮の第一圖は省く、第二圖より示すべし、偕

◎ 骨法

第 三 形

◎ Koppo Bone Manipulation
Third Kata
Second Illustration

The Tachi-rei 立禮, or Standing Bow of respect, from the first illustration will be abbreviated and the Kata will begin from the second illustration.

So then, as the two adversaries approach each other, you, armed with a Jutte in your right hand, strike Miken 眉間, or the area between the Opponent's eyebrows. The Opponent responds by dropping back to evade this blow. This is shown in the illustration above.

Following this, as the third illustration shows, the Opponent grabs both sides of your collar. You respond as shown in the fourth illustration, by raising your hands, as well as the Jutte, and slipping them between the Opponent's arms, which are holding your collar.

其十手にて左右へ劇しく打ちて、両手を切り掃ひ、第五圖のごとく、切り掃ふや否や、素速に受人の襟を、左の手にて取り、左の足を蹈み出し、同時に十手にて、受人の首すぢを打つなり、

此第三圖は、受人が両手にて、使人の襟を取りたる所なり、

是れよりは、前の第二圖の所に記したるごとく第四圖第五圖の働きぜなるなり、第四圖は両手にて、十手を受人の両手の間へ下よりさし入れ

（第三圖）

其十手にて左右へ烈しく打ちて、両手を切りはらひ、第五圖は切り掃ふや否や、素

Third Illustration

Next, you use the Jutte to do a Kiri-Harai 切り払い, or sharp sweep against both arms. The fifth illustration shows that as soon as you sweep his arms away you seize his collar with your left-hand using Shin-soku, Divine Speed. At the same time, step forward with your left foot and simultaneously strike Kubi-suji 首筋, or the tendons on the side of the neck, with your Jutte.

This third illustration depicts the point where the Opponent has taken a two-handed hold on your collar. From this point you should consider not only what occurred in the previous second illustration, but also how that movement changes in the following fourth and fifth illustrations.

The fourth illustration depicts both of your hands, as well as the Jutte, moving up from below to slip between the Opponent's two-handed grip on your collar. You free yourself by doing a violent Kiri-Harai using the Jutte to strike left and right on his arms.

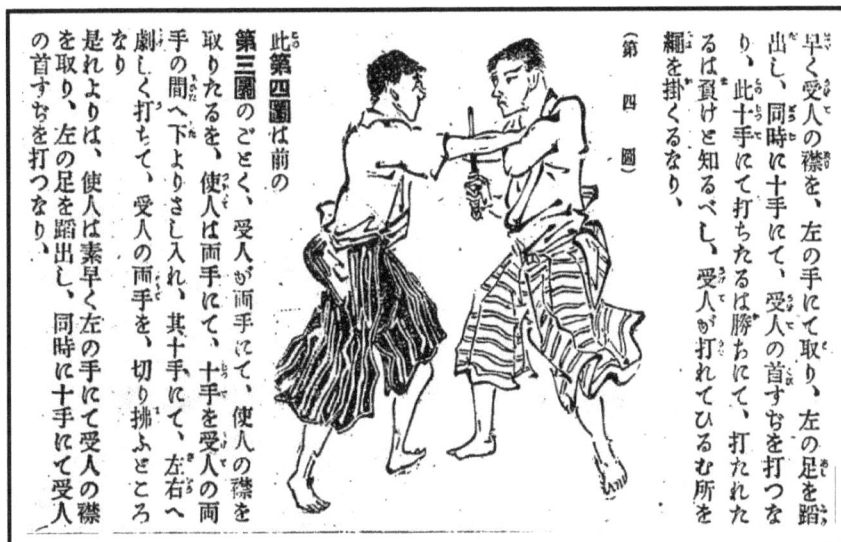

早く受人の襟を、左の手にて取り、左の足を蹈出し、同時に十手にて、受人の首すぢを打つなり、此十手にて打ちたるは勝ちにて、打たれたるは負けと知るべし、受人が打れてひるむ所を縄を掛くるなり、

（第四圖）

此第四圖は前の第三圖のごとく、受人が両手にて、使人の襟を取りたるを、使人は両手にて、十手を受人の両手の間へ下よりさし入れ、其十手にて、左右へ劇しく打ちて、受人の両手を、切り挑ふところなり、是れよりは、使人は素早く左の手にて受人の襟を取り、左の足を蹈出し、同時に十手にて受人の首すぢを打つなり、

Fourth Illustration

The fifth illustration, on the following page, shows how you rapidly take hold of the Opponent's collar as soon as you knock his arms away. Next, you step towards the opponent with your left foot. At the same time, strike the tendons in his neck with your Jutte.

Understand that the person striking this blow with the Jutte is the winner and the one being struck by it is the loser.[79] The next step would be to bind the Opponent with rope.

This fourth illustration follows what occurred in the third illustration. In response to the Opponent grabbing your collar with both hands, you slip both hands, along with the Jutte, up from below. Strike violently left and right with your Jutte, knocking the Opponents' hands away.

Next, you rapidly take hold of the Opponent's collar with your left hand while stepping towards the opponent with your left foot. At the same time the Jutte strikes to the Kubi-suji of the Opponent.

---

[79] Unless you like being struck in the neck-tendons by a metal bar, in which case everyone is a winner.

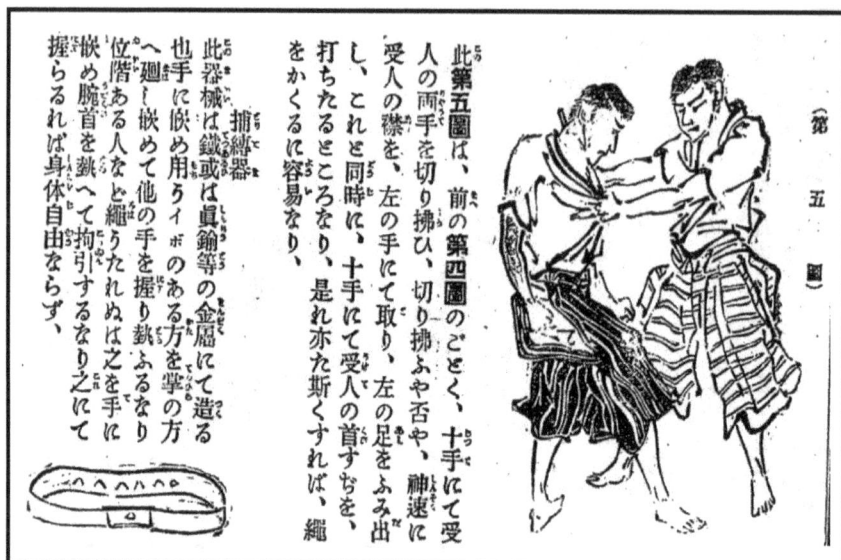

握らるれば身体自由ならず、

嵌め腕首を執へて拘引するなり之にて

位階ある人など縄うたれぬれば之を手に

へ廻し嵌めて他の手を握り鈎ふるなり

也手に嵌め用ラィボのある方を挙の方

此器械は鐵或は眞鍮等の金属にて造る

捕縛器

をかくるに容易なり、

打ちたるところなり、是れ亦た斯くすれば、縄

し、これと同時に、十手にて受人の首すぢを、

受人の襟を、左の手にて取り、左の足をふみ出

人の両手を切り拂ひ、切り拂ふや否や、神速に

此第五圖は、前の第四圖のごとく、十手にて受

Fifth Illustration

This fifth illustration, which shows how the movement proceeds from the previous fourth illustration, where the Jutte was used to perform a Kiri-hari on both arms. The moment the Kiri-Harai is finished, you grab the Opponent's collar with your left hand with Shin-soku, Divine Speed. Simultaneously, the Jutte strikes his Kubi-suji. Again if the Kata is executed in this manner, tying him up with rope will cause no undue hardship.

◎　捕縛機 **Hobaku-ki**　　**Arresting Aid**

This device is made of metal, typically iron but also sometimes brass or other such materials. You slip it over your hand with the rounded protrusions rotated onto your palm. Armed with this you use it to grip. When taking E-kai 位階, or those with court rank, into custody these can be affixed to your hand allowing you to take them by the wrist. If you grip a person while wearing these, they will be unable to resist.

Overview of Koppo Third Kata

1	2

3	4

5

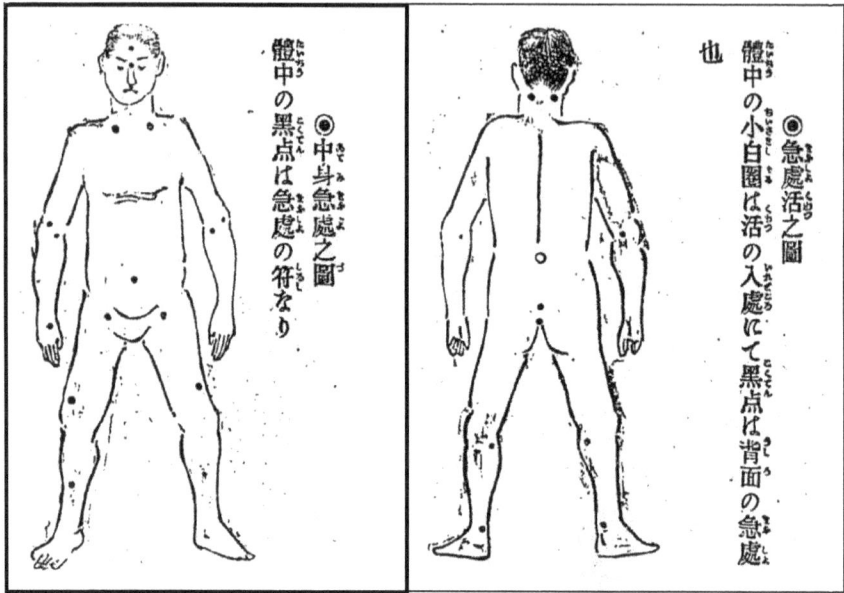

Left:

◎ **Atemi Kyusho   Diagram of Striking Points on the Body**

The black points indicate the placement of Kyusho, or vital points that can be struck, on the body.

Right:

◎ **Kyusho Katsu   Diagram of Resuscitative Points on the Body**

The small white circle indicates a Katso-wo-iru, or Resuscitative Point. The black points indicate a Kyusho, or striking point, on the back of the body.

◉活の入れ方

活を入るゝは左の圖のごとくすべし、氣絶した
る者あるときは、成るべく二人にて活を入るべ
し、活を入るゝは一人にて、一人は介しやく也
先づ氣絶したる者を抱き起し、活を入るゝ者は
後ろにて抱へ居り、介しやくは前に居りて、充
分に胸先を撫でおろし、倍て前の者は抱へ居り
後ろの者は前の急處活の圖の背中の小閣ある處
を、握り拳にて力を入れて打つべし、又呼吸を
詰めて、膝にて押すもよし、又た活を入るゝ者
一人なるときは、左の手にて喉元を抱き、膝に
て押すべし、此時は手と膝と、入れ力の齟齬せ
ぬやう、氣合をかけて入るべし、又二人の時も
前の者と後ろの者と、

活
之
圖

活
入

し、掛聲を合せて入るべし

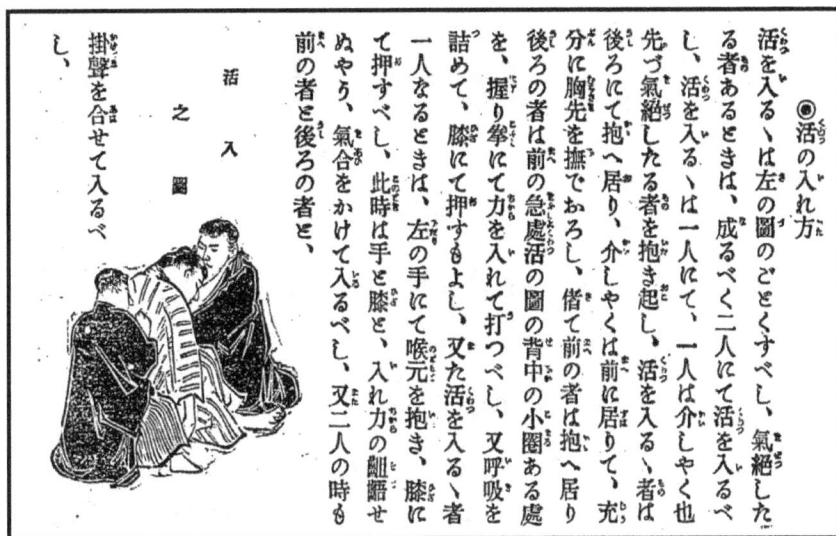

◎ **Katsu-wo-Ire Kata   Method for Resuscitating a Person**[80]
Illustration of Katsu wo Ire Being Performed

Katsu-wo-Ire, or Resuscitation, is done as shown in the illustration above. When a person has lost consciousness it is best that two people perform resuscitation. One person does the Katsu-wo-Ire while the other serves as the Kaishaku 介錯, or assistant.[81]

First the unconscious person is pulled upright. The person performing the resuscitation holds him from behind, while the Kaishaku sits in front and massages the chest.

---

[80] In this case "resuscitation" refers to how to revive a person who has been rendered unconscious during training. It was apparently used in a variety of situations (ie. after arresting someone.) Many Jujutsu schools had methods for reviving people. This is because they found that while certain points on the body were more vulnerable to strikes than others (see the Kyusho chart) other points on the body could be used to revive a person who was knocked out by training or some accident.

[81] The term Kaishaku is commonly used to describe the assistant in Seppuku 切腹, or ritual suicide. He is the person who lops the guys head off after he cuts open his belly..

So then the person sitting in front holds the unconscious person while the person behind should, according to the Kyusho Katsu Diagram, or the Diagram for Resuscitative Vital Points, press firmly into Katso-wo-iru, or Resuscitative Point. This point is indicated by the small circle on the back. Push with a closed fist.

In addition, artificial respiration[82] can be done by pushing the knees into the chest. This is also effective.

In case one must perform this resuscitation alone, use your left hand to hold the point where the neck meets the chest. Use your knee to push the Kyusho Katsu point that can be seen in the illustration on the previous page. Should this situation arise, be sure to use the same pressure with your knee as you did with your hand. Releasing a Ki-ai, or Shout, apply the pressure. When doing this with another person the Kake-goe of the two should be in unison.[83]

---

[82] Looking into the history of resuscitation I found such gems as:
In 1773, physician William Hawes (1736–1808) began publicizing the power of artificial respiration to resuscitate people who superficially appeared to have drowned. For a year he paid a reward out of his own pocket to anyone bringing him a body rescued from the water within a reasonable time of immersion. Previous methods, not all of which were discredited, (some of which occasionally worked) included:
- using bellows to put air into lungs
- rolling the drowned person on their torso over a cask
- putting the drowned person across a horse that was set to a trot
- bleeding
- rubbing with coarse salt
- applying heat (sometimes in the form of hot coals or heated excrement)
- tobacco smoke (or sage, rosemary, mint) forced up intestines
- ticking nostrils with a crow feather
- and suspension by the heels

[83] Ki-ai is the unification of the body and spirit moving into action. Kake-goe is the sound produced.

刀を抜き刀を收むるに居合抜の事を知らざれば
眞正に刀を利用すること能はず殊に抜打などは
出來ざるなり故に刀劍を撃つ者は一千抜きたり
二千抜きたり壹万抜きたり三萬抜きたりとて此
居合法に依りて數多く抜き習ふことなりされば
眞劍の勝負の時には勿論これを知らずばあらず
又當今劍舞といふもの流行す若し眞劍を抜きて
舞ふときには亦た此居合抜と收め方を心得置か
ずばあらず然をきときは刀劍を使ふ規則に適は
ざる故物識りたる人に觀られて笑はるべし務め
て修錬すべきことなり、

◎居合 一と形

（第 一 図）

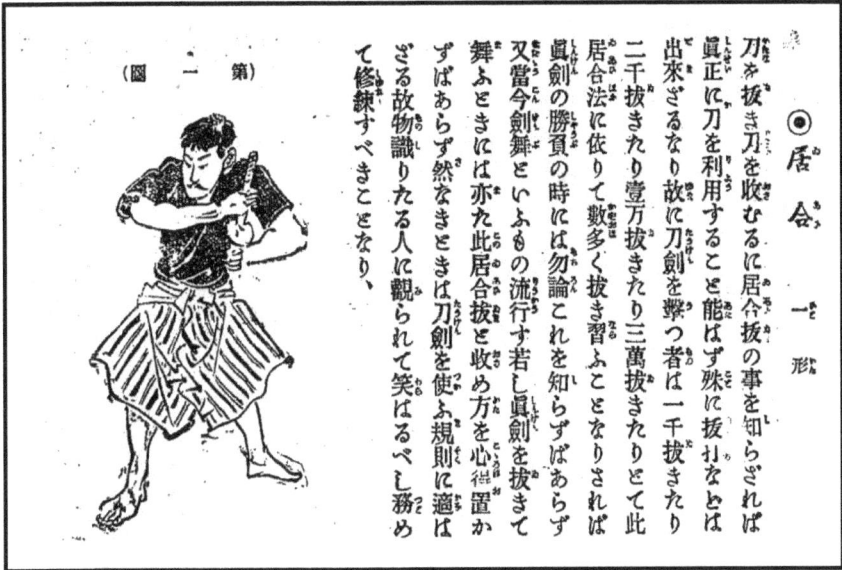

Iai Sword Drawing
One Kata
<u>First Illustration</u>

Katana wo Nuki 刀を抜き Drawing a Katana.
Katana wo Osamu 刀を収む Sheathing a Katana.

If you are not aware of the how to draw and sheathe a Katana, known as Iai-nuki 居合抜 , then you will not be able to properly use a Katana.

In order to be able to cut Nuki-uchi 抜き打ち, or Draw and Cut in One Motion, you must practice it one thousand times. This what people who train with To-Ken, or Swords, do. Sometimes they draw two thousand times, or ten-thousand times or they may even draw thirty-thousand times. This Iai-ho 居合法 , or method of practicing sword drawing, requires many repetitions the same actions.

Should you be in a Shin-ken Shobu 眞剣勝負, or actual combat situation with live blades, this knowledge would be absolutely essential.

Further, this training applies to Kenbu 剣舞, or the Sword Dance, which is quite in vogue these days. Should you consider performing such a dance, using a live blade you need to know about Iai. If you do not show awareness in how to handle a sword while doing a Kenbu performance you are likely to draw laughs.[84] You can ensure this is not a problem by doing Shuren 修練, or Rigorous Training and Repetition.

---

[84] According to *Illustrated Game Journal for Youths* 絵入幼年遊戯 published in 1893, Kenbu is:

A performance done before a seated audience whereupon acts of valor by men throughput history are portrayed through stirring poetry and sword drawing. Beginning after the (Meiji) Restoration period many youths began to do enactments of Kenbu.

Kenbu was around in a variety of forms before the Meiji Restoration in the 1860s, but the father of modern Kenbu is considered to be Hibino Raifu 日比野 雷風 (1864-1926.) He was also the founder of the Shinto School of Swordfighting 神刀流. In the 23rd year of the Meiji Emperor (1890) he combined the basic Kata of Iai, sword drawing, along with Jujutsu, Karate and Japanese dance into Shinto Ryu Kenbu "Sword Dance" School 神刀流剣舞術.

（第二圖）

偖て居合抜の初は左の手にて刀の鯉口を持ち出で其足を外八文字に踏み次に三足出でゝ居合腰になり右の手を右の膝に置き夫より立ちて刀を持ちかへ腰に佩し左の膝にて鯉口を持ち右の手を掌を仰向けて受くるやうにし左の肩の處へ上げ其手を下して掴へ掛け

第一圖のごとく其柄を握りて持上げ開と言ひて左の足を引きさまに抜き掴へ両手にて持ち一足進みて此に斬り、次の第三圖のごとく後とへ飛び歸りて大上段に上げ構へ第四圖のごとく柄を持下ろし第五圖のごとく持ちかへ第六圖のごとく收むるなり

第二圖のごとく

Second Illustration

So then, Iai-nuki 居合い抜き, or Practicing the Art of Sword Drawing, begins with the Katana being held at the Koi Guchi 鯉口 with your left hand. The Koi Guchi is the opening in the Saya 鞘, or Scabbard, that was thought to recall the open mouth of a Koi, or Japanese Carp. You should stand with your feet like the bottom of a Hachi Monji, or the Kanji for the number eight 八.

Next, step forward three paces and drop into Iai-goshi 居合い腰, or a Squat. Place your right hand on your right knee and your left hand on your left knee. Then rise, switch the sword to your other hand and slide your Katana into your Obi, or Belt. Finally, your left hand should return to the Koi Guchi.

Then next step is to raise the palm of your right hand up to the level of your left shoulder, as if you are receiving something from above. Then allow it to drop down and onto the Tsuka 柄, or Handle.

As you can see in the first illustration, you first grip, then raise the Tsuka up. Shouting "Ah!" step back with your left foot and draw. Then move your left hand to the Tsuka. With both hands on the sword you take a step forward.

The illustration above shows how your draw and cut should be done.

	As the following third illustration shows, jump back to the original position and raise your Katana up into Daijodan 大上段 Kamae.
	As shown in the fourth illustration the Tsuka is brought down in a cut.
	As the fifth illustration shows how your left hand releases the Tsuka and moves back to the Koi Guchi, Opening, of the Saya, Scabbard.
	The sixth illustration shows the Katana being sheathed.

此第三圖は後とへ一足飛かへりて大上段に構へ
たるところなり、尙又足つきに能く目を注くべ
し體のこなし方は基本にて太切なれとも手足は
此體のとなしに随ふもの故、或は抜き或は斬り
或は搆へ或は上げ或は下ろし或は持かへ或は收
むるといふ手つきのみならず、足は其初め抜く

（第三圖）

とさは大に開かずして直立外八文字に踏み夫よ
り一足進みて斬るときには右の足を出し此圖の
ごとく後とへ飛踏るときは右の足を引きたり

Third Illustration

This third illustration shows the moment after you have jumped back to the original position and gone into Daijodan no Kamae, Upper Stance. Pay attention to the way your feet are placed. The illustration shows the Kihon, or the basic body positioning when holding the Katana. It is important to understand this point.

The correct placement of the feet and legs rely on the correct positioning of the body. This is true when drawing, when cutting, when going into Kamae, when raising the sword, when lowering the Katana, when switching hands on the sword or when sheathing. This is not saying you should only pay attention to your hand positioning.

Your feet should not be spread overly wide during the initial draw, but rather your feet should be in an upright, proper, outward facing Hachi Monji 八, the character for "eight."

Further, when stepping forward to cut, your right foot should step forward. As this illustration shows, you pull your right foot back when jumping back to the starting point.

此第四圖は前の第三圖の
ごとく
大上段
に上げ
たる刀
を下ろしたる
ところなり、

（第
五
圖）

（第
四
圖）

Fourth Illustration

This fourth illustration continues the movement from the previous third illustration. It shows your positioning after you cut down with the Katana.

（第 六 圖）

此第六圖は持かへて刀を收むる所なり

Fifth Illustration

This fifth illustration shows your hand positioning before sheathing. The positioning of the right hand should be noted carefully.

此第五
圖は下
ろした
る刀を
持かへ
る所を
り、
右の持かへ方の手つ
きを能く見るべし

Sixth Illustration

This sixth illustration shows how the Katana should be held when doing Katana wo Osamu, or Sheathing Your Sword.

武藝心得歌

勝負とは深き淵瀬のうす氷わたる心のならひありける

稽古にも立たれる所先勝て身を浮島の松のみやかな

前うしろ左も右も一致とはわざとはなれし心法としれ

草の羽のはどはどしれや露の玉おもきはおつる人の身の上

ふしおがむいがきの内の氷なれや心の月もそめばうつるぞ

武藝全書中之卷大尾

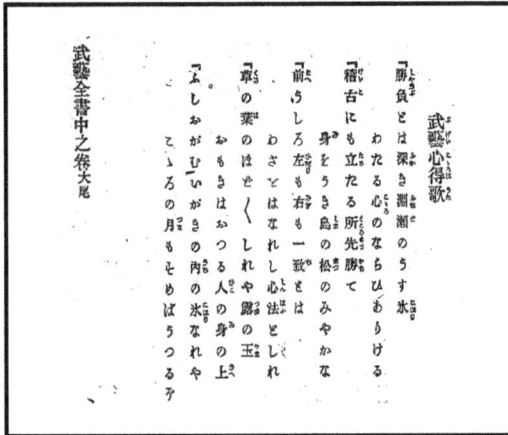

A Song Concerning the Important Elements of Martial Arts

勝負とは深き淵瀬のうす氷わたる心のならいありける

The difference between winning and defeat is like a thin layer of ice over the deepest, swiftest part of a river. How to cross over this point is something that must be learned deep inside.

稽古にも立たれる所先勝て身を浮島の松のみやかな

When doing Keiko, or training, the person who comes out victorious is one who stands like lone pine tree on a speck of an island.

前うしろ左も右も一致とはわざとはなれし心法としれ

The attention you place and the distance you keep from what is before you, as well as to the left and right should be equal. It is not Waza, or technique, that is the focus of Shin-gi-tai, or the mind, technique and body. It is the mind.

草の羽のはどはどしれや露の玉おもきはおつる人の身の上

Despite the weight of importance that people place upon themselves it is, in fact, no greater than that of dew upon a blade of grass.

ふしおがむいがきの内の氷なれや心の月もそめばうつるぞ

Know that a patch of ice within the boundary of the Shrine you pray at can reflect what is in your soul.

The Complete Martial Arts of Japan Volume III

Kenbu

Iai · Shikomi Zue

By Sadamoto Sugawara
Illustrated by Fujita Shiun
Translated by eric Shahan

Translator's Introduction:

I was not familiar at all with Kenbu before reading this volume. Though it no doubt has a long history, Kenbu seems to have become particularly popular in the post Meiji Restoration Era. It was a type of entertainment done at drinking parties both for people in the military as well as among the general population. A poem is composed about a famous Samurai or battle and acted out with a Katana like a short play. Other objects are sometimes also incorporated such as a Tenugui cloth or Ogi folding fan.

The poems are Kanbun, which means that they use Chinese characters, or Kanji, and Chinese word order. So the poem is written with Chinese word order and no Hiragana or Katakana alphabet. However, when recited and performed, the word order is "corrected" to Japanese.

武勇館蔵版

武藝全書

劍舞

菊判　全壹冊　正價貳拾五錢　郵送税四錢

本書ハ劍舞ノ外ニ居合、仕込杖、其外武藝ヲ實地ニ演習セ
タル、様記載セシ書ニシテ是迄他ニ出版セル劍舞書トハ月鼈
雲泥ノ相違ナル貴重ノ書ナリ

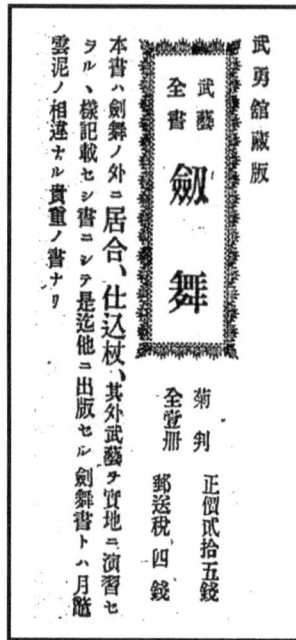

1898 Advertisement for
The Complete Martial Arts of Japan: Kenbu

This volume on Kenbu, or Sword Dance, also contains sections
on sword drawing and how to use a sword hidden in a cane. In
addition, this book provides practical information on Japanese
Bugei, or martial arts. The complete way in which Kenbu is
presented in this volume far exceeds that of any other publication
currently available. It is like the difference between cloud that float
across the heavens and mud on the ground, or the difference between
the moon and a turtle.[85] A valuable resource all around.

---

[85] 雲泥月鼈 *Unjo Getsubetsu* Cloud + Mud, Moon + Turtle
The first two Kanji *Clouds* and *Mud* is a phrase that indicates
two things that are completely different. The second two Kanji,
Moon and Soft Shelled Turtle, indicate things that, though they
share a single similarity (they are both round) in all other respects
they are completely different. The four Kanji together describe an
almost incalculable difference.

自序

軾今劍舞之技競行矣。夫劍
舞者。修武技餘興。而演慷慨
悲壯之詩歌演之舞之之間。
キ劍法諸科演習非徒爲戲
謳也。然則若夫俳優演戲柔
媚不規一塲戲謔者決非劍
舞也。不觀潔土史籍乎頃
會沛公於鴻門舞之以計非
戲也彼欲擊歆。我大前途有
欷。欲當之素行也。以是援劍
收劍由居合擊劍由劍法投

伏由柔術。以謂舞技抑亦異
他之演舞今之少壯者若演
劍舞冀演眞正劍舞徒行兒
戲者。不要須劍也。通覽本卷。
自知眞意所在。而上中二卷
共通覽之尚且得豁然而
方今代刀劍以杖劍。故亦說
之術。皆劍舞之本技也。述以
爲序。

明治戊戌春三月

浪速處士 菅原定基 撰

Introduction

Recently there are clubs devoted solely to who can put on the best Kenbu 剣舞,or Sword Dance, performance. Originally, Kenbu was a kind of pastime that part of martial arts training. Generally, the performances are tragic tales of heroism.

In order to perform a Kenbu, you need to learn three kinds of Kenpo 剣法, or Sword Fighting Methods. That being said, Kenbu is not something intended to be light entertainment as a play would be. If it is an actor up there on stage performing for the enjoyment of the audience then Kenbu it is not. The person on stage should be envisioning the enemy. Drawing his sword. This drawing of the sword must be in accordance with the precepts set down in Iai, or Sword Drawing. Of course blending in Waza, or Techniques, from Jujutsu is acceptable. Interweaving elements from other martial arts can also be done.

These days it is my fervent wish that young people study Kenbu seriously and enact it properly.

This volume completes the transference of my knowledge and intent that I started with volumes one and two. Note that using a stick to enact Kenbu instead of a sword is perfectly acceptable.

That is all.

March, Spring of 1898 Year of the Meiji Emperor
Nami wa sho shi or Citizen of the Land of Osaka
Sugawara Sadamoto

Table of Contents for Kenbu

武藝全書 下巻

右の剣舞第一形より第十一形迄は詩にして、第十三形は軍歌、第十二形は愉快節なり

目錄　終

Table of Contents For Kenbu

Be aware that Kenbu techniques 1 ~ 11 are poems. The Twelfth is a Military Song and no doubt the Thirteenth technique will give you a feeling of satisfaction.

居合一形は第二の巻に圖解したり其居合は柔術に係るを以てなり、然るに今一形を此巻首に掲げ

し故は書中の劔舞なし亦た必要なるを以てな

り、劔舞の譽は断に參けれども、居合の法にらな

のて抜き收めたうのは無きがごとし如何に

戴るべにせば劔舞と言ふからには武藝の餘興

となるものなれば功を知らず又た收む

る術それ知らず體の構へ方、刀劔の撃ち方、

は第一の巻に記してある大上段、上段、中段、下段、或

八相の刀の構へ方とも知らずして常に器用に任

せて舞ふときは事を識りたる人に親られて嗤は

るべし假令ば刀の構へ方、法にかなはずしては實よ可笑しきこと

なり、殊に抜き打などのとき或は刀を收むると

き或は刀を鞘ともに脱するとき或は置きさる刀

武藝全書　下巻

關口流天羽拙翁正傳

菅原定基著

藤田紫雲畫

◉ 居合　一形

The Complete Martial Arts of Japan : Third Scroll

Direct Transmissions from Sekiguchi Ryu Amaha Setsuo
Sugawara Sadamoto: Writer
Fujita Shiun : Illustrator

◎ Iai　Sword Drawing
One Kata

There was an illustrated breakdown of an Iai Kata 居合形, or a method for training sword drawing and cutting, in the second volume of *The Complete Martial Arts of Japan*. That Iai Kata was to be used as a reference for when doing Jujutsu against an armed opponent.

However, I am including another Iai technique at the beginning of this volume because it contains elements that are essential to learn for the Kenbu, Sword Dance, techniques. While there are numerous books on Kenbu available these days, those concerning the Iai no Ho 居合の法, or the way in which you draw, cut and sheathe your sword are few if non-existent. Without these crucial elements, Kenbu would be all but impossible to do.

Though Kenbu may have some aspect of entertainment in it, you should not turn Kenbu into a martial arts sideshow. If you want to put on a performance like a circus sideshow then do not familiarize yourself with how the Katana should be drawn, ignore how the Katana should be sheathed, pay no attention to the proper way to move, do not seek to learn the proper way to strike with a bladed weapon or even, as recorded in the first volume, study how to take the basic Kamae with the Katana. Daijodan, Jodan, Chudan, Gedan and Haso.

Simply relying on your own intuition as you dance about will likely draw laughter from those possessing real knowledge who happen to be viewing. Take, for example, a person going into Kamae with a Katana. The way he holds the Katana is wrong. The way he is standing is wrong. He looks completely ridiculous.

So, when reading this book pay attention to all the points. This is important when doing a Nuki-Uchi 抜き打ち, or Draw and Cut in One Motion. Follow the methods prescribed when sheathing the Katana, as well as when removing the Katana when it is sheathed in the scabbard.

Be sure to follow the instructions for how to pick up your Katana and doing a Koshi ni Sasu 腰に佩く, or sliding it in your belt and Hakama. Being unfamiliar with the Iai no Ho, Sword Drawing Methodology, will result in your performance being something that is completely divorced from the prescribed way. Such a performance is well and truly a thing painful to witness and those persons sitting in attendance will surely be presented with a dreary sight.

Iai is not just about drawing the Katana but it deals with the proper way the Katana should be handled both before and after your performance. All of this is essential to those seeking to take the stage and perform Kenbu, thus it shall be recorded here. Though clearly these instructions are of inestimable necessity when engaged in Shinken-Shobu 真剣勝負, or combat with live blades, however these days the skills introduced will be of more use when performing Kenbu.

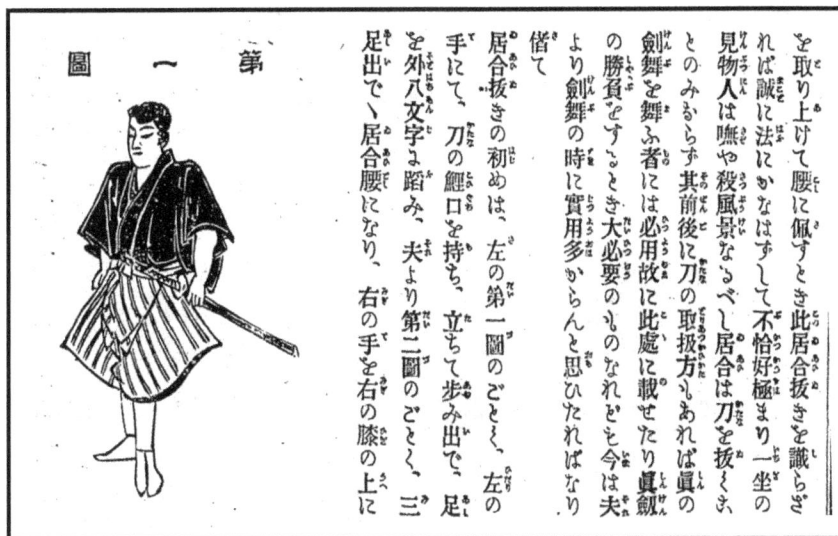

と取り上げて腰に佩すとき此居合抜きを識らざ
れば誠に法にかなはずして不恰好極まり一坐の
見物人は嘸や殺風景なるべし居合は刀を抜くさ
とのみあらず其前後に刀の取扱方もあれば眞の
剣舞を舞ふ者には必用故に此處に載せたり眞劔
の勝負とすゝとき大必要のものなれども今は夫
より劔舞の時に實用多からんと思ひたればなり
偕て
居合抜きの初めは、左の第一圖のごとく、左の
手にて、刀の鯉口を持ち、立ちて歩み出で、足
を外八文字ゝ踏み、夫より第二圖のごとく、三
足出でゝ居合腰になり、右の手を右の膝の上に

First Illustration

So then, the beginning of Iai-nuki, Drawing the Katana, is as shown in this first illustration. Step forward while holding the Katana in your left hand at the Koi Guchi, or the opening in the scabbard. Stand with your feet planted like the bottom of a Hachi Monji, or the bottom of the Kanji for eight 八.

From there, as shown in the second illustration, walk forward three paces and take Iai Goshi 居合い腰, a low squat. Your right hand should be on top of your right knee and your left hand, which continues to hold the Katana, is placed on the left knee.

置き、左の手は刀を持ちながら、左の膝の上に置
き、夫より第三圖のごとく立ちて、左の手にて
持ちたる鯉口の上を、右の手に持が、左の手
は刀の鞘を放さずに摺り下し、帶なる刀のさし
際に鞘を、握りながら置き、スーと佩すなり。
此時足元を集めて、スックと直立し、外八文字
になりたるところ、腰のスラリと伸びたっとこ
ろ、能々眼を着けて視るべし。又を鞘に收め、
又た刀を腰に佩すときは、何時にても此體勢を
思ふべし、夫よりは次の第四圖のごとく左の手
にて佩したるまゝ、刀の鯉口の所を持ち、次に
右の手の掌を上げながら抑向け。第五圖のごと

圖　二　第

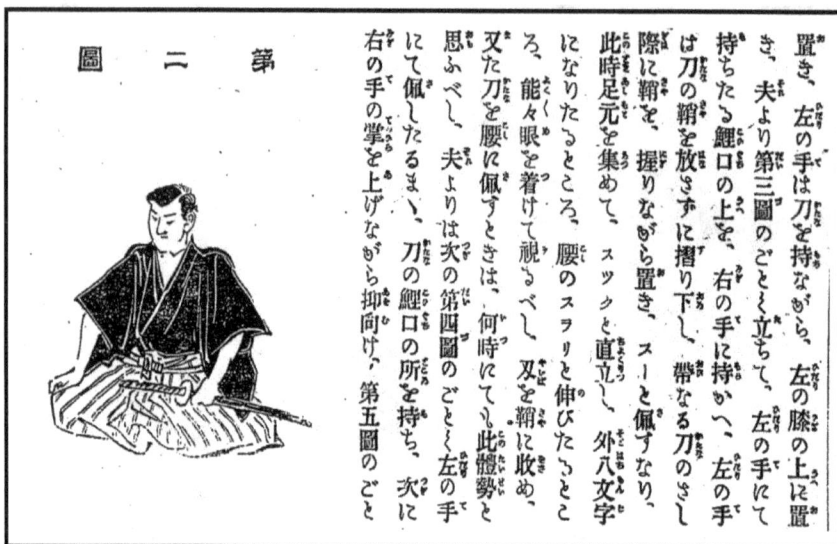

Second Illustration

Next, as depicted in the third illustration, you stand. Switch the sword to your right hand and hold it at the Koi Guchi, while keeping your left hand on the scabbard. Slide your left hand down to the end and slip the end into your Obi, or belt. Finally, the slide the Saya, or Scabbard, into your belt with a smooth Suu スー sound.

Throughout this, you should keep your feet together and your body upright and proper as if your back was making a Sukku スック sound of perfect posture.

You should focus your eyes on the drawing showing the feet being planted in an outward facing Hachi monji, as well as how the hips are squared with a Surari スラリ sound of perfect alignment, and your back is extended up to its full length. Whenever the Yaiba 刃, or blade, is being returned to the scabbard or when the Katana is stuck in the belt the body positioning shown in this illustration should be recalled and adopted.

The following fourth illustration depicts your Katana on your hip, with your left hand still on the Koi Guchi. Your next move is rotate your right hand over so your palm is up. You then raise your right hand, palm up, to the level of your left shoulder. This is shown in the fifth step, though there is no illustration.

第三圖

く、左の肩の所まで上げ、次に第六圖のごとく上げたる右の手を下ろして柄へ掛け、足をひらきて其柄を上げ、第七圖のごとく、左の足を一足引きて右の手にて抜き、第八圖のごとく、右の足を一足出でヽ突き、第九圖のごとく、體をかはして刀を擔ぎ、第十圖のごとく、右の足を一足踏み出し、體を左へかはして一刀斬り、夫より第十一圖のごとく、右の足を引くと共に體を引き、第十二圖のごとく右の手を放して上より伏せ、柄元の鍔際を持ちかへ、第十三圖のごとくに、刀を收め、前の第三圖の時のごとく、とくに、共に腰へ佩へ終るなり、

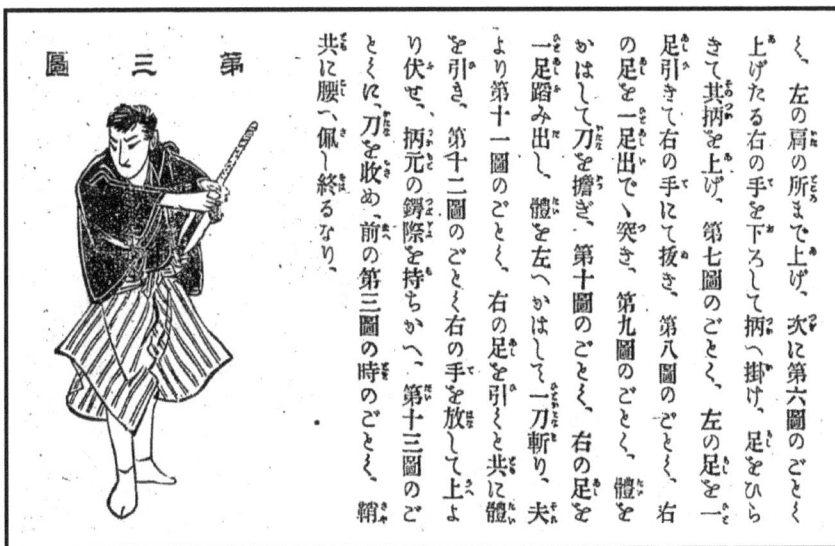

Third Illustration

The following sixth illustration shows how you lower your right hand and place it on the Tsuka 柄, or handle of your sword. You then spread your legs and raise the Tsuka.

As the seventh illustration shows step back with your left foot one step as you draw with your right hand. The eight illustration shows how you step forward with your right leg and Tsuki 突き, or attack with a straight thrust, at the same time. The ninth illustration shows your movement as you bring your Katana up to your shoulder.

The tenth illustration shows how you step out with your right foot and turn your body to the left. You then do a Hito-tachi Kiri, or a single cut.

From there, as shown in the eleventh illustration, take a step back with your right foot.

The twelfth illustration shows how your left hand releases the handle as you use your right hand to flip the blade upright. Your right hand should be gripping just at where the Tsuka meets the Tsuba 鍔, or hand guard.

The thirteenth illustration shows the Katana being sheathed, which closely resembles how the Katana was drawn out in the third illustration. With your sword returned to its original position in the belt the technique is over.

此第六圖は、前の第五圖のごとく、左の肩の所へ、上げたる右の手を、下して柄へ掛け、其柄を上げ、左の手は、鞘をすりて、腰にて其鞘を握り、足を開きて左の第七圖のごとく、左の足を一足引きて、抜かんとする所なり、

第五圖は、前の第四圖のごとく、左の手にて鯉口の所を持ちながら、右の手を上げ、掌を仰向け、左の肩の所へ上げ、其手を柄へ掛けんとする所(此處圖を略す)

第四圖

此第四圖は、前の第三圖のごとく、刀を佩し終るや否や、左の手にて鯉口の所を持ち、次の第五圖のごとく、右の手を上げんとする所なり、

Fourth Illustration

This fourth illustration follows the movement that occurred in the third illustration.

As soon as the sword has been fixed to your hip, your left hand takes hold of the Koi Guchi.

The following fifth illustration shows the movement after you place your left hand on the Koi Guchi. You rotate your right hand palm up. You then raise that hand to the level of your left shoulder before dropping it down and placing it on the Tsuka, or handle. This illustration has been omitted.

Sixth Illustration (right)

The sixth illustration follows what was described in the fifth illustration. Your right hand, which was raised up to the level of your left shoulder, is next lowered onto the Tsuka. You then raise the handle of your sword with your right, while your left hand allows the Saya to slide through it, but remains holding on to it at the hip. You should spread your feet slightly.

As the seventh illustration, on the left, depicts, you pull your left foot back one step as you draw.

Seventh Illustration (left)

The seventh illustration follows the Taisei, or Body Positioning, of the sixth illustration. You draw your Katana out with a smooth Surari スラリ sound of something moving like a snake. Next, step forward with your right foot and do a Tsuki 突き, or Straight Thrust.

Eighth Illustration (right)

The eighth illustration shows how you step forward with your right foot as you do a Tsuki, or Straight Thrust. From there, as can be seen in the ninth illustration to the left, you twist your body to the right as you bring your sword up to your right shoulder.[86]

Ninth Illustration (left)

The ninth illustration follows what happened in the eight illustration. Immediately following your straight thrust, twist your body to the right and bring your Katana up to your right shoulder. From there, as can be seen in the following tenth illustration, step forward with your right foot and cut as you twist to the left.

---

[86] The text says "left shoulder" both here and in the ninth illustration, but both have been corrected.

Tenth Illustration (right)

This tenth illustration follows what occurred in the previous ninth illustration. Bring your Katana up as you step forward with your right foot. Twist your body to the left as you cut.

The next movement is shown in the eleventh illustration. Pull your right foot back one step.

Eleventh Illustration (left)

The eleventh illustration follows what occurred in the previous tenth illustration.

As soon as your downward cut is completed, pull your right leg back and shift your weight back at the same time. Next, hold the Katana with your right hand at Tsuba-moto 鍔元, or where the handle meets the hand guard.

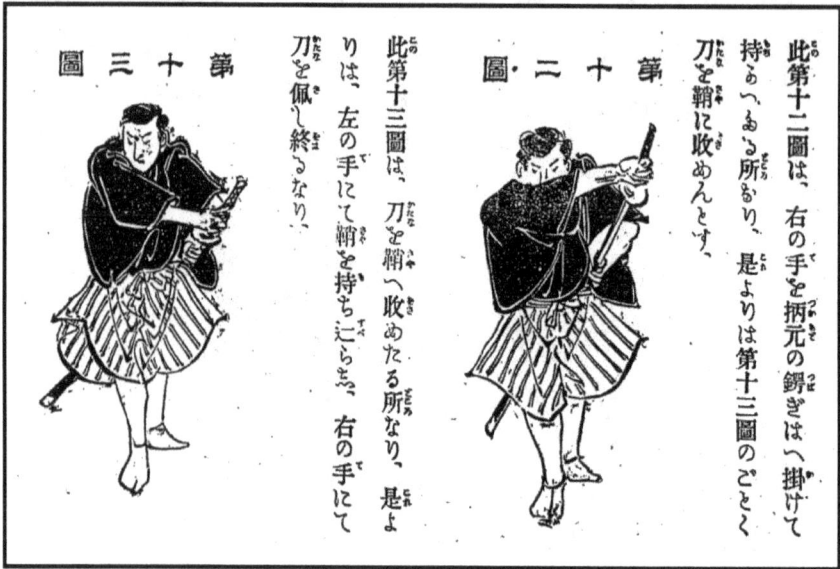

圖 三 十 第　　圖・二 十 第

此第十三圖は、刀を鞘へ收めたる所なり、是よりは、左の手にて鞘を持ち르らを、右の手にて刀を佩し終るなり。

此第十二圖は、右の手を柄元の鍔ぎはへ掛けて持ちへある所なり、是よりは第十三圖のごとく刀を鞘に收めんとす。

Twelfth Illustration (right)

This twelfth illustration show how your right hand should be holding the Katana at the Tsuba-moto after having flipped your Katana over so the blade is upright. The thirteenth illustration shows how you sheathe your Katana in the Saya, or Scabbard.

Thirteenth Illustration (left)

In the thirteenth illustration you are sheathing your Katana in the Saya. Next, your left hand allows the Saya to slip through your fingers while your right hand guides the sheathing of the Katana.

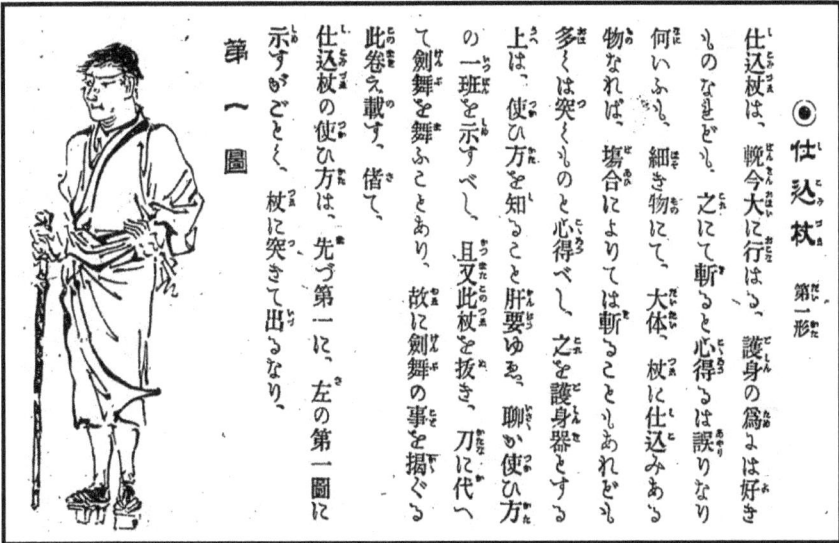

◉仕込杖 第一形

仕込杖は、輓今大に行はゞ、護身の為よは好きものなれども、之にて斬ると心得るは誤りなり何いふも、細き物にて、大体、杖に仕込みある物なれば、場合によりては斬ることもあれども多くは突くものと心得べし、之を護身器とする上は、使ひ方を知ること肝要ゆえ、聊か使ひ方の一班を示すべし、且又此杖を抜き、刀に代へて剣舞を舞ふことあり、故に剣舞の事を掲ぐる此巻え載す、皆て、仕込杖の使ひ方は、先づ第一に、左の第一圖に示すもゝごとく、杖に突きて出るなり。

第一圖

Shikomi Zue Sword Cane
First Kata[87]
First Illustration

The Shikomi Zue has, of late, become the weapon of choice for those seeking to protect themselves. That being said, thinking it is a weapon to cut with would be an error. The body of the blade is quite thin overall, since it is meant to fit inside a walking stick. While it may be used to cut in some situations, the reader should be aware that in most cases you use a Tsuki, or Straight Thrust.

If you desire to use this implement for self-defense it is essential you learn the correct way. Therefore a portion of this document will be devoted to its proper use.

On another note, as the sword within this Zue can be drawn and used in place of a Katana when performing Kenbu, an introduction to Shikomi Zue has been in included in this volume on Kenbu.

---

[87] In Japan the carrying of swords was banned in the Meiji Era. The Samurai class resorted to carrying Shikomi Tsue. The Meiji Government eventually banned such "Swords within canes.".

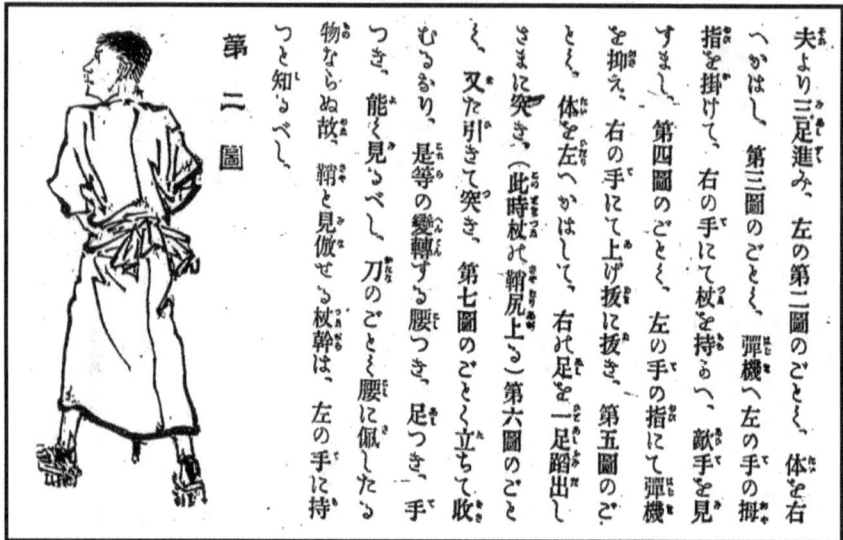

夫より三足進み、左の第二圖のごとく、体を右
へかはし、第三圖のごとく、弾機へ左の手の拇
指を掛けて、右の手にて杖を持る、歌手を見
すまし、第四圖のごとく、左の手の指にて弾機
を抑え、右の手にて上げ抜に抜き、第五圖のご
とく、体を左へかはして、右の足を一足蹈出し
さまに突き、(此時杖れ鞘尻上る)第六圖のごと
く、又た引きて突き、第七圖のごとく立ちて收
むるなり、是等の變轉する腰つき、足つき、一手
つき、能く見るべし、刀のごとく腰に佩したる
物ならぬ故、鞘と見倣せる杖幹は、左の手に持
つと知るべし

第二圖

Second Illustration

So then, first of all the Tsukai-kata 使い方, or Method of Using, the Shikomi Zue begins in the first illustration above. The Zue, or Walking Stick, is planted on the ground in front of you. Take three steps forward, as the second illustration shows, then twist your body to the right.

As the third illustration shows the Oya-yubi 拇指, or thumb, of your left hand should be resting on the Hajiki 弾機, or Release Mechanism, for the blade. Switch the way your right hand grips the end of the Zue, so it is holding it like a sword. Keep a careful watch on your opponent.

The fourth illustration shows how your left hand presses the Hajiki, Release Mechanism, and you pull the blade out with Age-nuki 上げ抜, or Rising Draw.

As can be seen in the fifth illustration, step forward with your right foot, rotate your body to the left and do a straight thrust. (at this point the Saya-jiri 鞘尻, or bottom of the scabbard, should be raised up off the ground.)[88]

---

[88] The brackets are by the author.

The sixth illustration shows how you pull the blade back and then do another Tsuki, or Straight Thrust.

As can be seen in the seventh illustration, when you sheathe the blade, you hold it upright.

Pay careful attention to all of the transitions as well as the placement of the hips, the placement of the feet and the placement of the hands. While this weapon is not fixed to the hip like a Katana, the body of the cane, the Zue-gara 杖幹, should be considered the equivalent of the scabbard, therefore hold it in your left hand[89].

---

[89] The man in the illustration is wearing Geta 下駄, traditional Japanese sandals (in addition to a simple Kimono.) The base of the Geta is called the Dai 台, while the cloth thong is called a Hanao 鼻緒, Nose Knot. The two pieces of wood underneath are called Ha 歯, or Teeth. The sound made by Geta scraping on the street is Karan-Koran からんころん or Karakoro からころ. The Geta are usually made out of wood from the Kiri tree 桐.

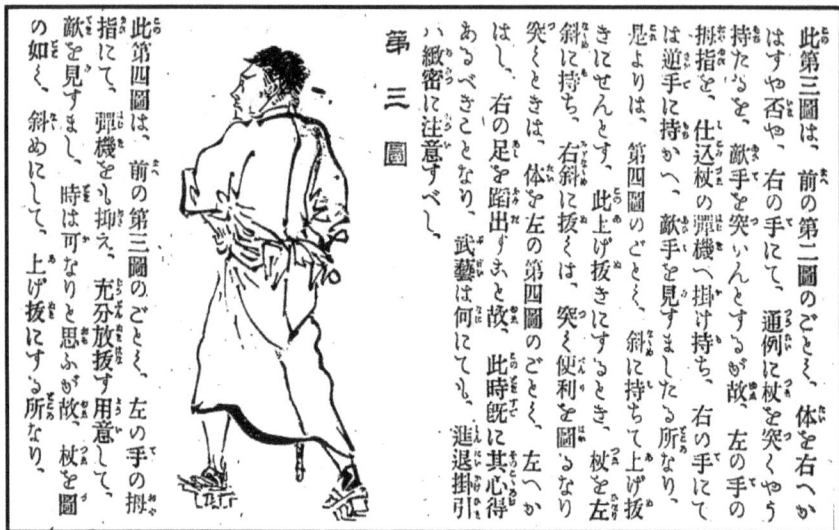

この如く、斜めにして、上げ抜にする所なり。

此第四圖は、前の第三圖のごとく、左の手の摳指にて、彈機をも抑え、充分放抜す用意して、時は可なりと思ふが故、杖を圖

第三圖

八緻密に注意すべし、

あるべきことなり、武藝は何にても、進退駆引

きにせんとす、此上げ抜きにするとき、右斜に持て、右斜に抜くは、突く便利を圖るなり、突くときは、體や左の足を踏出すと故、此時既に其心得はし、右の足を踏出すと

此第三圖は、前の第二圖のごとく、體を右へかはすや否や、欹手を突いんとするを、右の手にて、欹手を突いんとする故、左の手の摳指を、仕込杖の彈機へ掛け持ち、欹手を見すましたる所なり、右の手にて逆手に持かへ、欹手を見すましたる所なり、思よりは、第四圖のごとく、斜に持ちて上げ抜

第三圖

This third illustration follows the movement of the previous second illustration.

As soon as you twist your body to the right, switch the way you hold with your right hand so you are ready to do a Tsuki, or Straight Thrust. As your intent is to stab the opponent, your left Oya-yubi, or Thumb, should be on the Hajiki, Release Mechanism, of your Shikomi Zue. You should be keeping a sharp eye on your opponent the whole time.

The next step is shown in the fourth illustration. You draw the blade out diagonally as you do an Age-nuki, or Upward Draw. When doing this Age-nuki, hold your Shikomi Zue so the bottom is pointed diagonally to your left. You then draw it out diagonally to the right. Doing this will make you Tsuki, or Straight Thrust, easier and more effective.

When doing the Tsuki, the right side of your body should rotate forward as you step forward with your right foot. This is shown in the fourth illustration.

Within Bugei 武芸, or Martial Arts, you must pay special attention to the fine line drawn by Shin-Tai-Kake-Hiki 進退駆引, or *the strategy of when to advance and when to withdraw.*

此第五圖は、前の第四圖の
ごとく、上げ抜に抜くや否
や、體を左へのはしきまに
右の足を一足踏出し、踏出
す足と共に、鞘を左に持ち
て右にて突く所ん。

Fourth Illustration (right)

The fourth illustration continues the movement from the previous third illustration.

Your left Oya-yubi, or Thumb, presses the Hajiki, or Release Mechanism. Draw your blade back sufficiently while keeping a firm eye on your opponent. This may, in fact, take more time than you think, thus the Zue should be held diagonally as you do the Age-nuki, Upward Draw.

Fifth Illustration (left)

The fifth illustration follows the movement you did in the previous fourth illustration. As soon as you draw the blade out, step forward with your right foot, twisting your body to the left . As you step out with your right foot, keep your left hand on the scabbard as your right hand thrusts the blade forward.

Sixth Illustration (right)

The sixth illustration shown here follows what occurred in the previous fifth illustration.

The moment you thrust forward with the blade, pull it back and stab forward again with your right hand. You should pay close attention the Taisei 体勢, or Body Positioning, shown in this illustration.

Seventh Illustration (left)

The Taisei in the seventh illustration follows that of the sixth illustration. The Yaiba 刃, or Blade, should be sheathed vertically as this drawing shows.

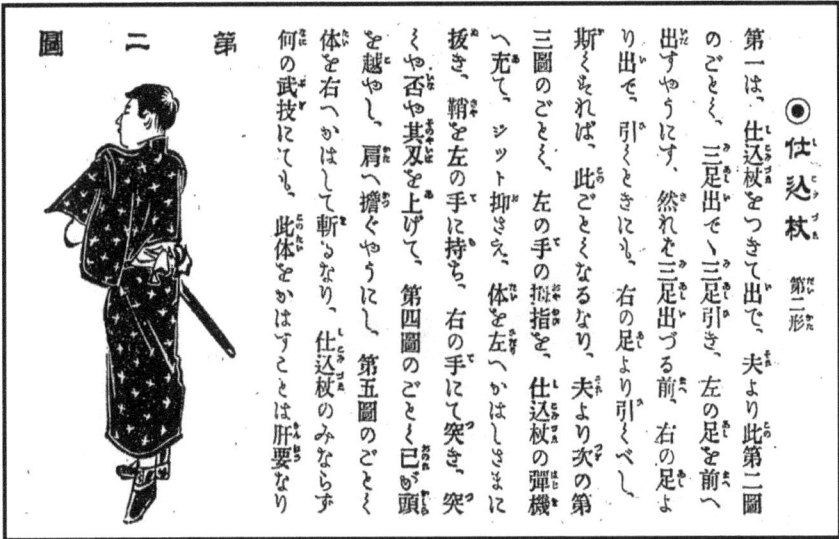

何の武技にても、此体をかはすことは肝要なり
体を右へかはしして斬るなり、仕込杖のみならず
を越やし、肩へ擔ぐやうにし、第五圖のごとく
くや否や其双を上げて、第四圖のごとく巳に頭
抜き、鞘を左の手に持ち、右の手にて突き、突
へ充て、ジット抑さえ、体を左へかはしさまに
三圖のごとく、左の手の擬指を、仕込杖の彈機
斯くされば、此ごとくなるなり、夫より次の第
り出で、引くときにも、右の足より引くべし
出すやうにす、然れを三足出づる前、右の足よ
のごとく、三足出で、三足引き、左の足を前へ
第一は、仕込杖をつきて出で、夫より此第二圖

◉ 仕込杖
第二形

◎ **Shikomi Zue Sword Cane**
Second Kata
Second Illustration

The first step is to hold the Shikomi Zue out in front of you. The next movement is shown in the illustration above. Take three steps forward and then three back, ending up with your left leg out in front. In order to accomplish this, start with your right foot. Further, when stepping back, your right foot moves first. Keeping this in mind will enable a correct execution.

Next, place your left Oya-yubi, or Thumb, on the Hajiki, Release Mechanism. Press with a steady pressure on the release, until it opens with a Jitto ジット sound. Draw the blade while rotating the left side of your body forward. Keeping the scabbard in your left hand, step forward with your right foot and attack with a Tsuki, or Straight Thrust with the blade in your right hand.

As soon as that Tsuki is done, raise the Yaiba, or Blade, up over your head. This is shown in the fourth illustration. This action is like trying to hoist a heavy load up on your shoulder. Next, rotate your right side forward and cut down. This is shown in the fifth illustration. Twisting your body as you cut is a Kanyo 肝要, a Fundamental Element, not only of Shikomi Zue, but in all martial arts techniques.

圖　三　第

此第三圖は、前の第二圖の体勢より、左の手の
拇指にて、仕込杖の彈機を抑さへ、体を左へか
はしさまに抜き、鞘を左の手に持ち、右の手に
て突きふるところなり。
是よりは、突くや否や其双を上げ、次の第四圖
のごとく、己が頭を越やして、肩へ擔ぐやうに
し、第五圖のごとく、体を右へかはして斬るな
り。
第二圖より第五圖に至るまで、体勢及び腰つき
手つき、足つきに目を止め、其變轉を能く視る
べし。又の鞘へ收め方え、第一形の第七圖を視
て知るべし。

Third Illustration

This third illustration follows the Taisei, or Body Positioning,
from the second illustration. Your left Oya-yubi, or Thumb, presses
the Hajiki, or Release Mechanism, of the Shikomi Zue. As you
twist your left shoulder forward, draw the blade. Your left hand
holds the scabbard while you step forward with your right foot and
attack with a straight thrust holding the blade in your right hand.

Next, the moment you finish the thrust, raise your blade up as
the fourth illustration shows. It should go up over your head so that
it ends up as if you have hoisted a large bundle onto your shoulder[90].
The fifth illustration shows how you twist your right shoulder
forward as you cut.

The reader should fix their eyes on the body positioning shown
in this illustration. Focus on the positioning of the hips, the hands
and the feet in illustrations two through five. Pay particular attention
to the transitions between pictures.

The seventh illustration of the first technique shows how to
sheathe the blade.

---

[90] The Kanji used here Katsugu 擔ぐ(担ぐ)generally means to "load
up" and is the verb used to describe the action of carrying the
portable Shrines, or Mikoshi 御輿 , one sees at festivals in Japan. I
think the writer is saying this action is a wind up for your cut.

第四圖

此第四圖は、前の第三圖のごとく、左の手にて
仕込杖の鞘を持ち、右の手にて突くや否や、其
又を上げ、已が頭を越やして、右の肩へ擔ぎた
る所なり。
是よりは、体を右へいはして斬り、斬り終りて
刀を鞘へ収むるなり。
能く圖を視よ、右にて突くときは左の足を前へ
出し、左の手にて鞘を持つに、便宜にす。
体を右へいるはして斬り、斬り終りて刀を鞘へ
むるは、次の第五圖に示すを見るべし。
尚又此第四圖の、左の手にて鞘なる杖を持ちた
る所、体勢、腰つき、手つき、足つき、能く心
を潜めて見るべし。

Fourth Illustration

This fourth illustration follows what occurred in the previous third illustration. Hold the Saya, or Scabbard, of the Shikomi Zue in your left hand. As soon as you finish the first straight thrust, raise the blade up over the head. It should look like you are attempting to load a heavy burden on your right shoulder.

Twist to your right side forward as you cut downward. The next step is to sheathe your blade.

Be sure to study these drawings with care. When preparing to do a Tsuki, or Straight Thrust, with your right hand, keep your left foot forward until you are ready to attack. The left side of your body rotates back as you step forward with your right foot and stab. Next, bring your blade up above your shoulder and twist your right side forward as you cut down. Then sheathe your blade.

The technique continues in the fifth illustration.

Returning to this fourth illustration, note how the illustration shows you holding the walking stick, which is actually the scabbard for your blade, in your left hand. Note the body positioning, the placement of the hands and the positioning of the feet. These are all crucial elements and be examined with great care.

此第五圖は、前の第四圖のごとく、右の肩へ
つぎたる刄を下ろし、下ろしざまに体を右へか
はして、斬り付くるところなり。
是よりも、刄を鞘に收むるところなれど、第一
形の第七圖に示したると同じことゆゑ、此處に
は圖を揚ぐるを省く。
圖を省けど、其收め方は、左の手にて、鞘
る杖を左斜に持ち、右の手にて、左斜に下ろし
て差し込み、收むるなり、其大体は、居合にて
刀を鞘へ收むる心持なるべし。

Fifth Illustration

This fifth illustration follows what occurred in the previous fourth illustration. After raising your blade above your right shoulder, cut down. As the blade comes down twist your right side forward.[91]

Finally, sheathe the blade back in your scabbard. However, as it is the same as the seventh illustration of the first Kata the drawing will be abbreviated here.

While the illustration itself will not be displayed the way in which the blade should be sheathed is as follows. Hold shaft of the cane, which is serving as the scabbard, on a left diagonal with your left hand. Use your right hand to slide the sword into the scabbard at a left diagonal until it is sheathed.

Be aware that the way you sheathe your blade in Shikomi Zue is the same as in Iai.

---

[91] The footwear has changed and the practitioner is shown wearing western style boots with heels.

第一圖ハ、同じき故に省く、夫より前形の第二
圖のごとく、三足出で、三足引くるれど、是も
前形に掲げたれば、此處に再び圖を出さず、次
に左の第三圖のごとく、左の足を一足踏み出し
仕込秘にて槲共に突き、それを引くや、第四圖
のごとく、左の手の拇指にて、彈機を抑さにて
外し、第五圖のごとく、右の手にて柄を持かへ
く、第六圖のごとく、右後ろへ抜き、第七圖のごと
く、右の足を出して突き、第八圖のごとく、上
段に振り上げ、斬り下し、而して收むるなり。

第 三 圖

◎ **Shikomi Zue Cane Sword**
Third Kata
<u>**Third Illustration**</u>

The first illustration is identical to the other Shikomi Zue techniques, so it will be abbreviated. Further, the second move of taking of three steps forward and three steps back is the same as the previous technique, so it too will not be reproduced.

The movement following those first two illustrations is continued in the third illustration, above. Step forward one pace with your left foot and attack with a Tsuki, or Straight Thrust, with the blade still in the scabbard. Step back and, as the fourth illustration shows, your left Oya-yubi, or Thumb, pushes the Hajiki, releasing the blade.

The fifth illustration shows how your right hand switches its grip around on the handle, taking hold of it like you are gripping a sword. The sixth illustration shows how you draw the sword out back and to the right.

The seventh illustration shows the right foot stepping out as a Tsuki is done with the exposed blade.

The eighth illustration depicts how you bring your blade up into Dai Jodan and then whip it down in a cut. Finally, you sheathe your blade.

此第四圖は、前の第三圖のごとく、左れ足を出し、鞘共に突きたる杖を引き、引くや否や神速に左の手の拇指にて、杖の彈機を抑さえ外に、拇指にて抑さえ方、能く見るべし。是よりは、右の手にて柄を持ち、右後ろへ抜き、右の足を出して突くるなり、此時左の手にて持ちたる鞘口は、左の股に當り、鞘尻ハ上れり。夫より上段に振り上げ、斬りて鞘に收むるなり。鞘なる杖に又を收むることは、左の手にて鞘を斜に持ち、右の手にて又を左斜に下ろしさし込み、收むるなり、其圖は第一形の第七圖を見るべし。

圖 四 第

Fourth Illustration

This fourth illustration follows the movement that occurred in the previous third illustration.

You stepped forward with your left foot and attacked with a Tsuki, Straight Thrust, with the end of your walking stick. The blade is still in the scabbard at this point. You pull your walking stick back and with Shinsoku, Divine Speed, press your left Oya-yubi, or Thumb, on the Hajiki release button. You should consider carefully how the thumb presses the Hajiki switch.

From there, your right hand switches its grip on the handle so you are holding it like a sword. Next, draw the blade back and to your right side. Stepping forward with your right foot attack with a straight thrust. At this point your left hand, which is holding the Saya Guchi, or the opening at the end of the Saya, should be on your left thigh. The Saya Jiri 鞘尻, or the end of the Saya, should be raised. Following this, you raise your blade into Dai Jodan and cut down. After that, you sheathe the blade in your scabbard.

The way in which the blade is sheathed in the body of the walking stick, which is serving as the scabbard, is to hold it diagonally in your left hand. Your right hand slides the blade into your left. Refer to the seventh illustration of the first Kata .

第六圖

此第六圖は、前の第五圖のごとく、柄を右の手に持かへてより、右後ろへ抜くとあるなり。

第五圖

此第五圖は、前の第四圖のごとく、左の手の拇指にて、彈機を抑さに外し、右の手にて、柄を持かへたるところなり。

Fifth Illustration (right)

The fifth illustration follows what occurred in the fourth illustration. Your left thumb presses the release which frees the blade, then your right hand switches around to hold the handle like a sword.

Sixth Illustration (left)

This sixth illustration follows what occurred in the fifth illustration. After switching your right hand to a sword grip, you draw the blade out back and to your right.

第七圖

此の第七圖は、前の第六圖のごとくに、右の足を抜き、の足を出して、突きたるところなり。

第八圖

此の第八圖ハ、前の第七圖のごとく、突きたる又一形第七圖のごとくに一振り上げ、斬下けところなり、是よりは、第七圖のごとくに鞘に収む。

Seventh Illustration (right)

This seventh illustration shows the movement after the sixth illustration. You draw your sword and step forward with your right foot as you do a straight thrust.

Eighth Illustration (left)

This eighth illustration follows what occurred in the seventh illustration. After the Tsuki, or Straight Thrust, has been done, you bring your blade up and then whip it down.

Finally, you sheathe your blade as shown in the seventh illustration of the first Kata.

剣舞なる者は武技の餘りを以て舞ふものなり故に
酒席の餘興と雖も其體武技を演ずる法に稱は
ず又た刀釼を構へ斬下し斬上げ斬拂ひ薙ぎ廻り
或は追取刀にて駈げ出し或は抜打にいるなど夫
々武藝の心得なくばあらず又た置きたる刀の取
上げ方、これを佩す儀、之を脱く樣、脱きて置
くやう、捧ぐるやう皆心得るくばあらず此第一
得而して舞ふは眞の劍舞なりと知るべし此第一
形を始とをして次を逐ぬて左に舞ひ方を記をべし

Kenbu Sword Dance

When you do Kenbu, or Sword Dance, you are employing elements of every martial art as you perform. Kenbu is known as a form of entertainment, done whilst people sip Sake, however if you do not stay true to Bugei, or Martial Arts, in your performance, it can hardly be said to represent them.

How does one go into Kamae, or Proper Stance, with a sword? How should the Kiri-sage, or Downward Cut, be done? What does a proper Kiri-age, or Upward Cut, look like? What should a Kiri-harai, or Sweeping Cut, look like? How then is a Nagi-mawari, or an Overhead Downward Sweeping Cut, done? Do you know how to do an Ottori Katana, or Drawing Quickly When Under Attack? Can you do a Nuki-uchi, or Draw and Cut, in one quick motion? You will not be able to answer in the affirmative to any of the above without first becoming knowledgeable in each of these martial arts.

Further, how do you pick up a sword that has been placed on the ground? How do you wear the sword? How do you take it off? How do you present the Katana and place it on the ground after you have taken it off?

This book will introduce how Kenbu and the sword arts are meant to be done. The original Kenbu song will be written in its entirety first, and then each line and the associated movements will be described.

不識庵撃機山圖　頼山陽

鞭聲肅々夜過河
曉見千兵擁大牙
遺恨十年磨一劍
流星光底逸長蛇

此詩は上杉謙信が武田信玄を撃つ圖即ち信州川中島の合戰の圖を見て頼山陽先生作られたり詩の意味は乘りうる馬を鞭うつ聲肅々として夜中に謙信は河を渡り曉になりて敵軍を望むに一千有餘の軍勢が主將の大旗を持ちて居るを見る今指折り算ふれば十年の永き間戰むに遺恨がある依て佩ぶる所の一劍を磨ぎて旗本に入りて斬り付けたるに天を見れば

Kenbu First Kata

不識庵擊機山圖

On the Topic of the Illustration of Fushikian Attacking Kizan
By Rai Sanyo 頼山陽 (1780～1832)

鞭聲肅肅夜過河

The Shuku-Shuku sound of the whip,
Crossing the river at night.

曉見千兵擁大牙

By dawn's light a thousand troops come into view,

遺恨十年磨一劍

Ten years of built up enmity!

流星光底逸長蛇

Beneath the blinding light of the Katana Ryusei,
The great serpent succeeds in its escape.

This poem was composed while viewing an illustration of Uesugi Kenshin's attack on Takeda Shingen. The poem was composed by Rai Sanyo Sensei as he viewed *The Battle of Kawanaka Island Illustration*. The meaning of this poem is as follows:

Urging his horse on with light brushes with the whip, making a soft, encouraging Shuku-Shuku 粛粛 sound Kenshin crosses the river. As dawn breaks they come in sight of a thousand plus troops all under the Ohata 大旗, or main banner, of the enemy commander in chief.

Kenshin clenched his fists so tight it seemed it would break his fingers. This was due to the enmity that had built up day after day over the past ten years as he sought combat with Takeda. Yanking his sword from the scabbard at his waist he charged for the base of the enemy's banner, where Takeda's headquarters was sure to be. If you were to look to the heavens, under the shooting stars a great snake is allowed to escape. Shingen is saved by one of his troops. Kenshin's enemy is not obliterated as was desired.

Translators note:

In this poem Uesugi Kenshin 上田謙信 is referred to as Fushikian 不識庵 and Takeda Shingen 武田信玄 is referred to by his Dogo 道号,or monks name of Kizan 機山. There were a total of five battles between the famous adversaries beginning in 1553. The battle discussed here is the fourth one which occurred in 1561. There are many illustrations of the Battle of Kawanaka Island the one on the following page is an example.

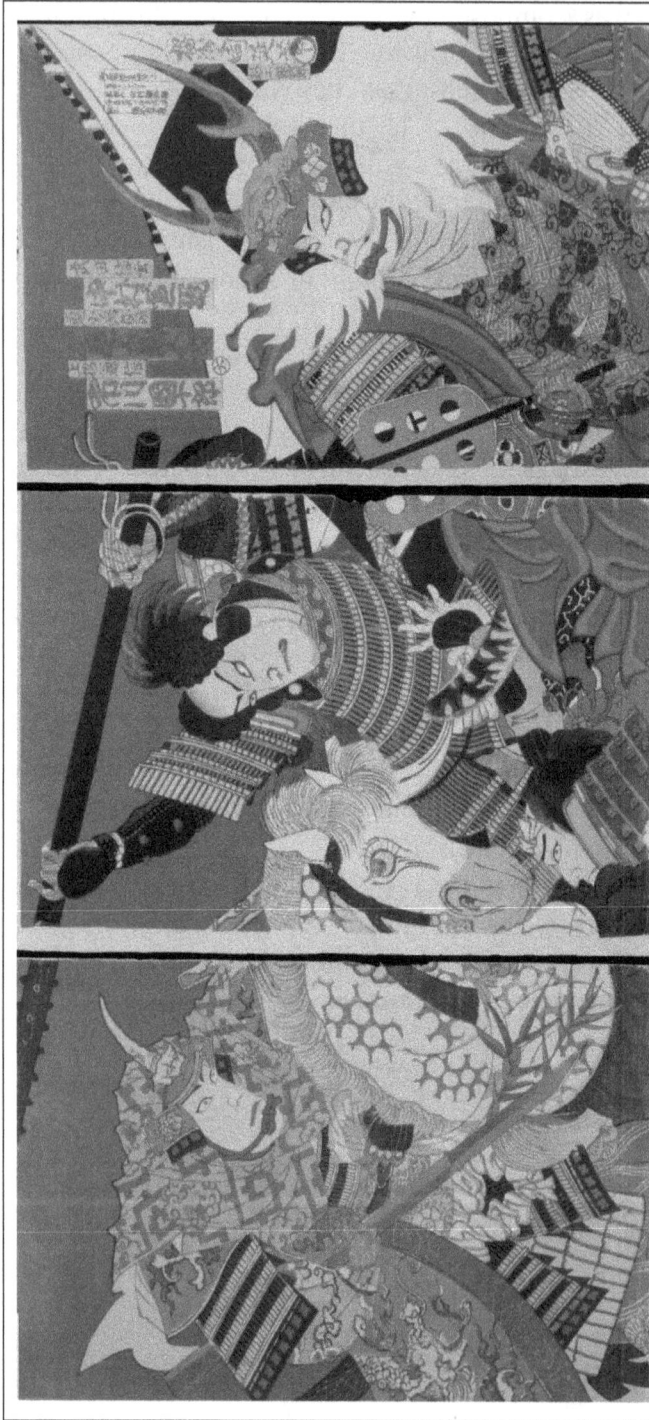

Illustration of the Battle of Kawanaka Island 川中島東都錦 by Yoshu Chikanobu 楊洲周延 Meiji 15 (1882) In this scene Kenshin is attacking Takeda, who is seated and has no time to draw his sword. In this famous encounter Takeda blocks Kenshin's strike with his war fan and Kenshin is driven off by Takeda's Samurai, resulting in an indecisive encounter.

First Illustration

When you perform you should be wearing a Hakama and have a Katana sheathed in your belt. Usually another person chants while you perform, though you can both chant and perform it as well.

The way it is performed is to chant: *Ben Sei Shuku Shuku* or *The Shuku-Shuku sound of the whip striking your horse*, as you pretend you are Kenshin atop his horse. As the illustration above shows, your left hand holds the Te-tsuna, or reins, and your right hand makes as if striking the horse's rear with a whip.

While reciting: *Yoru Kawachi Wataru* or *Crossing the river at night*, move your body from thigh to waist as you hold the reins and strike with your whip, as if you are riding a horse across a river. (Many people that believe you can successfully sit atop a horse and ride it across a great river. Illustrations *The Vanguard Crossing Uji River* or *Akechi Sannosuke Crossing the Lake* should not be believed. In reality, such a thing would be all but impossible.

Horses aren't ridden as they swim in deep water. The reason for this is that the horse's body would be submerged with naught but the head above water spraying out water as it breathes with a Fu-Fu sound. Thus, when crossing deep water, you should dismount, grasp hold of the horse's mouth and swim alongside. Upon reaching shallow water, you can then remount.)

The Vanguard Crossing Uji River 宇治川先陣
By Utakawa Kuniyoshi 歌川国芳 This is a scene from the *Tale of the Heike* that occurred in the 12th Century. The Samurai's name is Sasaki Shiro. He is cutting arrows in half as he rides across the river.

第二圖

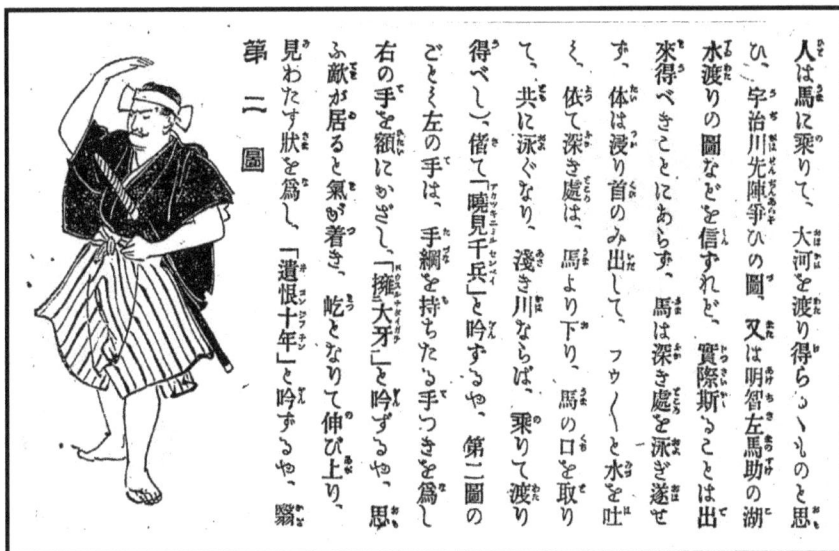

人は馬に乗りて、大河を渡り得らゝゝものと思ひ、宇治川先陣爭ひの圖、又は明智左馬助の湖水渡りの圖などを信ずれど、實際斯ることは出來得べきことにあらず、馬は深き處を泳ぎ遂せず、体は渡り首のみ出して、フウゝと水を吐く、依て深き處は、馬より下り、馬の口を取りて、共に泳ぐなり、淺き川ならば、乗りて渡り得べし、偖て「曉見千兵」と吟ずるや、第二圖のごとく左の手は、手綱を持ちたる手つきを爲し右の手を額にかざし、「擁大牙」と吟ずるや、思ふ歆が居ると氣が着き、屹となりて伸び上り、見わたす狀を爲し、「遺恨十年」と吟ずるや、翳

Second Illustration

So then, while incanting *Akatsuki ni Miru Sen Pei* or *By dawn's light a thousand troops come into view*, do as the second illustration above shows. Pretend you are holding the reins with your left hand while you shade your eyes with your right. You are now Kenshin searching for a glimpse of your enemy[92].

While chanting *Taiga wo Yo Suru* or *With the great fang*[93] *held aloft*, make as if realizing your long sought after enemy has appeared before you. Stretch your body up evaluating the scene about you.

---

[92] It appears Takeda Shingen's forces were startled to see Uesugi's forces approaching through clearing morning mist.

[93] The great fang, 大牙 Taiga, refers to Uesugi's battle flag. Uesugi's Gunki 軍旗, or flag, used the Kanji 「毘」 read as "Hi" referring to armor-clad god warrior and punisher of evildoers Bishamonten 毘沙門天, who holds a spear in one hand and a small pagoda in the other. Shingen's flag displayed a quote from Sun Tzu's *The Art of War*:

疾如風、徐如林、侵掠如火、不動如山

As swift as wind, as silent as forest, as fierce as fire, as immovable as mountain.

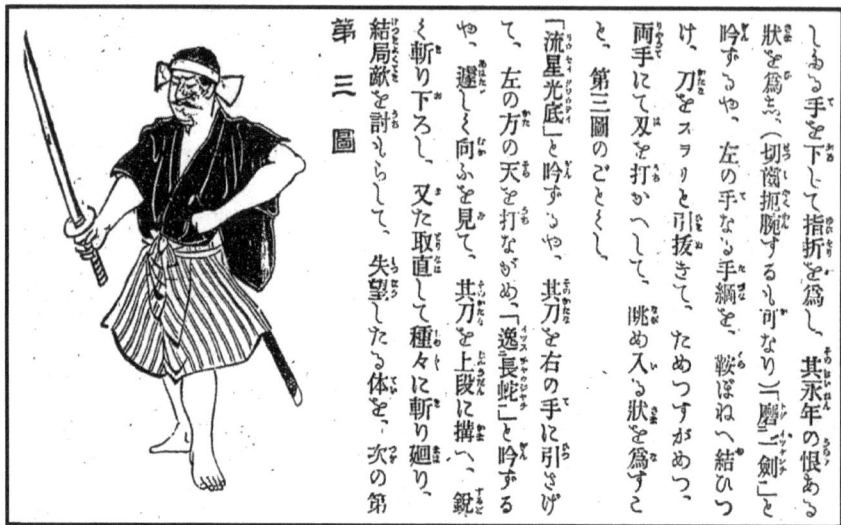

第
三
圖

結局欲を討えらして、失望したる体を、次の第

く斬り下ろし、又取直して種々に斬り廻り、

や、遲しく向ふを見て、其刀を上段に構へ、鋭

て、左の方の天を打ながめ、「逸長蛇」と吟ずる

「流星光底」と吟ずるや、其刀を右の手に引さげ

と、第三圖のごとくし、

両手にて又を打かへして、眺め入る状を為すこ

け、刀をスラリと引抜きて、ためつすがめつ、

吟ずるや、左の手なる手綱を、鞍ぼねへ結ひつ

状を為せ、(切齒扼腕するも可なり)「磨二劍」と

しある手を下して指折を為し、其永年の恨ある

Third Illustration

While chanting *Ikon Ju Nen* or *Ten years of built up enmity*, lower your raised hand. Your eagerness to attack that has built up over the past ten years should be on display. Clench your fists clenched tight enough to crack the finger bones. (Here one can display Sesshi-Yakuwan 切歯扼腕, or gnashing teeth and folded arms across the chest in barely restrained fury.)

While reciting *Ikken wo Togu* or *The sharpened sword is drawn,* your left hand, which holds the reins, now wraps them around the pommel of the saddle. Draw your Katana with a smooth Surari スラリ sound.

Flip the blade upright and, holding it with both hands examine it. Then, as the third illustration depicts, reciting *Ryusei Kotei* or *Beneath the blinding light of the Katana Ryusei*[94] lower the Katana down with your right hand and shift your gaze left in a hard stare.

While chanting *Choja wo Isu or The great serpent is allowed to flee*[95], make as if you are charging the enemy and, raising your Katana up in the air, cut down in a sharp, quick movement. Raise your blade again and revolve about while cutting in various ways all around you.

---

[94] Ryusei, or shooting star, is likely the name of his sword.
[95] The Choja, or Giant Serpent, refers to Takeda Shingen.

圖・四・第

四圖のごとくに爲し、居合の處に記しゝるごと
く、正式に刀を持かへて收め、坐上に一禮して
退くべし。
第一句を舞ふときは、勢ひ込で行進する心持
あるべく、
第二句を舞ふときは、思ふ敵に會ふをよろこ
び、いそいそといへる心持あるべく、
第三句を舞ふときは、是れ程の恨みがある
ゆゑ、其用意を充分にしたりとの意を含み、
第四句を舞ふときには、喜び勇み、勢ひこん
で打ち、志を得ずして大失望の体を示すべし
是等の所は、思入と見せる所なれば、注意し
て其れと見るべし。

Fourth Illustration

In the end, having laid into the enemy with your blade, present your utterly spent form as the fourth illustration depicts. Sheathe and put away the Katana in the Seishiki 正式, or the proper and prescribed manner, introduced in the section on Iai. Finally, do a Rei 禮, or Bow, to those seated in attendance and withdraw.

When enacting the first verse keep in mind you should move forward with vigor.

When enacting the second verse display the excitement you feel at encountering ones enemy at long last.

When enacting the third verse be prepared to exhibit how the depth of Uesugi's grudge has led to an inconsolable fury.

When enacting the fourth verse the zeal and bravery combined with the intensity of the strikes should be captured as well as the utterly dejected and spent body after you, as Uesugi, realize the goal you saw as your calling was not achieved.

All of these elements are crucial and care should be taken so that they are presented as described.

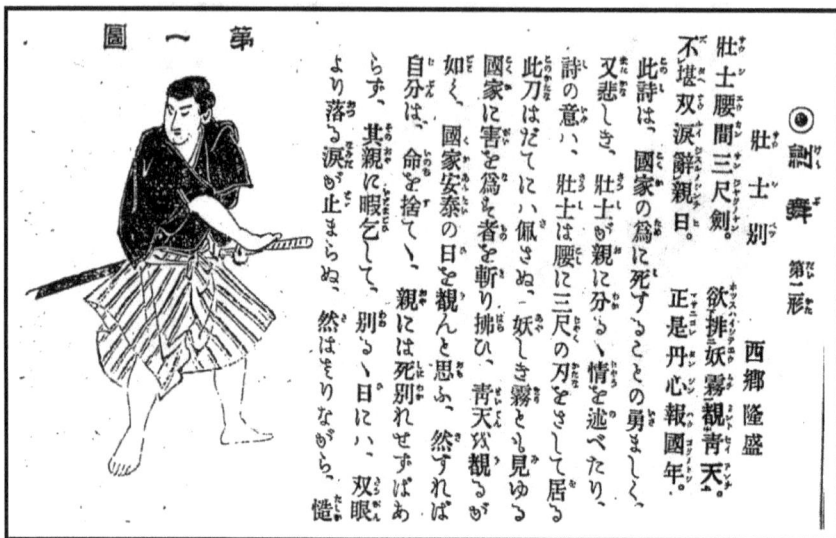

◎ Kenbu Sword Dance
Second Kata
First Illustration

壮士別 *Soshi Betsu*

What a Young Warrior is Comprised of

by Saigo Takamori 西郷隆盛 (1828 –1877)

壮士腰間三尺劍

A youth pauses to consider the blade at his hip, A three-foot sword.

欲排妖霧覩青天

Banishing the mysterious fog, Scanning for clear blue skies.

不堪涙辭親日

Resisting tears seeking to fall from both eyes proves impossible,
The day you depart from your parents.

正是丹心報國年

This is the true way, Sincerity and devotion.

This poem is about having the bravery to die for your county as a patriot. In addition, it describes the sadness young men feel when they take leave from their parents. Overall this poem describes a Shoshi 壮士, or a boy who has become a man, armed with a 3 Shaku 三尺, or 90 centimeter, Katana on his hip.[96] Fixing this Katana upon his hip is no light matter. Should a suspicious fog arise, threatening to harm your county, you would cut those that seek to imperil it with a great sweep of your sword.

The tranquility one finds when looking up at a clear blue sky is the kind of peace the patriot desires for his country. However, you are prepared to give your life in service of to your country and parting from your parents though death is the only path that remains.

The day you say goodbye to your parents, tears fall ceaselessly from both eyes. It is only when one you go to brush these tears aside that you realize in your heart what it means to have reverence for your country. To sacrifice for your country.

---

[96] As the blades on Katana for most Samurai were around two Shaku, or 60cm, including the handle the total length was 90 cm. Also, the length of a Shaku varied from region to region and from time to time. Previously one Shaku was about 35cm, but it was later standardized at around 30cm.

此舞ひ方は、「壮士腰間」と吟ずるや、左の手にて鯉口を持ち、腰なる刀を屹と見て、「三尺剣」と吟ずるや、右の第一圖のごとく、右の手を柄元に掛け、二三寸抜きかけ、鍔音はげしく金調、して收め、「排妖霧」と吟ずるや、左の第二圖のごとく、右の足を一足出すと同時に、刀を抜きて左右へ斬り開き、「欲親青天」と吟ずるや、左の足に繼ぎ、刀を收めて天をながめ、安心の体を為し、「不堪双涙」と吟ずるに是れ、ゆえなり。誠の心を以て、國恩を報ずる時であ

Second Illustration

Begin this Kenbu first reciting *Soshi Yoh Kan* or *A youth pauses to consider the blade at his hip.* Look with intensity at the Katana fixed to your hip. Next, while bringing your left hand up to the Koi Guchi 鯉口, or the end of your scabbard, intone *San Shaku Ken* or *A three foot sword.*

Next, as can be seen in the first illustration, your right hand goes to the Tsuak-moto 柄元, or the point where the hand guard meets the handle. You then draw the blade out 2 ~ 3 Sun, 6 ~ 9 centimeters. Then with a sharp quick movement, powerfully shove the sword back into the scabbard, causing the metal Tsuba to ring with the force of the impact.

While reciting *Yomu wo Haishite* or *Banishing the mysterious fog*, draw your sword as shown in the second illustration above. The way you do this is to take one step forward with your right foot and cut with a Kiri hiraki, or wide clearing cuts, to the left and right.

While reciting *Seiten wo Minto Hosu* or *Scanning for clear blue skies,* bring your left foot up beside your right foot. Then sheathe your Kanata and look up at the sky. Completely relax your body so it is at peace and intone *Taezu Sorui,* or *Resisting the tears that seek to fall from both eyes proves impossible,* as you wipe the tears away from both eyes with the downward facing thumb, of your right hand.

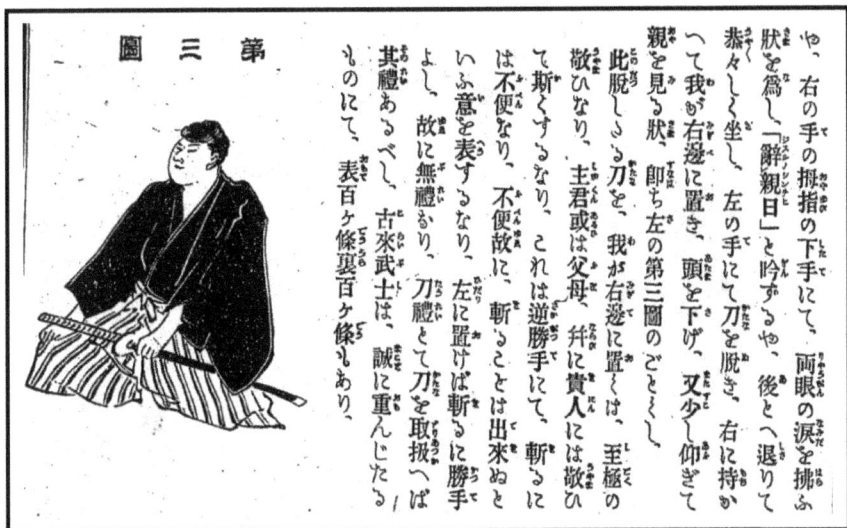

右の手の拇指の下手にて、両眼の涙を拭ふ
狀を為し、「辭親日」と吟ずるや、後とへ退りて
恭々しく坐し、左の手にて刀を脱き、右に持ち
て我が右邊に置き、頭を下げ、又少し仰ぎて
親を見る狀、即ち左の第三圖のごとくし、
此脱しゝる刀を、我が右邊に置くは、至極の
敬ひなり、主君或は父母、幷に貴人には敬ひ
て斯くするなり、これは逆勝手にて、斬るに
は不便なり、不便故に、斬ることは出來ぬと
いふ意を表するなり、左に置けば斬るに勝手
よし、故に無禮なり、刀體とて刀を取扱へば
其體あるべし、古來武士は、誠に重んじたる
ものにて、表百ヶ條裏百ヶ條もあり、

Third Illustration

While reciting *Shin wo Jizuru no Hi*, or *The day one departs from ones parents*, retrace your steps back and seat yourself reverently and with great ceremony. Pull your sword, still in its scabbard, out of your belt with your left hand. Then pass it to your right hand and place it down on your right side.

Lower your head and then raise it up slightly as if to bring your parents into view. This is shown in the third illustration, above.

Placing your sword on your right side is the ultimate sign of sign of respect and honor. It honors your lord, your parents as well as any assembled nobility. The reason is because your sword is Saka-gatte, or placed awkwardly. It would be difficult to pick up and draw when it is placed on your right, therefore it shows you cannot cut. However, placing your sword on your left side means you can pick it up and cut quite easily, and for that reason it is Burei, or Rude. Doing Torei, or Showing Respect with Your Sword, is important just as every aspect of sword handling should be done with respect. The Samurai of old went to great lengths to express their reverence. It is said,

There are a hundred chapters written on this and another hundred that are not.

第四圖

孝道にかなふと思ひ、死ぬると決心するなり。

此決心は、命を捨て、國此爲にするは、是が

第四句を舞ふには、決心しうら思入あるべし

第三句を舞ふは、充分孝道を思ひうか

第二句を舞ふは、刀劍の能を示し

第一句を舞ふは、刀劍を身の寶とする思ひあ

り、

して退くなり。

かへして見るべし、之を終れば刀を收め、一禮

と吟ずるや、左の第四圖のごとく刀を拔きて打

心」と吟ずるや、胸をひろげて見せ、「報國年」

「正是」と吟ずるや、正しく坐して屹となり、「丹

Fourth Illustration

Whilst chanting *Masa ni Kore,* or *This is the true way*, seat yourself properly and at attention. Then chant *Tanshin,* or *Sincerity and devotion*, as you puff your chest out. While reciting *Hokori no Toshi,* or *The year of your patriotism*, draw your Katana and do a cut, finishing as the fourth illustration above shows.

Next, sheathe your Katana and do a Rei, or Bow of Respect, then withdraw.

As the first verse is being chanted, fix the Katana to your body.

As the second verse is being chanted, show what the Token, or Sword, is capable of.

As the third verse is being chanted be sure to show how contemplation that leads to determination.

This determination represents your willingness to give up your life for your country, to feel that "now is the time" as filial piety wells up within you and you prepare yourself for death.

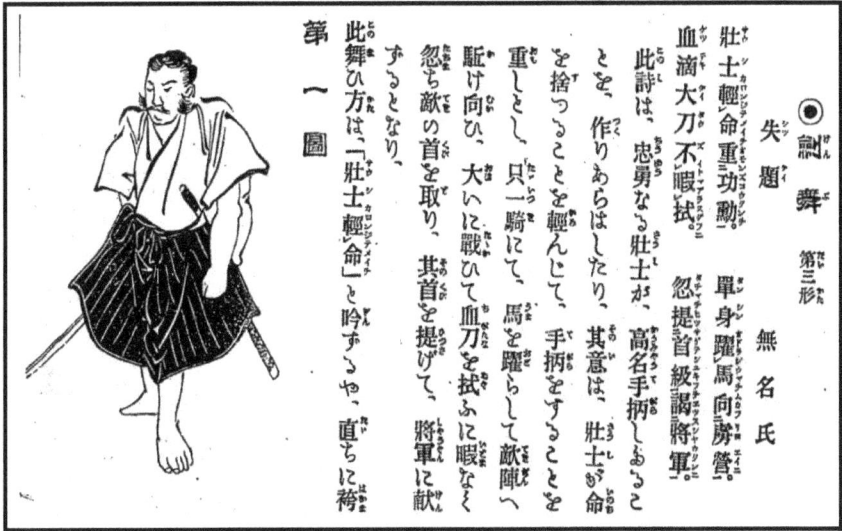

剣舞　第三形

◉ 失題　　　無名氏

壮士軽命重功勲

単身躍馬向虜営

血滴大刀不暇拭

忽提首級謁將軍。

此詩は、忠勇なる壮士が、高名手柄しあることを、作りあらはしたり。其意は、壮士の命を捨つることを軽んじて、手柄をすることを重しとし、只一騎にて、馬を躍らして敵陣へ駈け向ひ、大いに戰ひて血刀を拭ふに暇なく、忽ち敵の首を取り、其首を提げて、將軍に献ずるとなり。

此舞ひ方は、「壮士軽命」と吟ずるや、直ちに袴

第一圖

◎ Kenbu Sword Dance
Third Kata
First Illustration

失題 Shitsudai

Untitled

By Anonymous　無名氏

壮士經命重功勲

A young man has little concern for his life,
Focused entirely on achieving deeds of merit.

單身躍馬向虜営

Spurring his horse he moves out alone
Heading into the barbarians' encampment.

血滴大刀不暇拭

Daito soaked in blood,
There was not time even to wipe the blade.

忽提首級謁將軍

Presenting the enemy's severed head forthwith,
An audience with the Shogun

This poem was written to show how a brave and loyal Soshi, or young man, became famous through his deeds. The focus of this poem is how lightly the Soshi views putting his life in danger. At the same time great import is placed on achieving the kind of fame only bestowed upon those who perform meritorious deeds. This is known as Komyo-Tegara 高名手柄, Highest Class of Merit.

Alone, ahead of the others the young warrior spurs his horse into the heart of the enemy. The furious battle that ensues gives no time even to wipe the blood from his blade[97]. He is immediately able to take an enemy head. Carrying that Kubi 首, or Severed Head, it is presented to the Shogun[98].

The way this is performed is to intone *Soshi Mei wo Karonjite*, or *A young man has little concern for his life*, and immediately tuck the sides of your Hakama 袴 up under your belt. This is known as Momodachi 股立, which prevents your legs from getting tangled in your Hakama. You then rapidly fasten a Tamadasuki 玉襷 around your shoulders, which secures your loose sleeves.[99]

Hold yourself as if unconcerned about Uchi-jini 討死, or the prospect of dying in battle.

Intone *Kogun wo Omonzu*, or *Focused entirely on achieving deeds of merit*, and draw your sword. Make an offering of the sword with the blade facing downward.

(When offering your Katana to the Gods, even if it is done with your sword still in the scabbard, ensure the blade is facing you and the back of the sword facing away. You can also offer the sword by bowing as you hold it up.)

---

[97] A bloody sword doesn't cut well.

[98] Japanese say take the "neck" instead of take the "head" which is why the word Kubi 首, or neck, is used.

[99] 玉襷 The Tamadusuki, also known more simply as Tasuki, was a common item for men, women, old and young throughout the Edo Era and before. It was either a piece of string or a strip of cloth that was wrapped under both shoulders and made an X on the back.

第二圖

の股立を取り、手早く玉襷をかけ、討死は覺悟
といふ身輕の打扮を爲し、「重二功勵ニ」と吟ずるや
右の第一圖のごとく、刀を脱して又を下にして
捧げ、（すべて刀を捧ぐるに、縱ひ鞘に收まりた
りとも、双は我方にして、双背を向ふ、或は上
みするふと體なり、）「單身躍馬」と吟するや、刀
を佩して馬に乘りたる心持になり。左の手に手
綱を持ち、右の手にて馬臀を鞭うつさまを爲し
手綱を鞍の前輪に結ひ付け、「向ニ房螢ニ」と吟する
や、居合の形にて抜打に斬り、或は突き、劍術
の形にて種々に左の第二圖のごとく斬廻るなり。
此時にこそ、撃劍或は居合の諸手を見すべし

Second Illustration

While reciting *Tan Shin Uma wo Odorashi,* or *Spurring his horse he moves out alone*, sheathe your Katana and affect a manner as if astride a horse. Pretend you are holding your horse's reins with your left hand and a whip in your right hand. Make a show of striking the horse's rear with your whip. Next, make a show of tying off the Tezuna 手綱, or Reins, to the pommel of your saddle.

While reciting *Ryoei ni Muko,* or *Heading into the barbarians' encampment*, recall the previously introduced Iai no Kata and cut with a rapid Nuki-uchi 抜打, Draw and Cut.

Another possibility is to do a Tsuki 突, or Straight Thrust. Then you should twist about cutting around yourself while making use of the panoply of Kenjutsu techniques. This is shown in the second illustration on this page.

For more information on how to cut with the sword when doing Kenbu, you should refer to the first volume, Gekken 撃劍, or the section on Iai in this volume.

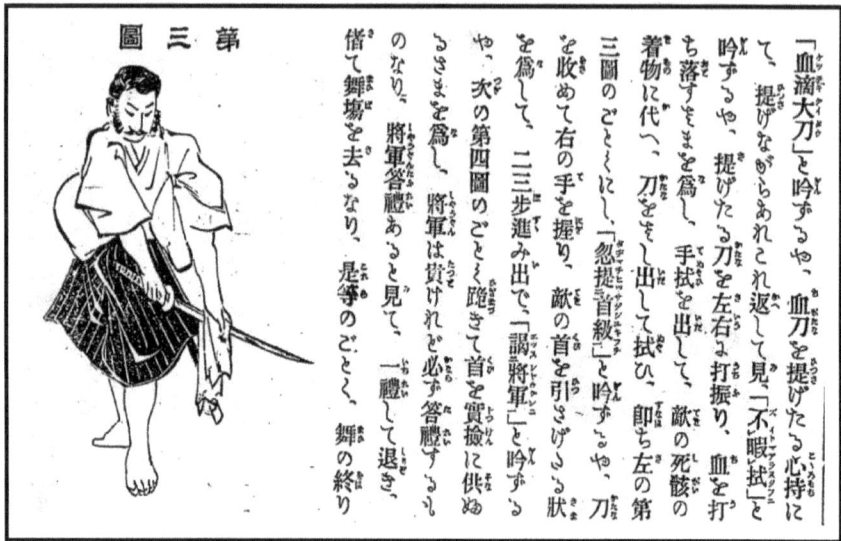

「血潮大刀」と吟ずるや、血刀を提げたる心持に
て、提げながらあれこれ返して見、「不眼拭」と
吟ずるや、提げたる刀を左右に打振り、血を打
ち落すさまを爲し、手拭を出して、敵の死骸の
着物に代へ、刀をさし出して拭ひ、即ち左の第
三圖のごとくにし、「忽提首級」と吟ずるや、刀
を收めて右の手を握り、敵の首を引さげゐる狀
を爲して、二三歩進み出で、「謁將軍」と吟ず
るや、次の第四圖のごとく跪きて首を實撿に供ぬ
さまを爲し、將軍は貴けれど必ず答禮するゝ
なり、將軍答禮あると見て、一禮して退き、
惜て舞墺を去るなり、是等のごとく、舞の終り

Third Illustration

While reciting *Chi-teki Daito*, or *Daito*[100] *soaked in blood*, show how you are brandishing a Chi-gatana, or a Katana drenched in blood. While carrying it look around for another adversary. While incanting *Nugui ni Itoma Arazu*, or *There was not time even to wipe the blade*, do a series of big arching strokes with a sudden stop at the end to the left and right to sling the blood from the blade.

Taking up a Tenugi, or a small multipurpose cloth, from one of the enemy dead lying about, draw the Katana through it. This is shown in the third illustration. While reciting *Tachimachi Shukyu Hisage*, or *Presenting the enemy's severed head forthwith*, sheathe your Katana and form a fist with your right hand and pretend you are holding the hair of a severed head.

Next, as the fourth illustration shows, take two or three steps forward and intone *Shogun Etsu*, or *An audience with the Shogun*. Then offer up the severed head for inspection and identification, This is known as Kubi-jikken, Establishing the Authenticity of a Head Taken in Battle. If the Shogun is a true noble he will certainly bestow praise. Upon receiving this from the Shogun, do a single bow and withdraw.

---

[100] 大刀 Daito is basically a Katana with a longer blade.

に一禮することあれば、別に再び看客へ一禮す
るに及ばず、是れ同じことを二つ重りて、見ること
とを厭ふ故なり。

第一句を舞ふときには、忠義心の身心に満ち
みちたる思入あり。

第二句を舞ふときには、勇氣凜々として、勇

第三句を舞ふときには、血戰して戰ひつかれ
み立ちゐる思入あり。

第四句を舞ふときには、志のごとくなりたる
を喜び、いかにも嬉しき思入あるべし。即ち

意氣揚々たる所を示すべきなり。

圖　四　第

Fourth Illustration

Having finished the performance you would typically do a bow and withdraw from the stage. This is true for all other Kenbu techniques. Here, however, repeating the bow to the assembled viewers is unneccssary as it repeats itself. This would make it redundant and somewhat off putting.[101]

When performing the first verse a sense of duty and honor should permeate your entire body.

When enacting the second verse you should be quivering with bravery and be infused with the essence of courage.

When enacting the third verse you should appear thoroughly wasted after the bloody battle.

When enacting the fourth verse, suffuse yourself with excitement and joy at having fulfilled your intended goal.

You should endeavor to convey the exuberance of this success.

---

[101] Note that the sword is placed on the right-hand side when before the Shogun.

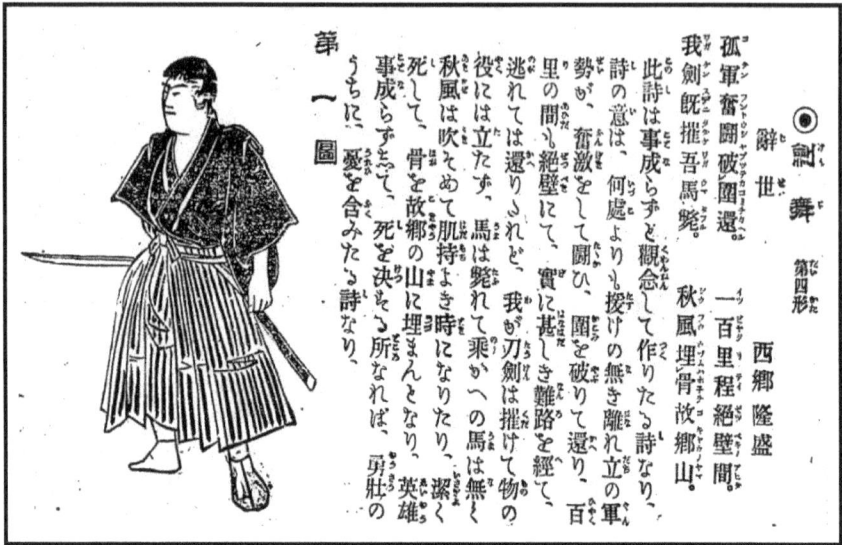

Kenbu Sword Dance
Fourth Kata
<u>**First Illustration**</u>

辞世

Death Poem

By Saigo Takamori 西郷隆盛 (1828 –1877)

孤軍奮闘破囲還
The solitary unit rallies its nerve and fights,
Breaking free of the ring of soldiers, they make their way home.
一百里程絶壁閒
A distance of a hundred odd Ri,
Between great, sheer cliffs.
我剣既摧吾馬斃
The blade of my sword is all but worthless,
My horse falters.
秋風埋骨故郷山
The autumn winds will buy my bones,
The mountains of home.

The subject of this poem is not based on a real event. The meaning of this poem is a military unit cut off and with no hope of rescue, rallies and breaks through the ring of enemy troops that have surrounded them. They travel a hundred Ri 里 along a trail between sheer cliffs and despite the extreme rigors of the road they can make their way home.[102] However, all their Katana are bent and good for nothing. Their horses are exhausted and no fresh mounts can be found.

The time of autumn winds has come. The cool light touch of that breeze is upon their skin. They seek a gallant death and to have their bones buried in the mountains of their hometown. Though they did not become heroes they seek an appropriate place to end their lives. This poem describes these warriors' delight in finding a grand location.

---

[102] The old unit of distance the Ri was equivalent to 3.927 kilometers or 2.44 miles. According to Manaka "Unsui" Sensei Kancho of the Jinenkan indicated that the term "a hundred Ri" does not refer to a specific distance but rather "a very long way".

此舞ひ方は、「孤軍奮闘」と吟ずるや、居合の形にて刀を抜き、其れより剣術の形にて上下縦横に斬り廻り、「破囲遁」と吟ずるや、詩の句のごとく、囲みを破る心持にて、前面のみを斬り立て、囲みを破りたる状さて、二三歩進み出づること、右の第一圖の如くにし、夫より「一百里程」と吟ずるや、後とをふりかへり見て、遠くのれ来りしものかなとの思入を爲し、「絶壁間」と吟ずるや、左の第二圖のごとく、左右の険阻なるを打るがむるさまを爲し、如何にも険阻なる間道にてあるとの、思入あるべし、軍敗れて退軍するには、斯る處を經ることあるゝのなり

第二圖

Second Illustration

The way this is enacted is to intone *Kogun Funtoshi* or *The solitary unit rallies its nerve and fights,* as you use the Iai no Kata, or the designated method for sword drawing, to take out your Katana. From there use Kenjutsu techniques to cut up, down, left, right and all around yourself.

While reciting *Kakomi wo Yabute Kaeru* or *Breaking free of the ring of soldiers, they make their way home,* do as this verse of the poem describes. Act as if you are attempting to break through the ring of opponent's around you by attacking only in front. Upon breaking out step forward two or three strides as the first illustration above depicts.

From there, while reciting *Ippyaku Ritei* or *A distance of a hundred odd Ri*, look back over your shoulder and affect the manner of one looking across a vast distance.

As you chant *Zeppiki no Aida* or *Between great, sheer cliffs* do as is shown in the second illustration above. Act as if you are penned in on two sides by walls of rock. Portray the actions of men passing down a trail bordered on the left and right by dangerous mountain faces. The fact that you are a group that was defeated and is now withdrawing should be portrayed.

第三圖

「我剣既摧」と吟ずるや、持つ所の刀を打かへし
て、鍔元より切先まで打ながめ、即ち左の第三
圖のごとくにし「吾馬斃」と吟ずるや、刀を投
びすて、澁りを見て、後居に堂と坐して、扇を抜き
の思入あり、「秋風埋骨」と吟ずるや、左の手
にて右の手に握り、「故郷山」と吟ずるや、
て衣服をひろげ、腹を寛げて切腹する状を爲
すべし。即ち次の第四圖のごとくするなり。
因に云ふ、切腹の事は、中々式あることにて
深腹を切り、臓腑を出すなどは、豪傑のごと
く思ふ者あれど、是れ正式に背きたる、無礼
の切腹なり。蕎圖などに、豪傑の切腹をあら
はさんとて、臓腑を引出し、向ふへ打付ける
などの状を描けり。亂暴なる切腹と謂ふべ
し

Third Illustration

While incanting *Waga Ken Sudeni Kudaku* or *The blade of my sword is all but worthless*, turn the side of your Katana towards you and examine it from the Tsuba-moto to the Ki-saki or point. This is as shown in the third illustration above.

While incanting *Waga Uma Taore* or *My horse falters*, throw your Katana away. Make as if observing your surroundings and then lower yourself into Za, or the formal way of sitting. Assume the air of one who is dejected.

Intone *Shufu wa Hone wo Uzumu,* or *The Autumn winds will bury my bones*, as you draw your Ogi, or folding fan and grip it in your right hand. You should intone *Kokyo no Yama,* or *The mountains of home*, while you open your shirt with the left hand. Relax your stomach and prepare for Seppuku, or ritual suicide. The body should be positioned as shown in the following fourth illustration.

Incidentally, when speaking of Seppuku, you should understand it is highly ritualized. There are those that believe slicing deep into the abdomen and flinging the intestines out is the mark of a great man, however this turns its back entirely on the correct, prescribed tradition. Doing such a thing is Burei Seppuku 無礼切腹, or a Seppuku without honor.

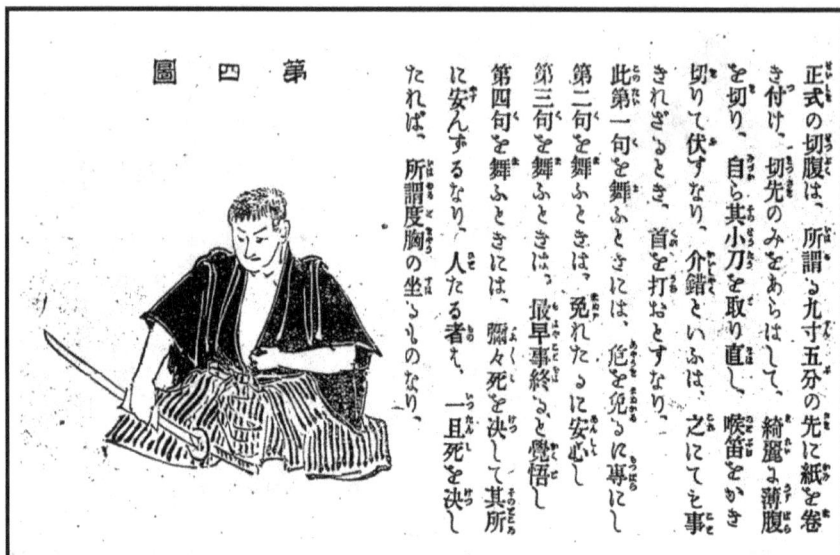

第四圖

正式の切腹は、所謂る九寸五分の先に紙を巻き付け、切先のみをあらはして、自ら其小刀を取り直し、切りて伏すなり。介錯といふは、之にても事きれざるとき、首を打おとすなり。

此第一句を舞ふときには、危を免るるに専にし
第二句を舞ふときは、免れたるに安心し
第三句を舞ふときは、最早事終ると覺悟し
第四句を舞ふときには、彌々死を決して其所に安ずるなり。人たる者も、一旦死を決したれば、所謂度胸の坐るものなり。

Fourth Illustration

Illustrations and so forth often depict masterful Seppuku scenes where a Samurai flings his Zofu 臓腑, or the innards, with such force they nearly strike those observing. However, this should be classified as utterly artless and undignified.

Correct Seppuku is done by wrapping a piece of paper around the blade of your so called Kusengobu 九寸五分, which is another name for the knife. Only the Kisaki 切先, or end of the blade, should be showing[103].

Then, a clean, beautiful, shallow cut is done along the abdomen. You would then bring your Shoto 小刀, short sword, up place it against the Nodo-bue 喉笛, or windpipe and draw it across.

---

[103] The term Kusengobu, which refers to the Tanto knife, is a combination of old Japanese measurements. Nine Sun 九寸 and five Bu 五分. A Sun, pronounced "soon" is 3.03 centimeters and a Bu is 0.303 centimeters. The total length of it being roughly 29 centimeters. This has come to be the preferred length of the Tanto, or knife.

Upon seeing this done, the Kaishaku, or second, would cut your head off.

When enacting the first verse, throw yourself into the role of breaking free of danger.

When enacting the second verse, depict the relief you feel after having broken through.

When enacting the third verse, show how you have prepared to end it all.

When enacting the fourth verse, show your satisfaction in finding a place to die.

Those that aspire to show that they are truly alive, once having decided to end their lives they become the very essence of bravery.

Translators note:

This poem is ostensibly by Saigo Takamori. In September of 1877 he was leading troops against the government. During the combat Saigo was shot twice, once in the thigh and once through the waist. According to a historical marker in Kagoshima, he was "650 steps from his hideout cave" (which you can still tour!) He then allegedly composed the above poem and then committed seppuku. His Kaishakunin, Beppu Shinsuke, cut his head off and hid it from the government troops.

According to the 1937 book *Famous Chinese Poem Appreciation* 名文鑑賞読本漢詩漢文, this poem, while extremely famous, is not actually by Saigo Takamori himself. The author actually Nishi Dosen 西道僊 (1836~1913). Dozen was an independent newspaper publisher who supported Saigo Takamori, he composed the poem upon hearing of Saigo's death in battle. Due to an editing error, when the poem was reprinted in *Past and Present Master Poets* 古今名家詩抄, the author was listed as Takamori.

Therefore, many assumed this was the poem Saigo Takamori composed before committing suicide. Though having been shot through the waist it seems unlikely he was in any condition to compose poetry. This poem was also listed as "author unknown" in some volumes on Kenbu.

The poem printed in this volume varies slightly from other versions as it uses the phrase 絶壁 "sheer cliffs" while other versions have it as 壘壁 "battlements." Another title of this poem is 詠西郷隆盛, a *Song of Saigo Takamori*. Below is a version of the Kanbun with arrows indicating inflection. The author is listed as Nishi Dosen and the title as Shiroyama 城山, *Castle Mountain*, the original name.

城山　西道仙

孤軍奮鬪破圍還

一百里程壘壁間

吾劍既折吾馬斃

秋風埋骨故郷山

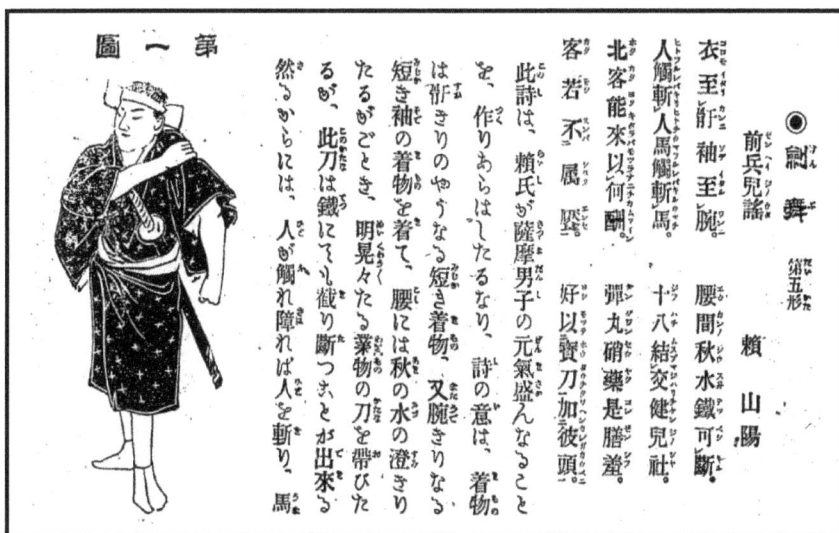

◎ Kenbu Sword Dance
Fifth Kata <u>First Illustration</u>

Song of the Youthful Vanguard 前兵児謠
By Rai Sanyo 頼山陽 (1780～1832)

衣至骭袖至腕 腰間秋水鐵可斷

The Kimono only covers the shins, sleeves stop above the forearms
On the hip a blade as still as the water of a lake in autumn,
That can cut right through steel.

人觸斬人馬觸斬馬 十八結交健兒社

If a person challenges, that person will be cut down,
If a horse is encountered, a horse will be cut down.
Eighteen-year olds encounter others of the same mind.

北客能來何以酬 彈丸硝藥是膳羞

Should visitors from the north appear, What is it going to take?
Bullets and gunpowder! Your fine meal is all ready!

客猶不屬饜 好以寶刀加渠頭

Should our visitors be not satisfied with their feast, Ready!
With your treasured sword,
You bring your Katana down on their heads

This poem was crafted by Rai Sanyo[104] to invigorate the young men of Satsuma, in the lower island of Kyushu. This poem describes a person in a Kimono short enough that it doesn't even cover the shins. The upper shirt is also short enough so that most of the arms are showing. They have slid a gleaming, glittering Waza no Katana 業物の刀, or a Well-forged and Razor-Sharp Katana, which was crafted by a master.[105] It lies resting on the hip as serene as lake water in autumn.

Further, should a person seek to obstruct its way this blade could cut right through them. Should a horse obstruct your way, you could use it to cut the beast in two.[106]

---

[104] Sanyo, pictured below, studied Chinese and wrote essays about history and politics. He is most famous for Nihongaishi or *The History of Japan From the Outside,* which collected foreign writings about Japan.

[105] The Satsuma area has been famous for sword forging since the Heian Era (794 to 1185).

[106] The title of this Kanbun uses the term Zenpei 前兵, or vanguard, which is a designation from the former Imperial Army of Japan. They are the part of the vanguard that goes out *beyond* the very front lines, so it is kind of like the vanguard of the vanguard, alerting the main force of attack and defending.

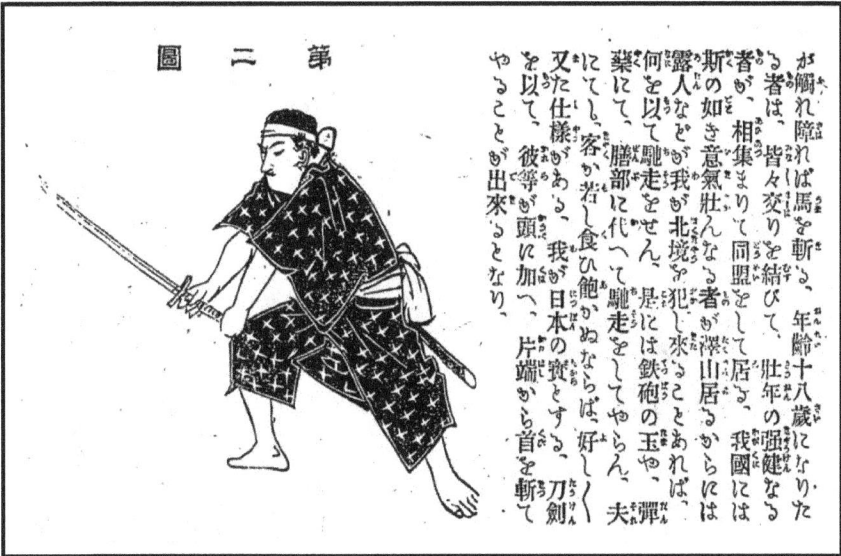

第二圖

が倜れば障れば馬を斬る、年齢十八歳になりた
斯者は、相集まりて同盟をして居る。壮年の強健なる我國には
者は、皆々相集まりて同盟をして居る。澤山居るからには、夫れ彈
露人などが我が北境を犯し来ることもあれば、是には鉄砲の玉や、
何をもて馳走をせんや、膳部に代へて馳走をしてやらん、
藥にて、客か若し食ひ飽かぬならば、好しく
又仕様はある、我日本の寶とする、刀劔から
を以て、彼か若し食ひ飽かぬならば、頭に加へ、片端から首を斬りて
やることが出來るとなり。

Second Illustration

Those youths set to turn eighteen years of age are all intermixing and forming relationships. The strongest of these young warriors are meeting each other and finding the same warrior spirit exists within all of them. There are many nowadays who are passionately devoted to our country. This is in no small part due to Rojin 露人, or Russians, and others seeking to invade out northern borders. [107]

Therefore, we will use any means necessary to send them scampering. We will fire musket balls and use gunpowder. If that does not suffice then, very well, very well, we have another method. The treasure of Japan, the edged weapon known as the Katana will be brought forth. We will bring it to their necks and cut across from one side to the other.

---

[107] The Russians were "invading" parts of China that Japan sought to control. Russia was after a warm water port on the Pacific, and found what they were looking for in Port Arthur. Later, the Russo-Japanese War (1904–1905) was fought for the possession of Port Arthur. The Russians were soundly defeated in this war, much to the surprise of the western powers.

此舞ひ方を、「衣至肝」と吟ずるや、
く袴の股立を取りて、刔までに至らせ、「袖至腕」
と吟ずるや、前の第一圖のごとく、兩袖を腕ま
くりして短くし、兩腕を張りて、一二歩進み出で
「腰間秋水」と吟ずるや、居合の形にて腰なる刀
をスラリと引き抜き、大上段に眞向にかざし
「鐵可斷」と吟ずるや、鐵をも斷る心持にて、
藥切の手にて、勢ひ込んで斷ること、第二圖の
ごとくにすべし。
此處の大上段の構へ方、及び卷藁の切り方、
正式にかなへば、嘸喝采を得ん。

Third Illustration

This is performed by reciting *Koromo Kanni Itaru* or *The Kimono only covers the shins,* as you draw your Hakama up Mata-dachi, or "revealing your lower legs style," which keeps your feet from getting tangled. Thus, you stand bravely with your shins exposed.

While incanting *Sode wan ni Itaru* or *The sleeves stop above the forearms,* do as is shown in the first illustration. Namely roll the excess fabric of your shirt up above your elbows, and then flex both arms.

Taking one or two steps out intone *Yoh Kanno Shusui* or *On the hip, a blade as still as the water of a lake in autumn.* Then, using the Iai techniques, draw your Katana from your hip with a Surari ス ラ リ, or the sound of something being done smoothly.

Raise your Katana overhead in Daijodan Kamae as you face the audience intone *Tetsu kiru beshi,* or *Can cut right through steel.* While holding the image of yourself cutting through steel in your heart, slice down with furious inertia through an imaginary Maki-wara, or rolled grass mat used for cutting practice. This should be done as shown in the second illustration.

If you can take proper Diajodan stance and demonstrate a textbook cut of the Maki-wara, you are sure to draw great applause.

「人觸斬人」と吟ずるや、居合の形にて拜み打に刀を振り上げ斫おろし、「馬觸斬馬」と吟ずるや第三圖のごとく神速に八相に搆へ、右より左へ斬りて、馬の前足を斬り拂ふ狀を爲す。是等の處にて、居合劍術の手を充分にあらはし、八相に搆へて、横に彼り拂ふなど、誠に脚肉にて、譯知りたる者は、思はず妙々の聲を發し、大喝采を爲すに至るべし。「十八結交」と吟ずるや、刀を鞘に收め、左を指さと、又右を指さし、一先づ兩手を廣げて、胸の邊りに寄せ、兩手を合せて握りしめ、(これ

第四圖

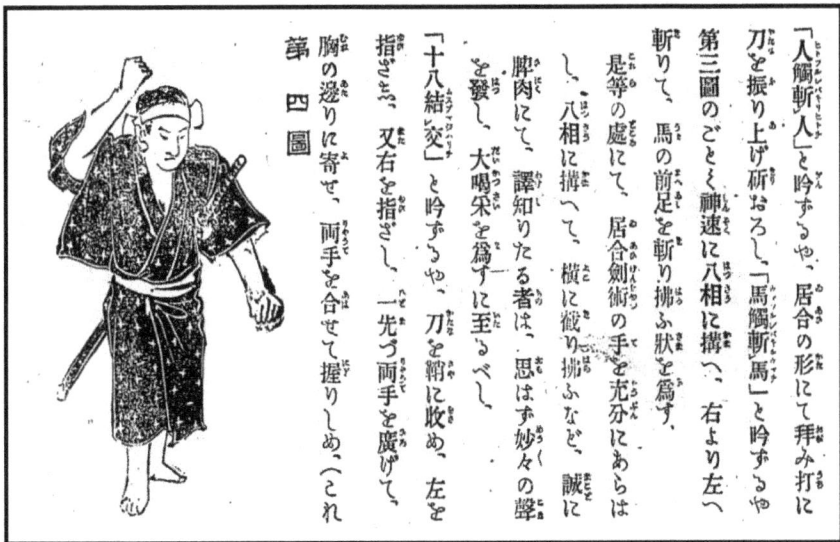

Fourth Illustration

While reciting *Hitofureba Hito wo kiru*, or *If a person challenges, that person will be cut down*, bring your Katana up with both hands and cut down in a sharp strike. This is an Iai technique known as Ogami Uchi 拜み打, or hands together as if praying strike.

While reciting *Uma Suwareba Uma wo Kiru*, or *If a horse is encountered, a horse will be cut down*, go into Haso no Kamae with Shinsoku, Divine Swiftness. Swing your Katana from right to left in a huge arc, as if you were trying to take out the legs of a horse.

At this point is prudent to note that you should be presenting all the finer points of Iai, Sword Drawing as well as Kenjutsu, Sword Fighting. When entering Haso no Kamae, or when doing the great arcing cut, there is a subtlety that is often overlooked. Those that are far along the path of swordsmanship make an exclamatory sound that is timed deftly with the cut. If done properly this will result in an explosion of approving cheers.

While reciting *Juhachi Majiwari wo Musubu*, or *Eighteen-year olds encounter others of the same mind*, return your Katana to the scabbard. Gesture, first with the fingers of the left hand then with the fingers of the right. Spreading both hands wide in an all-encompassing expanse move as if bringing all to your breast and join both hands together (This gesture indicates how many like-minded are brought together and unified).

は廣く友を集め、圓結するの形ちを示すなり。）

「健兒社」と吟ずるや、第四圖のごとく、左の手にて拳を固めて、右の腕こぶを打ち、右の手の拳にて、左の腕瘤を打ち、兩足を廣げ、又る兩足を集めて坐上を踏み鳴らし、いかにも強健なる男兒なるを示し、

「北客能來」と吟ずるや、左の第五圖のごとく、左の手ぇて鯉口を持ち、右の手を翳して遙かの方を望み、スワと言はべ抜き打ちにせんと、居合の腰つきを爲し、「以何酬」と吟ずるや、頭を左右ゝ傾げ、腕を叉み、暫し考ふる狀を爲し、此恩案中に、先には怒りて、後々は莞爾する所あるべし。

第五圖

Fifth Illustration

While reciting *Kenji no Sha,* or *Society of healthy youths,* do as shown in the fourth illustration. Tighten your left hand into a fist and strike your flexed right arm, then make a fist with your right hand and strike your flexed left arm. Stand with your legs spread wide, then bring them together with a loud stomp. The reverberations of this on the ground show the vigor of the young men.

While reciting *Hokukaku yori Kitaraba,* or *Should visitors from the north appear*, do as shown in the fifth illustration above. Take the Koi Guchi 鯉口, or the opening of the Saya, with your left hand while raising your right to shield your eyes. Make as if gazing off into the distance. To put it simply, you are prepared to do Nuki-uchi 抜き打ち, or draw and cut in one motion, as you have your legs spread and hips lowered.

While reciting *Nani wo Motte Mukuin,* or *What is it going to take,* tilt your head first to the left then to the right as you consider. Then cross your arms and assume the pose of one deep in thought for several beats.

Be sure to note that you should first display anger, then, during your introspection, allow it to evolve into amusement.

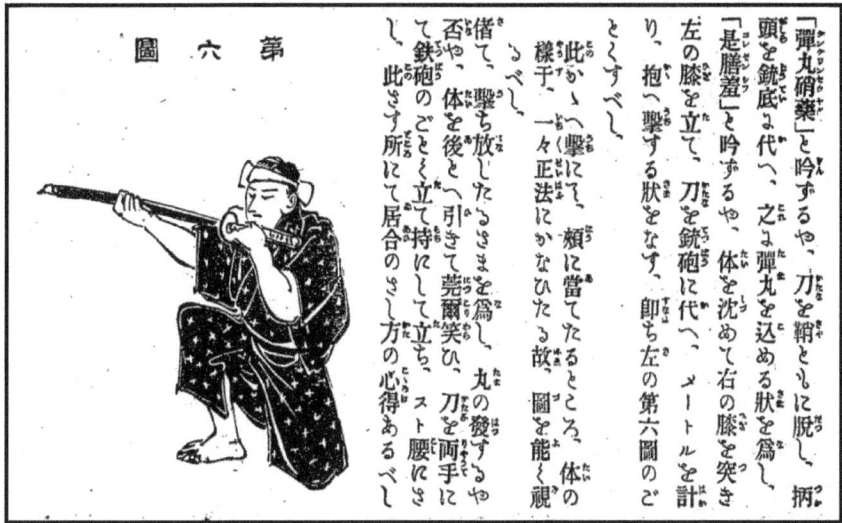

第六圖

「彈丸硝薬」と吟ずるや、刀を鞘ともに脱し、柄
頭を銃底の代へ、之に彈丸を込める状を爲し、
「是膳澄」と吟ずるや、之を
左の膝を立て、刀を銃砲に代へ、メートルを計き
り、抱へ撃する状をなす、即ち左の第六圖のご
とくすべし。
此かゝへ撃に、頬に當てたるところ、體の
様子、一々正法にかなひたる故、圖を能く視
るべし。
偖て、撃ち放したるさまを爲し、丸の發するや
否や、體を後へ引きて莞爾と笑ひ、刀を兩手に
して鉄砲のごとく立て持にして立て、スト腰にさ
し、此出す所にて居合のうしろ方の心得あるべ
し

Sixth Illustration

While reciting *Dangan Shoyaku*, or *Bullets and gunpowder*, take your Katana, still in its scabbard, out of your belt and make as if the Tsuka-Gashira, Pommel, is the butt of your rifle. Mime loading rounds into your gun.

While reciting *Kore Zenshu*, or *Your fine meal is all ready!*, drop down, sticking your right knee on the ground. With your left knee still up, use the Katana as if it were a rifle and judge the distance. Make as if firing the rifle, in other words, as shown in the sixth illustration above.

Ensure that you have proper form, with the gun on your cheek and all the points of the body positioned correctly. Scrutinize the illustration above.

So then, as soon as you finish "firing your rifle," step back one pace and allow a grin to spread on your face. Still holding the Katana as if it were a rifle, rise to a standing position.

Slip the Katana back onto your hip with a smooth Suto スト sound of something sliding cleanly in. Stop when your Tsuba, or Hand-guard, meets your belt.

When doing this one should be following the manner prescribed in Iai [108].

---

[108] There were two main rifles used by Japan around this time. Japan developed and introduced the Murata Rifle 村田銃 in the 13th Year of the Meiji Emperor, in 1880.

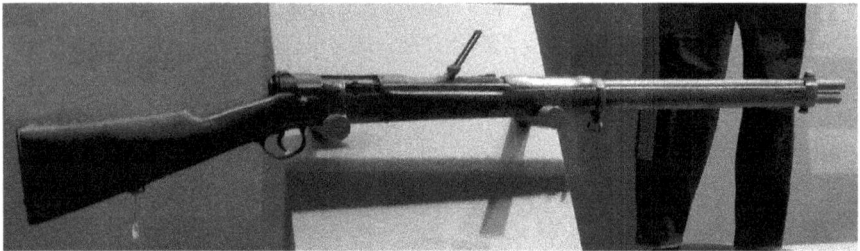

The Arisaka rifle 有坂銃 came into use around 1897, and eventually replaced the Murata. It was used up through the end of World War II, and by the Japan Self-defense forces from 1952-61.

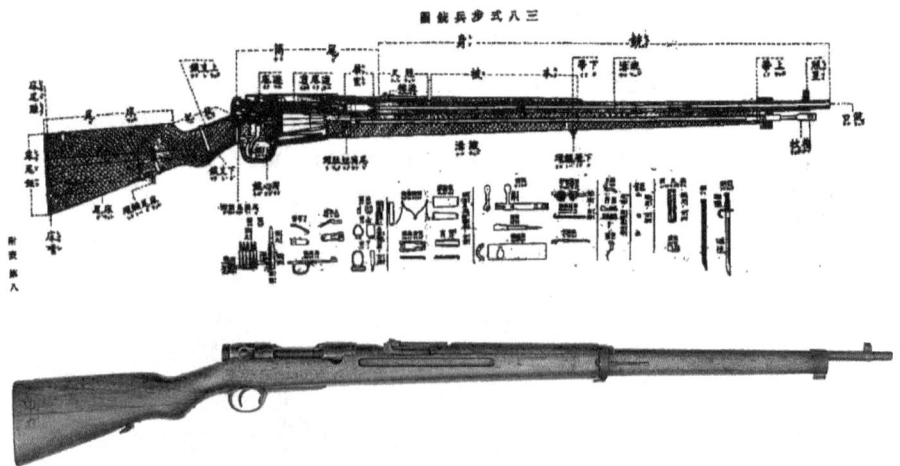

Seventh Illustration

　　Consider the situation for a while as you intone *Kaku Moshi Shokuen Sezunba*, or *Should our visitors be not satisfied with their feast.* Placing your left hand on the Koi-guchi, slowly draw out a portion of the blade. Next, placing your right hand on the handle, near the Mekugi peg that holds the handle together, draw the blade out more. Then, as shown in the seventh illustration ferociously slam it back into the scabbard, making a dramatic ringing sound.

　　At this point it would also be prudent to take off the Sageo, or cord attached to your Katana, and use it to tie up the sleeves of your Kimono in Tama-Dasuki style. While reciting Yosh!, or *Ready!*, allow your forehead to drop in a nod as if saying "all is good."

　　While chanting *Hotowo Motte*, or *By means of a treasured sword*, use the Iai technique previously introduced to draw your sword with a Surari スラリ sound of something being done smoothly.

　　As soon as you finish your draw, immediately bring your Katana overhead. While reciting *Kare ga Kobeni Kuwahen*, or *Bringing the sword to their heads*, step out one pace and, at the same time, cut down with your Katana. This is shown in the following eighth illustration. In other words, you should be going into Daijodan Kamae and then cutting down.

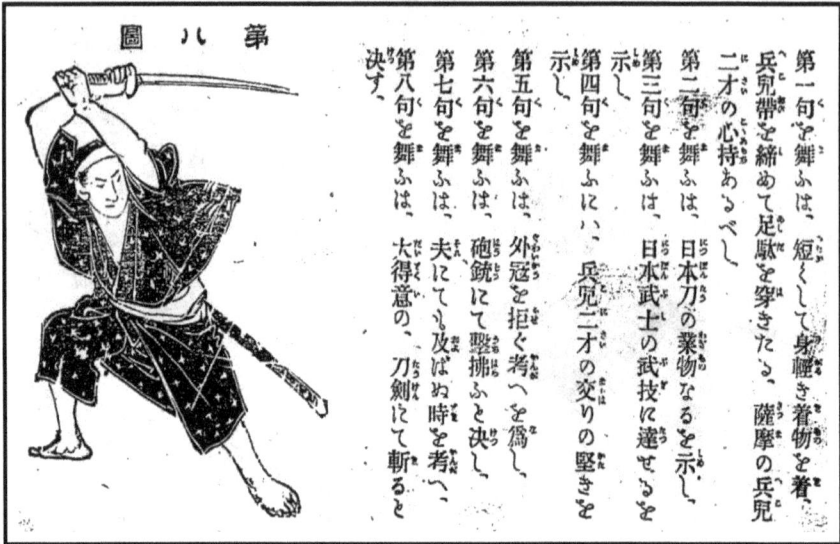

第八圖

第一句を舞ふは、短くして身軽き着物を着、兵児帯を締めて足駄を穿きた。薩摩の兵児二才の心持あるべし

第二句を舞ふは、日本刀の業物なるを示し、

第三句を舞ふは、日本武士の武技に達せるを

第四句を舞ふに、兵児二才の交りの堅きを示し、

第五句を舞ふは、外冠を拒く考へを為し、

第六句を舞ふは、砲銃にて整排ふと決し、

第七句を舞ふは、夫にても及ばぬ時を考へ、

第八句を舞ふは、大得意の、刀剣にて斬ると決す。

Eighth Illustration

When enacting the first verse you should have on a shortened Kimono, a Heko Obi tied about the waist and Ashida sandals on. All the while you should be positioning yourself as an example of a Heko ni Sai, or a youth from fourteen to twenty years old.[109]

---

[109] A Heko Obi 兵児帯 is a wider Obi worn by young soldiers of Satsuma (not in uniform, but when wearing Kimono) and it became fashionable after the Meiji Restoration. It eventually became common on children and currently is fashionable for both men and women when wearing Yukata, summer Kimono. The knot at the back is typically a simple affair, nothing like the complex ones used on formal Kimono.

The Ashida 足駄 are a kind of Geta with big Ha, or teeth, tall enough to keep the wearers' clothing away from the muddy ground.

The people of Satsuma used these terms to describe people:

兵児山: Hekosan (soldier + young + mountain) 7~14 years old

兵児二才: Hekonisai/Hekonise 14~20 years old

中老: Churo 20~30 years old (this is defined as "middle aged" as most people were only expected to live to 50)

When enacting the second verse you should display how your sword is a Waza Mono 業物, or a razor-sharp blade crafted by a master swordsmith.

When enacting the third verse the military arts of the Bushi 武士, or Samurai, should be on display.

The intermingling of the Hekonisai, or youth of Satsuma, should be on display when enacting the fourth verse.

In the fifth verse you must show the act of repelling foreign invaders.

When enacting the sixth verse show that you have decided to sweep the invaders away with rifle fire.

When enacting the seventh verse you should consider that your bullets were not enough of a response.

When enacting the eighth verse you have decided to attack with the technique you have perfected, cutting with a bladed weapon.

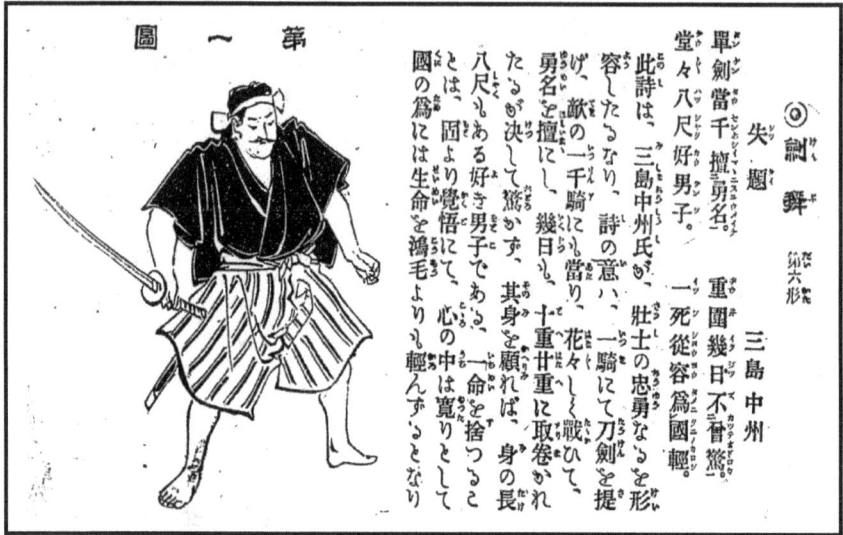

◎ **Kenbu Sword Dance**
Sixth Kata
First Illustration

失題

Untitled

By Mishima Chushu 三島 中洲 (1831-1919)

単剣当千壇勇名

A single sword meets a thousand opponents,
Allowing fame to come to your name unabated.

重囲幾日不曾驚

Being doubly surrounded by the enemy for several days,
Something hardly surprising.

堂々八尺好男子

An impressive frame of eight Shaku, A fine youth.

一死従容為國經

To face your one and only death serenely,
Giving my life for my country is a simple thing.

This poem was written by Mishima Chusho describing the loyalty and bravery of young men in the prime of their lives. What this poem describes is a lone warrior slashing with his Katana, striking down a thousand riders in a magnificent spectacle of swordsmanship.

It comes as no surprise that you have become renowned for your bravery as, over the course of several days, you have been surrounded by multitudes of opponents.

Looking down at your own form, you find a body eight Shaku in height, nearly two and a half meters tall. Having already committed to giving your life away, your spirit is at ease. The reason being is that one feels light as a feather knowing your life will be given up for the good of the country.

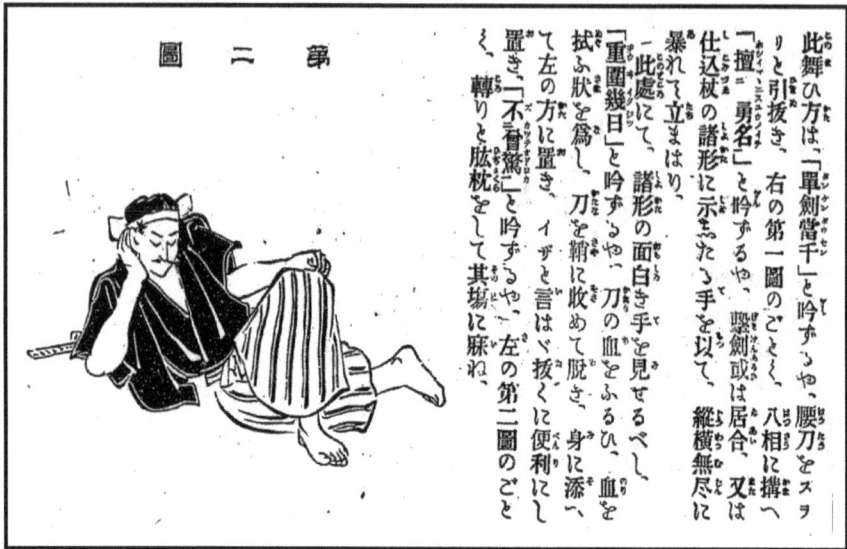

此舞ひ方は、「單劍瞥千」と吟ずるや、腰刀をスラりと引抜き、右の第一圖のごとく、八相に搆へ「擅ニ勇名」と吟ずるや、撃劍或は居合、又は仕込杖の諸形に示されたる手を以て、縦横無尽に暴れて立まはり。一此處にて、諸形の面白き手を見せるべし。「重圍幾日」と吟ずるや、刀の血をふるひ、血を拭ふ状を為し、刀を鞘に収めて脱ぎ、身に添へ、て左の方に置き、イザと言はゞ抜くに便利にし置き、「不覺鴬」と吟ずるや、左の第二圖のごとく、轉りと肱枕をして其場に臠ね。

第二圖

Second Illustration

This dance begins with you reciting *Tanken tosen*, or *A single sword meets a thousand opponents*, as you draw your Katana from your waist with a smooth Surari スラリ sound. As is shown in the first illustration, go into Haso no Kamae.

Intone Yumei wo *Hoshi-mamanisu*, or *Allowing fame to come to your name unabated*. As you speak those words, use Kata from either Gekken, Iai or Shikomi Zue to cut all round you with your Katana. Cut Juomujin 縦横無尽, or in all directions indiscriminately.

For this section the points that make each Kata interesting and unique should be emphasized. While reciting *Jui ikujitsu*, or *Being doubly surrounded by the enemy for several days*, shake the blood off the blade and then make as if wiping clean your Katana with a cloth.

Return your Katana to its scabbard and then remove it from your hip. Stretch out on the ground and lay your sword down on your left, in a position when it can be easily taken up and drawn.

While reciting *Katsu Odorokazu*, or *Something hardly surprising*, do as shown in the second illustration above, namely to prop your head up on your elbow and make as if going to sleep.

第 三 圖

とくすべし。

種々の手にて血戰する狀、即ち次の第四圖の

「爲國輕」と吟ずるや、圍みを破りて還るも爲め

他を願はず、心中は泰然たりとの意を示し、

食指にて、自分の胸を指ざし、其分に安んじて

ことを示し、「一死從容」と吟ずるや、右の手の

かり、是れこそ立派なる日本男兒であると云ふ

つるぎ、腹を出し、足を八文字に廣げて蹈はだ

男子」と吟ずるや、左の第三圖のごとく、胸を

手を上下して、其身の寸尺を取る狀をなし、「好

「堂々八尺」と吟ずるや、立ちて左右の手にて、

Third Illustration

While reciting Dodo Hashaku, or *An impressive frame of eight Shaku*, show how you are measuring yourself by marching your hands, left over right, up your body. Originally the size of the Shaku was the distance between the tip of your thumb and the tip of your forefinger.

While reciting *Kodanshi*, or *A fine youth*, open up your Kimono, exposing first your chest and then your stomach. Spread your legs outward in a Hachi monji, planting your feet firmly like the outspread bottom stroke of the Kanji 八. This is showing how this Japanese youth will become exemplary.

While reciting *Isshi Juyo*, or *To face your one and only death serenely*, point to your chest with your Hitosashi Yubi, or Index Finger, thereby relaxing that part of the body. This demonstrates how you are calm to the core of your being.

While reciting *Kuni no Karoshi Tameni*, or *Giving my life for my country is a simple thing*, use a variety of hand gestures to describe the bloody battles you were in. Show how you broke through the enemy forces surrounding you and were able to return home. In other words, do as is depicted in the following fourth illustration. To be unconcerned about your own death is to feel truly at ease.

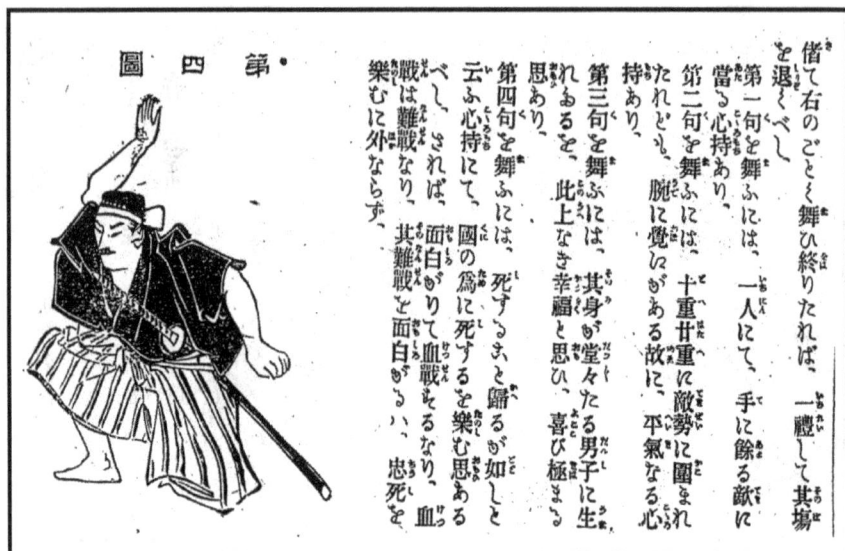

第四圖

偕て右のごとく舞ひ終りたれば、一禮して其場を退くべし

第一句を舞ふには、一人にて、手に餘る敵に當る心持あり、

第二句を舞ふには、十重廿重に敵勢に圍まれたれど、腕に覺ゆがある故に、平氣なる心持あり、

第三句を舞ふには、此上なき幸福と思ひ、其身が堂々たる男子に生れ、喜び極まる、

第四句を舞ふには、死するあと蹈るが如しと思ふ心持にて、國の為に死するを樂む思ある、べし、されば、面白りて血戰するなり、其難戰と面白がるハ、忠死を血戰は難戰なり、樂むに外ならず、

Fourth Illustration

So then, having finished the sections on the previous page, do a Rei, or bow, and withdraw from the stage.

When enacting the first verse, show how you are joining battle with an uncountable number of enemies.

When enacting the second verse project that though you are surrounded by countless enemies, your Ude 腕, or Arm, has remembered many techniques so you are calm and focused.

When enacting the third verse show how you were born into an impressive body of a young man. Due to this you are the height of satisfaction and bliss.

When enacting the fourth verse show how you are prepared to return home dead, yet the thought of giving your life up for your country only gives pleasure. Thus a fabulous bloody battle, a bloody battle is a difficult battle and the spectacle of a difficult battle does not diminish the joy of dying honorably.

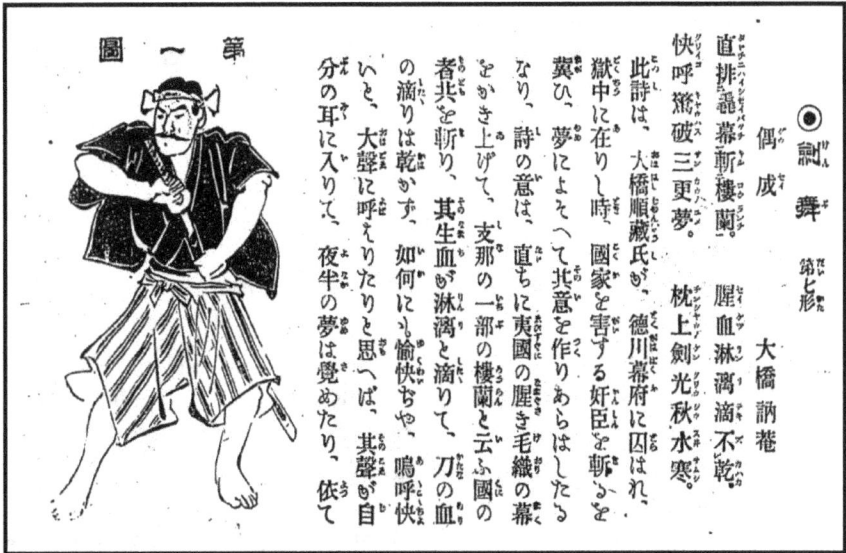

第一圖

◉訓舞　第七形

偶成

大橋訥菴

腥血淋漓滴不乾
枕上劍光秋水寒。

直排毳幕斬樓蘭。
快呼驚破三更夢。

此詩は、大橋順藏氏が、徳川幕府に囚はれ、獄中に在りし時、國家を害する奸臣を斬るを冀ひ、夢によそへて此意を作りあらはしたるなり、詩の意は、直ちに夷國の腥き毛織の幕をとき上げて、支那の一部の樓蘭と云ふ國の者共を斬り、其生血も淋漓と滴りて、刀の血の滴りは乾かず、如何にも愉快ちや、嗚呼快いと、大聲に呼えりたりと思へば、其聲自分の耳に入りりて、夜半の夢は覺めたり、依て

Kenbu Sword Dance
Seventh Kata
First Illustration

偶成

Impromptu
Ohashi Totsuan 大橋訥庵 (1816-1862)

直排毳幕斬樓蘭
Immediately lift the woolen curtain off and discard it!
Cutting into Roran.
腥血淋滴不乾
Awash in fetid blood overflowing the ground,
The Blood has no chance to dry.
快呼驚破三更夢
A dream during the third watch of the night.
枕上劍光秋水寒
The sword by your pillow shining brightly,
As calm as a lake in autumn.

This poem was written by Mr. Ohashi Junzo, as he was called by his friends, while in his cell after having been imprisoned by the Tokugawa Bakufu government. It deals with his hope that Kanshin 奸臣, or disloyal retainers to the emperor, who obstruct patriots be cut down. This poem crafts an ideal dream world.

This poem encourage us to immediately yank off the fetid wool curtain that has been lain across a certain unsophisticated county. Further, the those who are part of the Bakufu government should all be put to the sword.[110]

The freshly spilt blood should leave the ground awash and spilling over, the blood on swords not allowed to dry. All around an ideal outcome. To such degree that you spontaneously exclaim "Indeed!" out loud. That same sound travels to your ears in the deep of night, causing one to awaken.

Having been startled awake, one draws the Katana kept above the pillow. The blade shines like the light off still autumn water, and just as cold.[111]

---

[110] The word "Roran" refers to the Bakufu Government.

[111] Ohashi Totsuan was a big player in the 尊王攘夷 Sonnojoi "honor the emperor expel the foreigners" movement. Perhaps inspired by the Sakuramongai Incident in 1860, he initially helped organize a similar assassination of Ando Nobumasa 安藤信正 in 1862. The attempt failed despite a surprise attack involving pistols and swords. All of the would-be assassins were dispatched at the scene. Though not directly involved Ohashi had been an initial proponent of the assassination, thus he and others were rounded up and thrown in the slammer. It turns out this particular Gokusha 獄舎, or jail was a "hell prison" and the would-be assassins began to die. Ohashi was released after a short time but died shortly thereafter from infection. He was 47 years old.

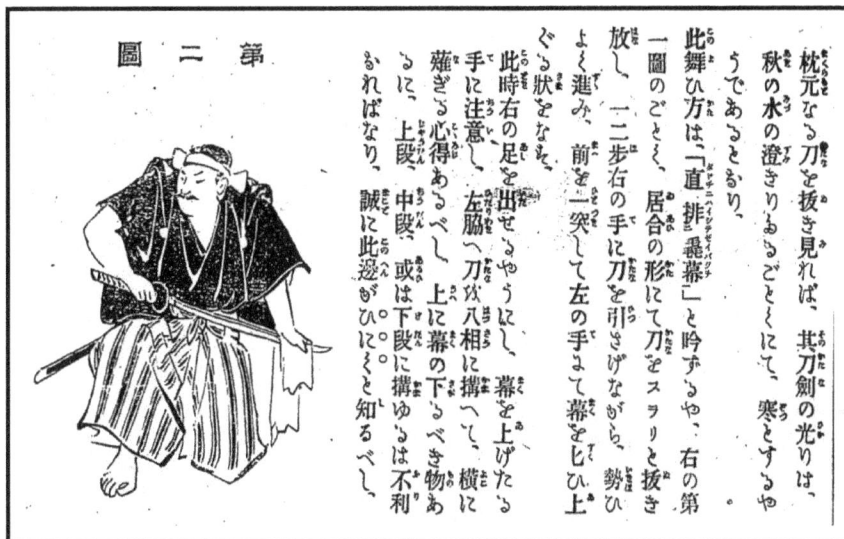

第二圖

枕元なる刀を抜き見れば、其刀劍の光りは、秋の水の澄きりゐるごとくにて、寒とするやうであるぞるぞ。

此舞ひ方は、「直に排し毳幕」と吟ずるや、右の第一圖のごとく、居合の形にて刀をスラリと抜き放し、一二歩右の手に刀を引きさげながら、勢ひよく進み、前を一突して左の手もて幕を七ひ上ぐる状をなせ。

此時の右の足を出せるやうにし、幕を上げたる手に注意し、左脇へ刀次八相に搆へて、横に薙ぎる心得あるべし。上に幕の下るべき物あるに、上段、中段、或は下段に搆ゆるは不利ればなり。誠に此邊がひにくると知るべし。

Second Illustration

This Kenbu is done by first reciting *Tadachi ni Keibaku wo Haishite*, or *Immediately lift the woolen curtain off and discard it!*, while doing as shown in the first illustration.

As the illustration on the previous page shows, draw your Katana out with a smooth Surari スラリ sound in accordance with the manner prescribed in the section on Iai. Rapidly advancing forward one or two steps, raise your Katana up with your right hand as you reach out with the left hand toward a cloth on the ground. Make as if whipping it off the ground.

When enacting this scene, your right leg should be out in front and you should show great caution when lifting the imaginary curtain up. Your Katana should be in Haso no Kamae, with your left side forward, ready to make a great sweeping cut.

As there are all manner of vile things under the curtain you are yanking away, Jodan Kamae, Chudan Kamae, as well as Gedan Kamae are not appropriate to this situation. Note that all of this is satiric or ironic.

327

第三圖

「斬穢蘭」と吟ずるや、直ちに幕を後ろへ跳ねる狀を爲し、跳ぬるや否や、二歩進みて右へ斬りはらひ、神速に上段に搆へて斬おろし「腥血淋漓」と吟ずるや、其血刀を左右へ打ち振り、刀の血を振り落し、「滴不乾」と吟ずるや、腰なる手拭を取り、敵の衣服として、是にて刀を拭ひ即ち右の第二圖のごとくし、又其刀㒵鞘に收めて、脱して下に臥き、自分は其右に添ふて横に麻ね、「快呼驚破」と吟ずるや、ムックと起きて驚きたる狀を爲し「三更夢」と吟ずるや、左の第三圖のごとく起きて四邊りを見まはすべし、即ち「ハテ今のは夢で有ったが」との思入るり、夢でなかりしるらばよいもと、失望の意あり。

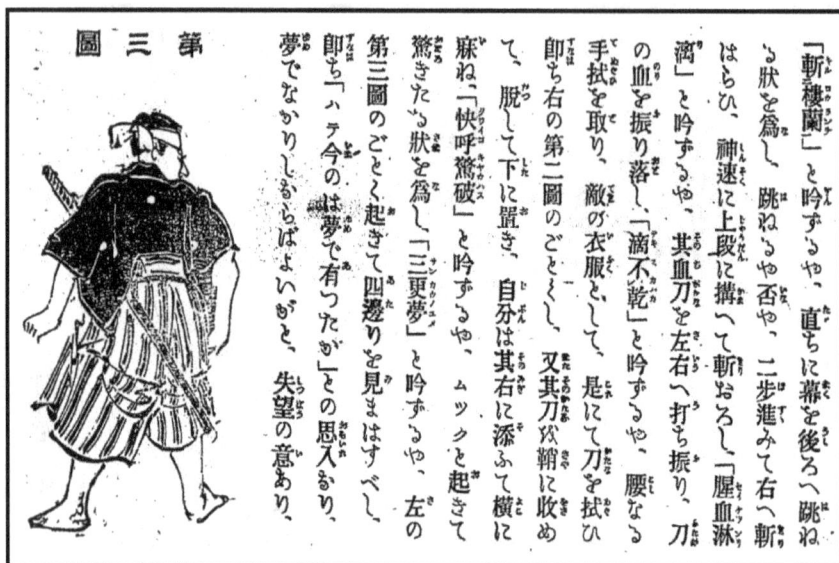

Third Illustration

While reciting *Roran wo Kiru,* or *Cutting into Roran,* immediately fling the curtain behind you. As soon as it is cast off, proceed two paces forward in rapid succession and do a sweeping cut to the right. With Shin-soku, Divine Swiftness, shift to Jodan Kamae and cut down.

While reciting *Seiketsu Rinri,* or *Awash in fetid blood overflowing the ground,* sling the Katana left and right to knock the blood off with a Uchi-furi 打ち振り, Strike and Fling, movement. While reciting *Teki Kawakazu,* or *The blood has no chance to dry,* take your Tenugi cloth from your hip. Use this as if you have taken a cloth from the enemy and wipe off your Katana. This is all depicted in the second illustration on the previous page.

From there, return your Katana to its Saya, or Scabbard. Removing it from your hip, place it on the ground. Next lay down to the right of it and make as if you have gone to sleep.

While reciting *Sanko no Yume,* or *A dream during the third watch of the night,* do as shown in the third illustration above. Wake up and check in all four directions, in other words as if realizing "So then it was a dream I saw?" and then, following that, show you are somewhat dejected at the fact that the dream was not reality.

第 四 圖

「枕上劍光」と吟ずるや、左の第四圖のごとく、刀に氣の付きたる思持にて、其刀を取上げ、坐ながらスラリと居合の形にて抜き、左に鞘を持ち、鐔元より尖頭まで打ち返して見、「秋水寒」と吟ずるや、刀を鞘に收めて腰にさし、少しく身を震はし、又これがあする心持にて、少しく抜きかければ大夫丈といふなごしあり、鍔音はげしく收め、偕て一禮して場を退くべし第一句は冀望を遂げんとし、遂げたるを喜び、第二句は冀望を第四句は刀を見て、第三句は夢なるに失望し氣を取直す心得あるべし

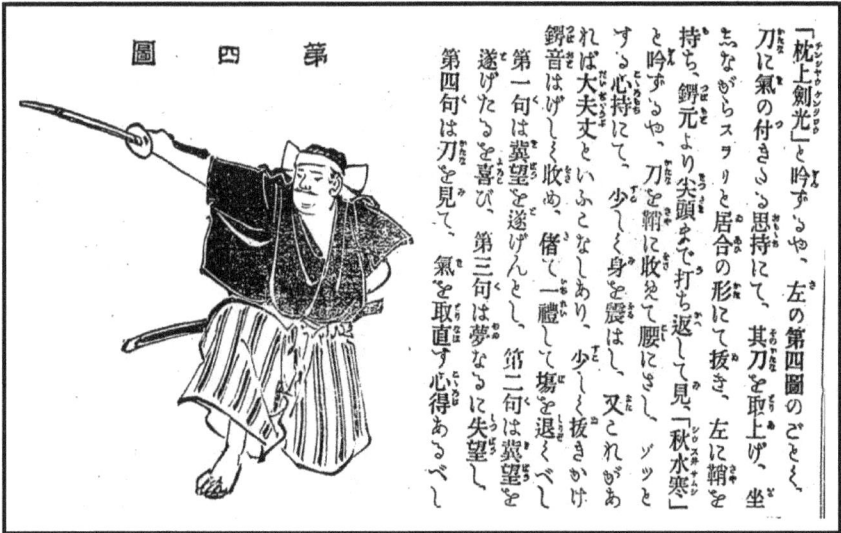

Fourth Illustration

While reciting *Chinjo Kenko,* or *The sword by your pillow shining brightly,* do as is pictured in the fourth illustration. You pick up your Katana, after first having examined it carefully. From a seated position rise up and draw in accordance with the precepts of Iai with a smooth Surari スラリ sound. Your left hand is holding the scabbard while you look the Katana up and down from the Tsuba-moto, or where the blade meets the hand guard, to the Kisaki, or tip.

While reciting *Shusui samushi,* or *As calm as a lake in autumn,* sheathe your Katana and slide the scabbard into your belt. While doing this, show you are looking deeply inward while a slight shudder passes through your body. While imagining how it would be most agreeable if it all came to pass, slide the sword out a bit and then slam it forcefully back in producing a sharp ringing sound as the scabbard connects with the hand guard. Doing a Rei, you should remove yourself from the stage.

In the first verse you should attempt to realize your hopes. In the second verse you are joyous at having achieved your goal. In the third verse, having realized it is a dream your hopes are dashed. In the fourth verse, upon seeing your Katana you are restored to your previous vigor.

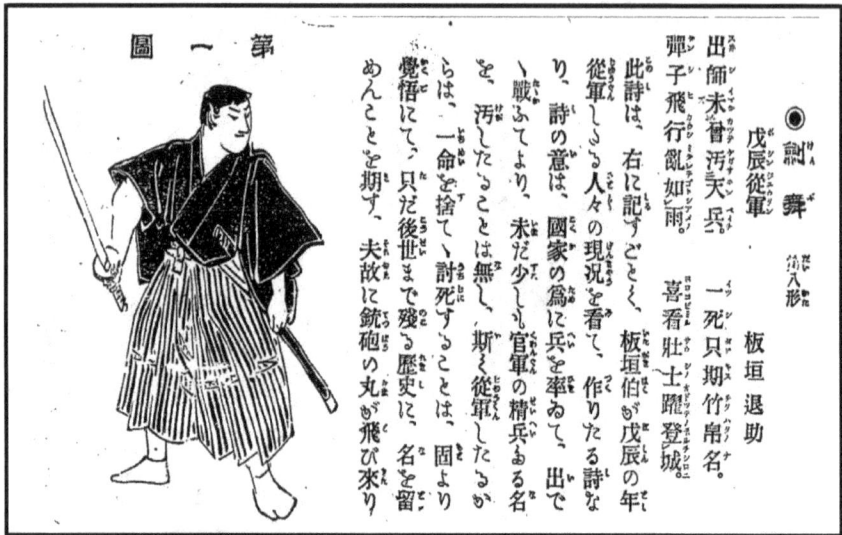

第一圖

◎ 劍舞
　戊辰從軍

板垣 退助

出師未曾汚天兵　一死只期竹帛名。
彈子飛行亂如雨。　喜看壯士躍登城。

此詩は、右に記すごとく、板垣伯が戊辰の年、從軍しるる人々の現況を看て、作りたる詩なり、詩の意は、國家の爲に兵を率ゐて、出でゝ賊ふてより、未だ少しも官軍の精兵ある名を、汚したることは無く、斯く從軍したるからは、一命を捨てゝ討死することは、固より覺悟にて、只だ後世まで殘る歷史に、名を留めんことを期す、夫故に銃砲の丸が飛び來り

◎ Kenbu Sword Dance
Eighth Kata
First Illustration

戊辰從軍
The Boshin Campaign
Itagaki Tasuke 板垣 退助 (1837-1919)

出師未曾汚天兵

The leader steps out,
Never allowing the name of the Heavenly warriors to become
sullied!

一死只期竹工之帛

This one life, this one death I leave to the ages,
Inscribing your name in a Chikuhaku book of bamboo strips.

彈子飛行亂如雨

As the bullets fly hither and yon, Like rain in a wild storm,

喜死壯士躍登城

Seeing pure joy before one's eyes,
The young warrior leaps up the wall of the castle

This poem by Count Itagaki is, as can be gleaned from what is written above, a poem about the state of the people involved in the campaign during the Boshin years of 1868-69. This poem talks about leading troops into combat as part of your patriotic duty. Further, not allowing the hitherto unblemished name of our forces to become sullied during the course of this campaign and, moreover, the fact that you are wholly prepared to give your life up whilst fighting.

This is a chance to have your name be inscribed in history by the following generation. Thus despite the bullets flying, even should they fall like a lashing rain, you do not flinch or hesitate even a little. Through the pain and suffering , the young warrior leaps up to be the first at the castle wall and seeing this brings join and makes ones heart light.[112]

---

[112] Born into the Samurai class Itagaki was a student of Muso Jikiden Eishin School Sword Drawing and the Doteki Takeuchi School Jujutsu. His martial arts skills were called into play when he was attacked by Aihara Nofumi 相原尚褧 after a speech. According to Osa Taketekki's 尾佐竹猛 1929 book *Secret History and Difficult Mysteries of the Meiji Era*『明治秘史疑獄難獄』 *Aihara drew his Tanto and screamed Robber of the Future! He grabbed Itagaki's arm and thrust to the center of his chest. Two thrusts thrust caught Itagaki in the chest, but Itagaki launched an elbow with all his body weight behind it into the midsection of the Opponent, knocking him off balance. Aihara stabbed with the Tanto again, but Itagaki caught it. The action of Aihara twisting the blade and pulling it back sliced Itagaki's thumb off."* Itagaki is alleged to have said: "Itagaki may die, but liberty never!" *Itagaki later credited the teachings of his Jujutsu instructor Yamamoto Danzo* 本山団蔵 *for his being able to fend off his Opponent.*

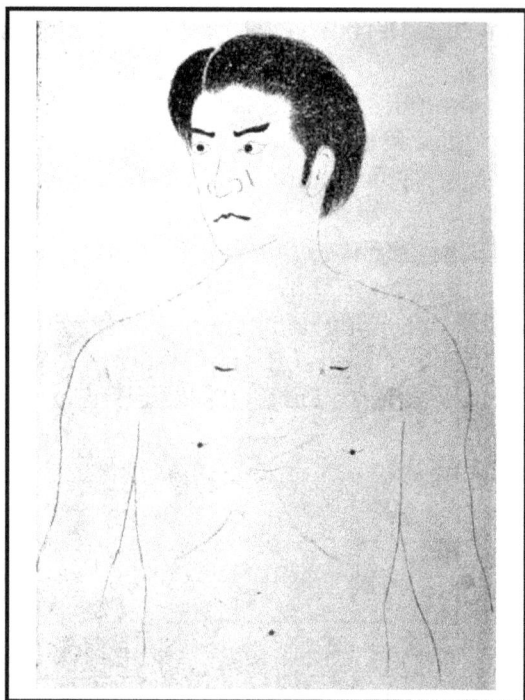

An illustration of the chest wounds Itagaki received during the
attack by Aihara.
Image from Osa Taketekki's 尾佐竹猛
Secret History and Difficult Mysteries of the Meiji Era
『明治秘史疑獄難獄』

するが肝腎なり。

但し、此處は、優然として、隊長の貫目を見

第一圖のごとくし、刀を鞘に收め。

事を喜び、甚だ得意なる樣子を示すこと、右の

是まで數度の戰爭に、一たびも敗を取らざりし

左の手の指を折り、指折り終りて莞爾と笑ひ、

と吟ずるや、後を顧み、目くばせして立止まり

進む狀にて、二足三足進み出で「未嘗汚天兵」

り、刀を拔きて司令刀に搆へ持ち、兵を率ゐて

此舞ひ方は、「出師」と吟ずるや、袴の股立を取

となり、

躍り上つて、城壁に先登するを、喜んで看る

は、之を苦とも困りとも爲で、却て壯士が

て、雨のごとくに亂れかゝりても、少しも厭と

Second Illustration

The way this Kenbu is done is to first recite *Sui Shi,* or *The leader steps out to give orders*, and hoist the sides of your Hakama up and tuck them into your Obi. This keeps your legs from getting tangled in your Hakama. Draw your Katana and take Kame with your Shireito, or sword of command, and make as if leading soldiers.

Proceed forward two or three steps, look over your shoulder and recite *Katsute Tenpei wo Kegasayu Imadazu* or, *Never allowing the name of the Heavenly warriors to become sullied.*

Show that your eyes have become unfocused and count on your fingers. When all the fingers of your hand have been bent in from counting, allow a grin to spread across your face. You, having counted back all the wars, are delighted to find no defeats and you revel in your prowess.

Next, as shown in the first illustration on the previous page, sheathe the Katana in its scabbard. All this should be done with an air of composure, reflecting the gravity of your position as Taicho, or Division Leader.

While reciting *Isshi tada Kisu, or This one life, this one death I leave to the ages*, point to your chest with your right hand. Then, draw your Katana, the symbol of your command, and go into a Kamae.

第 ・ 三 ・ 圖

「二死只期」と吟ずるや、右の手にて我が胸を指
ざし、續いて刀を抜きかけ、右の第二圖のごと
く、金調を爲し、「竹帛名」と吟ずるや、矢立を取
りて名を書き記す狀を爲し、

「弾子飛行」と吟ずるや、刀を抜きて、飛び來る
丸を烈しく左右へ拂ふ狀を爲し、「亂如雨」と吟
ずるや、左の第三圖のごとく、左の手にて扇を
腰より脱き持ち、竹たばに代へ、丸の來るを拒
ぎつゝ、刀をふるひ進む狀を爲し、「喜看」と吟
ずるや、左の手の扇を捨て、右の手に刀を提げ
左の手を額にかざして、遙か向を望み見るべし

Third Illustration

While reciting *Chikuhaku no Na, or Inscribing your name in a Chikuhaku book of bamboo strips*, make as if recording your name with a brush pulled from your Yatate, or portable brush case.

While reciting *Danshi Hikoshi, or As the bullets fly hither and yon*, draw your Katana and make as if vigorously deflecting the flying bullets to the left and right. While reciting *Midarete Ame no Gotoku, or Like rain in a wild storm*, do as is shown in the third illustration above.

With your left hand, take your Ogi, or folding fan, from your waist and is used in place of a Taketaba, or roll of bamboo strips, as a shield to protect from the bullets. As you block the oncoming fire with it, swing your Katana and make as if proceeding forward.

While reciting *Yorokobi miru, or Seeing pure joy before one's eyes*, throw the Ogi in your left hand away. Lowering your Katana in your right hand, raise your left hand to your forehead, sheltering your eyes. You should be looking off into the far distance.

第四圖

「壯士踊登城」と吟するや、左の第四圖のごとく、にこゝと笑ひて、己も引さげ刀にて、進てむさまと為し、蹈止まりて常坐へ引き、刀を收めて一禮し、夫より退くべし、
第一句は、心中の滿悦を示し、
第二句を舞ふときには、名譽を重んじて、死を輕んずる意あり、
第三句を舞ふは、砲烟弾雨を物ともせぬ意あり、
第四句を舞ふときは、已一人の功名を忘れ、全軍の功名をよろこぶ意あるべし、實際勢として斯くなるものなり、

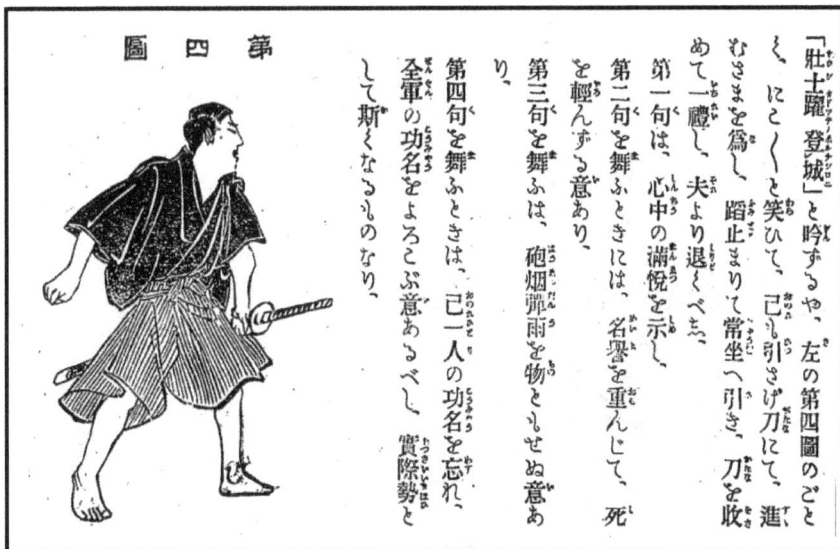

Fourth Illustration

While reciting Soshi Odoteni Shiro ni Noboru, or *The young warrior leaps up the wall of the castle*, do as is shown in the fourth illustration above, gradually change your expression from a grin to outright laughter. You yourself then raise your lowered Katana and make as if advancing.

Following this remove yourself to Joza 常座 , the right edge of the stage. Then, sheathe your sword, execute a Rei and depart the scene.

The first verse consists mainly of displaying great satisfaction.

When enacting the second verse show how honor coming to your name should be revered, just as dying should be seen as something trivial.

When enacting the third verse, understand that it is about not becoming unnerved by the Hoendanu 砲煙弾雨, or a hail of gunfire, bullets and smoke.

When enacting the fourth verse show how you are dismissing all thought of your own successes in battle but, rather, are showing your delight in the success of your entire company.

You should show energy and movement that would be present in an actual combat situation.

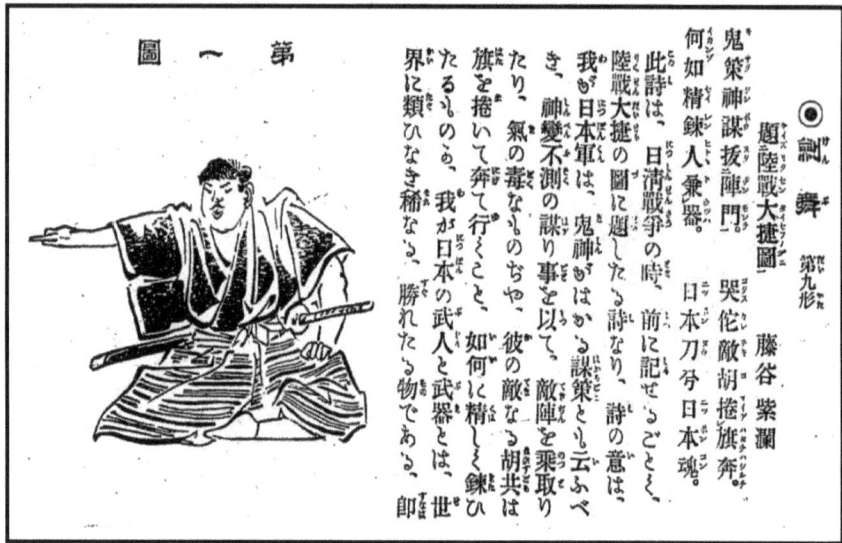

Kenbu Sword Dance
Ninth Kata
<u>**First Illustration**</u>

題陸戰大捷圖

Description of a Great Victory for the Army
By Fujitani Shiburan 藤谷紫瀾 (1867-1944)

鬼策神謀抜陣門
A Devil's tactics with God's plan,
The door holding back the forces is breached.
哭佗敵胡捲旗奔
The once proud barbarian enemies now weep,
Running with their flag wrapped about them.
何如精錬人兼器
The high level of training and spirit is on display,
The person and the instrument together.
日本刀兮日本魂
The sword of Japan, The soul of Japan.

This poem takes place during the Nishin War. As can be seen in the lines above, it is a poem describing a great victory for the ground forces. The poem tells of how our Japanese military utilized a stratagem that can perhaps only be described as otherworldly in its cunning. It was the stratagem of a Kishin 鬼神, a fierce god.

Through this strategy nearly miraculous in its unexpectedness, the enemy forces were overrun. Quite unfortunate for them. Those barbarian groups that are our enemies were seen fleeing with their flags wrapped around them.

This itself is evidence of the detailed training undergone by the troops. The military men and weapons of Japan, which have no equal or counterpart elsewhere. A superior thing overall.

The superior weapon carried by our warriors mentioned in the lines of the poem refer to a weapon without parallel in the world. A refined thing. This superior weapon referred to is of course the Nihonto, or the Japanese sword. The reason for the superiority of the military men is of course due to Yamatodamashi 大和魂, the soul of the Japanese warrior.

The fact we hold these two things has allowed victory after victory in battle after battle. Through the picture drawn by this poem we can envision these great successes[113].

---

[113] It appears that Fujitani was only about thirty years of age when this book came out. That seemed quite young for such weighty verse. However, Fujitani's father was a famous writer of Kanbun, or Chinese poems, and he passed this knowledge onto his son. His father, Fujitani Chikukei, apparently said on his deathbed,

日露戦争の今日なれば葬費を除き、僅少（きんしょう）たり
とも、軍資に献納せよ

If war between Japan and Russia were to start today, take the money saved for my funeral, however trifling it may be, and donate it to the war fund.

The war with Russia started the same month the father died.

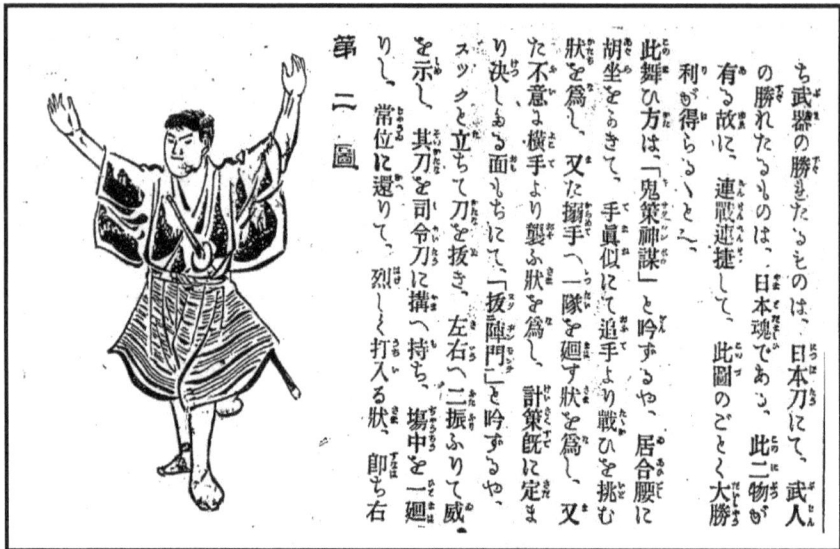

第二圖

Second Illustration

This Kenbu is done by first reciting, *Kisaku Shinbo*, or *A Devil's tactics with God's plan*, as you drop down into Iai Goshi 居合腰, or a squat, and then shift to Agura 胡坐, or a crossed leg position.

Using gestures indicate that the Oute 追手, or your pursuing force, is rapidly approaching from behind, seeking to engage the enemy. Further, show that the Karamete 搦手, or the force exploiting a chance, is moving around in front of the enemy. Finally show that an unexpected attack on the Yokote 横手, or the flank, is set to begin.

Setting your face in an expression showing that your plan of attack is already set recite *Jinmon wo Nuku*, or *The door holding back the forces is breached*, as you stand up sharply with a Sukku! スック sound.

Draw your Katana and make two great cuts to the left and right to demonstrate your intensity. Hold the Katana in a commanding pose as it is your Shireito 司令刀, or sword of command. Then revolve slowing around the center of the dais. When you return to the starting position do a sudden, violent cut.

For a better understanding of this, refer to the first illustration.

の第一圖のごとくし、蹈止まりて刀を收め、両手を上げて萬歳を唱へ、「哭佗敵胡」と吟ずるや右の手を額にかざして、向ふを望み、哀れなものぢやといふ顔つきをして、其手を下げて指さし、「捲旗弈」と吟ずるや、即ち右の第二圖のごとくし、心地よく笑ひ、即ち右の第二圖のごとくし、「何如精錬」と吟ずるや、刀を抜きて打ちへし、鍔元より尖頭まで篤と見て、感ずる面持し、「一人象器」と吟ずるや、左の第三圖のごとく、左の手の食指にて、自分の顔と抜きたる刀とを指さし、即ち人も兵器も善きを示すなり。

第三圖

Third Illustration

At the end of the cut, stop your feet where they are and sheathe the Katana. Raising both arms shout Banzai!万歳! After that recite *Kokusu Kare Tekiko*, or *The once proud barbarian enemies now weep*. Raise your right hand to your forehead as if to shield your eyes. Look off into the distance and grimace as if saying "This is quite a piteous sight!"

Lowering that hand point and intone *Hata wo Hashirkaite*, or *Running with their flag wrapped about them*. Put both hands on your belly add laugh heartily. In other words, as shown in the second illustration on the previous page.

While reciting *Ikanzo Seiren*, or *The high level of training and spirit is on display*, draw your Katana. Flip the blade upward and study it in earnest from the Tsuba-moto to the Kisaki, or from the sword guard to the tip. Show on your face that you are sensing something as you intone *Hito Utsuwato*, or *The person and the instrument together*. This is all depicted in the illustration above.

Use the Hitosashi-yubi 食指, or index finger, of your left hand to point at your own face and then point to your drawn Katana. This indicates that both you and your weapon are in fine order.

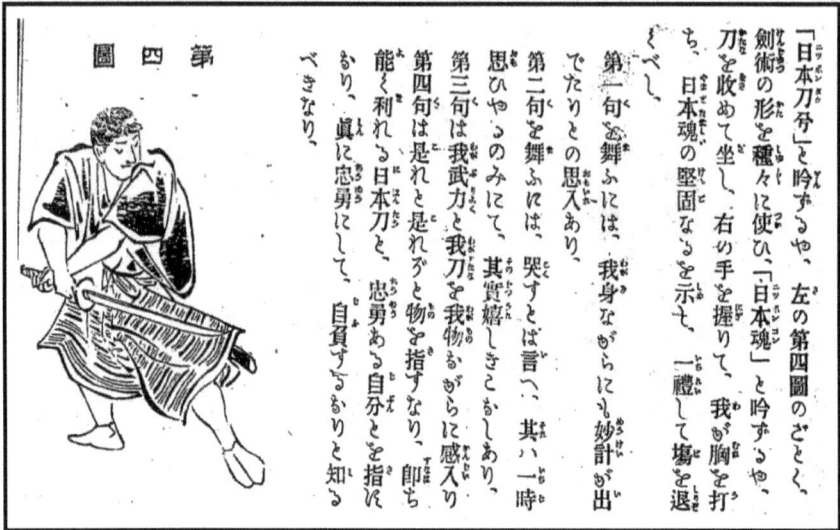

「日本刀号」と吟ずるや、左の第四圖のごとく、剣術の形を種々に使ひ、「日本魂」と吟ずるや、刀を収めて坐し、右の手を握りて、我が胸を打ち、日本魂の堅固なるを示て、一禮して場を退くべし。

第一句を舞ふには、我身ながらにも妙計が出でたりとの思入あり、

第二句を舞ふには、哭すとは言へ、其は一時思ひやりのみにて、其實慘しきことおしあり、

第三句は我武力と我刀を我物ながらに感入り、

第四句は是れと是れぞと物を指すなり、即ち能く利れる日本刀と、忠勇ある自分とを指べるり、眞に忠勇にして、自負するなりと知るべきなり。

Fourth Illustration

While reciting *Nihonto*, or *The sword of Japan*, do as shown in the fourth illustration above. You should do a sequence of several Kenjutsu techniques.

While reciting *Nipponkon*, or *The soul of Japan*, sheathe your Katana and seat yourself. Closing your right hand in a fist, strike your chest. This shows how Yamatodamashi, the spirit of Japan, is firmly within you.[114]. Do a Rei and remove yourself from the stage.

When enacting the first verse, show that you have come up with a clever little plan.

When enacting the second scene show that while you feel pity, it is only fleeting and it is overcome by the thrill of success.

The third verse is about our pride in both our military prowess and the swords that are so closely associated with Japan.

The fourth verse is saying "it is this and this" as we indicate ourselves and our sword. In other words, speaking proudly of the highly effective Nihonto as well as our own true loyalty and bravery.

---

[114] Nihonkon is the same word as Yamatodamashi. The Kanji are the same but the modern name for Japan, Nippon, is used instead of the historic one, Yamato. Damashi (Tamashi), soul or spirit, can also be read Kon, and that is used here.

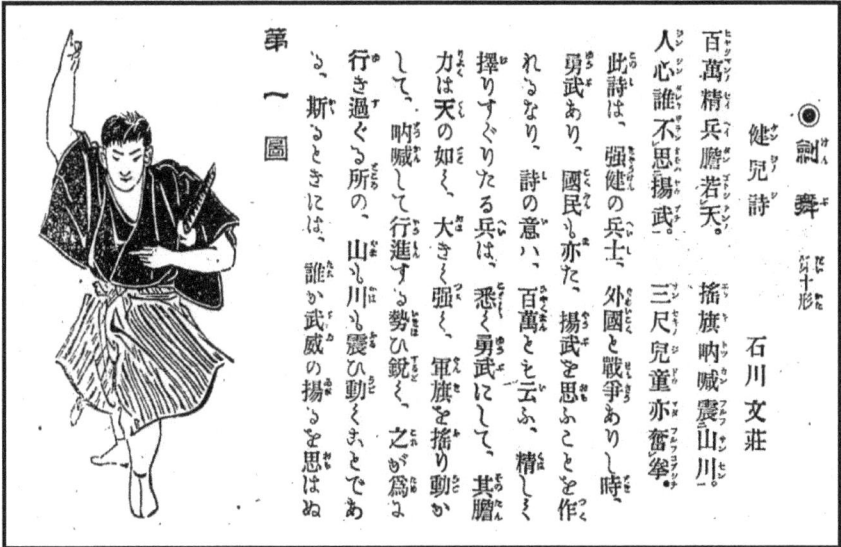

◉ 剣舞
健兒詩
三十形
石川 文荘

百萬精兵膽若天。
搖旗吶喊震山川。
人心誰不思揚武。
三尺兒童亦奮拳。

此詩は、強健の兵士、國民。亦た、揚武を思ふことを作れるなり、詩の意ハ、百萬と云ふ、悉く勇武にして、軍旗を搖り動かして、吶喊して行進する勢ひ鋭く、之が爲に、行き過ぐる所の、山も川も震ひ動くまとである、斯るときには、誰か武威の揚るを思はぬ

勇武あり、國民。亦た、外國と戰爭ありし時、擇りすぐりたる兵は、悉く勇武にして、力は天の如く、大きく強く、其膽

第一圖

◎ **Kenbu Sword Dance**
Tenth Kata
First Illustration

健兒詩
Poem of a Healthy Youth
By Ishikawa Bunzo 石川文荘 (?-1943)

百萬精兵膽若天
One million elite warriors,
Courage unparalleled under the heavens.
搖旗吶喊震山川
Waving flags and throaty calls,
Mountains and rivers alike are shaken.
人心誰不思揚武
Who does not desire this?
There are none amongst them who thinks such.
三尺兒童亦拳
Children of only three Shaku in height,
They too clench their fists in excitement.

This poem is about robust soldiers. When they are called upon to serve overseas, they will prove themselves valiant and, further, the people of Japan will continue to hoist up the ideal of the marital warrior.

What this poem relates is how the combined military prowess of Hyakuman 百萬, or One Million, of the finest soldiers as well as the nerve they possess, is quite nearly divine in nature. Large and strong. The Gunki 軍旗, or Battle Flag, wafting in the breeze as we advance with piercing force and throaty calls.

Proceeding in this way mountains and rivers quake as we pass. Who amongst us then at the sight of this should seek not the continued rise of our military might?

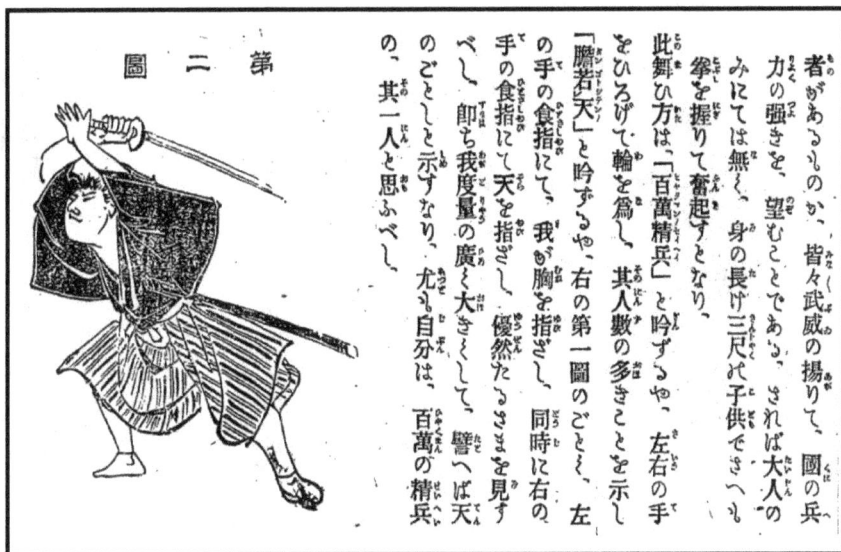

者があるものか、皆々武威の揚りて、國の兵、力の強きを、望むことであい、されば大人のみにては無く、身の長け三尺れ子供できへい拳を握りて奮起すとなり、此舞ひ方は、「百萬精兵」と吟ずるや、左右の手をひろげて輪を為し、其人數の多きことを示し「膽若天」と吟ずるや、右の第一圖のごとく、左の手の食指にて、我が胸を指ざし、同時に右の手の食指にして、天を指ざし、優然たるさまを見すべし、卽ち我度量の廣く大きくして、譬へば天のごとしと示すなり、尤も自分は、百萬の精兵の、其一人と思ふべし。

Second Illustration

Everyone from every strata of society cheers the might of our military forces. And this is not limited to the full-sized adults, but those whose bodies do not exceed three Shaku, or ninety centimeters. By this I am referring to the children who also clench their fists in building excitement.

This Kenbu is done by first reciting *Hyakuman Seihei*, or *One million elite warriors*, as you spread your arms out to the left and right encircling the area about you. This is showing the sheer number of people.

While reciting *Tanten no Gotoshi*, or *Courage unparalleled under the heavens*, do as is shown in the first illustration above. Specifically, you should use the Hitosashi-yubi 食指, or index finger, of your left hand to indicate your own chest. At the same time, the Hitosashi-yubi of your right-hand points to the heavens.

Here, you should be completely calm and composed. The performer should, in other words, have the length and breadth of their abilities on display, as you yourself are one of those Hyakuman Seihei, One Million Warriors, under the heavens.

第三圖

「搖旗吶喊」と吟ずるや、腰刀を抜き放し、吶喊して斫入る状、即ち右の第二圖のごとくし、「震山川」と吟ずるや、立止まりて震動の響を聞すまし、これに驚きたる状をなし、「人心誰」と吟ずるや、右の手にて刀を引さげ、左の手にて右より左へ一文字を畫き、一般にといふ意を示し「不思揚武」と吟ずるや、左右前後を斬るびけ武の尊きを左の第三圖のごとくして示し、刀を收め、「三尺兒童」と吟ずるや、左右の手を以て子供の脊たけを示し、「亦奮拳」と吟ずるや、次ての第四圖のごとく拳を振上る状を為し、坐して

Third Illustration

While reciting *Yuki Tokkan*, or *Waving flags and throaty calls*, draw the Yoto, or the Katana at your waist. With a great cry do a mighty downward chop. In other words, as shown in the second illustration on the previous page.

While reciting *Sansen Furu-u*, or *Mountains and rivers alike are shaken*, stop and make as if sensing the vibrations from the earth quaking. This can all be seen in the second illustration on the previous page.

As you show surprise at this chant, *Jinshin Dareka*, or *Who does not desire this?*, lower your right sword hand. With your left hand draw an Ichimonji 一文字, or the Kanji for "one," from left to right. This refers to the Ippan, or the average people, being unified.

While reciting *Yobu Omonwazaran*, or *There are naught amongst them who thinks such*, cut Sayuzengo, or left, right, front and back, with your Katana. This is a display that shows why Bu 武, or Military Prowess, should be revered and can be seen in the third illustration above.

As you sheathe your Katana, recite *Sanshaku Jido*, or *Children of only three Shaku in height*. Use your left and right hands to indicate a child's height.

一禮して退くべし

第一句を舞ふには、一兵として翳兵なきの意あり、

第二句を舞ぬには、行進して生還を期せず、思ぬ限り戰ふ心持あり、

第三句を舞ふには、武威の揚るを嬉しく思ひて、人の上をと推測し、

第四句を舞ふには、子供の上までも推測して其實況をあらはし示すなり、依ては子供できへも、左様であるに、大人は何とて、武の揚るを悦ばずに、居られやうやとの、意を含むべし。

Fourth Illustration

While reciting *Mata Kobushi wo Fururu,* or *They too clench their fists in excitement,* do as is shown in the following fourth illustration. Raise your clenched fist as you crouch down in a squat, as if you were a child. Finally do a Rei, or bow and withdraw.

When enacting the first verse show how, as you look among the soldiers, you find no cowards.

When enacting the second verse show how you march into battle intent on fighting to the best of your ability and how you are not expecting to return home alive.

When enacting the third verse, show the pleasure you feel as the status of the military is raised up and up and how you guess this feeling extends to all your countrymen.

When enacting the fourth verse you should convey how you believe that this is felt even by the smallest children. What should be on display here is that you cannot find anyone who is not delighted by the rise of the military.

第一圖

◎劔舞　第十一形

偶成
大久保利通

王師一到忽摧兇
戰克三千兵氣雄
請看皇威及異域
石門縣上旭旗風

此詩は、故參議大久保公が、戊辰の函館の戰爭の狀を、作られたるならん、詩の意と、軍が一たび蝦夷地に行きて、忽ちに朝歆の惡者共を討ち挫き、其戰ひに勝ちたる、三千の官兵え、如何にも兵氣が雄きことである。先づ人々看よ、皇室の御威光が、蝦夷のやうる外國同樣の土地にまで及びて、石門縣の邊りには、朝歆共は降參して居らず、官軍な

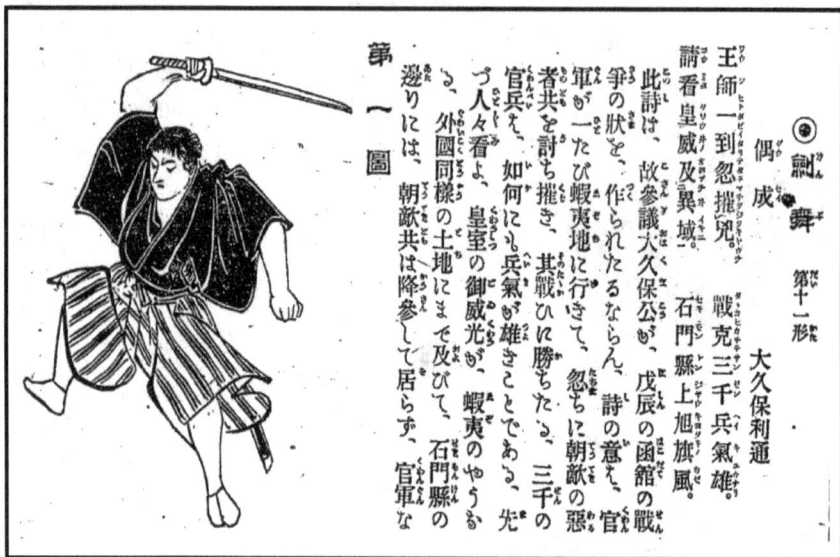

◎ **Kenbu Sword Dance**
Eleventh Kata
First Illustration

偶成

Impromptu

By Okubo Toshimichi 大久保 利通 (1830 –1878)

王師一到忽推兇

The servants of the crown make their arrival,
Immediately set about striking down the evil doers.

戦克三千兵気雄

The masterful attack of three thousand,
The unrestrained bravery of the soldiers.

請看皇威及異域

Look how authority emanates from the imperial throne,
Extending even to alien shores.

石門頭上旭旗風

Standing above Sekimon Prefecture,
The wind on the Rising Sun flag.

This Kenbu is by the deceased Councilor Lord Okubo, who crafted this poem to describe the battle of Hakodate from the Boshin War.

This poem is sometimes mistakenly associated with how the loyalist forces made their way to the northern island of Hokkaido, and battled at Hakodate. In fact, this story is about how our forces travelled to Ezochi 蝦夷地, the Barbarian Lands. There they immediately engaged crushed the wicked Choteki 朝敵, or Enemies of the Throne, who were hiding there. The three thousand soldiers loyal to the emperor who won that battle were filled to overflowing with military vigor and strength. Look upon them! The royal authority of the imperial throne extends to the Ezochi, Barbarian Lands, the same way they cover Japan. The Choteki in the area around Sekimon Prefecture were unable to resist the mighty Rising Sun Flag of the Imperial Forces as it flapped mightily in the wind.

Translator's Note:

Okubo Toshimichi 大久保利通, was Samurai from the Satsuma area of Kyushu and was considered one of the three main founders of modern Japan. And like two of the other authors of Kenbu in this book he died badly.

On May 14, 1878, Okubo was assassinated by six Samurai while on his way to meet with the Emperor. The attack, known as the Kioisaka Incident 紀尾井坂の変 consisted of the assassins first cutting off the legs of the horses pulling his carriage. They then killed his retainer, drug Okubo out in the street and cut his head off.

The blow that decapitated him was so strong the attacker's sword dug a hole in the ground. The police officers that arrived on the scene found Okubo dead from 16 cuts. There was blood and bone everywhere and his brainpan had been cut open and the contents scattered about.

This act was preceded by the delivery of an Ansatujo 暗殺状 or a letter describing why a person was assassinated. The letter stated the reasons for the assassination were (loosely translated):

- Rapid changing of laws in one day
- Misuse of public funds for projects
- Not revising agreements between Japan and foreign governments

● Causing chaos within Japan

The leader of the assassins was Shimada Ichiro 島田 一郎 (1848 –1878). After the completion of their attack the entire party turned themselves in and all were executed in July of the same year.

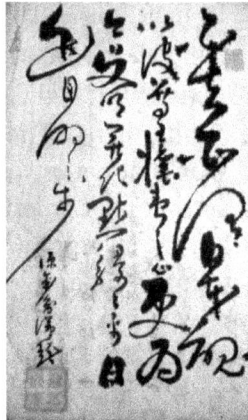

This is the final page of the nine page Ansatsujo sent by the assassins. A newspaper called The Choya Shimbun 朝野新聞 published the entirety of it and was punished by having its publication banned for five days.

A newspaper illustration of Okubo's assassination from May of 1878.

第二圖

て刀を抜き、指揮官の積りにて、兵を率ゐて到り

と云ふ處あり。孰れが是なるを知らず、借て此舞ひ方を、「王師一到」と吟ずるや、立ち

縣え彼土の縣名ならん、現に生蕃地には、石門。丹人にて、異域と云ふは、臺灣の生蕃地、石門、

伐の時の詩とも思へり、されぞ兇と云ふは、牡併し又思ふに、前の明治七年、臺灣征

今こそは、北海道となりて、内地に異らぬやうに思へど、其頃は異域とも謂いたるや

るとるなり、旭の御旗が、凰に飜りて勇ましく、立てあ

Second Illustration

Nowadays Taiwan considered to be along the same lines of the island of Hokkaido, not that different from the inner islands. At that time, however, it was still considered to be a different land all together.[115] While speaking of foreign lands, let us look at this poem about the punitive expedition to Taiwan in the seventh year of the Meiji Emperor[116]. In this caste the "evildoers" are the Botanjin 牡丹人, or the indigenous Paiwan inhabitants of Taiwan.

The "alien shores" refers to the aboriginal areas of Taiwan, specifically in a place called Sekimon Prefecture, if such a place could be called "a prefecture." At any rate, in the midst of this savage place there is an area known as Sekimon, or Stone Gate.

So then, the way this dance is enacted is to first incant *Oshi Hitotabi Itaru,* or *The servants of the crown make their arrival,* while you draw your Katana. Taking on the role of a commander, make as if leading troops in the landing.

---

115 Taiwan was under Japanese control from 1895 until 1945.
116 This occurred in 1874. It was launched in retaliation for the capture and beheading of 54 shipwrecked sailors by head-hunting aborigines in Taiwan in 1871.

第 三 圖

着したる状を為し、「忽攘兇」と吟ずるや、其刀
を揮ひて種々に戦ふ状を、前に出せる第一圖の
ごとくし、「戦克三千」と吟ずるや、右の第二圖
のごとく、手拭を出し、之を敵の戎衣として、
刀の血を拭ひ、さて左右を見わらして、莞爾と
笑ひ、「兵氣雄」と吟ずるや、一旦刀を収めて、
又左の手にて鯉口を持ち、右の手を柄に掛けて
二三寸抜きかけ、烈しく音させて收め、勇氣凛
々たるところを示し、「謝香皇威」と吟ずるや、
左の第三圖のごとく、刀を抜きて右斜めに見せ
掛け、「及異域」と吟ずるや其刀の尖頭にて、
ふを指ざし、左より右へ一文字に引き、向。

Third Illustration

While reciting *Tachimachi Kyo wo Kujiku,* or *Immediately set about striking down the evil doers,* use your Katana to cut all around you with various attacks. This is shown in the first illustration.

While reciting *Tatakai Katsute Sanzen,* or *The masterful attack of three thousand,* take out a Tenugui cloth. This is shown in the second illustration on the previous page. This is used to represent Jui 戎衣, or the clothing worn into battle by the barbarian warriors. You use it to wipe the sticky blood from your blade.

Next, looking to the left and right allow a grin to spread across your face. Recite *Heiki Yunari,* or *The unrestrained bravery of the soldiers,* as you sheathe your Katana. Keep your left hand on the Koiguchi, the mouth of the scabbard, and keep your right hand resting on the handle. Draw your sword out 6 ~ 9 centimeters and then violently force it back in. This should produce a ringing sound which serves to demonstrate the intensity of your bravery.

While reciting *Koumiru Koui,* or *Look how authority emanates from the imperial throne*, do as is shown in the third illustration on the previous page. Draw your Katana and, holding it diagonally down to the right, look at it. Intone *Iiki Oyobu,* or *Extending even to alien shoes,* indicating a distant land and trace an Ichimonji 一文字, the Kanji for "one," with the tip of your sword from left to right.

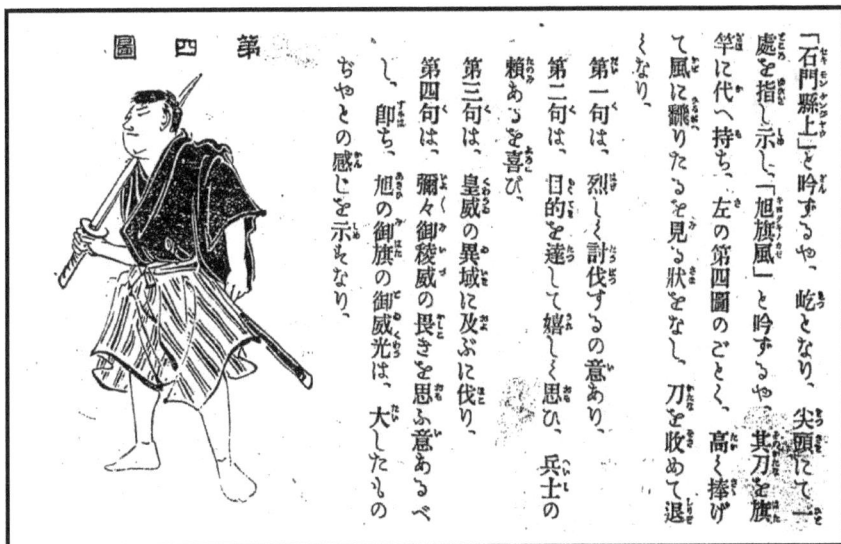

第四句は、旭の御旗の御威光は、大したもの
し、即ち、旭の御旗の御威光は、大したもの
ちやとの感じを示ぜなり。
第三句は、皇威の異城に及ぶに伐り、
彌々御稜威の畏きを思ふ意あるべ
第二句は、目的を達して嬉しく思ひ、兵士の
頼みを喜び、
第一句は、烈しく討伐するの意あり、
くなり、
て風に飄りたるを見る狀をなし、刀を收めて退
處を指し示し、「旭旗風」と吟ずるや、尖頭にて一
竿に代へ持ち、左の第四圖のごとく、高く捧げ
「石門縣上」を吟ずるや、屹となり、其刀を旗

Fourth Illustration

As soon as you intone the next line, *Sekimon Ken Jo,* or *Standing above Sekimon Prefecture,* indicate a place with the tip of your sword.

While reciting *Kyokuki no Kaze,* or *The wind on the Rising Sun flag,* hold your Katana as if it were the pole of a flag. This is shown in the fourth illustration above. Show how the flag, hoisted up high, is being buffeted by winds. Following this, sheathe your Katana and withdraw.

When enacting the first verse, show a violent subjugation of the enemy.

The second verse is about the joy of having achieved your goal along with the joy felt by the soldiers entrusted to carry out this task.

The third verse is the pride in how the authority of the Imperial Throne reaches to foreign lands.

The fourth verse conveys how at long last the honorable and majestic authority has arrived in this foreign land. In other words the great authority held by the mighty rising sun flag is something to behold indeed.

◉ 劍舞　第十二形　　大庭景陽

日本刀の歌

氷か雪か將た霜か
光も寒く又すごく
實に尊き日本刀

水より清く潔く
凛然万古に輝きし
世界に類なかりけり

百錬千磨の功を經て
忠魂義膽は鐵壁の
勳あぬ君が大御代と

きたひ出せし丈夫の
城より堅き賴もしさ
世界に類なかりけり

抜けば閃く青蛇が
霜雪飛ばす心地よさ
日本刀の斬れ味は

揮ひ來れば烈日が
奸臣賊子を斬斃す
世界に類なかりけり

我國勇氣の存亡は
此寶刀のなかりせば
實も尊き日本刀

此寶刀に因るぞかし
日本魂地に墜ちむ
世界に類なかりけり

此歌は、日本刀の功能を、軍歌に作り爲した
るなり。
此舞ひ方は、意は自ら解し得らるれば、別に解かず
るなり、「氷か雪か將た霜か」と歌ふや、刀を
を抜きて右に上げ出し、左の袖を拂ひて、氷を

◎ **Kenbu Sword Dance**
Twelfth Kata

This poem concerning the virtues of the Nihonto has become a song used by the military. The meaning of the song is more or less self-evident so there will be no explanation.

日本刀の歌
Nihonto no Uta
Song of the Japanese Sword
By Oniwa Keio 大庭景陽(?-1915)

Ice, snow and even frost,
More pure and undefiled than water.
The brightness and the cold are also intense.
Shining gloriously with eternal command,
It's worth is greater than that of money,
Without parallel the world over.

The result of a hundred temperings and a thousand polishings.
A warrior straight out of the forge,
The iron wall formed by the loyal and the just,
A wall that can be relied on to be stronger than a castle.
You who are immovable lay at the side of the Emperor,
In the whole world there is note that can compare.

If drawn it is akin to a blue snake of lightning,
Should it wave in your direction it will be like the blazing sun.
The blissful feel of snow and frost scattering about you,

Cut down the rebels and traitors to the throne.
The cutting edge of the Yamato Katana,
Without parallel the world over.

The Know that the fate of bravery in our country,
By means of this treasured sword.

Should this treasured sword become lost
The whole of the lands infused with Yamataodamashi will sink.
It's worth is greater than that of money,
Without parallel the world over.

除け、雪霜を挑ふ状を為し、「水より清と源く」
と歌ふや、両手にて差出し、鍔元より想頭に
透と見て、其清らるのに感ずる状を為す。
も寒く又凄く」と歌ふや、右の手のみにて刀を
提げ、左の手は袖の中へ入れて寒くして震ひ
状を為し、「凛然万古に輝きし」と歌ひ、左の
第一圖のごとく、剣術の形を使ひ、「賓の身を
本刀」と歌ふや、双を我方に向けて、両手に
立て、捧げ、「世界に類なかりけり」と歌ふや、
持かへて、居命の収め方のごとく、刀を鞘に収
むべきなり。頬なしといふところなれば、
自賁の心持ありて可なり。

図一第

First Illustration

The Kenbu is done by first reciting *Korika, Yukika Mata Shimoka,* or *Ice, snow and even frost,* as you draw your Katana and cut up and to your right. Brush away at your left Sode 袖, or sleeve, as if ridding it of ice, then make another sweeping motion to banish the snow and mist.

As you recite *Mizu yori Kiyoku, or purer and More undefiled than water,* thrust out both hands and admire the blade from the Tsuba to the tip. The way in which you hold yourself here should convey how you are sensing this purity.

Sing *Hikari mo Samuku mata Sugoku,* or *The brightness and the cold are also intense,* as you raise only the right hand. Next, slip your left hand into the sleeve of your Kimono and make as if shivering from the cold. Recite *Rinzen Bankoni Kagayakishi, or Shining gloriously with eternal command,* and perform a Kata from Kenjutsu. This is as shown in the first illustration above.

Recite *Zeni mo Totoni Nihonto, or Its worth is greater than that of money,* and turn the blade towards your face. After that, raise it up with both hands. Recite *Seikai ni Tagui Nakarikeri, or Without parallel the world over.* After doing that flip the blade back and return your Katana to its scabbard in the manner prescribed in Iai. Be sure to infuse pride in the line *Without parallel the world over.*

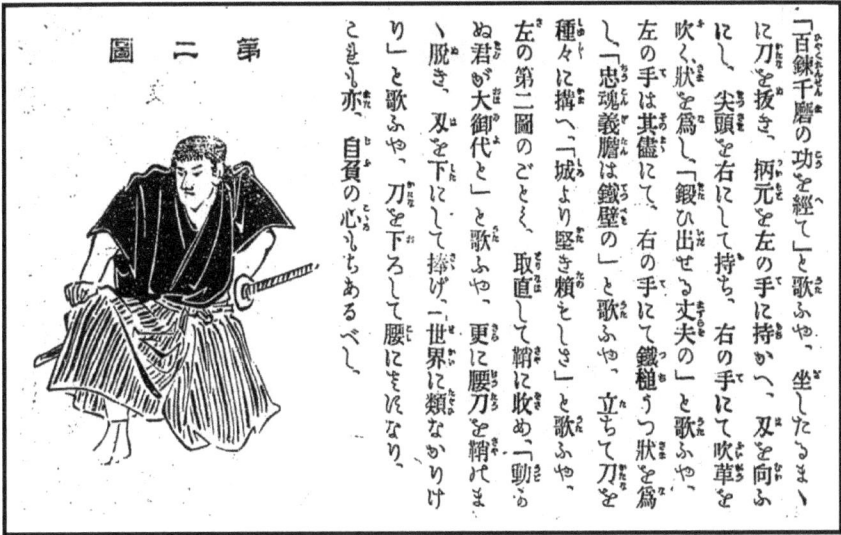

「百錬千磨の功を經て」と歌ふや、坐したるまゝに刀を抜き、柄元を左の手に持かへ、又を向ふに尖頭を右にして持ち、右の手にて吹革を吹く、狀を爲し、「鍛ひ出せる丈夫の」と歌ふや、左の手は其儘にて、右の手にて鐵槌うつ狀を爲し、「忠魂義膽は鐵壁の」と歌ふや、立ちて刀を種々に搆へ、「城より堅き賴をしさ」と歌ふや、左の第二圖のごとく、取直して鞘に收め、「動る君が大御代と」と歌ふや、更に腰刀を鞘代まゝ脱き、又を下にして捧げ、一世界に類なかりけり」と歌ふや、刀を下ろして腰にさたなり、こも亦、自貴の心いちあるべし

Second Illustration

Recite *Hyakurensenma no Ko wo Ete,* or *The result of a hundred temperings and a thousand polishings.* From a seated position draw your Katana. Switch the Tsuka, or handle, to your left hand and rotate the blade toward yourself, taking the point of the Katana in your right. Your right hand should hold the blade in a kind of pinch, like you would use if you were holding a blade of grass to make a whistle.

Then, leaving your left hand where it is, use your right hand to mimic a hammer pounding metal while you recite *Kitai Idaseru Masurano,* or *A warrior straight out of the forge.*

Rise to a standing position holding the Katana and take several different Kamae, one after the other as you recite *Chukon Gitan wa Tetsubekino,* or *The iron wall formed by the loyal and the just.*[117]

Recite *Shiroyori Kataki Tanomoshisa,* or *A wall that can be relied on to be stronger than a castle,* as you return the sword to a proper grip and sheathe. This is shown in the second illustration above.

---

[117] The word used here is a four character combination 忠魂義胆. The first two characters mean to maintain devotion and loyalty while the last two mean to maintain a just and honest heart/spirit.

Following that, take your Katana, still in its Saya, from your waist and offer it up with the blade facing downward as you recite *Ugokanu Kimiga Omiyoto,* or *You who are immovable lay at the side of the Emperor*.

Recite *Siekai ni Tagui Makarikeri,* or *In the whole world there is note that can compare* and lower your Katana and return it to its position on your hip. Again, this should be done with palpable pride.

第三圖

此處にても、亦自負の心もちあるべし。

界に類なゝりけり」と歌ふや、りうくと空を斬り、持かへて收むるなり。

前後左右に斬まくり、「奸臣賊子を斬斃す」と歌ふや、一刀の下に首斬落す狀を爲し「日本刀の斬れ味は」と歌ふや、

ばす心地よさ」と歌ふや、左の第三圖のごとく

ぶ」と歌ふや、殊に烈しく振りなびけ、「霜雪飛

きを見て、驚きたる狀を爲し、「揮ひ來れば烈日

捧げ、其双の光りの搖つきて、青蛇の匍ふごと

「抜けば閃く青蛇ぞ」と歌ふや、立ちて刀を抜き

Third Illustration

Rise up and draw your Katana from the scabbard as you recite *Nukeba Hirameku Aohebizo*, or *If drawn it is akin to a blue snake of lightning*. Hold it aloft so the reflected light shifting off the blade should recall a snake crawling along. At the sight of the light playing along the blade you should appear startled.

While reciting *Furuikitareba Retsujitsuzo*, or *Should it wave in your direction it will be like the blazing sun*, cut all about you with the Katana in great violent swings. Recite *Shimo Yuki Tobasu Kokochiyosa*, or *The blissful feel of snow and frost scattering about you*, as you do as shown in the third illustration above. Use the Katana to cut Zengosayu 前後左右, or front, back, left and right.

Recite *Kanshinzokushi wo Kiritaosu*, or *Cut down the rebels and traitors to the throne*, and swing your sword straight down, as if decapitating villains. Following that, slice the air about you with a whipping Ryu-Ryu sound as you recite *Yamato Gatana no Kiriaji wa, or The cutting edge of the Yamato Katana*.

Repeat again *Seikai ni Tagui Nakarikeri,* or *Without parallel the world over*, and return to your original position and sheathe the Katana.

All of this should be done with palpable pride.

357

圖四第

二、「我國勇氣の存亡は」と歌ふや、立ちて右の手の拳にて、左の腕ぶぶを打ち、左の手の拳にて、右の腕ぶぶを打ち、「此寶刀に因るぞかし」と歌ふや、左の手にて鯉口を持ち、右の手にて柄を持ち、二三寸抜きて烈しく収め、「此寶刀のなかりせば」と歌ふや、刀を脱し、跪きて地に置きたりせば」と歌ふや、其身を仆れ、「實に尊き日本刀」と歌ふや、置きたる刀を取上げ「日本魂地に墜ちむ」と歌ふや、双を下にして捧げ、「世界に類なかりけり」と歌ふや、刀を取直して、腰にこゝにしても、自負の心持あるべし。

Fourth Illustration

Recite *Wagakuni Yuki no Sonbowa,* or *The Know that the fate of bravery in our country,* and stand with your right hand closed in a fist. Strike the bicep of your left arm with it and then make a fist with your left hand and strike your right bicep. Placing your left hand on the Koiguchi, or the opening of the scabbard, and the right hand on the Tsuka, or handle, recite *Kono Hotoni Yoruzokashi,* or *By means of this treasured sword.* Draw the sword out two or three Sun, about 6 to 9 centimeters, and sheathe it again with a violent ring.

As you remove your Katana from your belt, squat down and place it on the ground as you recite *Kono Hoto no Nakarisebe,* or *Should this treasured sword become lost.* Make as if collapsing as you sing *Yamatodamashi Chiniochimu,* or *The whole of the lands infused with Yamataodamashi will sink.* Finally lay down on the ground.

Recite *Zeni mo Totoni Nihonto,* or *Its worth is greater than that of money,* as you pick up your Katana. Offer it up with the blade down. This is shown in the illustration above. Return the Katana to a normal grip as you recite *Seikai ni Tagui Nakarikeri,* or *Without parallel the world over.* Then, sheathe the sword and return it to your waist. This section should also be done with palpable pride.

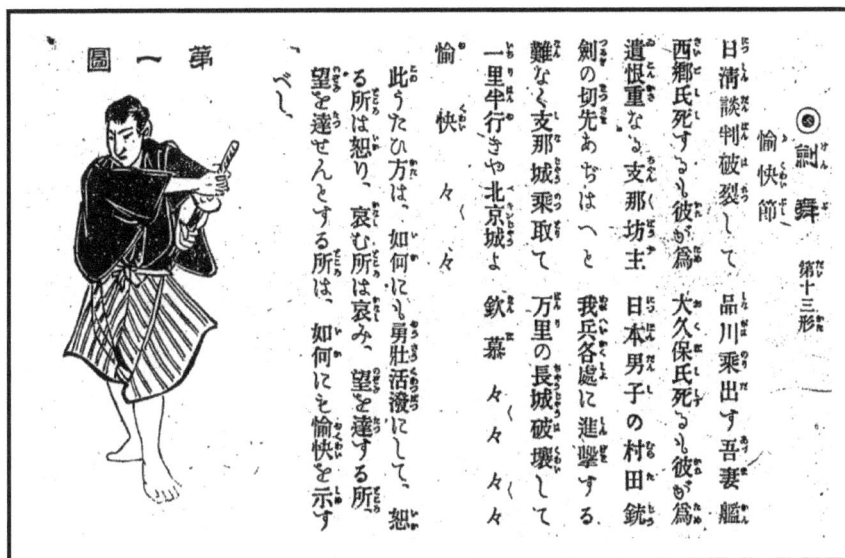

第一圖

◎試舞　愉快節　第十三形

日清談判破裂して　品川乗出す吾妻艦

西郷氏死するも彼が為　大久保氏死するも彼が為

遺恨重なる支那坊主　日本男子の村田銃

剣の切先あぢはへと　我兵各處に進撃する

難なく支那城乗取て　万里の長城破壊して

一里半行きや北京城よ　欽慕々々々々々々

愉快　々々　々

此うたひ方は、如何にも勇壮活溌にして、怒る所は怒り、哀む所は哀み、望を達する所は、如何にも愉快を示すべし。

◎ **Kenbu Sword Dance**
Thirteenth Kata
First Illustration

愉快節
A Pleasant Feeling
By Wakamiya Banjiro 若宮万次郎[118]　（1866-?）

---

[118] There is no author listed however, I was able to find his name. Miyakawa was an actor and playwright in Edo/Tokyo.

愉快節
A Pleasant Feeling
By Wakamiya Banjiro 若宮万次郎

日清談判破裂して
Negotiations between the Ming dynasty and Japan have broken off.

品川乗り出す吾妻艦
The battleship Azuma riding out of the mouth of the Shinagawa river.

西郷死するも彼が為　大久保殺すも彼が為
To do as the great Saigo Takamori died trying to do. For the same reasons Okubo died.

遺恨重なる支那坊主　日本男児の村田銃
A grudge has built up against the Chinese wanna be monks, The Murata rifle of the Japanese young warriors.

剣の切っ先味わえと　我が兵各地に進撃す
We will give them a taste of the tips of our swords as our forces fight their way into every area,

難無く支那共打ち倒し
Capturing castles in China with no undue trouble,

万里の長城乗っ取って
Bring down the Great Wall of China!

一里半行きゃ北京城よ
The city of Beijing is but a Ri and a half away!

欽慕欽慕欽慕 愉快愉快愉快
Reverence! Adoration! Admiration! Delightful! Exhilarating!

This song should have the epitome of the young warrior on display. Sections of the Kenbu that are tolerable should appear as such. You must impart anger in places that are angry. Places that are sad should show sadness. Places where the goals strived for are achieved, display the feeling that would occur if a long sought after goal is attained. Demonstrate the pleasant feeling this gives. [119]

---

119 The Azuma 吾妻 refers to a ship originally known as Kotetsu (甲鉄, literally "Ironclad.") The Azuma was built in France in 1864 for the Confederacy and christened CSS Stonewall. Japan bought it from the United States in February 1869. The style was an "ironclad ram warship." The ship served in the naval battle of Hakodate in 1869, which ended the Boshin War.

I could find no mention of the Azuma serving in China, but it appears it did participate in operations around Taiwan. She was scrapped in 1888.

此舞ひ方は、「日清談判破裂さて」と歌ふや、立ちて左の手にて刀の鯉口を持ち、右の手を柄に掛けて、イザと言はゞ斬らんとする身構へを、

右の第一圖のごとくに爲し、

「品川乗り出す吾妻艦」と歌ふや、軍艦號令橋上の司令官の心持にて、刀を向ふへ出し、抜錨して進航せよとの、號令をかけ、即ち左の第二圖のごとくし、

「西郷氏死するも彼が爲め」と歌ふや、刀を右に相に構へ、、目前に敵あらば、今にも斬はらはん、にと、足ずりして逆り、之が爲に人物を失ひた

Second Illustration

This Kenbu is performed by first signing *Nishin Danpan Harretsu,* or *The negotiations between the Ming dynasty and Japan have broken off.* You should stand and place your left hand on the Koiguchi of your Katana. Following that, place your right hand on the handle. You should be in a Kamae like the one demonstrated in the first illustration on the previous page.

Recite *Shinagawa Noridasu Azumakan,* or *The battleship Azuma riding out of the mouth of the Shinagawa river* and make as if you are the commanding officer of on the bridge of a Gunkan 軍艦, or Battleship. Thrust your sword out at the opponent and make as if giving the order for Batsubyo 抜錨, or Raising Anchor, and moving out. This should be done as is shown in the second illustration above.

Recite *Saigoshi Shi surumo Karega Tame,* or *To do as the great Saigo Takamori died trying to do.* Go into Haso no Kamae on your right side. Should an enemy appear before your eyes you feel an overwhelming urge to cut him down. Moving rapidly forward with Suriashi, a quick shuffling step, you find that the person in front of you has vanished. This fills you with a sense of regret. This is portrayed in the third illustration on the following page.

第三圖

「る、惜む狀、即ち左の第三圖のごとくし
「大久保氏死するも彼も爲め」を歌ふや、左の手
にて、引捕へんとする狀を爲し、
「遺恨重なる支那坊主」を歌ふや、齒切りをなし
て、屹と向ふを睨みつめ、
「日本男子の村田銃」と歌ふや、銃砲のごとく刀
を持ち、
「劍の切先きあぢはへ」と歌ふや、縱橫に種々
斬り廻る、即ち次の第四圖のごとくし。
但し、此斬まはりに、劍術居合の手を、充分
出すべし。

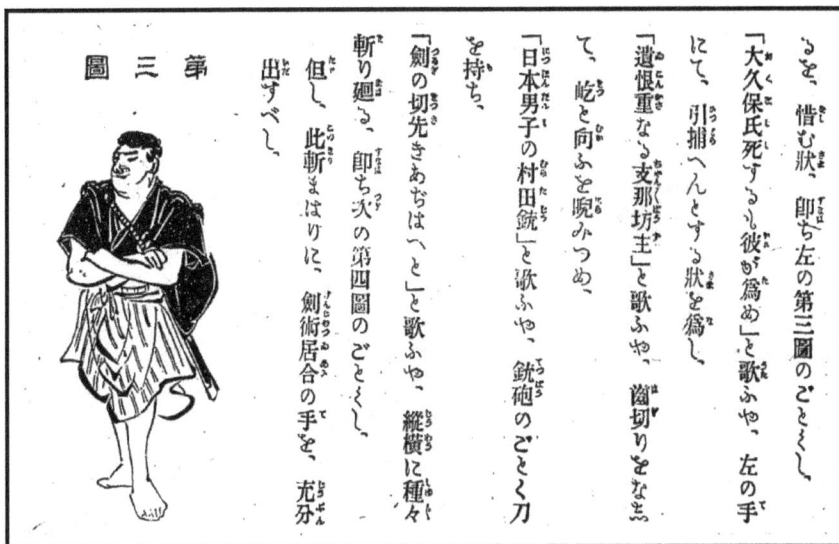

Third Illustration

Pretend someone has seized your left hand as you recite *Okuboshi Shisuruno Karegatame,* or *For the same reasons Okubo died.* Recite *Ikonkasanari Chanchanbozu,* or *A grudge has built up against the Chinese wanna be monks,* and gnash your teeth as you glare off towards them.

Hold your Katana as if it were a rifle and recite *Nihondanshi no Murataju,* or *The Murata rifle of the Japanese young warriors.*
Next recite *Tsurugi Kisakiajiwaeto, or How does the tip of my sword taste?,* as you cut in all directions with a variety of techniques. This is shown in the following fourth illustration.

It is important to note that the cuts should be plentiful and all conform to the manner prescribed in Iai and Kenjutsu.

第四圖

「我兵各所に進撃する」と歌ふや、刀を司令刀に擬へ、将校の心持にて、場中を一廻りし、隊兵を引率して、行進するに擬し、
「難なく支那城乗取て」と歌ふや、烈しく戦ふ状を為し、
此時此書中にて心得ある、剣術及び居合等の手をあらはすべし。
即ち次の第五圖のごとくに為すべし。
「万里の長城破壊して」と歌ふや、砲兵将校の心持にて、刀を司令刀に擬へ、砲撃せよとの指揮を為す状を為し

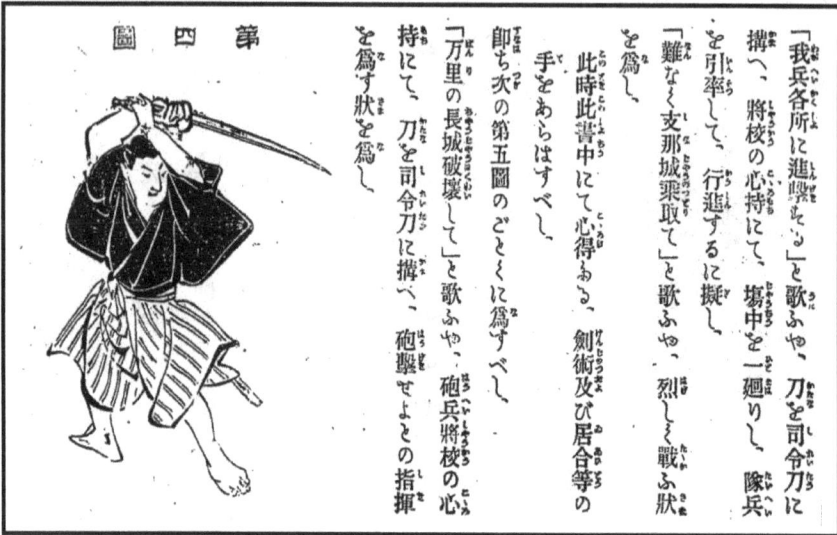

Fourth Illustration

Recite *Wagahei Kakushoni Shingekisuru,* or *Our forces fight their way into every area*, and raise your Katana up in a commanding manner. Like a commissioned officer take a turn around the center of the stage and make as if leading a division of soldiers.

Recite *Nannaku Shinajo Noritori, or Capturing castles in China with no undue trouble*, as you enact the manner of an intense battle. At this point, as well as throughout this volume, one thing to bear in mind is the importance of doing correct Kenjutsu and Iai-jutsu. In other words, do as is shown in the fifth illustration on the following page.

Use your sword to direct cannon fire as you take the manner of the commander of an artillery unit and recite *Banrinochojo Hakaishite,* or *Bring down the Great Wall of China.*

While reciting *Ichirihan Yukiya Peikingjoyo,* or *The city of Beijing is but a Ri and a half away,*[120] you should again take up your Katana as if it were your Shireito 司令刀, or sword of command, and make as if leading troops in an advance.

---

[120] One Ri is equivalent to approx. 3.9 km or 2.4 miles.

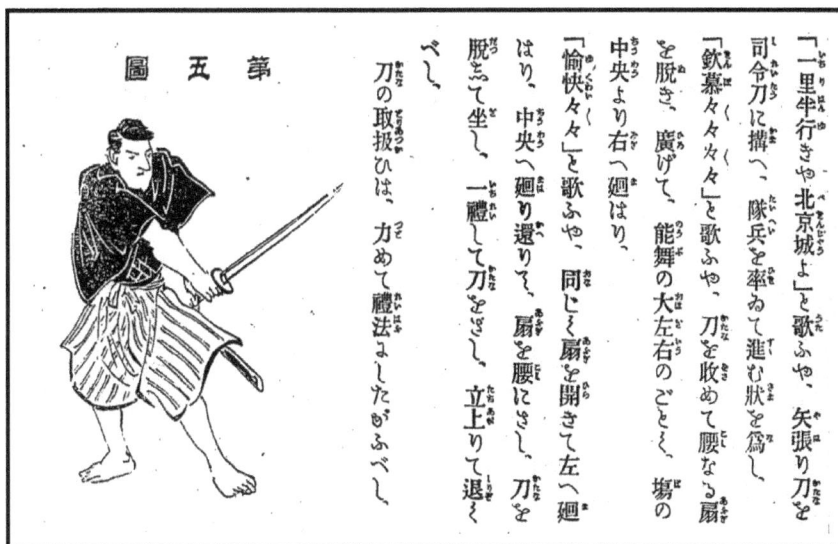

第五圖

一里半行きや北京城よ」と歌ふや、矢張り刀を
司令刀に携へ、隊兵を率ゐて進む状を爲し、
「欽慕々々々々」と歌ふや、刀を收めて腰なる扇
を脱き、廣げて、能舞の大左右のごとく、娚の
中央より右へ廻はり、
「愉快々々」と歌ふや、同じく扇を開きて左へ廻
はり、中央へ廻り還りて、扇を腰にさし、刀を
脱をて坐し、一體して刀をさし、立上りて退く
べし、
刀の取扱ひは、力めて禮法をしたがふべし

Fifth Illustration

Sheathe your Katana and take out your Ogi 扇, or Folding Fan, from your belt and recite *Kinbo, Kinbo, Kinbo or Reverence, Adoration, Admiration!* Opening it up move clockwise around the center of the stage much as is done in the Kabuki Kata Osayu[121] 大左右.

Recite *Yukai Yukai, or Delightful! Exhilarating!* as you open the Ogi again and turn around to the left. Eventually you should return to the center of the stage, collapse the Ogi and return it to your waist. Then, take your sword from your belt and sit. Do a Rei, return the sword to your belt, stand, and remove yourself from the stage.

The use of the Katana should be strong and be in accordance with the proper Reiho 礼法, or Etiquette.

The Complete Martial Arts of Japan
Third Volume : Kenbu
End

---

[121] This is an action done by Kabuki actors to take in the entire audience.